FORWARD

FARM BUREAU

NINETY YEAR HISTORY OF THE
AMERICAN FARM BUREAU FEDERATION

BY

STEWART R. TRUELSEN

Dedication

To the memory of my grandparents, James C. and Mary B. Truelsen, of Pocahontas County, Iowa. They heard the call of "Forward! Farm Bureau" in the 1920s and joined the march.

Copyright © 2009 by American Farm Bureau Federation

ISBN: 978-0-615-25908-6

Library of Congress Control Number: 2008939751

Printed in the United States of America.

Table of Contents

Acknowledgments

I'D LIKE TO EXPRESS MY SINCERE APPRECIATION TO PRESIDENT BOB STALLMAN AND the AFBF board of directors for giving me the opportunity to research and write the history of the American Farm Bureau Federation, and my special thanks to Executive Vice President Dick Newpher who first proposed the idea and Director of Public Relations Don Lipton who asked me to do it. To my friends at American Agricultural Insurance Company, Schaumburg, Illinois, thank you for providing me with workspace and office support for the time it took to complete the project.

There are four places in AFBF history that are quite special: Chicago, Illinois; Washington, D.C.; Broome County, New York; and Muscle Shoals, Alabama. I had never been to Muscle Shoals and neighboring Florence, Alabama, before this project. The family of AFBF General Counsel and Secretary Julie Anna Potts—her grandfather Frank and uncle Frank Potts who have a law practice there—gave me a wonderful tour of this historic area. While in Florence, I spent a couple days with the family of AFBF's fourth president, Ed O'Neal. Their scrapbooks from his years as president were a great source of information.

I worked for four of the eleven AFBF presidents, beginning with Allan Grant and knew the two previous presidents. My work experience covered roughly thirty years of Farm Bureau history. That left only sixty years with which I had to become a lot more familiar! Fortunately, many important documents were retained—annual reports and convention transcripts, board minutes, binders of old newsletters, and magazines. Two people had a lot to do with maintaining these collections—Corporate Secretary and Deputy General Counsel Dave Mayfield and librarian Sue Schultz.

My former colleagues in Public Relations were very helpful with the completion of the book, especially Director of Graphic Design Mary Burns and Graphic Designer Jordan Cutler who were responsible for the cover design and some of the photographs. I also appreciated the help I received from Deputy Director of Public Relations Mace Thornton and Assistant Director of Public Relations Phyllis

Brown. In the Schaumburg office, Patricia O'Brien helped me in the final phases of the project. Lauren Schoenherr, Jim Benes, and Spencer Lawrence did some of the legwork in finding magazine articles and other research material. Jamie Reid transcribed the interviews I recorded.

Libraries are one of our greatest public resources, in my opinion, and I made ample use of them, both online and in person. The collections and librarians at these libraries were most helpful: USDA National Agricultural Library, Beltsville, Maryland; Herbert Hoover Presidential Library, West Branch, Iowa; Cornell University Library, Ithaca, New York; State Historical Society of Iowa, Iowa City; Chicago Public Library; and the northwest suburban public libraries of Arlington Heights, Barrington, and Schaumburg, Illinois.

The first history of the American Farm Bureau Federation, *The Farm Bureau Movement,* was published in 1922, when the organization was barely three years old. The author, O. M. Kile, wrote a second history, *The Farm Bureau Through Three Decades*, in 1948. Melvin Woell, a colleague of mine, covered four decades of history in the 1990 book that he authored, *Farm Bureau Architects*. Their books were particularly helpful.

One of the most encouraging people I visited early in my work was Woodrow Luttrell who retired to Nashville after a long career at AFBF. "Woody" was a wealth of information and saved some of his files from organization work. I'm indebted to Woody, and all the other retirees I visited with in person or on the telephone. More than a few rummaged through their files to find some bit of information that I could use.

On a personal note, I want to thank Patrick Batts and the late Joe Fields for deciding to make me part of the expansion in broadcast journalism at AFBF in 1977. My greatest encourager of course was my wife Judie who was always willing to read a chapter and tell me what she liked best, and what I might want to correct. To all who contributed at some level of this project, I give a heartfelt thank you.

Foreword

FORWARD FARM BUREAU CHRONICLES THE EVENTS, PEOPLE, AND POLICIES THAT HAVE transformed this great organization from a simple "movement" led by farmers in the early twentieth century, to the nation's most vital and respected farm and ranch association today. During this ninety-year span, Farm Bureau has united millions of farm and ranch families under a common banner—doing together what they cannot do alone.

During this time, Farm Bureau has been forward-thinking. Agriculture's response to changing world dynamics, market conditions, and advances in technology and tools has helped dictate this organization's character. The same also is true of our innovative, grassroots-driven policies, developed by Farm Bureau's people, altering the face of our industry. Agriculture is better off because of the long line of farmers and ranchers through the years who have invested time, toil, and trust in Farm Bureau.

I count myself fortunate to be among the many people who have been touched by Farm Bureau. Members of Farm Bureau reap the rewards of involvement, whether that's nuts-and-bolts information to improve your place in the profession of agriculture, thoughtful insights into personal development and leadership training, or simply enjoying the benefits offered by the many outstanding services available to Farm Bureau members. There is something for everyone in our organization. The techniques, methods, and services may have changed over the years, but the one constant is that Farm Bureau and its people continue to move agriculture forward.

On the pages that follow, you will read a number of stirring chapters that cut to the heart of how the people behind Farm Bureau developed this organization, transitioned during challenges, and continued to position the organization to lead. You will gain insights into the fabric of the people who started, sustained, and continue to lead this movement. The stories of inspiration of those who came before us in this organization are empowering, as told by one of the best storytellers to dedicate his professional life to Farm Bureau, Stewart Truelsen.

This story of Farm Bureau and agriculture, however, is one that continues to be written today. It is playing out along the main streets of our rural towns that are more connected than ever to the world around them. It is being directed by the modern signals of high technology that are allowing us to farm even smarter and make more informed business decisions. And, it is being cast in the research facilities that are even now unlocking breakthroughs that will help us carry out our mission of feeding a growing world.

Through all of these developments, Farm Bureau is helping to lead the way. Our people, our member-service programs, and our grassroots policy process are establishing the new look and feel of agriculture today. As you read the following pages, know that Farm Bureau will continue to be steadfast in caring for its members, the natural resources on which they rely for success, and the multitude of consumers they serve, both here at home and around the world. Farm Bureau will continue to lead as we progress toward our centennial. And, the professional pursuit of agriculture, our nation, and our world will surely be better due to the repeated call of that enduring directive first proffered by AFBF's second president Oscar Bradfute—"Forward! Farm Bureau."

Bob Stallman, President
American Farm Bureau Federation

Preface

"FORWARD! FARM BUREAU" WAS A RALLYING CRY OF THE AMERICAN FARM BUREAU Federation (AFBF) in the early 1920s and was used on membership posters and in publications. The illustration that went with it was a long line of farmers marching on a country road. But marching to what you might ask? Where were they headed?

The answer is pretty simple. The American Farm Bureau Federation has been the collective voice of the nation's farmers and ranchers since 1919 and, together, Farm Bureau members of several generations have marched on that long road to realizing their hopes and aspirations. They were truly courageous people. Farming and ranching have never been easy work. The job is physically and mentally exhausting, economically risky, and subject to the vagaries of weather. This is a book about that march of progress and the building of the most powerful and influential farm organization in the world.

After the First World War, farmers who were part of the American Expeditionary Forces and those who stayed home to produce food for the war mobilized one more time—this time to give American agriculture a national voice in public affairs. It is hardly any wonder that Farm Bureau borrowed from the military command, "Forward March!" for its early membership drives. It would take a great army and great farm leaders to achieve social and economic equality for rural America and to solve the myriad of other problems along the way.

Of course, the job is not done. It never will be done as long as the nation and the world depend on American farmers and ranchers for food, fiber, and fuel. As long as that is the case, there will be a role for the American Farm Bureau Federation as the Voice of Agriculture. Remarkably, AFBF and our nation's agriculture stand at the pinnacle of success at a time when many other industries are struggling to find a place in the global economy.

I worked for the American Farm Bureau Federation in public relations for twenty-eight years before taking an early retirement. Always, I was greatly impressed by Farm Bureau member families. It was an honor to serve the members who welcomed me into their homes and shared their personal stories. I sat at many a kitchen table with farm families who were incredibly gracious hosts. I left more eager than ever to pass their stories on to the non-farm public. My coworkers felt the same way about our members. Farm Bureau is first and foremost a family organization.

When I reached the end of my career, I left with a feeling that the story of the American Farm Bureau Federation and its influence on food, agriculture, and rural America had not been fully told or appreciated. I was reminded of the fact while doing research for this book. At the 1952 AFBF annual meeting in Seattle, one of the speakers at the general session was Sen. Clinton Anderson of New Mexico. Anderson had earlier been secretary of agriculture and was a good friend of the organization. I don't know what kind of speaker he was, but probably no match for another speaker on the program, Rep. Walter Judd of Minnesota. "We get mad at Stalin because he won't live by our Christian virtues," Judd roared to the audience. "Well, he never said he would live by them! This was wishful thinking."

Senator Anderson's speech was not a stem-winder like Judd's and chances are a few people nodded off before he finished. He said the last hundred years were unlike any farmers would see again. There would never be another Homestead Act, and hopefully not another Great Depression, Dust Bowl, and two World Wars. Despite the crushing difficulties, agriculture had made tremendous progress.

The reasons he gave for the progress were the establishment of a Department of Agriculture in 1862 by President Abraham Lincoln; the Morrill Land Grant College Act the same year; the Hatch Experiment Station Act of 1867; and the Smith-Lever Act of 1914, which set up the Cooperative Extension Service and played a role in the development of Farm Bureau. He stopped after naming those four government acts, ones that laid a foundation for the agriculture we have today.

I was hoping, however, that he would finish by saying the fifth important reason for the progress of American agriculture was the founding of the American Farm Bureau Federation in 1919. I'm sure the audience would have responded well to that, but Sen. Anderson was finished. A respected public servant, he probably thought just in terms of what government had done to secure a place for agriculture. The thesis of this book is that the founding of the American Farm Bureau Federation should be considered one of the great events in any timeline of this nation's agricultural progress. Should it be ranked as high as the four actions Anderson listed? I certainly would not replace any of those, but the list should be expanded to include Farm Bureau.

There is one major difference between the four events Anderson listed and the founding of the federation. Farm Bureau is the story of how farmers took control of their own future, not how the government controlled it for them.

Whatever you may think, the story of American agriculture would be decidedly different without an American Farm Bureau Federation.

Farm Bureau fought to secure equality for agriculture with labor and industry in the first half of the twentieth century. It was the power behind the Farm Bloc in Congress that passed important farm credit and marketing legislation in the 1920s. Farm Bureau helped write the New Deal farm programs that rescued farmers from financial disaster. It pushed for development of fertilizer production and hydroelectric power at Muscle Shoals, Alabama, the beginning of the Tennessee Valley Authority.

Farm Bureau promoted an expansion of world trade after World War II, and was the leading proponent of a competitive, market-oriented farm policy for America's farmers. It defended the private property rights of rural Americans and fought the excesses of a big federal government and its regulatory bureaucracy. Farm Bureau sought a level playing field for farmers in world trade negotiations. It was an early supporter of biofuels. Farm Bureau developed several generations of the nation's top farm and ranch leaders. The list could go on and on. But what Farm Bureau is proudest of is the simple fact that it is the Voice of Agriculture. Its accomplishments are based on what farmers say and do.

When I was asked to write this book, I appreciated the opportunity and had many wonderful experiences researching and writing it. I recall the visit I paid to a former public relations staffer, Don Donnelly, whom I had known briefly in the late 1970s. I had just gotten to AFBF when he was about to retire. Don was in his nineties when I located him at a nursing home in Richmond, Virginia. The first AFBF president he ever met, in 1946 or 1947, was Ed O'Neal, the federation's fourth president.

When I arrived, Don was sitting on the edge of his bed dressed in a suit with vest and a tie. He was blind and in failing health, but his mind was sharp, his recollections quite good. He was looking forward to the visit. During our interview, I asked Don, "When do you think the American Farm Bureau reached its peak?" I figured that an old-timer would say something about the good old days. But without a moment's hesitation, he responded, "Hasn't come, it's still gaining members, still gaining influence." I came to the same conclusion after writing this book. Don expressed confidence in my work and was most anxious to read the final product. Unfortunately, he passed away not long after our visit.

I feel an obligation to Don Donnelly and other Farm Bureau leaders and staff, past and present, to give Farm Bureau members and the public a chance to read the history of the American Farm Bureau Federation. This is not a nostalgic look at the people and programs of the past ninety years, interesting though that might be to some who know the organization well. Instead, I have tried to write about the major themes affecting AFBF throughout the last ninety years. Bob Dole, the longest serving Republican leader in the Senate before he retired, used to say, "If you don't eat, don't worry about the farmers' problems." We all eat and most of us have ties to a farm or ranch somewhere in our own family history. Therefore, you don't have to be a farmer or Farm Bureau member to find this history interesting. At least, that is my hope.

Stewart R. Truelsen

Mission Statement

AMERICAN FARM BUREAU FEDERATION IS THE UNIFIED NATIONAL VOICE OF AGRICULTURE working through our grassroots organizations to enhance and strengthen the lives of rural Americans and to build strong, prosperous agricultural communities.

Adopted October 2006

1 | The Roots of Farm Bureau

THE SMOLDERING EMBERS OF ROWDY POPULISM WERE NEARLY EXTINGUISHED BY the end of the nineteenth century. Only the milder Grange survived to be of any consequence as a farm organization in the twentieth century, but its strength was greatly diminished. Into this lull was born a new kind of farm organization, one that wrote the book on grassroots lobbying and became the voice of American agriculture.

Farm Bureau was the first truly modern farm organization. It had no ties to the Agrarian Crusade that tried to correct the economic injustices perpetrated by robber barons, and it was not a secret or fraternal organization like some of its predecessors. Those that passed into history included the Farmers' Alliance, Agricultural Wheel, Ancient Order of Gleaners, American Society of Equity, Brothers of Freedom, Farmers' and Mutual Benefit Association. Both the National Grange (1867) and National Farmers Union (1902) preceded Farm Bureau and are active today, though much smaller in membership and more regional.

If the American Farm Bureau Federation (AFBF) is indebted at all to early farm organizations, it is in learning from their mistakes. Although it pursued some of the same goals, Farm Bureau avoided political partisanship and radicalism and had a better organizational model for growth. It also benefited from excellent timing, as we shall see later.

The Gilded Age was not good for farmers. They were spared a depression in name only. Economic collapses were called panics, and the Panic of 1873 and the Panic of 1893 hit farmers hard. Farm commodity prices dropped after the Civil War and continued down until the mid-1890s. Farmers were certain they were the victims of powerful monopolies, greedy speculators, and corrupt politicians.

The National Grange of the Patrons of Husbandry was formed before rural discontent boiled over. Oliver H. Kelley, a Washington, D.C., government clerk, founded the Grange along with a few associates. Kelley, an easterner by birth, had farmed in Minnesota and was sent by the U.S. commissioner of agriculture in 1866 to do survey work in the South. He returned with an idea for an organization to improve rural conditions, and because he and others interested in the organization were Masons, the Grange adopted Masonic lodge rituals.

The Grange sought to attract farmers interested in self-improvement and social advancement. Initially, it did not focus on political action, but the Grange became associated with the wider granger movement to reduce the economic power of railroads and grain elevators over farmers. A number of state granger laws were enacted, only to be ruled unconstitutional by the U.S. Supreme Court. However, federal regulation followed with the Interstate Commerce Act of 1887.

Grange members disliked middlemen and monopolies so they formed cooperatives and demanded discounts from manufacturers of farm equipment. When some of the harvester companies refused to go along, the Grange bought up a bunch of patents to manufacture its own line of farm machinery. Many of the patents were worthless and the failure of this and other commercial enterprises contributed to a loss of members. The Grange once had close to a million members but was down to around 100,000 by the century's end.[1]

The Farmers' Alliance was more rebellious and radical than the Grange and grabbed the lead of agrarian discontent in the latter part of the nineteenth century. Known for its firebrand leaders, some of whom were women, the Farmers' Alliance began at Lampasas, Texas, about 1875. Two years later, the Southern Farmers' Alliance was formed ostensibly for educational purposes. Part of the curriculum was to teach farmers about the evils of unrestrained capitalism.

Lecturer-organizers went throughout the South speaking at gatherings and signing up members at 25¢ a head. They took a percentage for their efforts and went on to the next town. The dues remittance never came close to matching the membership numbers, however. The Alliance also failed to come together as a national organization. The Southern Alliance and later the Northern Alliance held meetings aimed at consolidation but differences prevailed.

The Alliance formed cooperatives and even sold insurance, but commercial activities were secondary to its political agenda. It demanded free coinage of silver to inflate the currency, abolition of national banks, an end to all futures trading in agricultural commodities, and government ownership of both railroads and telegraph and telephone companies.

In July 1892, the Northern and Southern Alliance and Knights of Labor sent more than 1,300 delegates to a national convention at Omaha, Nebraska, to adopt a platform for the People's Party (also called the Populists). Alliance chapters or suballiances were converted into political organizations, spelling doom for the Alliance as a farm organization.

The Democratic national convention of 1896 in Chicago marked the end of the line for the Populists. The Democrats absorbed their platform and nominated a candidate who stole their rhetorical thunder, William Jennings Bryan. His "Cross of Gold" speech is one of the most famous in all political history. "You come to us and tell us that the great cities are in favor of the gold standard; we reply that the great cities rest upon our broad and fertile prairies. Burn down your cities and leave our farms, and your cities will spring up again as if by magic; but destroy our farms and the grass will grow in the streets of every city in the country."[2]

The heir to the Alliance was the National Farmers Union (NFU) founded in 1902 by Newton Gresham, a former Alliance organizer. The Farmers Union proposed security, equity, and justice for farmers, and said it intended "to garner the tears of the distressed, the blood of the martyrs, the laughter of innocent childhood, the sweat of honest labor, and the virtue of a happy home as the brightest jewels known."[3]

Farmers Union expanded throughout the South and absorbed several smaller organizations. In 1907, NFU was organized in twenty states and claimed a million members or more. Membership was open to farmers and other rural citizens with the exception of bankers, lawyers, and speculators.[4] In 1909, NFU President Charles S. Barrett feared that politicians and unscrupulous businessmen were infiltrating the organization. "Our ranks contain some of the noblest and purest hearted and ablest men in the country," he said. "They also contain some of the gravest, shrewdest, and most consummate villains who have managed to escape the penitentiary . . . one reason they are not to-day wearing ball, chain and stripes is that they can run just a little faster than the detective and the sheriff."[5]

From the start, Farmers Union emphasized cooperative marketing and other economic measures to help farmers. Initially, it did not have any important effect on national policies or legislation. It built cotton warehouses in the South and tried to influence farm prices through withholding actions and a 1907 campaign to plow up 10 percent of the cotton crop. Always more sectional than national, Farmers Union moved northward and westward. In 1919, an NFU treasurer's report indicated there were around 125,000 dues-paying members. Kansas, Nebraska, and Iowa accounted for the largest share of the membership.[6]

Third party politics lingered in farm country at the start of the twentieth century. The Non-Partisan League spread from North Dakota to a dozen northwestern states. It focused on seizing political control of state government and pushing for reforms. The Non-Partisan League favored state ownership of grain elevators, flour mills, and other farm infrastructure. League organizers went to Minnesota and joined with labor supporters to form the Farmer-Labor Party.[7]

The roots of Farm Bureau are not found in the early farm or political organizations. Farm Bureau grew out of recommendations from President Teddy

Roosevelt's Country Life Commission; the arrival on the American farm scene of the county agent and extension system; and the demands on agriculture resulting from the First World War. All of these played crucial roles in the Farm Bureau Movement and formation of the American Farm Bureau Federation.

In 1908, President Roosevelt appointed a four-member Country Life Commission to gather information on the condition of rural life and farming. "No nation has ever achieved permanent greatness unless this greatness was based on the well-being of the great farmer class," said the president. The number of Americans engaged in agriculture was at its peak at the time, but better living and business conditions were necessary to keep them interested in farming. "There is too much belief among all our people that the prizes of life lie away from the farm," Roosevelt added. When the commission's findings came out a year later, one of the suggestions was the need for unity and organization to solve farm problems. "There must be a vast enlargement of voluntary organized effort among farmers themselves," the report said."[8]

A dreaded agricultural pest also played a supporting role in the early history of Farm Bureau. After 1900, the cotton boll weevil made its way north from Mexico threatening southern agriculture. Cotton farmers needed to share information and make production changes if they were going to survive. The boll weevil problem was brought to the attention of a distinguished agricultural educator, Dr. Seaman A. Knapp.

In 1902, Knapp made several visits to Texas, and drawing on his broad experience, he came up with ways to adapt production patterns to the boll weevil. His plan included planting earlier varieties of cotton and diversifying crops. In the spring of the following year at a meeting in Terrell, Texas, Knapp encouraged a demonstration on the farm of a prominent local farmer. Knapp had been a rural editor and minister in Iowa, a background that no doubt served him well in convincing farmers. Nevertheless, the farmer he chose must have had reservations about experimenting with his cotton crop. Other farmers and businessmen put up money to cover any losses. None occurred, and the demonstration under Knapp's supervision was a big success. It convinced southern farmers that they would not have to give up raising their number one crop.

With money from an appropriation by Congress for the boll weevil emergency, Knapp took charge of farm demonstrations through the U.S. Department of Agriculture (USDA) in what was called the Farmers' Cooperative Demonstration Work, a forerunner of the Cooperative Extension Service. From a headquarters in Houston, Texas, in 1904, Knapp began his job by traveling on an agricultural lecture train to reach farmers at stations along the route. He and the cadre of farmer-demonstrators he enlisted found farmers willing to listen.

At this time throughout the country there was a wave of interest in better farming practices—a period of "agricultural evangelism," as Farm Bureau's first historian O. M. Kile called it. Farmer institutes, lecture trains, and demonstrations were popular methods of getting the word out to the country. Farmer institutes were often held in the winter months and lasted one or two days. The speakers were successful farmers or faculty from the state agricultural college. Lecture trains were usually a joint venture of the college and the railroad.[9]

Knapp, however, made sure the farmer was not merely an interested bystander but one who learned by doing. "What a man hears, he may doubt; what he sees he may possibly doubt, but what he does himself, he cannot doubt," was his observation.[10] After trying demonstrations on a district basis of ten or more counties, Knapp became convinced that the best method was to employ demonstration agents in a single county.

The first county agent in the country was W. C. Stallings who started work in Smith County, Texas, in November 1906. He was paid through local government funds and contributions from businessmen and farmers. The idea of placing a man in a county or district caught on so quickly that by 1910 there were nearly 500 agents in twelve southern states.

The farm adviser or county agent was described by Gladys L. Baker in *The County Agent* as an "agricultural missionary preaching the gospel of good farming which was based on a few well-established methods of farming."[11] Knapp valued practical farming experience in his agents rather than "book farming," and therefore did not enlist the aid of specialists at the state agricultural colleges. Upon his death in 1911, his son took over and sought cooperation from the colleges.

The county agricultural agent got his start in the South, but the North first linked the agent to a group of farmers that was the basis for Farm Bureau. Unlike the South with the cotton boll weevil, the North had no single adversary to provide an impetus for demonstration work. In New York, however, there was growing concern about the abandonment of small farms on the southern hills of the state. This came to light during a visit by Secretary of Agriculture James Wilson. He also personally inspected the Texas farm used by Knapp for his demonstration.

In submitting the report of the Country Life Commission to Congress, Roosevelt warned that the rapid advancement of city life was not the true measure of America "for our civilization rests at the bottom on the wholesomeness, the attractiveness, and the completeness, as well as the prosperity, of life in the country."[12] The commission concluded that farmers could not be left behind if the whole nation was to prosper. Business leaders who heard the news agreed, or at least they did in Binghamton, New York. In 1910, the secretary of the Binghamton Chamber of Commerce, Byers H. Gitchell, proposed a farm department in the chamber "to extend to farmers the same opportunities for cooperation now enjoyed by the business men of this city." A few progressive farmers responded by taking out memberships in the chamber.[13]

The chamber also had the cooperation of the Delaware, Lackawanna and Western Railroad and its traffic manager, George A. Cullen. The railroad was hauling freight for farmers and naturally had a stake in any plans to help its customer base. A tour was made of farms in Broome County by representatives of the chamber, College of Agriculture at Cornell University, and state and federal agriculture departments. The tour confirmed the need for assistance, especially to small, hardscrabble farmers. One idea was to set up a public demonstration farm as an object lesson in good farming.

A lack of agreement and need for more advice resulted in Cullen going to Washington, D.C., to consult with Dr. W. J. Spillman, chief of USDA's Office of Farm Management. Spillman who pioneered the field of farm management also was supervisor of Knapp's work in the South. He discouraged the demonstration farm idea because a number of these public farms had been unsuccessful. Instead, he recommended a county demonstrator or agent to work with farmers on their own farms.

At this time there already was an agent in Bedford County, Pennsylvania, A. B. Ross, a lawyer who left his profession in Cleveland for health reasons and moved to rural Pennsylvania. While recuperating he became interested in agronomy and found a calling as a self-educated farm adviser. Armed with USDA bulletins, Ross wore down his clientele until they would try new farming methods. On a trip to Washington, he encountered Spillman who put him on the payroll in 1910 to conduct field demonstrations as the first county agent in the North.

The county demonstrator idea appealed to Cullen and the rest of the committee in Binghamton, and they found the right man in John H. Barron, a graduate of the state college of agriculture. Raised on a farm and a member of the Grange, Barron opened an office in the Binghamton Chamber of Commerce on March 20, 1911. His salary was paid jointly by the chamber, railroad, and USDA. The college provided no money but gave advice and encouragement. Later the state authorized county boards of supervisors to appropriate money for farm improvement work.

In a newspaper advertisement or broadside, a message was delivered to farmers in Broome County that "an expert agriculturalist has been employed, whose services you may have free of charge." Barron was available to answer questions about farm management, soil fertility, dairy production, plant diseases and insect infestation, and anything else pertaining to farming. The notice promised that he would speak to groups of farmers, carry on experiments and demonstration work, and interest schoolchildren in farming. For further information, they were to contact "John H. Barron, agent for the Farm Bureau, Binghamton, N.Y."[14]

Farm Bureau was the logical choice of a name because the chamber already had a traffic bureau and manufacturing bureau. Barron initially covered several counties traveling in a fifty mile radius of Binghamton, often on poor roads. Naturally, there was skepticism about the involvement of businessmen and the railroad in this Farm Bureau, but Barron's solid farm background overcame a lot of concerns. He also appointed county chairmen from among the best and most cooperative farmers. In this way, he gained farmer participation and extended the knowledge from his work. Barron didn't stay long though; he resigned in 1913 and a replacement was named.

On October 10, 1913, farmers gathered at a county meeting to form the Farm Improvement Association of Broome County. Why this was done is not exactly clear. It could have had something to do with Barron's departure or a desire to separate from the chamber.[15] In 1914, this group became the Broome County Farm Bureau Association and took over the agricultural responsibilities of the chamber. The agent was responsible to the Farm Bureau and to the college of agriculture which administered state and federal funds.

James Quinn, the first president of the Broome County Farm Bureau, was elected in October of 1914. Quinn also was master of the local Grange. A plaque honoring Quinn as president of the nation's first Farm Bureau is located in a suburban area of Broome County on land that was once part of Quinn's farm. The county has retained farms and its rural character, and Broome County Farm Bureau is an active part of the community.

In March 1912 in Sedalia, Missouri, a farmer institute was so successful that it inspired the Sedalia Booster's Club to investigate hiring a county agricultural agent for Pettis County. A month later, Sam H. Jordan of the Missouri Board of Agriculture took a leave of absence to become farm adviser and manager of the Pettis County Bureau of Agriculture.

Broome County, New York, clearly used the name "Farm Bureau" first and is considered the first county Farm Bureau in the nation, but Pettis County was perhaps more of a farmer organization from the start.[16] It had representation of farmers by townships, school districts, and several honor committees that pledged to conserve soil, use purebred sires, and maintain roads. Funds for the Pettis County agent came partly from the county court. The first Farm Bureaus were funded from a number of sources in addition to small dues from the farmers themselves. The other sources included boards of supervisors, boards of education, and the Crop Improvement Committee of Chicago.

The Crop Improvement Committee of the Council of Grain Exchanges received a generous pledge from Julius Rosenwald of Sears, Roebuck and Co. for agricultural development. The centerpiece of the plan was a grant of $1,000 to any county willing to raise additional money to employ an agricultural agent.

Bert Ball, secretary of the committee, said there were a lot of plans for agricultural improvement but no concerted effort. He said the committee wanted to "awaken enthusiasm and action" in rural America and bring the best plans and teachings to the farmer in the remotest counties of every state. "Farm science is twenty-five years in advance of its practical application. Farming is a business and farmers should be business men or business men will be compelled to put a little farming into their business."[17]

Additionally, there were other sponsors motivated by self-interest, goodwill, or philanthropy. The size of the farm population in 1910 was thirty-two million and farmers were important buyers of goods and services. The Great Northern Railway provided funds through the Better Farming Association of North Dakota to employ a number of county agents in North Dakota and Minnesota. In the South, the Rockefeller family was a large contributor to the work of Knapp and his demonstration agents through its General Education Board. The board was established by oil tycoon John D. Rockefeller in 1903 to promote public school education. One reason businessmen were so eager to help the farm population was they feared an exodus from the farms would lead to food shortages and higher prices that would drive up wage demands. It certainly was not all altruism.

Critics charge that the American Farm Bureau Federation was born in the Chamber of Commerce or started with money from big business, the Rockefellers, and boards of trade. The truth is these contributions were for the services of a county agricultural agent and educational work, not to build a farm organization like Farm Bureau.

Agricultural extension was one of the main recommendations of the Country Life Commission. It called for off-campus work by the state colleges of agriculture to reach every farmer with "both information and inspiration."[18] The issue came up in Congress with more than a dozen bills seeking to bring federal aid and uniformity to extension.

On May 8, 1914, President Woodrow Wilson signed the Smith-Lever Act establishing the Cooperative Extension system as a partnership between USDA and the land-grant colleges and universities. It began the task of uniting the two divisions of extension work in the South and North through the State Relation's Service in 1915. Farm Bureau dues and contributions from local businessmen continued to support the county agent, but the big donor contributions stopped after the Smith-Lever Act.[19]

In 1921, historian Kile said, "The Smith-Lever Bill was an epoch-making event in agricultural development. It made available the funds necessary for the rapid extension of the County Agent system into every agricultural county of the nation."[20] In 1914, at least 700 counties in the South had agricultural agents. They included home demonstration and club agents assigned to work with women and young people. In the North and West (the terms then used for the north-eastern and midwestern parts of the country) a little more than 200 agents were employed, but their numbers increased dramatically.[21]

A pattern that emerged was to place greater responsibility on the farmers being served. In some states, farmers were required to organize to support the work of an agent before one could be assigned. Farmers helped the agent carry out his plans and provided supplemental financial assistance through their dues, which were usually a dollar. In the North and West, this county organization became Farm Bureau, the name that originated with Broome County and found favor with USDA and Extension leaders. Early on, other names were used for county organizations too. In Illinois and Iowa they were sometimes called crop improvement associations, and in the South they were known as councils of agriculture.

Farmers weren't always sure what to make of the young, college-trained men who showed up at their farms. An agent who served a Pennsylvania county recalled how he was mistaken at various times for a vaudeville trouper, horse doctor, fertilizer salesman, or the son of a county agent because of his youthful appearance. An agent's duties extended from teaching and demonstrating to judging agricultural fairs and organizing clubs for young people taking vocational education courses. The salary at the time was about $1,600 a year.[22]

As the county agent system spread so did the Farm Bureaus. New York's vice-director of extension, M. C. Burritt, published a definition of a Farm Bureau in his 1922 book, *The County Agent and Farm Bureau*. "A county farm bureau is an association of people interested in rural affairs, which has for its object the development in a county of the most profitable and permanent system of agriculture, the establishment of community ideals, and the furtherance of the well-being, prosperity, and happiness of the rural people through cooperation with local, state and national agencies in development and execution of a program of extension work in agriculture and home economics."[23]

An early supporter of the Farm Bureau was Liberty Hyde Bailey, dean of the College of Agriculture at Cornell University and chairman of the Country Life Commission. In 1914, Bailey said, "I like the idea of a public-membership organization on which Farm Bureau rests, every member paying his annual dues." He also observed that the control of Farm Bureau was in the hands of farmers, something he liked very much.[24] The name Farm Bureau was formally adopted for the farmer organizations supporting Extension work in the North and West beginning in 1916.

State federations of county Farm Bureaus formed as a result of yearly meetings of county agents and farmers at state agricultural colleges. The meetings were usually held during farmers' week celebrations and brought county Farm Bureau representatives to share ideas and concerns. Missouri organized the first state Farm Bureau in March 1915, and Massachusetts followed in May.

In December 1918, a resolution encouraging federations of county Farm Bureaus was passed at a meeting of the National County Agents Association. The agents believed that state Farm Bureaus promoted and strengthened the programs and objectives of the county Farm Bureaus. Indiana became the ninth state Farm Bureau in March 1919.[25]

There were twenty-two state federations of Farm Bureaus by the end of 1919, 800 county Farm Bureaus, and around 300,000 farmer members. Twenty-nine northern and western states recognized Farm Bureau as part of their Extension organization. There was some catching up to do in the South, but a number of southern states were represented at the first AFBF convention that year.[26] The Grange and Farmers Union got left behind by the Cooperative Extension Service because USDA required that farmer organizations in a supportive role be nonpolitical, nonsectarian, and nonsecretive. This definition excluded the Grange, Farmers Union, and potentially others.[27]

Endnotes

1. Harlow, *The Growth of the United States*, 86.

2. "Paragraphs from Speech that Nominated William Jennings Bryan for President," *Chicago Tribune*, July 11, 1896.

3. Kile, *The Farm Bureau Movement*, 31.

4. Benedict, *Farm Policies of the United States, 1790–1950*, 134.

5. Kile, *The Farm Bureau Movement*, 36.

6. Kile, *The Farm Bureau Through Three Decades*, 10; Benedict, *Farm Policies of the United States*, 134.

7. Hicks, *The American Nation*, 465–466.

8. "Roosevelt Plans Better Farm Life," *New York Times*, Aug. 9, 1908; Rasmussen, *Agriculture in the United States, A Documentary* History, vol. 2, 1869.

9. Kile, *The Farm Bureau Through Three Decades*, 25.

10. L. R. Simons, "New York State's Contribution to the Organization and Development of the County Agent–Farm Bureau Movement," *Cornell Extension Bulletin 993* (1957): 4.

11. Baker, *The County Agent*, 30.

12. Rasmussen, *Agriculture in the United States, A Documentary History*, vol. 2, 1863.

13. Simons, "New York State's Contribution," 5.

14. Ibid., 7.

15. Ibid., 9.

16. Baker, *The County Agent*, 16.

17. "$1,000,000 Crop Gift Stirs Farm Counties," *New York Times*, May 20, 1912.

18. Rasmussen, *Agriculture in the United States, A Documentary History,* vol. 2, 1870.

19. Baker, *The County Agent,* 39.

20. Kile, *The Farm Bureau Movement,* 86.

21. Baker, *The County Agent,* 29, 35.

22. Bezilla. "Pennsylvania's County Agents: The Early Years of the Agricultural Extension Service." 107–108.

23. Kile, *The Farm Bureau Through Three Decades,* 41.

24. Kile, *The Farm Bureau Movement,* 103.

25. Baker, *The County Agent,* 17.

26. Ibid., 16–17.

27. McConnell, *The Decline of Agrarian Democracy,* 48.

2 | The Great War and the American Farm Bureau Federation

THE FIRST WORLD WAR (1914–1918), ALSO KNOWN AS THE GREAT WAR, ADDED new words to the American lexicon: aerial dogfights, tanks, U-boats, mustard gas, trench warfare, no man's land, and the "unknown soldier." It is difficult to think of anything good coming from a war like that, but it also awakened Americans to the importance of agriculture. They read every day in newspapers about the grim specters of malnutrition and starvation in Europe.

Farm production was absolutely vital to national security and the outcome of the war. To fail was to fall under the Kaiser's boot. "Who the hell speaks for agriculture anyhow?" wondered Herbert Hoover, the Food Administrator charged with marshalling the forces of America's heartland.[1] Hoover soon realized that farmers had no collective national voice, but his exasperated query would be answered by the time he became president of the United States.

An American Farm Bureau Federation was the next logical step after county and state Farm Bureaus, but the war gave it greater impetus. AFBF Secretary John Coverdale confirmed this in the first annual report when he said, "The American Farm Bureau Federation is the direct result of the teamwork done by the individual county Farm Bureaus during the war period in helping stimulate food production and food conservation."[2]

Herbert Hoover biographer George Nash said that Henry C. Wallace, editor of *Wallaces' Farmer,* also credited World War I with AFBF's founding. But Wallace said it resulted from farmer discontent over Hoover's wartime manipulations of commodity prices and food supplies.[3] Both Coverdale and Wallace were right. Farmers exhibited great teamwork in producing enough food to win the war, but they also were dissatisfied with the voice they had in national affairs.

During the war, the Extension Service expanded with an emergency appropriation that increased the number of county agents from 1,436 to 2,435. Farm Bureaus expanded right along with the Extension Service. So-called "emergency

Farm Bureaus" were started while local appropriations and farmer dues were being arranged. The farm adviser went from being agricultural missionary and book farmer to patriotic leader of wartime campaigns to raise food production. Some of the conservation measures farmers had learned were discarded or downplayed in a determination to produce more foodstuffs, especially wheat. Agents traveled farm-to-farm soliciting cooperation from farmers who greatly increased their plantings and fed more hogs.[4]

Hoover, a successful mining engineer, initiated food relief to Belgium after it was invaded by Germany in 1914. This great humanitarian effort made him the logical choice of President Woodrow Wilson to head the U.S. Food Administration after America entered the war in 1917. An adept planner, Hoover clearly saw the task at hand. "If we cannot maintain the Allies in their necessities, we cannot expect them to remain constant in war. If their food fails, we shall be left alone in the fight, and the western line will move to the Atlantic seaboard," said Hoover.[5]

The Allies and Central Powers had not given enough consideration to feeding large armies and civilians during a protracted war because a short war was expected. Europe was fairly self-sufficient in food, and Russia was the world's largest agricultural exporter, so food got little attention from military planners. The mistake soon became apparent. Food production dropped by one-third across Europe because farmers were permitted to enter the military or jobs in industry. Horses were commandeered by armies, farm machinery broke down, and fertilizer ingredients were used for explosives.[6] The British blockaded food from reaching Germany, and U-boats torpedoed ships destined for Allied nations.

At a closed meeting of the House Agriculture Committee in May 1917 after returning from Europe, Hoover described the seriousness of the situation. England, France, and Italy with a combined population of 120 million people had two months of breadstuffs available. They were cut off from pre-war sources like Russia and Romania. Argentina had a crop failure and embargoed its food exports. France lost half of its winter wheat due to a frost.

Hoover proposed feeding the Allies without creating food shortages at home or resorting to rationing. The U.S. winter wheat harvest was the smallest in thirteen years and USDA warned that there was barely enough wheat for domestic consumption. In April 1917, May wheat contracts in Chicago were $1.29 a bushel. After the crop report, wheat futures soared to $3 a bushel, an all-time high. Wheat was highly prized because it was a durable grain and shipped well.

In August 1917, the federal government took unprecedented control over the nation's food and agriculture to stop speculation in commodities, stabilize consumer prices, and supply the needs of the Allies. Hoover considered it profit control not price control. "We can only use influence on both the retailer and producer, and depend upon their patriotism," he said in a speech to a business convention in Atlantic City. "In this area we can only regulate the flow of trade and hold it to moderate profits and excise speculation."[7]

The farmer received a "fair price" for his wheat, fair by Hoover's standards. A government commission set the price at $2.20 per bushel for Chicago delivery, considerably below the market price. A barrel of flour was comparable to a barrel of oil in today's terms of economic importance, and Hoover said that without government intervention, the price of a barrel of flour would have gone from $10 at the mill door to $30 or $50 instead.[8]

Hoover courted farmer favor wherever he could find it. He issued a news release from his office that voiced support from the secretary of the National Council of Farmers' Cooperative Marketing Association, J. W. Shorthill. "Who is afraid to permit our government to control the product of his labor or his genius in order that ruinous speculation in that product may be curbed? Certainly not the grain growers of this country?" said Shorthill.[9]

Nonetheless, Hoover frequently was in hot water in farm states. On one occasion he was accused of wanting to drop the price of wheat at $1.65 a bushel. Then he tried to adjust the corn/hog price ratio to convince farmers to raise more hogs. Hogs were the greatest source of fats that were needed in Europe. His attempt at price manipulation in the hog market ended badly and earned him a rebuke from Wallace and his farm magazine. Hoover was accused of breaking promises made to farmers.

Farmers were never formally licensed and regulated, but the government maintained unprecedented control over farm production and distribution. Poultry farmers were prevented from selling laying hens in order to increase egg production, and the Army and Navy were told not to buy tomato products from processors who paid eastern growers more than Hoover's price. Farm-state senators, congressmen, and rural advocates like Wallace spoke up, but there was no national voice for farmers, aside from government advisory committees with a few farmer representatives.

Hoover also forced down food prices through his conservation program. Never before had there been a nationwide campaign to get Americans to pay attention to the food they ate. In October 1917, a house-to-house canvass of twenty-two million families was begun. Every household, restaurant, and food dealer was asked to make a pledge to sacrifice and conserve food. A "pledge of loyalty" was printed on reminder cards so families would not forget at mealtime. "One meal every day and all day Wednesday in every week, I eat no wheat. One meal each day and all day Tuesday in every week, I eat no meat. Also on Saturday I eat no pork. Also I will use no more than ¾ pound of sugar every week—I and others of my household."[10]

Hoover enlisted 750,000 volunteers, mostly women, to serve on various committees at local, state and national levels. The housewife was Hoover's chief agent in food conservation. "Of our own free will we can send wheat for liberty; out of our love for our fellows we can eat potatoes for democracy," proclaimed a Food Administration bulletin. Americans got used to eating Victory bread which used one-fourth less wheat flour.[11]

Rural sociologist Ernest R. Groves said the war taught many lessons about agriculture. One of the most important was a realization that farming is the nation's most basic industry and without its success, the whole nation was in jeopardy. "National leaders as never before will consider every possible method by which farming can be made profitable, satisfying and socially appreciated," said Groves. "This policy will be undertaken not merely for the sake of the farmer, but also as a means of providing national safety."[12]

Not only had food won the war, but a third of American doughboys came from farms. Who could deny the importance of American agriculture and the need for farmers to be fully represented in the nation's councils with business and labor? The timing was right for an American Farm Bureau Federation.

The most detailed account of the beginning is found in *Cornell Extension Bulletin No. 993* by Lloyd R. Simons, Director of New York State Extension. According to Simons, talk of a national Farm Bureau first started around 1915 in Missouri, New York, and West Virginia. Then in November 1917, a group of New York county Farm Bureau presidents went to Washington to seek military draft exemptions for farm workers.[13]

Simons was assigned to take the group around to meetings with Food Administrator Hoover, Secretary of Agriculture David F. Houston, and others. The conferences proved worthwhile and afterwards at the Raleigh Hotel, the county presidents discussed the future. "What we need is a national Farm Bureau with the State Federations as member units," said E. V. Titus of Nassau County. Simons agreed with Titus. No mention was made of whether the topic came up with Hoover.[14]

A conference to explore forming a national federation of state Farm Bureaus took place on February 12–13, 1919, at Ithaca, New York. The twelve states represented were Delaware, Illinois, Iowa, Massachusetts, Michigan, Missouri, New Hampshire, New York, Ohio, Pennsylvania, Vermont, and West Virginia. Two future AFBF presidents, James R. Howard of Iowa and Oscar E. Bradfute of Ohio, were among the twenty-one farmers present for the Ithaca meeting.

The official minutes left no doubt that this was a grassroots movement of farmers even though it had the endorsement of Extension leaders. New York Farm Bureau President S. L. Strivings said the national organization must be " . . . democratic, thoroughly representative of actual farm conditions, and close to the farmers of the nation. Superimposed agriculture, however well constructed, is sure to fail," he said. In Striving's opinion, farmers would not accept a top-down organization. The marching orders had to come from the grassroots.[15]

A small committee drafted a constitution and bylaws over the summer for a meeting to take place in November at Chicago. The committee was headed by Bradfute and included Chester Gray of Missouri, E. B. Cornwall of Vermont, Frank M. Smith of New York, and J. C. Sailor of Illinois. States without a federation of county Farm Bureaus were urged to organize one immediately.

Anticipation ran high according to historian Kile. "The possibility of creating a great, new, national farmers' organization on a basis different from anything that had preceded and with elements of strength never before possible, was suddenly borne home alike in professional agricultural circles and to the practical farmer. It was recognized by all that here was a sleeping giant that might be awakened to full power almost immediately."[16]

AFBF was founded at one of the most significant times of the twentieth century. Cultural historian William Klingaman referred to 1919 as "the year our world began."[17] In March, Benito Mussolini addressed a small group of followers in Milan and started the Italian fascist movement. Vladimir Lenin's Third International or Comintern was staged in Moscow to plot the overthrow of the capitalist system. A German army corporal was ordered to check out a small political gathering at a Munich beer hall. Adolph Hitler joined the group he was supposed to monitor and turned it into the Nazi Party. The American Legion also was founded that year, and fortunately only the Legion and Farm Bureau are intact today.

As the Farm Bureau leaders prepared for the big Chicago meeting at the LaSalle Hotel in early November, the city was still in shock over the White Sox loss to the Cincinnati Reds in Major League Baseball's fall classic. Suspicions were running high that gamblers had paid a few of the best Sox players to throw the World Series. Detectives working for Sox owner Charles A. Comiskey were investigating leads, and Comiskey offered a huge reward for proof of the Black Sox scandal.[18]

A bigger story was the nationwide strike by 600,000 coal miners that began that month. Winter was fast approaching and Chicagoans were gripped with fear at not having coal to heat their homes. Under a wartime agreement, coal miners worked an eight-hour day, six days a week. The United Mine Workers charged that this contract expired with the signing of the armistice a year earlier. The union demanded a six-hour day, a five-day week, and a wage increase of 60 percent.

The Farm Bureau wasn't the only farmers' meeting in Chicago at that time. A meeting of state agricultural commissioners a few days earlier heard John McSparren, master of the Pennsylvania Grange, say, "We are the greatest capitalists in the world. We are also the greatest laborers in the world. Yet we have no single organized mouthpiece working for our interests in the nation's capital."[19]

The first annual meeting of the American Farm Bureau Federation began on November 12, 1919. The general session was in the Red Room of the LaSalle Hotel and was called to order by Bradfute. There were 500 Farm Bureau leaders and visitors from thirty-two states present. More than 200 attendees were from the host state. By the time the convention was over, a couple more state representatives were credentialed. Each state was allowed one voting delegate. Illinois, with so many farmers present to observe the meeting, agreed to have its contingent refrain from applause or shouts that might steer the delegates in their decisions.

The first of three keynote addresses was by Harvey J. Sconce, president of the Illinois Agricultural Association (original corporate name of Illinois Farm Bureau). "The inception of this national farm bureau association is taking place at a most opportune time," he said. "The United States is at present experiencing the greatest period of industrial unrest in its entire history. It is now just one year since the signing of the Armistice. During this interval more than 3,000 strikes have been inaugurated in this country. Is it any wonder that production has dwindled and cost of living has so greatly increased?"[20]

The second address by Silas L. Strivings, president of the New York Farm Bureau, expressed the viewpoint of eastern states. Their members wanted the national organization to be primarily educational, but educational in a way that promoted understanding between farm and city people. "Farmers must get past their own gateways and get out and see what is going on in the world. We must put agriculture into proper relationship with the rest of the world."[21]

The third address was by James R. Howard, president of the Iowa Farm Bureau, who later emerged as the first AFBF president. "The East and West, the North and the South, have agricultural problems which are different only in their external aspects," said Howard. "These problems are basically similar or identical. We need to create a national spirit in our agricultural life. The farm bureaus enabled us to look over our line fences, the state organizations enabled us to work on our state problems, and now we have before us the possibility of a national association to create the national agricultural spirit."[22]

Howard ended his speech with a remark important in the context of the times. "I stand as a rock against radicalism, but I believe in an organization which strikes out from the shoulder." A week earlier on the second anniversary of the Bolshevik Revolution, the U.S. Attorney General's office raided radical organizations in eighteen cities. Hundreds of anarchists and socialists were deported. AFBF founders had no interest in radical politics, strikes, or disruptive behavior, but Farm Bureau would not "pussy-foot" around, as Howard put it. He said it would be a straight-shooter in public affairs.[23]

Robert P. Howard wrote a biography of his father in which he described the delegates as "upper-middle class landowners, forward-looking, hard-headed, and bipartisan, convinced that agriculture needed national leadership and hopeful that they could establish a Farm Bureau Federation that would provide it, then and in future years for the good of rural America."[24]

Sconce said the same thing about the sort of person who would become a member. "The membership of Farm Bureau represents the very cream of American farmers. They are the real progressive, intelligent, energetic leaders of their community, who are public benefactors in every way. He is not the disgruntled individual who has a grudge against his neighbor, his government or the Farm Bureau."[25]

Strivings described the average farmer as "a very plain, matter-of-fact man" who is especially loyal to his country. "He has been talking at home with his neighbors at the places of meeting; he has been conversing in his little assemblages where he met his neighbors and friends, and his discussion has been sane and sound, but there is no national effort or welding process by which that organized sanity and that constructive thinking and that nationalistic program of building up the national good could find expression," he added.[26]

The name American Farm Bureau Federation was proposed for the new organization, but it was hardly a unanimous choice. One delegate thought the word "bureau" would remind farmers of "bureaucratic methods to which the farmer is unalterably opposed." Some states and counties already had adopted other names. Howard was one of those who didn't like the name Farm Bureau. He had been president of the Marshall County Iowa Farm Improvement Association when it changed its name to conform to the national movement. Bureau reminded him of a subordinate government agency or a piece of bedroom furniture.[27]

A farmer from Colorado told the meeting he understood the name to stand for "a plan of work whereby farmers thrash out their individual problems from the ground up." The name American Farm Bureau Federation won out because it was distinctive, unlikely to get confused with other organizations and "Farm Bureau" was already in use. The names discarded included National Agricultural Society, American Agricultural Association, and American Chamber of Agriculture. It was agreed that a state need not call itself a Farm Bureau so long as it worked along the lines of the Farm Bureau plan.[28]

A lesser dispute arose over the location of the headquarters. The Ithaca committee recommended Chicago. Illinois poet and newspaperman Carl Sandburg called Chicago "Hog butcher for the world, tool maker, stacker of wheat."[29] Indeed it was an agricultural hub in 1919 with the Chicago Board of Trade, Chicago stockyards, and other connections to agriculture. Washington, D.C., Indianapolis, Kansas City, Topeka, Atlanta, and a couple other sites were discussed and rejected.

The real sticking points of the convention had nothing to do with name and location but were the purpose, financing, and representation of the organization. The purpose was resolved by the adoption of a statement amended from the Ithaca meeting: "The objects of this organization shall be to correlate and strengthen the State Farm Bureaus and similar State organizations of farmers of the several states, in a National Federation, to promote, protect and represent the business, economic, social and educational interests of the farmers of the nation, and to develop agriculture."*30*

The issue was whether the purpose of AFBF should be primarily educational or economic. States also were divided over financing the organization. Eastern, southern and western states went along with an educational emphasis while the Midwest wanted an organization that could help them solve marketing problems through national cooperatives. The latter would require more financing.

The original dues proposal was 10¢ per Farm Bureau member family in the first year, 25¢ the second year, and 50¢ in the third year. This was seen as inadequate by a number of states. "You put a 10¢ stamp on anything and you don't get it very far. That is very objectionable to a lot of men in this audience today," said Sconce. Instead, he proposed that the national organization be financed at 20 percent of all membership dues received by the state and an initiation fee of $1,000.

His feelings were echoed by Ralph Snyder of Kansas, who stated, "I want to impress on you this fact that we are merging into the greatest organization that these United States have ever seen and we must have sufficient money to get us sufficient prestige so that we go into it with some dignity." John Coverdale of Iowa referred to a telegram he received from a membership drive back home. "We have 104 men today who are running through the mud, slush and snow and cold throughout seven counties, working there with the Farm Bureau, putting on a campaign and a drive in which over 90 percent of our farmers have come in." He too urged delegates not to sell short the organization by failing to sufficiently fund it.

Dr. W. H. Walker of California was afraid of just the opposite—that the organization would start with too much money and that would invite "vultures" in to wreck it. "My suggestion is that we ought to be careful and moderate in our plans, because in our experience every organization that we have looked up that has been wrecked, one of the things that contributed to wrecking it was too much money." Walker was joined by delegates from states with small, less prosperous producers.

In the end, a compromise was reached that AFBF would receive 10 percent of the membership dues paid to each state Farm Bureau. Dues varied considerably at the time, even within a state; they were anywhere from $1 to $10 per member family. A provision also was made for state Farm Bureaus that collected no dues from county memberships.

Representation in the governing body boiled down to two choices: one vote per state, as was the rule at this convention, or representation based on total state membership. States that were smaller agriculturally and therefore would have fewer members favored one vote per state. They thought this would stop the agricultural center of the country from dominating the organization. But midwestern states had a good argument; they said there would be less incentive for farmers to join Farm Bureau if their state was held down to one vote regardless of size. They also questioned the fairness of this unless AFBF's budget expenses were likewise shared equally.

The one-vote-per-state group could have held sway at this convention but decided it was best not to risk a walkout from the larger states that were insisting on greater representation. Thus the outcome was one-vote per state plus an additional director for every 20,000 paid-up members. This board later became the House of Delegates or simply voting delegates of the American Farm Bureau Federation. They elected an executive committee of twelve members, three from each region (the regions were Northeast, Central, Far Western, and Southern), but not more than one from a state. The executive committee also included the president and vice president. This executive committee later became the board of directors.

The constitutional debate took up much of the time of the three-day convention, but a resolutions committee headed by Howard simultaneously met and was ready on the final day, November 14, with its proposals. After amendments and discussion, the resolutions were passed, including one that recognized "that the strength and origin of the American Federation of Farm Bureaus has been achieved through co-operation with the State and Federal Department of Agriculture, upon a sound educational program of local work." The rest of this resolution was a hope for continuing cooperation with the Extension Service as Farm Bureau moved into legislative activity and business enterprise. It was now a fact that Farm Bureau was no longer an educational plan, but a broader movement.[31]

The final business of the first meeting was the election of a president and vice president. The chairman of the convention, Bradfute, seemed like a shoo-in. In the interest of time, nominating speeches were dispensed with. The nominations from the floor were Bradfute and Strivings of New York, but Bradfute magnanimously nominated Howard who by then was packing his bags in his hotel room to return to the farm.

Howard won with a clear majority on the first ballot. Apparently, he had impressed the delegates with his keynote speech and work as chairman of the resolutions committee. Coverdale, his friend and fellow Iowan, quickly ran to get him. Howard hesitated a bit but returned to the convention and entered the room to applause. The first president had no platform or promises to make except one. "I only promise you that I will work at the job, not on an eight hour day basis and five days a week basis, but I will put in full farmer time." This brought more applause and laughter.[32]

Reaction in the press was generally favorable. The *Chicago Tribune*, in addition to mistaking Bradfute for the elected president, labeled the organization a "new farmers' union" and said it represented five million farmers. This was a generous assessment perhaps based on the number of farmers in the states represented.[33]

The *Chicago Herald Examiner* also called it a farmers' union and said the purpose was to "teach capital and labor a lesson." A Missouri delegate told the reporter, "The fundamental purpose of the national association as I see it is to take both capital and labor by the seat of their pants and the nape of their necks and crack their heads together so they'll learn a little sense." He toned it down a little in an afterthought that of course Farm Bureau would try to work with them first.[34]

The *Prairie Farmer* was mildly disappointed. The farm publication said that the American Farm Bureau Federation "took to the water with its hull stove in and its engines hitting on two cylinders. Instead of being born to the enthusiastic vision of big service to the business of American agriculture with which many of the delegates were inspired, it was born of the suspicion and conservatism which others brought to the meeting." The editorial added, "The important thing, of course, is that it was born at all. Never before have farmers from New Hampshire to Mississippi and California been able to meet for such a purpose and find any common ground at all on which to set their feet. The new association, imperfect as it is, is a great step forward . . ."[35]

The newly minted American Farm Bureau Federation was a temporary organization when the delegates left Chicago. The constitution or bylaws had to be ratified by ten state Farm Bureaus over the next few months. Another convention was scheduled for the LaSalle Hotel in March 1920 to finalize a permanent organization.

Endnotes

1. Victor J. Albjerg, "Allan Blair Kline: 'The Farm Bureau 1955,'" *Current History* (June 1955): 362–368.

2. *AFBF Annual Report of 1920*. For the first twenty-five years or so, AFBF produced an annual report to members that summarized the organization's accomplishments. Bound copies are maintained by the American Farm Bureau Federation.

3. Nash, *The Life of Herbert Hoover; Master of Emergencies*, 401.

4. Baker, *The County Agent*, 40–41; L. R. Simons, "New York State's Contribution to the Organization and Development of the County Agent–Farm Bureau Movement," *Cornell Extension Bulletin No. 993*, 20.

5. USDA, Woman's Committee, *Council of National Defense Bulletin*, March 1918.

6. DeGroot, *The First World War*, 149–150.

7. "Hoover Sees Peril of Socialism Here," *New York Times*, September 20, 1917.

8. "Hoover Sees Plenty of Food This Year," *New York Times*. May 1, 1918.

9. News Release, Herbert Hoover, Washington, D.C. Monday, July 15, 1917, Pre-Commerce Papers, Hoover Library.

10. "A Pledge of Loyalty," U.S. Food Administration pledge card, Pre-Commerce Papers, Hoover Library.

11. "Potatoes for Wheat," *U.S. Food Administration Bulletin*, April 1918," Pre-Commerce Papers, Hoover Library.

12. Groves, *Rural Problems of Today*, 173–174.

13. Simons, *Extension Bulletin No. 993*, 26.

14. Simons, *Extension Bulletin No. 993*, 26. Simons was recognized in 1945 with AFBF's highest honor, the Distinguished Service Award. He was modest in writing about his own contribution to the idea of forming a national Farm Bureau.

15. Simons, *Extension Bulletin No. 993*, 31.

16. Kile, *The Farm Bureau Movement*, 114.

17. Klingaman, from the title of his book, *The Year Our World Began 1919*.

18. "Comiskey Refutes Charges Against White Sox," *Chicago Tribune*, December 15, 1919.

19. "Farmers Cheer Plan to Enter Industrial War," *New York Times*, November 11, 1919.

20. Transcript, AFBF Annual Meeting, November 12–14, 1919, Chicago, Illinois. A transcript of the annual meetings was prepared by a court reporter. The transcript usually included speeches at the general session and debate in the House of Delegates. These unpublished transcripts are maintained solely by the American Farm Bureau Federation.

21. Ibid.

22. Ibid.

23. Ibid.; Renshaw, *The Wobblies*, 191.

24. Howard, *James R. Howard and the Farm Bureau*, 108.

25. Transcript, AFBF Annual Meeting, November 12–14, 1919, Chicago, Illinois.

26. Ibid.

27. Howard, *James R. Howard and the Farm Bureau*, 65.

28. Transcript, AFBF Annual Meeting, November 12–14, 1919, Chicago, Illinois.

29. Sandburg, *The Complete Poems of Charles Sandburg*, 3.

30. Transcript, AFBF Annual Meeting, November 12–14, Chicago, Illinois.

31. Ibid.

32. Howard, *James R. Howard and the Farm Bureau*, 3, 113–114; Transcript, AFBF Annual Meeting of November 12–14, 1919, Chicago, Illinois.

33. "Farmers Union Formed to Act for 5,000,000," *Chicago Tribune*, November 14, 1919.

34. "Farmers' 'Union' Told to Beware Nonpartisans," *Chicago Herald Examiner*, November 13, 1919.

35. Kile, *The Farm Bureau Movement*, 121.

3 | The Farm Bureau Movement

At the start in 1919, farmers showed great enthusiasm for this new farm organization that represented their legislative interests and upheld their fundamental beliefs. "The farm is the basic source of every national function—material, moral, spiritual," said AFBF President Howard at the 1921 AFBF annual meeting in Atlanta. "The American Farm Bureau Federation's job is to guard the fountainhead that the waters may be kept pure and clean for the well-being of all." Farm Bureau became keeper of the flame for Jeffersonian agrarian beliefs that had been reaffirmed by Roosevelt's Country Life Commission.[1]

Farm Bureau also was no longer just an educational plan to spread better farming methods, but a movement for economic and social advancement. The Farm Bureau Movement benefited from near perfect timing in 1919. The war was over, but Americans were used to volunteering and mobilizing to be part of something big, whether the expeditionary forces in Europe or Hoover's "Food Will Win the War" campaign at home.

Now there was a chance for them to mobilize as farmers for their own interests. The Farm Bureau membership drive in the winter of 1919 was especially exciting. According to Kile, "Big things were expected of Farm Bureau and big things were promised." There were speeches in every county, headlines in local newspapers, and prominent mentions in the farm press.[2]

An Illinois farmer gave an account of a whirlwind Farm Bureau membership drive. "I remember the day I was tackled by one of Sailor's solicitors (Jacob Sailor of the Illinois Farm Bureau). He jumped out of my neighbor's 'flivver,' hopped the drainage ditch and tried to stand me up in a fence corner and make me listen to his whole rigamarole of reasons why and wherefore. I cut him off rather short, by asking if I looked like the sort of customer who had to be sold on a farm organization. Didn't he suppose I read the papers? Didn't he know I saw the need of it every day of the year? Didn't he think I had any brains at all? Where was there a farmer who surmised that he was going to get full measure of economic and social justice without organization? I'd sign up right then and there and he could save his furious spiel for the man across the road."[3]

AFBF delegates met again in Chicago on March 3, 1920, to finalize the organization. Indiana was the first of 28 states to ratify the constitution and bylaws mailed out ahead of the meeting. Howard was elected president of the permanent organization. The job was a full-time commitment that came with great sacrifice. He had to turn over his farm business to others in his absence and give up a good deal of family life. Silas Strivings was elected vice president, John Coverdale became secretary, and Gray Silver of West Virginia was named Washington representative.

A clarification was made right from the start that the president, who had to be a bona fide farmer, was the chief officer of the organization. Further discussion about dues and office location settled matters. The American Farm Bureau Federation share of member dues would be 50¢ per member family. Chicago was selected for the AFBF headquarters and Washington, D.C., for a legislative office. There was more unanimity at this meeting than the one a few months back. Delegates were more comfortable with each other and were anxious to get to work.[4]

Increased membership was the first priority. Farmers joined Farm Bureau at the county level; the counties belonged to the state federation; and the states belonged to the American Farm Bureau Federation. Technically speaking, only the state Farm Bureaus were members of the national federation, but in reality a Farm Bureau member family was represented at all three levels.

Coverdale suggested the way farmers should be approached to join. Ask them, "Are you standing together with the farmers of your state and other states of this nation on a national organization? If you are, we want you with us." Yearly dues were $5 up to as much as $10 in more prosperous states. Typically, a $10 membership was divided into 50¢ for the national organization, $3.50 for the state, and the remaining $6 spent at the local level. Because the county agent was supported mainly by public funds, Farm Bureau and Extension agreed that soliciting Farm Bureau memberships was not part of the agent's job. That was a job for volunteers and to a lesser extent, in the early years, paid solicitors.

The automobile age arrived just in time for the Farm Bureau Movement and made it easier and more thrilling perhaps to go from farm to farm to recruit members. After introducing his Model T in 1908, Henry Ford became one of the most famous men in all America. Ford produced one million automobiles in 1921 and two million by 1923. Born on a Michigan farm, Ford was a folk hero in the eyes of many Americans especially farmers.

The best time of the year for a Farm Bureau membership drive was before spring fieldwork. Howard's biography recalled that " ... even if it might be inconvenient, winter was the ideal time for traveling from town to town and farm to farm. Spring rains would make roads impassable, forming mudholes deeper than Model T axles. It was better to dress warmly, put side curtains on the open car, and start out over ruts that could cut tires to shreds." A team of horses was kept handy for when the car broke down.[5]

Whenever possible, a three-year membership was secured by having the farmer write three checks. One check was for this year's dues, and two were post-dated for payment in the following years. Once members were recruited, they were invited to Farm Bureau meetings, usually held in churches or schoolhouses where films, spelling bees, ciphering matches, or other simple forms of entertainment were used to guarantee a good turnout.

Farm Bureau shattered conventional wisdom that farmers could not organize on a national basis. Rural sociologist Groves theorized that farmers were not like-minded enough. "In this country at present there is no mind that can be fairly said to represent a group so lacking in substantial unity as the farming class." He attributed the lack of unity primarily to geographical differences and the isolation of farming. "The work of the average farmer brings him into limited association with his fellows as compared with the city worker. This fact also operates upon him mentally. He has less sense of social variations and less realization of the need of group solidarity." The only time farmers got together, in Groves' opinion, was during hard times when discontent spilled over briefly into radicalism. He didn't see the automobile as a uniting factor either, but a way off the farm for those dissatisfied with "slowly acquired property, impersonal success and non-dramatic activities of farming."[6]

Such negative thinking about farmers was not uncommon. Farm Bureau, on the other hand, wanted to give members a sense of pride in themselves and their farming profession—to lift them up. Doing so, it was believed, could even stem the tide of people leaving the farm for jobs in the city. The "Farm Bureau Platform" was a simplification of what the organization sought to accomplish: (1) efficient production, (2) better merchandising methods, (3) higher living standards, (4) a well-rounded community, and (5) an equal opportunity.[7]

Farm Bureau was built on solid ground as a grassroots organization with sound principles and strong leadership from the top ranks of agriculture. There was just one problem: the Farm Bureau Movement sailed directly into the headwinds of the worst farm depression the country has ever known. Farm Bureau's survival in the 1920s and 1930s, while not a miracle perhaps, was at least a major accomplishment and indicative of its staying power.

Before the First World War, there were the so-called "parity" years of 1910–1914 when farmers felt reasonably prosperous and thought farm prices were in equilibrium with prices for manufactured products. Then in response to wartime demands, farmers plowed up forty million additional acres and planted almost three-fourths of it to wheat. Exports soared, mechanization increased farm productivity, and farm prices rose faster than non-farm prices.

Prosperity came to a crashing halt shortly after the war's end. Government price guarantees, which had been more like price ceilings during the war, ended abruptly and prices fell. Competition from Canada, Australia, and other countries cut exports in half. The purchasing power of farmers declined sharply, taxes rose, and farmers were hard-pressed to make mortgage payments on farmland purchased at inflated prices. An economic adjustment had been expected, but farmers were surprised by its severity and how agriculture seemed singled out by it.

"The prices of farm products have gone back far below pre-war prices, while the prices of other things have remained high," said Secretary of Agriculture Henry C. Wallace at the 1921 AFBF annual meeting. "All in all, this depression is the most severe the farmers have ever experienced."[8] The numbers bore this out. Wheat was $2.16 a bushel in 1919 and fell to $1 two years later. Hog prices similarly were cut nearly in half from $16.10 per hundredweight to $8.50. Cotton dropped from 35¢ a pound to 16¢ in one year, and the gross income of farmers was reduced from $15.8 billion in 1919 to just $9.55 billion in 1920.

There were two ways to look at this development. Farmers obviously needed Farm Bureau more than ever, but were they too discouraged by the farm economy to join and volunteer their time? Farm Bureau claimed to have a membership of one million farm families. The 1920 AFBF annual report listed more than 800,000 members in thirty-seven states, and there were 85,000 members in states not yet affiliated with the national organization. The number got rounded up to a million, but paid-up memberships were another matter. They were 317,108 in 1920, and most were in the Midwest. Officially, AFBF membership did not reach the one million mark until 1946.[9]

While the Washington office concentrated on legislative issues, the Chicago general headquarters was concerned with building membership, which meant supporting the efforts of state and county Farm Bureaus. "If a permanent membership is paramount, if Farm Bureau is to function in an educational, social and economic capacity, then the program of securing and maintaining membership should be the leading objective of every local Farm Bureau," said Coverdale.[10]

Beginning in 1920, the organization department assisted in membership campaigns by sending out AFBF's limited staff and leadership to make appearances at meetings and producing membership handbooks and other materials. Farm Bureau was likened to a giant wheel in an early handbook. In the center was the hub or the county Farm Bureau. The spokes were the member state Farm Bureaus that carry on the service programs demanded by its members. The rim and tire holding the entire structure together was the American Farm Bureau Federation.

"If any part of this wheel is weak, injured or missing, the whole thing is shaky and unsafe."[11]

Because it boldly proffered to speak for all of agriculture, the Farm Bureau Movement never lost sight of its goal of representing all regions and commodities. Other farm organizations eventually retreated to parts of the country where they had strength. Farm Bureau could have done this too, because the Corn Belt was clearly its stronghold, but AFBF leadership was determined to keep everyone in the fold. One concern was the South which needed additional attention because Farm Bureaus and Extension got off to a slow start there.

In 1921 AFBF paid membership was up to 466,422, but as farmer worries mounted over farm prices, it dropped down to 363,481 in 1922. Most of the losses were in the Midwest. The other three regions actually posted gains. There was good news especially in the South which jumped from only 7,928 members to 25,275, but negatives outweighed the positives.

"None of us hope, of course, or even anticipate that Farm Bureau has reached its zenith, although in a national way and in many of our states at the present time everything does not look absolutely in a rosy atmosphere," said Missouri Farm Bureau President Chester Gray at an AFBF board meeting.[12] The organization department reported a feeling of pessimism out in the country on the part of Farm Bureau membership chairmen. "The inspirational enthusiasm coming from the working out of a new idea in agricultural organization has somewhat subsided," it noted.[13]

The Roaring Twenties were not roaring for families in rural America. The decade only served to heighten economic and social disparity between cities and farms. Addressing the 1927 AFBF annual meeting at Chicago, AFBF president Sam Thompson of Illinois noted, "While the average citizen is reported to have attained the highest standard of living ever attained in this or any country, or an average of income per citizen of $2,010, the farm income decreased from $922 in 1925 to $853 in the year 1926–1927."[14]

Thompson, the third AFBF president, was concerned about the sociological aspects of the farm problem which he said were acute. He cited the exodus from the country to the city, an increase in tenant farming, reduced financial ability to maintain rural schools, churches and community institutions, and a loss of interest by young people in the farming vocation. Rural churches in Illinois, he noted, had reduced the annual salaries paid to pastors from $1,000 to $500.[15]

The AFBF leader vowed that Farm Bureau would find a remedy for the farm situation, and added, "The farmers have no desire to deprive others of the benefits of prosperity. They do not overlook the fact that Americans consciously and deliberately adopted a high standard of living as a national policy."[16] The Illinois "dirt farmer" tipped his hat to urban prosperity which was outstripping farm profitability. Catching up was a major Farm Bureau goal that consumed much of its attention through the New Deal years.

Rural America also lost ground to the cities in population growth, as reported by the 1920 U.S. Census. The nation exceeded 100 million people, and for the first time there was an urban majority of 51 percent. The interpretation of what constituted an urban community was a loose one, but this still marked a milestone in American society.

Music, film, and radio transformed American culture in the 1920s. This was the beginning of the consumer culture with mass advertising, installment buying, lay-away plans, and door-to-door salesmen. Families bought exciting new electronic gadgets—refrigerators, washing machines, sewing machines, vacuum cleaners, toasters, irons, radios, and phonographs or Victrolas. The AFBF headquarters city just happened to be the center of the nation's film distribution industry. The major filmmakers moved to Hollywood for sunnier weather, but many movies were still produced in Chicago. Throughout its ninety-year history, Farm Bureau made excellent use of mass communication, and it wasn't long before the young organization discovered motion pictures.

In April 1922, AFBF signed a contract with Homestead Films to produce Farm Bureau motion pictures. The production studio was located in Peoria, outside Chicago. More than a dozen silent films were produced in the 1920s. Titles included: "Spring Valley," "The Farm Bureau Comes to Pleasant View," "Horse Sense," "Layers and Liars," "Golden School Days," "The Homestead," and "Forward Farm Bureau." The movies promoted Farm Bureau membership, better farming, and rural homemaking. They were educational, inspirational, and even humorous. Unfortunately, only one or two of these films survived the years.

Best of all, the Farm Bureau message was on the screen at no cost to the national organization, because it certainly couldn't afford to be making movies. Homestead Films produced the films using Farm Bureau approved scenarios for the scripts. It recovered costs and presumably made money from distribution and advertising. For example, the White Sewing Machine Company was the underwriter of a film about the role of farm women. Homestead Films arranged with small town theaters to hold a Farm Bureau night at the movies so farmers could see the films on the "big screen." County Farm Bureaus also received the movies on loan to show at meetings. The county agent got the job of locating and operating a projector.

Farm Bureau also was a pioneer in radio and farm broadcasting. In 1922, an agreement was made with radio station KYW in Chicago to broadcast Farm Bureau news on a nightly basis. The station went on the air in 1921 as the seventh radio station in the nation. Its call letters were moved to Philadelphia in 1934. Calvin Coolidge was the first U.S. president to use radio, about the same time as Farm Bureau. Even in the worst of times, farmers hung on to radios. The radio was said to be the last thing to go when the sheriff came to foreclose on the farm. It took some time for modern conveniences to make their way to farm homes, particularly in the South. Farm Bureau promoted rural electrification to end the drudgery of everyday farm life which it feared was sapping members of the energy needed to build the organization.

As early as 1920, the Washington office issued news releases and op-ed pieces for newspapers and magazines. The first Farm Bureau newsletter was a mimeographed sheet, but by 1921 an information department was started and the *American Farm Bureau Federation Official News Letter* was printed. The *Bureau Farmer* monthly magazine was started in 1926 as a cooperative arrangement with state Farm Bureaus so they could include individual state supplements. There were quite a number of farm publications, but they generally reflected the editorial opinions of the publisher and editor. The *Bureau Farmer* was the "Voice of Agriculture."

There was no question that the American Farm Bureau Federation got off to a good start, but the farm depression threatened to drag it down. At the 1925 AFBF annual meeting in Chicago, Organization Director E. P. Taylor warned delegates, "It is fairly easy to induce men to sign membership contracts and pay their initial membership dues, especially if a noisy campaign is put on with lots of jazz music, passionate appeals and a big feed." But he feared that members obtained in this manner would not stay around long. The farmer that Farm Bureau wanted to reach was not the one given to emotional appeals, but the farmer imbued with a cooperative spirit who joined with fellow farmers to develop the policies and plans of the Farm Bureau.[17]

Through the 1920s, Farm Bureau had carefully refined its membership drives. There were as many as twelve steps to a successful campaign beginning with a county Farm Bureau board meeting. Local publicity was obtained through newspapers and the farm press, and direct mail was used to reach prospects. Solicitors were given their materials at a banquet-school, and told, "Those who make the canvass should be prepared to intelligently present the plan and aim of the organization and to answer questions regarding the past history as well as present policy of the Farm Bureau."[18]

Meetings were held throughout the county just before the drive. They featured a Farm Bureau membership talk and one of the movies. The membership drive was conducted in all the townships at once or on a rotating basis. After the drive, it was important to put as many members as possible to work on committees. The Farm Bureau Membership Creed in 1925 used these words: "I believe I will get out of this organization just exactly what I put into it. I therefore pledge my energy and support to make it a success."[19]

One of the first activities that members rallied around was the Gift Corn Project of 1921. In the aftermath of the war, people in Europe and Asia were still in desperate need of food. The Illinois Farm Bureau came up with the idea at a winter meeting to help with donations of corn. In a few weeks, a dozen trains with 431 carloads of corn were traveling east by rail. The corn was ground into corn meal and by May was on a ship bound from New York to Poland. This was the first of many charitable efforts by Farm Bureau members over the years.[20]

In the first book written about the American Farm Bureau Federation in 1921, author Kile was excited about the possibilities of the Farm Bureau Movement and said this enthusiasm was only tempered by "his observation of the ease and regularity which farmers' organizations of the past had speedily arrived at a state of somnolence and inaction after a brief period of promising, albeit somewhat feverish activity."[21] It was too early to tell if this farmers' organization was going to be any different, but the founders sure hoped so.

Endnotes

1. Transcript, AFBF Annual Meeting, November 21–23, 1921, Atlanta, Georgia.
2. Kile, *The Farm Bureau Movement*, 127.
3. Ibid., 126.
4. Ibid.
5. Howard, *James R. Howard and the Farm Bureau*, 64.
6. Groves, *Rural Problems of Today*, 120–124.
7. *AFBF Annual Report of 1926.*
8. Transcript, AFBF Annual Meeting, November 21–23, 1921, Atlanta, Georgia.
9. *AFBF Annual Report of 1920.*
10. Ibid.
11. *American Farm Bureau Community Handbook.*
12. Minutes, AFBF board of directors, 1921.
13. Minutes, AFBF board of directors, 1921, 1922.
14. Transcript, AFBF Annual Meeting, December 5–7, 1927, Chicago, Illinois.
15. Ibid.
16. Ibid.
17. Transcript, AFBF Annual Meeting, December 7–9, 1925, Chicago, Illinois.
18. *American Farm Bureau Community Handbook.*
19. *AFBF Annual Report of 1925.*
20. Kile, *Farm Bureau Through Three Decades*, 75–76.
21. Kile, Author's Preface, *The Farm Bureau Movement*, v.

4 | Two Paths: Farm Bloc and Cooperative Marketing

THE FARM BUREAU MOVEMENT NEEDED BIG ACCOMPLISHMENTS IN ORDER TO SUSTAIN the momentum it had at the end of 1919, and Farm Bureau leaders thought they saw two ways for this to happen. One was legislative activity, getting long-stalled farm legislation passed by Congress. The other way was cooperative marketing on the national level to regulate the flow of commodities, establish fair prices, and reduce the role of the middleman. One way was so successful that it established Farm Bureau's reputation as a powerful, influential organization. The other almost led to disaster.

The American Farm Bureau Federation was not the first interest group to attempt grassroots lobbying on Capitol Hill. The lobbies for women's suffrage and Prohibition preceded it, but Farm Bureau was the first organization to perfect grassroots lobbying (informing and activating its members) and to practice it so effectively on a wide range of issues.

Immediately after the March 1920 meeting that set up the permanent organization, AFBF opened its legislative headquarters in a rented office at 1411 Pennsylvania Avenue. The man in charge was Gray Silver, referred to as "Senator" by colleagues. Silver had served in the West Virginia Senate and had a farm in Martinsburg. He was the only member of the AFBF executive committee with any political experience and represented his state at the 1919 convention.

Congress initially paid little attention to the Farm Bureau while it was setting up shop. As Silver recounted later, "Committees of farmers had been going to Congress for these many years, always getting a dinner, sometimes a ticket to the theater, and the occasion of their trip was often forgotten shortly after they left. But the farmer in this case had taken up headquarters in Washington, he was there to stay and see whether these things so close to his heart were forgotten."[1]

On the surface it would seem that a single lobbyist without great favors to dole out would not create much of a stir, particularly one representing farmers, a fairly disorganized and docile bunch compared to organized labor. The original legislative staff consisted of Silver, assistant O. M. Kile and three stenographers or secretaries. Silver's demeanor may have caused congressmen to underestimate him. He was soft-spoken, unemotional, and was described as having the appearance of "a shrewd but benign Yankee trader."[2]

Most of the bills close to the farmer's heart had been languishing in Congress for years, losing out from one Congress to the next. Farmers couldn't understand how the packers, textile industry, and other interests were so successful in stopping farm legislation. They weren't looking for special favors, just the same consideration that businessmen got. Industry lobbyists operated quietly and effectively out of the public eye. However, Farm Bureau was determined to operate in the open and play its cards face up. "There is no secret about it; the farmer representative doesn't take a congressman by the coat and pull him around the corner and whisper in his ear," said Silver.[3]

The lack of interest in farm legislation was due partly to the committee structure. In the 66th Congress, Republicans from the Northeast controlled the House, and even in 1920, only nine of 435 House members were real farmers. As Silver described the problem, "There had been a system in Congress for many years that when measures were offered on the floor and referred to a committee, they would go to a subcommittee and two men in the Senate or three in the House . . . would determine whether that measure would be heard on the floor or not, and that was where so many measures died." Farm Bureau's legislative strategy was to break the logjam and hold members of Congress accountable for their decisions.[4]

Gray Silver was the master at bringing grassroots pressure to bear on elected leaders. Farm Bureau's policy process was not yet fully developed, but member attitudes were obtained from polls and questionnaires distributed by county Farm Bureaus. President Howard also made appeals through farm publications asking for letters on specific issues that he could show Congress.

With the member wishes in hand, Silver would visit a wavering congressman or one who voiced opposition to a Farm Bureau-backed bill. The senator or representative had a hard time ignoring the well-documented opinions from his constituents. If fast action was needed, Silver alerted state and county Farm Bureaus by telegram, and they responded with a flood of wires.

Before long, Silver noticed that he was being followed on his visits to Capitol Hill by a large man with a round face and dimpled grin. He presumed the man to be a private detective. After this went on for awhile, the Farm Bureau lobbyist approached the man and struck a deal. Silver gave him a full report of his daily schedule in exchange for some privacy. The detective, Gaston Means, was one of the most colorful rogues of the Harding years in Washington. He worked for the Justice Department and later wrote a book claiming that Mrs. Harding killed the president with poison because of his philandering. Means achieved notoriety in the 1930s when he was arrested for taking money from a wealthy friend of the Lindbergh family to arrange the return of their kidnapped baby. He ended up spending the rest of his life in prison.[5]

Farm Bureau's Washington activities also were monitored by wiretaps. Silver and AFBF President Howard suspected as much and concocted a fantastic story that they shared over the office phone. The story soon made its way back to them from other sources.[6] When Silver had the tap traced by the telephone company, it led to a political office used by Sen. Boies Penrose (R-Pennsylvania), chairman of the Republican National Committee. Silver went with phone company technicians to the office and confronted an apologetic Penrose.[7]

The Eighteenth Amendment to the Constitution was passed by Congress and ratified by the states in 1919, and went into effect just before Farm Bureau opened its legislative office. Alcoholism was a problem in Congress despite Prohibition. The Senate even had its own private bootlegger. Horse racing, professional baseball, and golf were popular diversions that kept members of Congress from getting down to business. Also, there was no air conditioning in the House or Senate, and lawmakers weren't anxious to stay around in hot weather to address farm legislation.[8]

Silver explained his approach to lobbying so farmers could understand it. He likened it to a farmer and a team of plow horses. "Congress is the team I have in mind, and you are the farmers at the plow, and the Washington office is the jerk line. What is the jerk line for when you hook up a team? It is to get across to the leader what your wishes are." One way congressmen felt the jerk line was when Farm Bureau published their voting records in the AFBF official newsletter, something unprecedented in the history of Congress.[9]

In the last session of the 66th Congress, the top two Farm Bureau issues were a packer control bill and conversion of the munitions plant at Muscle Shoals, Alabama, to the production of chemical fertilizers. In the Muscle Shoals matter, Farm Bureau was up against the fertilizer trust and GOP congressmen. Republicans wanted to hold up Muscle Shoals as a white elephant, an example of waste and extravagance by the Wilson administration. They were in no hurry to make anything useful out of it.

Therefore, the House voted against a Farm Bureau-backed proposal, and because it was a voice vote and not recorded, congressmen thought they would not have to explain their votes back home. That was until Howard wrote a letter to each member of the House. "We regret that the vote yesterday was not one of record. In order that we may do justice both to Representatives in Congress and to our membership, will you kindly notify our Washington representative, Mr. Gray Silver, 1411 Pennsylvania Avenue, whether you voted for or against the proposition."[10]

Congressmen howled at the demand from the upstart Farm Bureau. They couldn't believe the audacity. Howard had not finessed the points of his letter either. He said the defeat of the Muscle Shoals proposition was because of the influence of the fertilizer lobby and its selfish interest in maintaining high fertilizer prices. Clearly, he was impugning the integrity of the Congress.

As a result, both Howard and Silver were hauled before a Congressional investigating committee. The AFBF leader was asked point blank if he was implying that Congress was corrupt, and if so, where was his proof? Howard could not understand what was wrong with asking a congressman to explain his vote. The inquiry continued for several hours with the farm leader pressed to name anyone from the fertilizer lobby who might have unduly influenced the legislators. Howard eventually came up with a name, and within a minute or two that man walked into the hearing room to angrily defend himself. He had been listening from an anteroom the whole time.[11]

Farm Bureau's foes then tried to undermine confidence in the small AFBF legislative staff. Word was spread to Farm Bureau leaders outside Washington that AFBF was misinformed and behaved antagonistically. An AFBF committee investigated and found nothing wrong but decided to make a change for appearance's sake. As a result, Silver was given more supervision and his assistant Kile was let go. Kile went to work for *Wallaces' Farmer* and authored two histories of the American Farm Bureau Federation. Relations between AFBF and Congress were patched up at a meeting in a House caucus room attended by more than 100 senators and representatives. Thereafter, a cooperative spirit prevailed.

The crowning achievement of the American Farm Bureau Federation in the 1920s was formation of the Farm Bloc in Congress. The bloc literally controlled both houses of Congress and passed twenty-six laws of interest to farmers by the time the 67th Congress adjourned in 1923. This remarkable feat earned AFBF a lasting place in American political history.

The Farm Bloc was formed on May 9, 1921, when a bipartisan group of senators from the Midwest and South met in Farm Bureau's office. The original group of twelve senators quickly grew to twenty-two. There were thirty members from the House of Representatives. Senator William Kenyon (R-Iowa) was the Senate leader until President Harding nominated him to a federal judgeship in an attempt to break the power of the bloc. Kenyon's place was taken by Sen. Arthur Capper (R-Kansas). The leader in the House was Rep. Lester J. Dickinson (R-Iowa). Farm Bloc members caucused separately and divided into groups by issue—adequate warehousing and storage, credit, taxation, transportation, and the like.

The deteriorating farm economy and President Harding's reliance on an "old guard" leadership to move his legislative program made it possible for the Farm Bloc to coalesce, but it would not have happened without Farm Bureau and its clever lobbyist. "It was only when organized agriculture came into the field that the real friends of the farmer saw an opportunity to make a stand against the dictators. Previous to that time it would have been political suicide . . . " wrote Kile.[12]

The 67th Congress that met for the first time in the spring of 1921 had a big Republican majority but little party unity. When Sen. Henry Cabot Lodge (R-Massachusetts) sought to adjourn the upper house for the month of July without acting on farm legislation, the Farm Bloc refused to go along. Harding summoned both Howard and Silver to the Oval Office. According to Howard, the president greeted them with, "Well, boys you have us. What do you want us to do?"[13] They wanted Congress to stay in session and pass the bills of interest to farmers. From that point on, the Farm Bloc took charge of the legislative agenda.

Farm Bureau adopted a policy against the short-selling of commodity futures contracts in 1920. As farmers saw it, sales of "phantom grain" were driving down market prices, except for the occasional attempt by a big speculator to corner the market and squeeze the short sellers. Senator Capper claimed that the Chicago Board of Trade was "the greatest gambling house in the world" with "wagers" amounting to $15 billion annually.[14] Will Rogers agreed with the need for a law prohibiting short sales. "We are continually buying something that we never get from a man that never had it," he wrote in one of his newspaper columns.[15]

In late August 1921, Harding signed the Capper-Tincher Futures Trading Act to dampen commodity speculation. The government imposed a per-bushel tax on grain sold for future delivery, unless the sale was by an individual farmer or a producer association. A number of forms of speculation, including puts and calls, were prohibited. Board of Trade members challenged the Futures Trading Act and were successful in getting the law overturned by the Supreme Court because of the tax feature, but a revised bill signed by Harding in 1922 was upheld on judicial review. Federal regulation of commodity futures trading thus was firmly established.

Another Farm Bloc victory was the Packers and Stockyard Act of 1921 that prohibited meat packers from engaging in unfair, noncompetitive practices to control supplies and rig the prices paid to stockmen. Stockyard rates and practices also were brought under the regulation of the secretary of agriculture who gave packers the benefit of the doubt by saying he wouldn't assume they all were "rascals" until it was proven to him.

There were several noteworthy victories in farm credit and financing too. The Emergency Agricultural Credits Act of 1921 revitalized the War Finance Corporation and authorized it to lend up to a billion dollars to dealers, exporters, banks, and farmer cooperatives for marketing, storage, and export of farm commodities. The interest rate on Federal Farm Loan bonds was increased by a half percent to attract more buyers while the lending rate to farmers was left unchanged. The working capital of the Farm Loan Banks was increased. Agriculture was given a representative on the Federal Reserve Board, and bills were passed to finance farm-to-market roads and construction of irrigation projects.

The greatest achievement of the Farm Bloc was the Capper-Volstead Act in February 1922 that gave legal protection to farmer cooperatives. Otherwise state and federal antitrust laws could be used to forbid the joint activities of farmers through cooperatives to market, price, and sell their products. Prior to the act, dairymen had been harassed by lawsuits for selling their milk cooperatively. The new law encouraged the development of large, well-capitalized marketing cooperatives.

The cooperative bill passed easily in the Senate despite some fears that it would lead to price-fixing. Bernard Baruch, financier and White House adviser, defended the cooperative law in a letter to Sen. Capper. "The farmers have not asked for any special privilege, nor has it been accorded to them. Certain laws have been passed and others sought, to enable them to do in their way— co-operation—what other producers, the makers of steel, for example, do by means of great corporations."[16]

While eastern newspapers typically were critical of the Farm Bloc, the *Chicago Tribune* reprinted an editorial from *Wallaces' Farmer* that praised it. "The farmers are coming on. They are getting stronger in national councils—so strong that they must be reckoned with. If this were not so, gentlemen in various parts of the country would not be wearing out their typewriters denouncing the activities of the farm organizations." The editorial expressed amusement that farmers were criticized for exerting the same kind of influence and political pressure that manufacturers, labor, and financial interests had long exerted in Washington, D.C.[17]

In January 1922, Harding called an agricultural conference in Washington and invited representatives of farm organizations, agribusiness, and labor. More than 300 delegates took part. It was a way for Harding and his Department of Agriculture to get in front of the Farm Bloc by showing concern for farm problems. "The administration has been keenly alive to the situation, and has given encouragement and support to every measure which it believed calculated to ameliorate the condition of agriculture," said Harding.

Howard himself was not entirely comfortable with the idea of special interests or blocs, and he told the 1922 AFBF annual meeting in Chicago, "I have said many times, and I repeat that I deplore a condition whereby a bloc or a faction in government becomes a necessity. But that condition existed and it was the only means that we could see to get agricultural justice from our national legislature, and we have just as good a right to have a bloc as have bankers or manufacturers or fertilizer people or railroads or anybody else." Howard was afraid farmers would be reduced to peasantry or serfdom without the intervention of Farm Bureau through the Farm Bloc.[18]

Harding, however, continued to do his best to make the Farm Bloc go away. In March 1922, he noted an increase in farm prices and said further work by the Bloc was unnecessary. Corn was at 50¢ a bushel which was up from as little as 20¢ six months earlier. Wheat rose to $1.40 a bushel from $1. Senator Capper's response was that the higher prices validated the usefulness of the Farm Bloc. On another occasion, Harding unveiled a statue of Alexander Hamilton and attacked factions and blocs during the ceremony. "Hamilton warned us that however such combinations or associations may now and then answer popular ends, they are likely to usurp the reins of government," he said.[19]

Although AFBF rang up a series of legislative victories in quick succession, its lobbying over the years has been characterized more by patience and persistence than lightning-fast results. It took twenty years for Farm Bureau to succeed in getting truth-in-fabrics legislation passed. The law required honest labeling of woolen cloth by making manufacturers indicate the presence of reworked wool also known as "shoddy" wool in their products. Woolen and worsted manufacturers formed the Fabric Labeling Legislation Committee to defeat bills that differentiated between virgin and reworked wool. Farm Bureau's persistence paid off, however, and the public adopted the term "shoddy" to mean anything of inferior quality.[20]

Warren G. Harding died of a stroke on August 2, 1923, three months before his fifty-eighth birthday. A month before his death, the president traveled out west and stopped in Kansas to call attention to the administration's efforts on behalf of farmers. Under a blazing sun, Harding helped a farmer near Hutchison harvest his wheat. The president knew how to make a shock of wheat and operated a McCormick-Deering grain binder in the field. "There senator," he said to Arthur Capper who accompanied him, "don't you think that ought to admit me to the Farm Bloc?" Harding's legacy was ruined by Teapot Dome and other scandals, but the amount of farm legislation he signed because of Farm Bureau and the Farm Bloc was surpassed only by the New Deal.

Despite its legislative success in Washington, the American Farm Bureau Federation made cooperative marketing its central theme in the early 1920s. The voting delegates put their stamp of approval on it at the 1922 annual meeting in Chicago, and Oscar E. Bradfute, the second AFBF president, was determined to carry out their wishes. Bradfute had been prominent in the national organization right from the start. He also came from Ohio, a state that was a leader in cooperative organizing among Farm Bureaus.

In a New Year's message to all Farm Bureau members, Bradfute said, "The Farm Bureau poses as a service organization. Without doubt the greatest and most immediate service which can be rendered is help in more successfully and profitably marketing farm products." He ended the message with a muster call,

"Forward! Farm Bureau." The theme was used on a widely distributed member-ship poster and is the source for the title of this book.[21]

AFBF moved forward on cooperative marketing but faced strong opposi-tion from grain merchants and almost fell under the influence of a manipula-tive cooperative organizer. The subsequent retreat on cooperative marketing was a painful, trying experience that nearly short-circuited the national organization.

The Rochdale system was borrowed from England before 1900 to set up small-scale producer cooperatives in the United States. After World War I, there was a new wave of interest in "orderly marketing," and Herbert Hoover suggested to AFBF that it send representatives to Belgium and Denmark to study coopera-tive marketing.

The Department of Agriculture collected data on cooperatives in the early 1920s and estimated as many as 10,000 grain elevators, creameries, cheese factories, and other cooperatives existed. As farm policy historian Murray Benedict pointed out, "As yet, farm sentiment, as well as business sentiment, favored solutions that did not require direct government action and financing."[22]

Midwestern states were the most interested in marketing and were the stron-gest state Farm Bureaus at the time. The sharp drop in farm prices after the war served to strengthen their hand in directing the organization. In July 1920, the first AFBF conference to discuss large-scale cooperative handling and selling of farm products was held in Chicago, and representatives of farmer cooperative associations, farm organizations, and the Department of Agriculture were invited to attend. The first speaker was Aaron Sapiro, a young California lawyer. Sapiro was the attorney for several California cooperatives handling specialty crops. He was convinced that these practices could successfully be transferred to handling basic commodities on a nationwide basis. A dynamic speaker, Sapiro won a num-ber of converts with his enthusiasm and sparked heated discussion among the 500 participants.

The Sapiro plan called for strong, centralized producer cooperatives, organ-ized on a commodity basis that entered into multi-year, ironclad contracts with members for delivery of all they produced. National or regional cooperatives were anticipated for the major commodities. They would enter terminal markets and take over selling, warehousing, and other functions normally handled by commis-sion merchants, elevator companies, and other middlemen. If a majority of farm-ers producing a commodity signed binding contracts, the cooperative would have enormous power over marketing and prices.[23]

General agreement was obtained at the meeting on doing something along national lines, but organization rivalries and jealousy prevented AFBF from taking the outright lead. In the end, the whole matter was turned over to the Committee of Seventeen, carefully appointed by Howard to give every organization a voice. The chairman was C. H. Gustafson, president of the Nebraska State Farmers Union.[24]

After months of hearing from experts and visiting cooperatives, the committee came forward with recommendations on April 6, 1921. Howard called the day "the sun-up for American agriculture." He viewed it as the end of the uneconomic and speculative marketing system which had left farmers powerless. He also promised that this new day dawning would not mean cutbacks in farm production. A commonly held belief among farmers at the time was that overproduction was not a problem so long as there were hungry people in the world.[25]

The report of the Committee of Seventeen placed the responsibility for inadequate farm profits squarely on a faulty marketing system. Commodity exchanges were blamed for price manipulation by speculators intent on driving down prices. The report noted that the total amount of grain sold annually on the Chicago Board of Trade (CBOT) was fifty times the amount of actual deliveries.

The committee's plan called for a central sales agency, the U.S. Grain Growers, Inc. Membership was limited to grain producers who paid $10 each and signed a contract to market grain for a period of five years. This was a nonstock, nonprofit organization with a board of twenty-one members, largely from farm organizations. The farmer's contract was with the local cooperative elevator, and the elevator's contract was with the national corporation. Sales and pooling arrangements required all grain marketed off the farm to end up under the control of the national sales agency. Divisions were set up to provide warehousing, financing, and export sales.

Committees soon followed to develop marketing arrangements for other commodities: The Committee of Fifteen for livestock; Committee of Twenty-One for a national dairy marketing plan; Committee of Twenty-One for a national fruit marketing plan; Committee of Ten for a vegetable marketing system; and the Committee of Twenty-five to develop a cooperative wool pool.

U.S. Grain Growers stumbled from the outset because of internal dissension and outside opposition. The Chicago Board of Trade denied its application for a seat on the exchange, which was necessary to trade large volumes of grain. At one point, a prominent CBOT member pledged $1 million to help farmers get a seat but nothing came of it. Membership was finally secured on the Minneapolis exchange.[26]

In August 1922, the American Farm Bureau Federation stepped in and asked the entire board of the U.S. Grain Growers to resign because the cooperative was a quarter million dollars in debt. E. L. Cunningham, secretary of the Iowa Farm Bureau, became the head of the grain cooperative. At the AFBF annual meeting that year, Cunningham tried to rally support for the marketing efforts. "Gentle-men, everything on our program must be secondary to the question of a market-ing system for the farm products of the land. A solution will enable the whole program of the American Farm Bureau Federation to carry on," he said.[27]

President Howard, exhausted and ailing from the tough task of getting the national organization off to a good start, declined a second term, and Bradfute was elected. After issuing his muster call in 1923, Bradfute told leaders and staff, "Commodity marketing is trumps. All departments, all the officials, and all the employees of the American Farm Bureau Federation will be expected to play the trump card." At least half of the national organization's income was to be spent on cooperative marketing, and state Farm Bureaus wanted an educational campaign to promote the advantages of cooperative marketing to farmers.[28]

Bradfute's first year in office was as difficult as that experienced by any presi-dent since. He immediately felt pressure from a meeting that took place at the same time as AFBF's annual meeting. Aaron Sapiro held a conference of com-modity marketing organizations in Washington from which the National Coun-cil of Farmer Cooperative Marketing Associations emerged. Farm Bureau sent a delegation to the meeting and obtained a pledge that the new organization would not overlap with Farm Bureau and other farm organizations, but the council broke the agreement and adopted its own policy resolutions on farm credit.[29]

Walton Peteet, secretary of the Texas Farm Bureau, was appointed to head AFBF's Cooperative Marketing Department in January 1923. A few months later, Sapiro was retained as a legal counsel to placate a few members of the AFBF board. Bradfute acknowledged that Sapiro was "the ablest proponent of coopera-tive marketing in America," but soon developed doubts about his loyalty, motives, and methods of doing business. Sapiro wanted so much control over marketing and finances that Bradfute said it would strip the AFBF president of much of his authority. Sapiro also demanded a large retainer and other compensation. This prompted a frustrated Bradfute to tell the board, "Mr. Sapiro does not seem to have the ability—while he is a great proponent of cooperation—does not seem to have the ability to cooperate quite as well as I would like to see."[30]

In a cryptic telegram to Peteet, Sapiro tried to hatch a plot. "We cannot leave the grain growers of country to mercy of present incompetent leadership." He suggested that they should form a national grain committee with the help of other Farm Bureau leaders in the Sapiro camp. Fractures within AFBF worsened. In September, a motion was made by Gen. E. H. Woods, president of Kentucky Farm Bureau, to accept the resignation of each and every AFBF employee so the board could reorganize the work and hire new and presumably lesser-salaried personnel to stay within budget. The motion was defeated as unfair and inconsistent with the way a hired-man was treated on the farm.[31]

By December, the Sapiro forces in Farm Bureau gained enough control to force the resignation of Secretary Coverdale, who maintained that Farm Bureau should have a balanced program and not concentrate solely on marketing. Sapiro had little time to celebrate, however. The 1923 AFBF annual meeting in Chicago resulted in a big turnover on the board. Sapiro backers were ousted and Coverdale was restored to his position as secretary. Sapiro, Peteet, and Information Director Sam Guard all left. Indiana Farm Bureau withheld its dues money for a year or two, and several other states threatened to do likewise.[32]

Sapiro's fortunes went downhill in years that followed. Many of the cooperatives he helped organize collapsed because they had been organized too quickly, from the top down with high-pressure salesmanship. Sapiro filed a million dollar lawsuit against Henry Ford in 1925 accusing Ford of libel for a story in his Dearborn, Michigan, weekly journal. The lengthy article began, "This is the story of the effort of Aaron Sapiro to seize control of the American Farm Bureau Federation."[33]

Perhaps Sapiro tried to hijack Farm Bureau. If so, he underestimated it. Farmers were not about to give up control. Sapiro's genuine accomplishments were acknowledged in time. He was inducted into the Cooperative Hall of Fame for developing the commodity method or "California Plan" of cooperative marketing and for his work on contracts and commodity marketing legislation.

By 1925, cooperative marketing was losing favor with AFBF leadership. Utah Farm Bureau President Frank Evans said the organization's emphasis on it was not resulting in membership gains. In fact, it was having the opposite effect. Where Farm Bureaus were active in forming cooperative associations, members concluded that Farm Bureau had finished its work and membership was no longer required. Evans said it was necessary to reeducate farmers about the difference between the cooperative association and the Farm Bureau.[34]

The organization director of the Illinois Farm Bureau, G. E. Metzger, offered a similar opinion. "If I may criticize the present 'sales' method of too many of our Farm Bureau leaders," he said, "it is to say that I am afraid we are allowing ourselves to be led astray in a desperate attempt to secure actual dollar and cent results, usually from the cooperative buying of farm supplies or the marketing of farm products." The problems of farmers go much deeper than purchasing feed and fertilizer, said Metzger, and he added, "No organization should lay stress on individual service. Its big job is not to help the member individually, but rather to aid him in doing in co-operation with his neighbors what he cannot do alone."[35]

The crippled U.S. Grain Growers never got a seat on the CBOT. In 1923, it became part of a new cooperative set up to buy the warehouses and other physical assets of five commercial grain companies. Two brilliant staff leaders, Washington lobbyist Gray Silver and Secretary John Coverdale, left AFBF to join the newly constituted grain corporation. Coverdale departed with these words, "My heart is with Farm Bureau and it is there all the time."[36]

Endnotes

1. Transcript, AFBF Annual Meeting, December 11–14, 1922, Chicago, Illinois.

2. Carleton, "Gray Silver and the Rise of the Farm Bureau," *Current History,* 1955, 347–350.

3. Transcript, AFBF Annual Meeting, December 11–14, 1922, Chicago, Illinois.

4. Ibid.

5. "Gaston Means Held in Lindberg Fraud," *New York Times,* May 6, 1932.

6. Howard, *James R. Howard and the Farm Bureau,* 133.

7. Ibid., 134.

8. Gould, *The Most Exclusive Club: A History of the Modern United States Senate,* 96–97.

9. Transcript, AFBF Annual Meeting, December 6–8, 1920, Indianapolis, Indiana.

10. Kile, *The Farm Bureau Movement,* 21, 180.

11. Howard, *James R. Howard and the Farm Bureau,* 137.

12. "The Agricultural Bloc, Is It a Menace or Blessing?" *Wallaces' Farmer,* March 1922.

13. Howard, *James R. Howard and the Farm Bureau,* 65.

14. "Capper Brands Board of Trade Gambling Resort," *Chicago Daily Tribune,* April 10, 1921.

15. "Mr. Rogers's Views on Buying Things the Seller Hasn't Got," *New York Times,* September 24, 1930.

16. "Calls Gary Wrong on the Capper Law," *New York Times,* June 5, 1922.

17. "Editorial of the Day, The Farm Bloc," *Chicago Daily Tribune,* November 3, 1921.

18. Transcript, AFBF Annual Meeting, December 11–14, 1922, Chicago, Illinois.

19. "Farmer's Prices Greatly Helped, President Says," *New York Times,* March 9, 1922; "Blocs Must Go at Any Cost," *New York Times,* May 17, 1923.

20. "Misleading Ideas as to Virgin Wool," *New York Times,* February 29, 1920.

21. Kile, *The Farm Bureau Through Three Decades,* 114; *AFBF Official News Letter,* January 1923.

22. Benedict, "*Farm Policies of the United States,*" 194.

23. Benedict, *Farm Policies of the United States,* 195; Kile, *The Farm Bureau Through Three Decades,*" 83–84.

24. Ibid., 84–85.

25. Ibid., 157.

26. "Hales, Ex-Grain Operator, Co-op Market Angel," *Chicago Tribune,* June 13, 1922.

27. Transcript, AFBF Annual Meeting, December 11–14, 1922, Chicago, Illinois.

28. Kile, *The Farm Bureau Through Three Decades,* 114.

29. Ibid., 117.

30. Minutes, AFBF board of directors, April 1923.

31. Minutes, AFBF board of directors, September 1923.

32. Kile, *The Farm Bureau Through Three Decades*, 118.

33. Benedict, *Farm Policies of the United States*, 197; "Warns Ford of $1,000,000 Suit, Charging Libel," *Chicago Tribune*, January 8, 1925.

34. Minutes, AFBF board of directors, January 1925.

35. *AFBF Official News Letter*, April 1925.

36. Minutes, AFBF board of directors, September 1924.

5 | Equality for Agriculture

ONE OF THE AMERICAN FARM BUREAU FEDERATION'S OVERRIDING CONCERNS IN ITS first three decades was finding a solution for economic inequality. Actually, it was a popular topic of conversation at the dinner table for a large section of the American public—all those who weren't rich. In the 1930s, Sen. Huey Long (D-Louisiana) popularized redistribution of wealth with his Share-Our-Wealth Society and plans for a sharply graduated income tax and confiscatory estate taxes.

But that's not what Farm Bureau meant when it talked about equality. Farm Bureau meant equality for agriculture with business, finance, and labor. Even today, economic opportunity is a fundamental belief of the organization. Beginning in the 1920s, the deck looked stacked against farmers. Farm prices had slipped badly after the war, but the prices farmers paid for goods and services remained high. Farmers suffered a loss of purchasing power.

Agriculture also was subject to what economists call "pure competition," whereby no individual seller controlled or influenced prices. Even while they were trying to remedy this through cooperative marketing, Farm Bureau leaders kept their options open. Thus, they welcomed hearing from George N. Peek who had a plan to restore equality to agriculture.

Peek worked for the War Industries Board when it was headed by financier Bernard Baruch. He came with an impressive agricultural lineage; his grandfather was the brother-in-law of John Deere. Later Peek became general manager of the Moline Plow Company of Illinois. His experience on the War Industries Board had a lasting impression on him. Biographer Gilbert C. Fite wrote that Peek saw how government could help or hinder businesses. "Within a short time he was arguing that the government should be used as an instrument to help American agriculture."[1]

In 1920, Peek wrote a lengthy analysis of farm problems that he asked AFBF staff to edit. He then gave copies to Republican Harding and Democrat James M. Cox during the presidential campaign. The next year he approached AFBF President Howard with his plan to "equalize" or raise farm prices in line with other goods. Howard must have given him encouragement because Peek and an associate, Gen. Hugh S. Johnson, drafted an outline of the plan. AFBF distributed it to Farm Bureaus in a pamphlet entitled, "Equality for Agriculture."[2]

The key to Peek's plan was an "equalization fee" to finance the sale abroad of surplus farm commodities through an export corporation of the federal government. The surplus would be sold at world market prices, and if a loss was taken it would be apportioned among farmers of that commodity and paid back. "Since we cannot prevent surplus, there are only two solutions," explained Peek. "One is to destroy all over prudent reserves; this is, of course impossible. The other is to sell surplus in world markets at what we can get for it."[3] Industrial manufacturers already were dumping excess production abroad in order to maintain higher domestic prices.

Peek hoped to prop up domestic farm prices at what he termed the "fair-exchange value," a price that reflected the ratio between farm and industrial prices existing before the war. "The formula for computing fair-exchange value is merely a means for expressing pure economic relation of values and preserving it from the subversive and disturbing influences of such artificial invasions of economic law as the tariff, pooled foreign buying, government wage-fixing, industrial and commercial combinations, and the like," explained Peek.[4]

Not all farmers understood or supported Peek's plan, but they were convinced that there was something unfair about the prices they were receiving, and they saw their purchasing power erode. Introduced as a bill in Congress in 1924, Peek's price equalization plan took the names of Sen. Charles L. McNary (R-Oregon) and Rep. Gilbert N. Haugen (R-Iowa). Haugen was chairman of the House Agriculture Committee, and McNary put his name on the bill because Senate Agriculture Committee Chairman George Norris (R-Nebraska) had his own bill. The McNary-Haugen bill applied to wheat, corn, cotton, wool, cattle, sheep, hogs, and rice.

Despite the encouragement given Peek, AFBF was lukewarm to the bill at first. The equalization fee concept was not popular in the South where cotton exports already amounted to almost half of the crop, and livestock producers and dairy farmers weren't sure it would help them. There also was the matter of an estimated $200 million in government funds to capitalize the export corporation.

The McNary-Haugen farm bill was viewed as too radical by its detractors. They thought of it as government paternalism at best and a socialist or communist scheme at worst. Rep. Henry T. Rainey (D-Illinois) got into a bitter exchange of letters with Sam H. Thompson, president of the Illinois Farm Bureau, a vocal supporter of the plan. "The bill you champion was drawn by a socialist in the department of agriculture," said Rainey. "It would make more real Bolsheviks in this country than Russia will ever be able to make."[5]

Once when Thompson was testifying before the House Agriculture Committee, his credentials were questioned by an unnamed member. "What right have you to speak in the name of Illinois farmers? I am told Illinois farmers are not interested in agricultural schemes being brought to us." Thompson stormed from the hearing, called ahead with instructions for his staff, and hurried home by train. Only 48 hours later, he was back with petitions signed by 67,000 Illinois farmers requesting passage of the McNary-Haugen farm bill.[6]

In February 1924, President Calvin Coolidge asked Secretary of Agriculture Wallace to call a conference of agricultural leaders at the White House. With an election coming up, Coolidge needed to respond to farm demands. He endorsed a bill to diversify crops in the nation's depressed wheat belt and said a higher tariff on wheat also appeared to be in order, but the president did not like the McNary-Haugen bill even though Wallace favored it.

An editorial in the conservative *Chicago Tribune* called it a "wild bill" and sniffed, "It (Farm Bloc) presented and obtained the passage of dozens of laws, large and small, designed to relieve the farmer. Yet, we find the farmer, especially the wheat farmer, insisting that he is unrelieved. The condition remains, but the experience of failure to remedy the situation by law is forgotten."[7]

A letter to the president and Congress signed in April 1924 by the American Farm Bureau Federation, National Grange, National Livestock Producers Association, and American Wheat Growers Association urged action. "More farmers were ruined in 1922 than in 1921, more in 1923 than in 1922 and during this year unless conditions are changed more country people will fail than in all the preceding four years," said the statement.[8]

The first attempt to pass the McNary-Haugen farm bill failed in the House in 1924. "It is a campaign year," noted the *New York Times,* "and in such a year party lines grow taut. Western Republicans and Southern Democrats who formerly composed most of the farm bloc have gone back to party folds for a time." The newspaper speculated that Farm Bloc members were weary of the repeated charges that Gray Silver was their "boss." There were suggestions too that Farm Bureau had not pushed hard for the bill.[9] Farm Bureau's statement after the defeat read, "Congress has freely admitted the plight of the farmer, but it has failed to take the steps dictated by simple justice toward correction of conditions that have precipitated nation-wide agricultural collapse."[10]

The following year the McNary-Haugen bill did not come up for a vote, and William M. Jardine, president of Kansas State College of Agriculture, became secretary of agriculture succeeding Wallace who had died in office. Although he was from the wheat belt, Jardine opposed the bill.

At the 1925 AFBF annual meeting in Chicago, voting delegates adopted a resolution of full support. "We endorse the enactment of a federal law based on the principle of a farmers' export corporation, providing for the creation of an agency with broad powers for the purpose of handling the surplus farm crops that the American producer may receive an American price in the domestic market, and we instruct our officers and representatives to work for the early enactment of such a law founded on solid economic policy and not involving government subsidy." McNary-Haugen supporter Sam Thompson was elected president and Edward A. O'Neal III of Alabama was elected as vice president.[11]

That year, President Coolidge became the first U.S. president to address an AFBF annual meeting. He was optimistic about the farm economy and showed great disdain for the McNary-Haugen bill. "No matter how it is disguised," he said, "the moment the government engages in buying and selling, by that act it is fixing prices. Moreover, it would apparently destroy cooperative associations and all other marketing machinery, for no one can compete with the government."[12]

Coolidge suggested that farm prices had reached a low in 1921 and were improving. "The future of agriculture looks to be exceedingly secure," he added. Humorist Will Rogers seized upon this remark from the convention in his newspaper column. "Agriculture is secure," agreed Rogers. "In fact it's secured by at least two mortgages."[13] Coolidge received scant applause, but surely even the most pessimistic farmers had no idea how bad things would get.

Thompson, O'Neal, and representatives from other farm groups went to the White House in the spring of 1926 to attempt to change the president's mind about farm relief. Vice President Charles G. Dawes was very receptive but not Coolidge. Despite the pep talk from Coolidge at the AFBF convention, the farm economy was not improving. "It is generally recognized now that an acute farm problem exists, whereas a year or two ago it was too commonly stated that the situation would cure itself if left alone," said AFBF.[14]

The South swung around to support the McNary-Haugen bill after cotton prices plunged in 1926. The bill was modified to emphasize orderly marketing through farm cooperatives rather than export dumping, and the equalization fee was going to be collected from middlemen instead of farmers. With these changes, the McNary-Haugen bill passed in February 1927 by a vote of 214 to 178 in the House and 47 to 39 in the Senate.

While the bill sat on the president's desk, Thompson, O'Neal, lobbyist Chester Gray, and several others went to see him. Thompson told the president that Farm Bureau members were solidly behind the bill. "Silent Cal" listened but with a stone face, no hint of a decision. Afterwards, Thompson went out on a limb with reporters. "I believe that the President understands and appreciates the merits of the bill, and I confidently expect that he will sign it."[15] Thousands of letters and telegrams from Farm Bureau members poured into the White House.

A veto was going to make it extremely difficult for Coolidge to win another term in 1928, but a week after Farm Bureau's visit he vetoed the measure. His views of farming from his New England boyhood were at odds with the way American agriculture was evolving. Later in 1931, Coolidge said, "The family that makes the farm an old fashioned home with diversified crops, fruits and domestic animals sufficient to meet the household needs will still find agriculture one of the most satisfactory forms of existence."[16] Coolidge grew up around farms that were never very profitable; that's just the way it was, he thought, and if a farmer couldn't make a living at farming, perhaps he should do something else.[17]

Many newspapers praised Coolidge on their editorial pages for his personal courage in vetoing the bill, but the *Omaha Bee* accused him of listening to industrial leaders and not farmers. "The fight for justice to the farmer will not be abandoned. It is not humanly possible to repress and restrict the great basic industry of agriculture and not invite disaster."[18] Coolidge tried smoothing things over in the farm belt by setting up a summer White House in the Black Hills of South Dakota.

In August 1927, less than six months after his farm bill veto, Coolidge dropped a bombshell with his famous announcement, "I do not choose to run for president in 1928," issued from Rapid City, South Dakota. Kile believed the decision was in response to the "farm revolt" over the McNary-Haugen veto.[19]

Congress again passed the McNary-Haugen bill in the spring of 1928, Coolidge's last year in office. The margin was even wider than before, but for the second time Coolidge vetoed the bill, and in even stronger terms. "It embodies a formidable array of perils for agriculture which are all the more menacing because of their being obscured in a maze of ponderously futile bureaucratic paraphernalia. In fact, in spite of the inclusion in this measure of some constructive steps proposed by the administration, it renews most of the more vicious devices which appeared in the bill that was vetoed last year."[20]

AFBF leaders resented the president's action, but their response was mild compared to that of Gov. Adam McMullen (R–Nebraska) who called for 100,000 farmers to march on the Republican National Convention in Kansas City. "Farmers arise as crusaders of old. Defend your families, property and freedom," urged the governor who described the march as a "living petition."[21]

AFBF was under great pressure to enter into presidential politics in 1928. Several Midwestern Farm Bureau leaders went to Thompson's home one evening and urged him to follow them to Des Moines to attend a political rally for Gov. Al Smith (D–New York). Thompson declined. The majority of the AFBF board agreed that the organization should stay out of partisan politics. They recalled disastrous results when Grange leaders took sides in the Bryan-McKinley presidential race of 1896.

In its recommendations to both parties, AFBF said farmers constituted one-third of the population but were receiving only 8 percent of national income. It wanted the party platforms to read, "We therefore pledge the party forthwith to initiate and enact legislation that will secure for agriculture a place of equality along with industry, finance, labor and other groups in our American system, thereby guaranteeing to the agricultural dollar a purchasing power equal to that of other groups."[22]

The Democratic convention virtually adopted the Farm Bureau plank, but the Republican convention flatly turned it down and nominated Hoover for president. At least two state Farm Bureau presidents couldn't take it any longer and resigned their positions to help Smith in his campaign. The rest of AFBF leaders were in a quandary. If they stood aside and did nothing, it would seem as though Farm Bureau interests could be ignored in an election.

A decision was reached to set up a separate campaign organization, "The Independent Equality for Agriculture League," headquartered in Chicago, AFBF's home base, and headed by Peek. The league adopted the slogan, "Vote as farmers, not partisans" and ran ads in all the major farm publications, including negative ads attacking Hoover for holding down wheat prices during the war. Al Smith, the "Happy Warrior," sensed that a miracle was taking place on election eve when he addressed farmers across the nation by radio. But the next day he lost and the McNary-Haugen plan to gain equality for agriculture was lost for good.

Coolidge's belief in *laissez-faire* economics caused him to ignore stock market speculation and what was happening to farmers. In his first veto message he said, "We must be careful in trying to help the farmer not to jeopardize the whole agricultural industry by subjecting it to the tyranny of bureaucratic regulation and control." But a hands-off approach wasn't the answer either. Coolidge also dragged his feet on federal flood relief after the Great Mississippi Flood of 1927, the worst natural disaster to hit the Gulf Coast before Hurricane Katrina. Four million acres of land were flooded by spring rains. As the farm economy failed to improve and farmers were going broke in the 1920s and 1930s, Coolidge refused to act; Hoover was slow to act; and AFBF had to wait for the man who nominated Al Smith in 1928, Franklin D. Roosevelt.

The American Farm Bureau Federation's drive for equality for agriculture was not limited to surplus removal and raising farm prices. Farm relief legislation was foremost, but Farm Bureau also wanted better living conditions for rural America and fair treatment for farmers from an old nemesis, the railroads.

In the summer of 1923, AFBF President Bradfute appealed to the National Electric Light Association, a forerunner of the Edison Electric Institute, to electrify

America's farms. In an address to the association in New York City, Bradfute said, "No one who was not born and reared on a farm can realize what it means to the farmer and his family when for the first time he presses the button and sees his home, lawn, barns and yards suddenly spring from darkness into full noonday light and the activities of the farm take on, as it were, new life."[23]

After the war, the electric industry considered what it would take to bring power lines out to farms, but it hadn't yet enlisted the aid of farmers. Farmer involvement began with the Committee on the Relation of Electricity to Agriculture (CREA) formed in September 1923 at AFBF's general headquarters. John Coverdale was named chairman. Represented on the committee were the departments of agriculture, commerce and interior; the National Grange, National Electric Light Association, the American Society of Agricultural Engineers, General Federation of Women's Clubs, National Association of Farm Implement Manufacturers and others.

The staff director was Dr. E. A. White, an electrical engineer who worked out of the AFBF office. White proceeded to set up state committees to promote rural electricity. On a Farm Bureau radio broadcast in January 1925, he suggested that electricity would make farmers happier. "In this day and age it is doubtful if man or woman can afford the time to carry water to say nothing of the inconvenience, and when father climbs into a sure-enough bath tub after a hard day's work, mother may not be able to recognize either his physical appearance or disposition when he comes out." Mother was a lot happier too because housework was easier with a washing machine, electric iron, sewing machine, and other appliances.[24]

However, in 1925 few farm families shared these happy moments of electric service. Of the more than 6.3 million farms that year, only 204,780 or 3.2 percent were receiving central station electrical service. Typically, these farms were located along major roads, or in California where the amount of power needed to run irrigation pumps made it profitable for utility companies to extend lines. Rural electrification was piecemeal and in the hands of private utility companies.[25]

Under White's direction, CREA conducted on-farm experiments with electricity in twenty-three states. It quickly determined that there were a hundred or more applications on farms around the barnyard or in the home. Nearly half of the power expended on the farm was in the field, so engineers went so far as to consider stringing trolley wires over fields for electrified tractors. It was estimated that five years of engineering research could solve any of the problems associated with making tractors similar to street cars; an idea whose time never came, thankfully.

At Red Wing, Minnesota, an experiment was done on ten farms, equipping them with all kinds of electric appliances in barns, chicken houses, and milk sheds. Each device was metered separately to check the power consumption, while the farmer kept close track of his operating costs. Even though the electric bills seemed high, the farmer came out ahead in time and labor.

"A new era in farming has dawned," reported the *New York Times* about rural electrification. "Agriculture will become an industry and farms an open-air factory. A power with new and different possibilities has been made available."[26] Years later the term "factory farm" would have a bad connotation. Then, in the pre-electrification 1920s, it was seen as a marvelous improvement.

Despite the good work done by CREA, the private power companies that controlled 90 percent of the electric power industry seemed unwilling to get involved in rural electrification. Their reluctance was based on a number of assumptions. They estimated that rural electrification would be a far larger and more costly project than even the Panama Canal. On average, there were three farms in a one-mile stretch of land, and it would cost $400 per farm to string wires and provide other necessary apparatus.[27] The power companies often expected the farmer to pay the cost of the distribution lines and guarantee his use of electricity at high rates. No concessions were made on rates in order to generate business, because power companies had plenty of growth already in the cities. CREA did its best to document the vast potential for rural electricity and farmer enthusiasm for it, but that wasn't enough.

Many local power, gas, and water companies also were controlled through large holding companies which were far removed from customers. They bought controlling shares in operating companies in order to drive up their stock prices. Centralized management had some real advantages, but spreading electricity to rural customers was not one of them. Holding companies and investment trusts contributed extensively to stock market speculation that ended abruptly and badly in 1929.[28]

Rural electrification finally received its biggest boost from Roosevelt's election. As governor of New York he was keenly aware of his own state's hydroelectric resources and arguments over private and public power development. Because of his polio, Roosevelt went to Warm Springs, Georgia, for relaxation and therapy. Roosevelt considered Warm Springs the birthplace of the Rural Electrification Administration (REA), because it was there that he discovered electricity for his small cottage was four times costlier than his home in Hyde Park, New York. Roosevelt believed electricity should not be a luxury but one of the necessities of modern life, including country life.[29]

According to Marquis Child, author of *The Farmer Takes a Hand: The Electric Power Revolution in Rural America*, AFBF President O'Neal was the first to suggest to Roosevelt that rural electrification should be part of the New Deal. The REA was created by executive order of the president in May 1935. It tied together several New Deal objectives—low-cost power, conservation of natural resources and the general improvement of farm life.[30]

A year later, Sen. George Norris (R–Nebraska) and Rep. Sam Rayburn (D–Texas) introduced legislation to give the REA the power and money to make loans to build transmission and generating facilities. Farm Bureau urged farmers to form rural cooperatives to take advantage of the low-cost financing—and they did.

Nothing revolutionized farming like electrification; it was part of Farm Bureau's quest for equality for agriculture. Even the *New York Times* questioned the propriety of leaving out rural America. "We have raised the standard of living in industrial centres, not only by increasing wages but by providing comforts that kings would have considered luxuries a century ago. Must the farmer forever maintain the standards of his great-grandfather?"[31]

REA borrowers used the loans to serve entire rural areas and not scatterings of farmers here and there, as had been the case with private power companies. Advances in technology by this time also helped make it possible to transmit electricity over longer distances to reach farmers. By the end of 1941, almost half of the nation's farms were receiving electricity. World War II interrupted the construction of power lines because copper was needed for the war, but by the end of the 1940s, electricity reached almost every farm.

The American Farm Bureau Federation also was a leader in securing better roads for rural America. "Get the farmer out of the mud," was a slogan in rural areas that helped turn attention toward building farm-to-market roads. Progress was slow. Farmers were told to wait in the dust or mud until main roads were built first. Beginning in 1935, the Works Progress Administration (WPA) built or improved hundreds of thousands of miles of rural roads, bridges, drainage ditches, and culverts. By the late 1930s, trucks replaced freight trains for many high-value commodities and short hauls.

Hatred of the railroads was the staple of the Agrarian Crusade, despite the key role they played in the settlement of rural America. Nineteenth century farmers found themselves at the mercy of the railroads for shipping crops and livestock to market. Freight rates fluctuated wildly without notice, and to avoid competition, railroads formed traffic pools and divided up the market. Eventually rate-setting was brought under the control of the Interstate Commerce Commission (ICC).

During the First World War, the railroads were nationalized and then returned to private hands after the war. Under the Esch-Cummins Transportation Act of 1920, the carriers were granted rates by the ICC that guaranteed them an adequate return on investment. When railway workers received a big wage increase through the Railway Labor Board, the ICC compensated the carriers with a rate increase averaging 35 percent. Farm prices were falling at the time, so it was a double-whammy for farmers.

In 1921, The American Farm Bureau Federation took the lead in getting costs revised downward at a general hearing before the ICC on farm conditions and freight rates. AFBF already had a transportation department by this time; it was the second department formed after the legislative department. The man heading the transportation department was Clifford Thorne, a highly capable Chicago attorney. Of course, the railroads also employed the best lawyers in the country.

Thorne organized the case and arranged for witnesses. Farm historian Benedict described the scene. "In a huge, sweltering hearing room, farm witness after farm witness, most of them having their first experience at testifying before such a tribunal set forth the desperate conditions of agriculture and the evil effects that would result if freight rate reductions were not granted."*32* Farm Bureau was fulfilling its role as the Voice of Agriculture. In the past, only rate experts and lawyers had been heard in such cases.

The ICC granted rate reductions amounting to around 10 percent which saved farmers millions of dollars annually. Thorne did not rely solely on the emotions of hard-pressed farmers to make his case to the ICC. He came amply prepared with all the relevant data and was able to show that the railroads were overvalued by nearly $2 billion, which of course affected the return on investment they were allowed. Thorne's successes were tallied up and reported to farmers as reason enough to join Farm Bureau.

The two largest industries in the 1920s were transportation and agriculture. The railroads were represented by the American Railway Association which later became the Association of American Railroads. Because of the American Farm Bureau Federation, farmers found themselves on more equal ground with their historic antagonist. Fairness and economic equality were the watchwords of Farm Bureau.

Endnotes

1. Fite, *George N. Peek and the Fight for Farm Parity*, 32.

2. Ibid., 43.

3. Peek and Johnson, "Equality for Agriculture," 1921.

4. Ibid.

5. "McNary-Haugen Bill Assailed as Almost Red," *Chicago Tribune*, April 16, 1924.

6. Kile, *The Farm Bureau Through Three Decades,* 129.

7. "A Wild Bill for Farmers," *Chicago Tribune*, April 11, 1924.

8. "Ask Protection of Farm Products," *New York Times*, April 6, 1924.

9. "Future of the Farm Bloc, A Washington Riddle," *New York Times,* May 18, 1924.

10. "Congress Quits Saturday, Farm Bloc to Arms," *New York Times*, June 4, 1924.

11. Transcript, AFBF Annual Meeting, December 7–9, 1925, Chicago, Illinois.

12. Ibid.

13. Sterling and Sterling, *Will Rogers Speaks*, 176.

14. *AFBF Annual Report of 1926.*

15. "Says Coolidge Will Sign," *New York Times*, February 19, 1927.

16. Hannaford, *The Quotable Calvin Coolidge*, 68.

17. Ferrell, *The Presidency of Calvin Coolidge*, 86.

18. "Coolidge Rapped and Praised by Editors for Farm Veto," *Chicago Daily Tribune*, February 26, 1927.

19. Kile, "The Farm Bureau Through Three Decades," 148; Ferrell, *The Presidency of Calvin Coolidge*, 193.

20. "Coolidge Vetoes Farm Relief," *New York Times*, May 24, 1928.

21. "West Is Aroused by Farm Bill Veto," *New York Times*, May 24, 1928.

22. Minutes, AFBF board of directors, May 1928.

23. *AFBF Official News Letter*, June 7, 1923.

24. *AFBF Official News Letter*, January 15, 1925.

25. USDA, *Yearbook of Agriculture 1940*, 790–791.

26. "Electricity Promises New Aid to the Farmer," *The New York Times,* July 3, 1927.

27. Ibid.

28. Childs, *The Farmer Takes Hand*, 39–43.

29. Ibid., 51.

30. Ibid., 54.

31. "Electricity Promises New Aid to the Farmer," *The New York Times,* July 3, 1927.

32. Benedict, *Farm Policies of the United States*, 192.

6 | Muscle Shoals

On a blustery December day in 1921, Edward A. O'Neal III, president of the Lauderdale County Farm Bureau and future AFBF president, waited expectantly for visitors at the railroad depot in O'Neal's hometown of Florence, Alabama. "I'll never forget it. What a beautiful private car Henry Ford had," said O'Neal years later. The distinguished visitors were Ford, son Edsel, Thomas Alva Edison, the only private citizen in America as famous as Ford, and their wives. The railcar was named Fair Lane.[1]

Ford and his party were there to study one of the most hotly debated political issues of the 1920s: disposition of the defense project at Muscle Shoals on the Tennessee River. Late in the war, the government spent more than $80 million on the construction of two nitrate plants and a partially completed dam to manufacture munitions.

The bulk of nitrates used in this country came from Chilean surface mines, but the cost of imported nitrates soared during the war, and there were obvious concerns about relying on a distant supplier. Nitrogen could, however, be separated from the air using the cyanamid process which required large amounts of electricity. The Haber process to synthesize ammonia for explosives and fertilizers was still experimental at the time.

The Muscle Shoals project contained at least four significant features. First and foremost of course was national preparedness; second was the production and distribution of fertilizers; third and fourth were the development of river transportation and hydroelectric power. The American Farm Bureau Federation was keenly interested in the second use, production of nitrogen fertilizer. AFBF wanted to see the government finish the dam and manufacture low-cost fertilizer. The Tennessee Valley was worn out and worthless; cotton and tobacco farmers were in need of fertilizer to bring it back to life.

Had the war continued a few more years, the nitrogen fixation project would have seemed like a prudent move, but now the Republicans seized on it as a wasteful expenditure and the Democrats wanted the facility sold for salvage value. When Harding became president in 1921, he decided Muscle Shoals should be privately operated so the government could get a return on its investment. That's how Henry Ford came into the picture. He first visited Muscle Shoals in June 1921, and toured the facilities with two engineers and an official of the Tennessee River Development Association.

A month later he submitted a bid that called for the government to complete Wilson Dam and another dam and lease them to him for 100 years. He would purchase the two nitrate plants and several steam electric plants for $5 million and produce nitrogen fertilizer. As part of the agreement, he would limit his profit on fertilizer to 8 percent. A board of farm representatives, including the American Farm Bureau Federation, would oversee the fertilizer operation. Commerce Secretary Herbert Hoover applauded the idea because Ford would be maintaining the nitrate plant in reserve for the government in the event the plant was needed again for munitions.

As he stepped off the train in Florence on that Sunday, Ford was asked by O'Neal if he wanted to attend church. "No, I'll worship the Lord seeing what He gave us," he replied. The Army Corps of Engineers had a narrow gauge railroad that ran out to the inspection site. On the trip out there, Ford and O'Neal sat on the back platform of the guest coach so O'Neal could smoke his pipe. Ford was inquisitive about farming in the area.[2]

Later, they all went to O'Neal's farm for a barbeque. Edison was deaf and wore a hearing device. Ford grabbed O'Neal's son Camper to show him around the farm. They visited the smokehouse where hams were hanging to be cured in hickory smoke. "Oh, come here, come here, everybody!" shouted Ford. Next he noticed two big iron kettles that were used for washing clothes in boiling water, and again he just "had a fit about it" recalled O'Neal.

After getting a drink of water from a cedar bucket with a gourd dipper, Ford said, "Ed, you know when I was a kid, I used to tote water for mother to wash our clothes once or twice a week. I'd have to tote water to drink. Sell me that kettle. Sell me that gourd." The Ford party left the farm with a kettle and gourd loaded in a car, a gift from the host.[3]

The three-day visit by Ford and Edison was big news around the nation. Before the trip from Dearborn, Michigan, hundreds of civic groups invited them to stop at towns and cities along the way, but they declined. At Florence, Ford revealed his entire plan which was truly astonishing; fertilizer production was just the beginning.

What Ford proposed to do with Muscle Shoals was make it the greatest industrial development in all America. The auto magnate wanted to build a dream city seventy-five miles long, from Florence on the west to Huntsville on the east. But even bigger than that, Muscle Shoals would be a step toward ending world wars because Ford proposed to use it as the basis for American currency. "It is very simple when you analyze it," he said. "The cause of all wars is gold. We shall demonstrate to the world through Muscle Shoals, first the practicability, second the desirability of displacing gold as the basis of currency and substituting in its place the world's imperishable natural wealth."[4]

Florida was undergoing a real estate boom in the 1920s, and speculators hearing of Ford's plan flocked to Alabama. Property infested with mosquitoes in the summer and bearing the scars of erosion was bought up and laid out in lots. "Real estate in the region across which Ford's 'farm-flung' city would be built is changing hands almost hourly, according to the latest reports from Muscle Shoals and its vicinity," reported the *New York Times*.[5]

Ford's utopian dream was clusters of small cities that in total would be larger than Detroit. There were going to be small factories and modern farms with electricity, and if that wasn't enough to whet public appetite, one million men would be needed to build it. Hardly any wonder that the entire plan was enthusiastically supported by AFBF, Chamber of Commerce, and the American Federation of Labor (AFL). Southern congressmen and senators were solidly for the Ford offer, but easterners, particularly those on Wall Street whom Ford often offended, called him a "mad hatter."[6]

The auto manufacturer's proposal was vague enough that he could probably opt out of producing fertilizer if it proved unprofitable, and that would still leave him with control of the hydroelectric power. "It would give Mr. Ford water power far greater than that developed at Niagara Falls," argued Gifford Pinchot, president of the National Conservation Association, who thought that Ford would reap "perpetual and gigantic profits."[7] Possibly Ford wanted to use the electricity to manufacture aluminum but was hesitant to say so because of Treasury Secretary Andrew Mellon, the founder of the Aluminum Company of America.

Farm Bureau's interest in Muscle Shoals was really twofold: it wanted to bring cheap fertilizer to farmers and boost Farm Bureau membership in the South. At a House Agriculture Committee hearing in late January 1923, AFBF Washington lobbyist Gray Silver said the Muscle Shoals nitrate plant would be able to produce nitrates at 6¢ a pound instead of 22¢ a pound charged by the Chileans.[8]

Between 1921 and 1924 there was a pitched battle in Congress over Ford's offer. Southern Democrats and AFBF were on Ford's side while the opposition forces were progressive members of Congress plus the power and fertilizer lobbies. Ford would have won had it not been for the dogged efforts of his most vigorous opponent, Sen. George Norris (R-Nebraska), chairman of the Senate Agriculture Committee.

Norris was a pugnacious battler and leader of the small progressive wing of the Republican Party. He was a holdover from the days of Teddy Roosevelt when first elected to Congress from rural Nebraska. Norris was not intimidated in the least by Ford. He was staunchly in favor of public ownership and operation of Muscle Shoals, while AFBF supported leasing it to Ford.

In March 1922, members of the Senate Agriculture Committee and the House Committee on Military Affairs visited Muscle Shoals and they too were hosted at a barbeque on O'Neal's farm. Years later, Norris told O'Neal, "That wet and dry party you gave on your place was the birth of the development of the Tennessee River, the real development of the Tennessee Valley Authority."[9] The host went to some length to see that liquor was served to those who wanted it, despite Prohibition. It was O'Neal's intention to sell the committee on the Ford proposal, but he only managed to convince them of the importance of Muscle Shoals.

During Senate Agriculture Committee hearings that followed, Sen. Oscar W. Underwood (D-Alabama) tried to enlist support for Ford's offer from outside the South. He noted that wheat production in the Northwest had declined from forty to fifty bushels an acre to fifteen to twenty bushels because the soil was depleted. "The necessity for renewing the fertility of our soil is as essential to our national welfare as is the maintenance of an adequate army and navy for the defense of the country," he said.[10]

Senator Norris blasted Farm Bureau for supporting Ford's offer. Addressing his remarks to lobbyist Silver, Norris said, "You know that if Rockefeller or the International Harvester Company was making the same proposition Ford makes, you would be here condemning it, charging that Congress was giving away the people's property to a corporation." Silver said that Ford's offer gave farmers more than they could ever hope for otherwise. Norris vowed that Ford would never get his hands on Muscle Shoals.[11]

In May 1922, Ford improved his offer and spelled out in more detail his plans to produce fertilizer. The next month the House Military Committee acted favorably on Ford's offer and reported it to the House. Senate hearings continued into July when a voluminous report written by Norris was issued by his committee. It was a scathing attack on the offer, describing it as "the most wonderful real estate speculation since Adam and Eve lost the Garden of Eden," and wondering sarcastically why Ford wasn't also receiving a deed to the Capitol.[12]

Not to be outdone by Norris, Farm Bureau asked financier Bernard Baruch to prepare a special report on the Ford offer from an engineering survey and make a recommendation. This was no small feat considering Baruch was Jewish and Ford had a reputation for being anti-Semitic. Baruch complied and made a positive recommendation with only a few adjustments to the offer. Around the same time, the Nebraska State Senate embarrassed Norris by inviting Ford to the senator's home state to survey water power and help develop it. The invitation was coupled with an endorsement of Muscle Shoals."[13]

Despite intensive lobbying on both sides, the 67th Congress adjourned in March 1923, without a decision. Farm Bureau concentrated mostly on the fertilizer aspects of Muscle Shoals, but also told members that acceptance of the Ford offer would lead to widespread rural electrification. The longer the issue was debated the more attention shifted to hydroelectric power and the whole Tennessee Valley.

Ford continued to stand by his offer, and added, "If I get Muscle Shoals we shall run power lines 200 miles in every direction from Muscle Shoals. We have been working and have learned how to send power long distances without losses by leakage."[14]

Harding's death brought Calvin Coolidge to the presidency and created a new controversy. Shortly after a meeting with Ford in late 1923, Coolidge announced that he favored sale of the Muscle Shoals properties and that a commission should be formed to consider the bids. Norris cried foul. The Nebraska senator surmised that a deal had been made between Coolidge and Ford who was prominently mentioned as a candidate for president in 1924. The alleged deal was Ford's sitting out the election in return for Coolidge's agreeing to sell Muscle Shoals. In December 1923, Ford announced his withdrawal from the race for president and backed Coolidge.

The following month, nine southern power companies including the Alabama Power Company, submitted a joint bid for Muscle Shoals. The power companies were not interested in fertilizer production, but Union Carbide Company was a possible lessee of the nitrate plants.

The closest Henry Ford and Farm Bureau got to winning the battle for Muscle Shoals came in the House during the first session of the 68th Congress in March 1924. Ford's bid was accepted by a vote of 227 to 142. The debate on the floor was rancorous with Rep. Fiorello LaGuardia (D-New York), a progressive like Norris, rallying the opposition. House leaders backing the measure pointed to the farm support delivered by Farm Bureau.

The Ford offer flopped in the Senate where it failed to make headway in 1924. Norris kept up his attack, accusing Farm Bureau and real estate speculators of spreading propaganda favoring the Ford proposal. His charges were usually leveled at Silver and not at AFBF leadership or members. Of course, Silver was just trying to implement the policy adopted by members. In May 1924, the Senate Agriculture Committee voted to report out the Norris bill, but the principle of government ownership and operation of Muscle Shoals was still unpopular and viewed as a step in the direction of socialism.

There is no figure in the business world today quite like Henry Ford; not Bill Gates, Warren Buffett, or Donald Trump. "Unlike robber barons such as John D. Rockefeller, J. P. Morgan, and Cornelius Vanderbilt, Ford emerged as 'the

people's tycoon,'" said a biographer. Ford also maintained a big interest in agriculture. His factories produced thousands of Fordson tractors in the 1920s and
his engineers and chemists experimented with alcohol fuels and new uses for
soybeans.[15]

Ford was a visionary, but his vision for Muscle Shoals was never to be realized by
him. In October 1924, he unexpectedly withdrew, probably out of sheer frustration
with Congress. With Ford out of the picture, the fight almost ended in 1925 with
the Underwood-McKenzie bill that provided for private leasing first and government operation as a last resort. Farm Bureau supported the bill because it met its
fertilizer requirements, but Norris and other progressives threatened a filibuster.

Next, AFBF backed a House resolution asking President Coolidge to appoint
a commission to study the cheapest and best way to produce nitrates at Muscle
Shoals. The five member commission was composed of two members of Congress,
two scientists, and a Farm Bureau staff member, Russell Bower. The commission
decided on private operation of Muscle Shoals, but the two scientist members
thought hydroelectric power should be emphasized over fertilizer production.
A joint committee of Congress was formed to accept bids from power and chemical companies. Farm Bureau sided with the chemical companies to deliver on
fertilizer production. The power trust or power combine was generally viewed
with suspicion.

In November 1926, former AFBF President Bradfute advised Coolidge at
the White House that Muscle Shoals could be the answer to badly needed farm
relief. Bradfute said the farm problem was due in part to high production costs
which Muscle Shoals could address by reducing the cost of fertilizer.[16] A year later
as Coolidge was getting ready to deliver his annual address to Congress, he was
apparently told by Hoover that the nitrate plants at Muscle Shoals were no longer needed for national defense and fertilizer production could be deemphasized.
Farm Bureau found out that Coolidge was going to say this in his speech, but
Chester Gray, Silver's successor as AFBF lobbyist, got to Coolidge in time to have
a new line inserted that gave preference to fertilizer production.[17]

By 1927, AFBF settled on the American Cyanamid Corporation as the best
option to develop Muscle Shoals. A bid by the chemical giant to lease Muscle
Shoals for fifty years was contained in the Willis-Madden bill introduced by Sen.
Frank Willis (R-Ohio) and Rep. Martin R. Madden (R-Illinois). Norris called it
a ploy by American Cyanamid to get its hands on cheap power. He substituted
his own bill for public ownership of Muscle Shoals with a provision for fertilizer
research.

Senator Norris had been in this fight as long as Farm Bureau and finally got his
first significant victory after seven years. The Norris bill passed Congress in 1928, but
not before Sen. Kenneth D. McKellar (D-Tennessee) delivered a twenty-one-hour

filibuster about fertilizer costs, states' rights, and water projects. One of the most powerful men in the Senate, William E. Borah (R-Idaho) personally went to the White House to urge President Coolidge to sign the legislation. Farm Bureau wanted a veto. Coolidge had not tipped his hand, but exercised a pocket veto by leaving the bill unsigned on his desk.

When Hoover became president, fertilizer production at Muscle Shoals received new support from the New England commissioners of agriculture. They feared a fertilizer shortage in the country. But two investigations, one involving Farm Bureau, diverted attention. At Sen. Norris' request, the Federal Trade Commission (FTC) launched an investigation of the power trust. Norris accused power companies of being behind the bad press he was receiving because they controlled a number of newspapers.

The investigation of the American Farm Bureau Federation was in front of a Senate Judiciary subcommittee headed by Sen. Thaddeus Caraway (D-Arkansas). Over four months in 1930, the subcommittee looked into ties between AFBF and American Cyanamid Corporation, and the pressure Farm Bureau put on Congress and the president. Letters from the files of the Washington office were subpoenaed, and lobbyist Gray was charged with using funds from American Cyanamid to produce publicity material bearing Farm Bureau's name. Gray saw nothing wrong with this collaboration because Farm Bureau supported the company's bid. AFBF also was accused of trying to arrange a secret meeting between the power and fertilizer companies at the request of President Hoover.[18]

There was nothing to the intrigue, and Gray denied doing anything unethical. The hearing revealed more about AFBF's effectiveness as a lobbying organization than anything else. Everyone agreed that Farm Bureau's honor was intact, and Norris himself was then accused of trying to discredit the organization. Meanwhile, Nebraska Republican leaders were tired of Norris and plotted to defeat him in the 1930 primary election. They placed on the ballot a grocery store clerk with the same name, George W. Norris. Farm Bureau had nothing to do with the "Grocer George" plot.

In February 1931, a Senate-House conference agreed on a bill that included the Norris plan for public ownership and operation of hydroelectric facilities at Muscle Shoals, but it provided for a private lessee to take over the nitrate plants and produce fertilizer. This time AFBF and southerners in Congress supported government operation because it looked like the only way anything would get done. Eastern Republicans still considered government involvement in the power business a bad option, and Hoover, always the engineer, raised a number of technical issues before vetoing it.

Next Hoover appointed yet another Muscle Shoals Commission; this one included the governors of Alabama and Tennessee and AFBF President Ed O'Neal.

In 1931, the commission reported that Muscle Shoals should be used for fertilizer research and production. The Army Corps of Engineers concluded that power generation was a money-losing proposition but did not calculate any benefits from flood control and river navigation.

The fight over Muscle Shoals involved five American presidents and four AFBF presidents before it stopped with Roosevelt and O'Neal. AFBF was involved every step of the way with Muscle Shoals, long after Ford, the fertilizer interests, and power companies gave up and dropped out. The end was in sight on January 21, 1933, when the president-elect announced on the portico of the state capitol at Montgomery, Alabama, that he supported a government operations bill in a special session of Congress that he intended to call. Muscle Shoals would be part of a much larger development he envisioned for the Tennessee River.

Norris snubbed the Republican Party to endorse Roosevelt in the 1932 election and was on hand as Roosevelt inspected Wilson Dam and the idle nitrate plants. "This should be a happy day for you, George," Roosevelt said while the two watched water passing unused through the Wilson Dam spillways. Norris replied, "It is Mr. President. I see my dreams come true."[19]

The maverick Republican senator from Nebraska is hailed as the "father of the Tennessee Valley Authority," but no national organization spent more time and energy than Farm Bureau in seeing Muscle Shoals through to completion, as the Tennessee Valley Authority (TVA).

Shortly after becoming president, Roosevelt asked for Farm Bureau's advice. O'Neal told him to accelerate rural electrification and institute a program to develop improved nitrogen and phosphate fertilizers.[20]

AFBF was given a chance to run the fertilizer program itself for a lease period of fifty years at only $1 per year, but the start-up and operational costs were prohibitive. Instead, TVA converted two old electric carbide furnaces to phosphate smelters and started the National Fertilizer Development Center (NFDC). According to TVA historians, "by 1934, the NFDC was churning out pumped-up phosphate-based fertilizers whose names sounded as if they were inspired by comic-book heroes: Triple Superphosphate, Calcium Metaphosphate. As the names implied, these new products had several times the potency of the stuff farmers had been buying by the ton."[21]

O'Neal referred to this as "using brains on the land." Farm Bureau and O'Neal personally were big supporters of fertilizer research.[22] The fertilizers were used throughout the Tennessee Valley and across a large part of the country. A test farm was selected in each area and the cooperating farmer received the fertilizer at no cost other than shipping. The results of using top-grade fertilizers were astonishing. "Forty years later, the farms of the once-ruined Tennessee Valley were twice as productive per acre as the average American farm," reported the TVA.[23]

TVA continues to provide more electricity than any other public utility in the nation. It operates a system of forty-nine dams and reservoirs on the Tennessee River and manages the river system for a wide variety of benefits, including transportation and flood control. Surprisingly perhaps, AFBF buried the hatchet with Sen. Norris and gave him its Distinguished Service Award for diligence in getting legislation passed to help rural America. As for Muscle Shoals, it forever merits a special place in Farm Bureau history.

Endnotes

1. Dean Albertson, Columbia University, Oral History Research Office, New York, New York, Interview with Ed O'Neal (June 1953), 49.

2. Ibid.

3. Ibid., 51.

4. "Ford Hopes To Use Muscle Shoals As Step to End Wars," *New York Times*, December 4, 1921.

5. "Rush for Muscle Shoals, Ford's Proposed Seventy-five Mile City Already Attracting Thousands," *New York Times*, February 12, 1921.

6. "Ford A 'Mad Hatter' Untermyer Says," *New York Times*, December 5, 1921.

7. "Opposes Ford Offer for Muscle Shoals," *New York Times*, August 29, 1921.

8. "For Ford's Nitrate Proposal, Farm Bureau Official Argues for It at Hearing on Chilean Purchases," *New York Times*, January 30, 1923.

9. Albertson Interview with O'Neal, 55.

10. "Underwood Backs Ford," *New York Times*, April 11, 1922.

11. "Norris Shows Anger over Ford's Offer," *New York Times*, May 10, 1922.

12. "Ford Offer Riddled in Senate Report," *New York Times*, July 21, 1922.

13. "Invites Ford to Develop Nebraska," *New York Times*, February 20, 1923.

14. "Ford Assails Weeks; Says Offer Stands for Muscle Shoals," *New York Times*, October 12, 1923.

15. Watts, *The People's Tycoon*, 315.

16. "Urges Prompt Action at Muscle Shoals," *New York Times*, November 27, 1926.

17. Hubbard, *Origins of the TVA*, 210.

18. Ibid., 257–263.

19. "Alabamans Cheer Him, In Montgomery Speech He Indicates Legislation in Extra Session," *New York Times*, January 22, 1933.

20. Albertson Interview with O'Neal, 91.

21. www.tva.gov/heritage/bloom/, accessed May 30, 2007.

22. Albertson Interview with O'Neal, 92.

23. www.tva.gov/heritage/bloom/, accessed May 30, 2007.

7 | The Spirit of Farm Bureau

Before winning the 1928 election, Herbert Hoover let it be known that his "greatest honor" as president would be to solve the most difficult economic problem facing the American people—the farm problem. That also was the year of wild speculation in the stock market. "The mass escape into make-believe so much a part of the true speculative orgy, started in earnest," recalled economist John Kenneth Galbraith about 1928.[1]

Hoover was wary of stock market speculation, much more so than Coolidge, but his landslide election only made matters worse. Investors were sure he was good for American business. After his inauguration in March 1929, the president called a special session of Congress to pass farm relief legislation. The farm plank in the Republican Party platform called for a Federal Farm Board to "stabilize" farm prices by making loans to farmer cooperatives to hold crop surpluses off the market.[2]

The McNary-Haugen bill for a government corporation to buy surplus stocks and sell them on foreign markets was dead. A somewhat similar export debenture plan passed the Senate but not the House. Hoover finally intervened at a meeting with congressional leaders to break the stalemate over farm relief. The Agricultural Marketing Act of 1929 was signed by the president in June and featured an eight-member Federal Farm Board.

Hoover was delighted by the outcome and called the new farm bill "the most important measure ever passed by Congress in aid of a single industry."[3] Indeed, it was the first major farm relief legislation, but Hoover did not regard it as a farm subsidy. He thought it gave farmers "equality of opportunity" so they could have access to the same tools industry used in controlling market supplies.

AFBF President Thompson accepted the possibility that farmers would find the economic justice they sought through the Farm Board.

"Signing of the agricultural marketing bill today by President Hoover was the final step in laying the foundation of a national agricultural policy," said Thompson. "Farming will become an increasingly profitable business." [4]

The Farm Board used a $500 million revolving fund to make loans to cooperatives so they could hold seasonal commodity surpluses in storage until the markets improved. Hoover appointed the president of International Harvester Company, Alexander Legge, chairman of the Farm Board. Farm Bureau was well-acquainted with him and the other members. Legge was convinced that what farmers lacked most was organized marketing. "We have 6,000,000 farmers, all or nearly all of them, competing with one another in a buyer's market, in which the buyers are relatively few," he said. The Farm Board could help cooperatives remove surpluses from the market but had no authority to limit farm production. Legge was already concerned that maintaining prices at artificially high levels would be courting disaster. [5]

"The Farm Board was not our baby," reminded AFBF lobbyist Chester Gray at a contentious congressional hearing about its operations in 1930, but the Farm Bureau did have ties to it. [6] William Settle resigned as president of the Indiana Farm Bureau to become the first general manager of the Farmers National Grain Corporation in Chicago, the national sales agency set up to help the cooperatives, and Thompson also accepted a position on the grain corporation's board. The agency was reminiscent of Farm Bureau's ill-fated U.S. Grain Growers Corporation. Additional agencies or super-cooperatives were set up to handle cotton, wool, livestock, and other commodities. Loans also were made to cooperatives that handled fruits and vegetables to improve processing and marketing.

Legge credited the Farm Board with preventing a collapse of the grain and cotton markets when the stock market crashed on October 29, 1929. The commodities market did not collapse but slid; wheat was below 99¢ a bushel a year later. Falling prices meant the cooperatives could not repay the loans. As a result, wheat and cotton stabilization corporations were set up to take a direct role in the market. The stabilization corporations acquired commodities from the cooperatives at the loan rate and bought additional grain and cotton on the cash and futures markets to shore up prices. In effect this was price-fixing, and it brought angry charges from commodity exchanges and commission houses. The stabilization corporations were owned by the cooperatives, but the risk and financial exposures were the federal government's responsibility.

The International Harvester executive was under frequent attack while running the Farm Board from critics like grain dealer Julius Barnes, head of the Chamber of Commerce. Farmers were not happy either, even though Legge and Secretary of Agriculture Arthur Hyde claimed wheat would be at least a dime lower without the board's market intervention. Hyde did not blame farmers for being upset. "It's enough to make a farmer cuss his grandmother as well as the Farm Board when, after a year's labor, he has to take a price for his product less than the cost to produce," he said.[7]

Thompson sent a letter to all state and county Farm Bureaus in which he called for a united front against the foes of the Farm Board. "Great selfish, speculative business groups have joined forces to secure repeal or nullifying amendment to the agricultural marketing act," he said. Thompson reminded farmers that the act "represents the results of seven years of toil, sacrifice, and bitter battle on the part of the farm people of this country." In closing, he urged Farm Bureaus to bring in more members so there would be a great army fighting for the farmer's economic justice.[8]

Both Hyde and Legge appealed to farmers to cut production of wheat and cotton but could do little more than jawbone about it. Southern farmers were urged to diversify and meet their own food needs first and those of people living in cities. Hyde declared, "Blind production for an unknown demand is now the bane of agriculture." Legge meanwhile suggested that farmers restore the old woodlot by planting 5 percent of cropland in trees.[9] These appeals were not popular, and they grew even less popular as the Depression worsened. At the 1930 AFBF annual convention in Boston, Massachusetts, Thompson said, "I recognize that there is a very genuine market surplus—goods that cannot be sold with adequate return to the producer. But in terms of human needs there is no surplus . . . multitudes are hungry."[10]

Legge quit the Farm Board in March 1931 as the board announced it was trying to sell thirty-five million bushels of wheat in foreign markets to make storage available for new crop wheat. The announcement led to heavy selling pressure in the futures market. A month later President Hoover called Sam Thompson to take a spot on the board. Another Farm Bureau stalwart, Frank Evans, was added a little later. The two men were boarding a sinking ship. At the end of May, the Farm Board announced it would stop making purchases of wheat. It had 200 million bushels on hand and paper losses amounted to $90 million, all occurring in a little over one year.[11] By the end of October 1931 it was holding 1.3 million bales of cotton.[12]

A major failing in the Agricultural Marketing Act of 1929, besides not having a mechanism to limit production, was not having a workable plan to dispose of surplus commodities. Foreign sales were arranged whenever possible through credit or barter, but the export market for American farm commodities was shrinking. The Farm Board also intended to curb speculation in the grain and cotton markets, but its dealings only added to the rumor mill that speculators thrived on.

Hoover must have thought his experience as food administrator during the First World War gave him a unique perspective on farm policy. As criticisms of the Farm Board grew louder, however, he stayed away, contending it was an independent agency. It is doubtful that Calvin Coolidge would have fared better. In March 1931, the former president entertained Farm Board members at a breakfast meeting while they dealt with the wheat surplus. The main dish was a steaming hot porridge of wheat and rye, which Coolidge heartily endorsed as though this was his answer to disposing of the wheat surplus.

The president who wanted to solve the nation's farm problem never realized his potentially greatest triumph, and the Great Depression and Dust Bowl made it far worse. For farm families living on the Great Plains, economic and ecological disasters occurring at the same time were especially devastating. They were the greatest calamities ever vested on American agriculture. The Dust Bowl was preventable to a certain degree—if soil conservation had been better understood and additional land had not been plowed up for wartime production. But the main instigator, a scorching multi-year drought, was not preventable and was a definite shift in pattern from generally good crop moisture in the 1920s.

Arguments have been made about the causes of the Great Depression. The American Farm Bureau Federation believed it was avoidable and a direct consequence of the nation ignoring agriculture. In a 1932 policy resolution, the delegates said, "Delay on the part of the government in facing the farm problem fairly and squarely has resulted not only in a greatly aggravated condition in agriculture, but finally has undermined the economic structure of the nation."[13]

The AFBF's 1939 annual report on the occasion of its twentieth anniversary came to a similar conclusion. "The boom days that other groups had enjoyed during most of the period of the [1920s] suddenly ended in 1929, partly at least because farmers could not buy industrial goods in normal volumes." Farm Bureau's point was that the nation could not go on half-booming and half-busted, particularly when the half-busted part, the farmers, made up one-fourth of the population.[14]

After paying production expenses, rent, interest, and taxes, the average farmer was left with about $230 for the year, which the Department of Agriculture said gave him nothing as a return on investment and much less pay than a common day-laborer. All capital employed in agriculture had a value of $38 billion in 1933, a tremendous decline from $58 billion in 1929 and $79 billion in 1919. Thousands of country banks closed, leaving communities without savings or credit.[15]

President Roosevelt measured the Depression's impact on farmers in a speech in September 1935 at Freemont, Nebraska. "From the Summer of 1929 to the time when I took office in 1933, the prices of farm products—that is the things that the farmer had to sell—had declined 62 percent, while the prices of the things the farmer had to buy had fallen 35 percent. Thus the farmer on the average had to use twice as many bushels of wheat, twice as many bushels of corn, twice as many hogs, twice as many bales of cotton, twice as much of all of his products, in order buy the same amount of the things he needed."[16]

The parity index was a popular measurement of a farmer's purchasing power and farm prices. The base period of 1910–1914 was said to be 100. Parity was measured at 58 in 1932, down from 110 in 1919. Parity did not reach 100 again until the start of World War II. Hard times were nothing new to farmers, but the Depression and Dust Bowl were different. A USDA account of farm life in the mid-nineteenth century described it this way: "Life might be hard and crude, but it was secure. There was nothing in the social code that forced a man to lose his self-respect because of poverty, for no one was far from hardship, and none had excess of ease; and when opportunity was not at hand, it could be found just over the horizon."[17]

For Depression-era farmers, there were no new lands freely available, no opportunity in farming just over the horizon. There was a pronounced lack of security and nature turned its back on the farmer. In a letter to my father dated April 5, 1930, my grandmother, Mary B. Truelsen, wrote from Gilmore City, Iowa, about "one of the worst dirt storms we ever had." She said, "You cannot see nearly to the corner of our fence and you get your mouth and eyes full of dust and dirt the minute you step outside." She decided the family would be better off in another line of work that didn't depend so much on rainfall. Farming was incredibly discouraging and hard. By the summer of 1930, newspapers were reporting a great drought taking hold of the land east of the Rockies.

In 1932 there were fourteen major dust storms, followed by twenty-eight the next year. One theory was that huge masses of ocean air became turbulent after crossing the Rockies and were digging down into the plains, scouring them out.[18] On May 11, 1934, a huge cloud of dust originating 1,500 miles away moved over New York City and left the city in half-light for five hours. The Statue of Liberty was described as just a smudge of gray, its outline barely distinguishable to New Yorkers.[19] A year later on April 14, a monstrous dust storm referred to as Black Sunday spread dust eastward until it became a curtain around Capitol Hill.[20]

Soil scientist Hugh Hammond Bennett was testifying before a Senate committee about the need for a permanent soil conservation agency. With the help of an aide, he timed his testimony for the skies to darken over the Senate Office Building as the dust cloud arrived. Senators, who had not shown much interest up until then, dashed to the windows to see for themselves. Bennett got what he wanted. The Soil Conservation Act of April 27, 1935, created the Soil Conservation Service.[21]

The Depression and Dust Bowl were hard times for Farm Bureau as well. A darkness fell over the organization in 1931, analogous to the darkness created by the dust clouds that occasionally moved over Chicago. December 1931 marked the end of a painful year. It was the same year that Thompson, encouraged by his board of directors, accepted a position on the Federal Farm Board. The Farm Board was headed for failure, but what else could Thompson do? The call had come from President Hoover and Farm Bureau was trying to be supportive of any efforts at farm relief. Thompson might have even welcomed the change; it wasn't any easier being head of a farm organization in times like this.

The new president, Ed O'Neal, was trying to get used to the Chicago winter, which was a far cry from anything experienced at his northern Alabama farm. At least the windows to his office in Chicago's Loop were closed during the winter, and he didn't have to listen to the rumble and screech of the elevated trains on Wabash Street.

The 1931 annual report to Farm Bureau members did not pull any punches in analyzing the farm outlook. "The continuing evil effects of the great drought of 1930 were intensified by renewed drought in 1931 in a large section of the country; the price of the products of the farm fell to the lowest level witnessed in more than twenty years; unsettled world conditions further restricted markets for American farm products; those opposing the progress of organized agriculture, consolidated their forces and launched a well-directed and well-financed drive to nullify the accomplishments of twelve years of organized effort."[22]

But the annual report tried to reassure members that everything was well with their Farm Bureau, despite what seemed like an utter collapse in agriculture. "The organization has gallantly met these conditions. Morale of the Farm Bureau from the individual farmer-member to the national office is the highest that it has ever been," said the report. Members were told that organizational activity increased in 1931 and programs were actually enlarged. The staff had been reduced 11 percent in keeping with the national farm situation, but the output of work was up an amazing 22 percent.[23]

There was no point in troubling members with a pessimistic report. The one organization that could help them was Farm Bureau and somehow it had to pull through. Therefore, the pleadings of Chester Gray for more help in the Washington office were left out. Missing too were the official membership numbers. Farm Bureau had 276,053 paid-up members on the rolls a 45,000 member decrease. It was generally thought that 300,000 members was the minimum number necessary to fund a national presence.

The AFBF budget for 1932 cut salaries across the board by 10 percent. Dues income of $140,000 was expected for the year ahead, but that had to later be revised downward to $100,000. A new lease on the office at 59 East Washington Street (the Garland Building) was signed at a savings of $150 a month. With so many businesses failing, landlords were willing to reduce rents to keep stable renters.

W. T. Martindale, director of field services, found hope in the fact that Farm Bureau had the most complete machine for service to agriculture ever voluntarily created by farm people. He counted 6,000 staff workers assisted by 50,000 volunteers across the country. Martindale stretched the truth only a little. There were 1,843 organized county Farm Bureaus at the end of 1931. The county units further divided into more than 16,000 community or township units. Indiana

Farm Bureau alone had 90 office workers and another 360 in the field. Illinois Farm Bureau also had a large staff and a wide range of programs and services. It even had its own baseball league, the Farm Bureau Baseball League, with thirty-four teams around the state.[24]

But Farm Bureau needed membership in order to survive, of that there was no doubt. Martindale kept the numbers updated on a blackboard in his office and the totals made him fear for his job. "It is unfortunate," he said, "that the membership department of any Farm Bureau is the one that suffers from all the ills of every other department." In a report that only the board of directors received, Martindale said some Farm Bureaus were practically dormant, and members were unlikely much longer to pay dues to a county organization that offered little or no services and direct benefits.

Martindale also reported a clamor out in the country for a dues reduction or, worse yet in his opinion, a moratorium. Some state Farm Bureaus had already cut their dues from $10 to $5 and even further to $1, but these desperate measures weren't adding new members as expected and certainly didn't help finances. Martindale predicted that dues moratoriums would result in "the complete ruination of our organization, both state and national."[25]

This was certainly the darkest hour in the history of American agriculture and the American Farm Bureau Federation. O'Neal, board members, and staff all pondered the fate of the organization. They could take solace in the fact that Farm Bureau had a good run of twelve years. If the organization failed at this point, who could blame any of them? The Great Depression and Dust Bowl following on the heels of a farm depression were almost insurmountable odds against which to build a positive, constructive organization. If the national organization failed now, surely some of the stronger state Farm Bureaus in the Midwest would survive and maybe one or two in the East.

Because farmers often do turn adversity around on the farm and come out ahead, no one at the national level was ready to throw in the towel. O'Neal probably thought that things couldn't get any worse, but he was wrong. Things did get worse. Shortly after delivering a gloomy report to the AFBF board of directors, Martindale was injured in an automobile accident in Indiana. He was expected to remain in a hospital there for two months. Mrs. Charles Sewell, head of the Home and Community Department, became ill as well and required a leave of absence.

In May 1932, Ward T. Martindale died of his injuries leaving behind a wife and two daughters. After his death, field services were suspended in order to save money. AFBF Secretary-Treasurer M. S. Winder was apologetic about the decision. "We must continue to regard organization as the first function of the Farm Bureau and not until we have developed in every part of the country a strong vigorous organization with an intelligent and informed membership, can we hope to achieve the goal we have set," he said.[26]

A year later in October 1933, Winder resigned and Director of Information H. R. Kibler was fired for questionable financial dealings involving a publicity contract with the General Asphalt Association, a road building trade association. The revelation came to light in a most embarrassing way at a public hearing on ship subsidies before a Senate subcommittee chaired by Sen. Hugo Black (D–Alabama). Winder and Kibler were conducting similar negotiations with two associations representing American shipping interests to run a similar campaign for a stronger merchant marine through the American Farm Bureau Federation. They were asking $94,000 from the shipbuilders and ship owners.

Further probing by the subcommittee and AFBF board of directors revealed unethical behavior. A former employee involved in the motion picture service, S. A. Van Petten, sold a publicity contract to the asphalt industry that was worth $135,000 over three years. The contract called for a Secondary Road Institute to be set up within the American Farm Bureau Federation. Van Petten received a hefty 25 percent commission for arranging this and gave a portion of the money to Winder and Kibler.

O'Neal acted swiftly and decisively to restore the integrity of the American Farm Bureau Federation. He decided that anyone remotely connected with the scheme would be let go. A bookkeeper barely escaped only because $50 she received had been charged against her salary by Winder. The board already decided not to accept any more publicity contracts, although it knew nothing of the unauthorized commission splitting. The scandal did not involve Gray and AFBF legislative activities. It was one of very few embarrassments for an organization that prides itself on its integrity.

Ed O'Neal used to tell new board members not to fail to register their opinions according to their consciences and as the Lord inspires them. Agriculture was contracting; Farm Bureau was contracting and no one knew where or when this was going to stop. One measure the board considered in 1933 was a consolidation of the two offices into one Washington office.

It was at this time that AFBF Vice President Earl Smith of Illinois issued a challenge to his fellow board members. Smith suggested they pledge to increase their state membership by 25 percent. "Increase our membership; then we will save agriculture, also the nation," said Smith. O'Neal heartily concurred. "It delights me to see our strong leaders face these things straight. Let's get out of the peanut business and face the big things to be done." [27]

The hit song of 1931 was "Brother, Can You Spare a Dime?" It captured the mood of the Great Depression. Farm Bureau was looking for a song too, but that sort of song wouldn't do. It had to be something positive and uplifting. Tin Pan Alley realized the same thing and came out with "Life Is Just a Bowl of Cherries" and "We're in the Money," cheery songs to make people forget their troubles.

Ideally the Farm Bureau song would be inspirational and would invoke a feeling of kinship that comes with being a Farm Bureau member. Contests were a popular diversion, so in the middle of the Depression, the Home and Community Department decided to sponsor a songwriting contest. The director of the women's department, Mrs. Charles Sewell, put together a contest with help from Homer Rodeheaver, the well-known musical director for evangelist Billy Sunday and a pioneer in the recording of sacred music. His most recorded piece and Sunday's theme song was "Brighten the Corner Where You Are." The Rodeheaver Recording Company was located in downtown Chicago, not far from the AFBF headquarters.

Rodeheaver happened to be looking for a Farm Bureau song to include in a new songbook. His songbooks were popular sellers with farm families and already included one Farm Bureau song, a march called "Boost the Farm," with the lyrics "We'll treat you square, let's do our share, to boost the Farm Bureau." This time he wanted a sing-along song with more sweep and dignity for the new book.[28]

Most of the contest entries were disappointing. They merely added Farm Bureau lyrics to existing popular music. Rodeheaver found only two entries that he liked and decided to combine them. One was submitted by Mrs. Lillian Atcherson of Mankato, Minnesota, an established poet, who was inspired by her first airplane ride over Minnesota farmland. Mrs. Catherine Wilson, also of Mankato, worked with her on the music.

> 'Neath the great blue dome of Heaven
>
> Lies a country fair and free
>
> With its fertile hills and valleys
>
> Stretching out from sea to sea . . .

Rodeheaver chose for the chorus the words and music of Florence Cheadle of Indianapolis.

> There's a guiding ray
>
> That leads the way
>
> As farmers forward go,
>
> We love the name of world-wide fame
>
> The American Farm Bureau.
>
> Farm Federation,
>
> The watchword of our Nation
>
> United we, in strength shall be
>
> Throughout this glorious land.[29]

Together, the moving words of poet Atcherson and the powerful chorus of Cheadle made "The American Farm Bureau Spirit" the perfect song, honoring America's farmland and the spirit of its farmers. The "American Farm Bureau Spirit" was recorded in 1949 by Harry Kogen and the Homesteaders and later by a Purdue University men's chorus.

Music always brought smiles to the faces of the thousands of farm families at the annual meetings. For many, many years, Frank Pierce of the California Farm Bureau was song leader. He was then followed by Murray Miles of the Tennessee Farm Bureau. More recently, Chicago White Sox organist Nancy Faust has provided music for the conventions.

The wonderful story about an Iowa farm community coming together to form a marching band brings one thing to mind—"The Music Man." The Meredith Willson musical comedy opened in December 1957 at the Majestic Theater on Broadway. Robert Preston starred as "Professor" Harold Hill, the glib con man and traveling salesman who sold musical instruments and uniforms to schools with the promise to form a marching band. Hill was no music professor and had no intention of staying around once he collected the band money, but his stop in River City, Iowa, was unlike the rest. He fell in love with the town's pretty librarian, Marian, and stayed to face the music.

"The Music Man" became one of America's best-loved musicals with its signature march, "Seventy-Six Trombones," and the memorable song "Ya Got Trouble." Willson said the musical was inspired by his own life; he was born in Mason City, Iowa, played the flute and piccolo, and traveled with the legendary John Philip Sousa's marching band in the early 1920s.

But before Willson's "Music Man," there was a real marching band from Iowa that bore a few striking resemblances to the musical. The Southern Iowa Farm Bureau Band was assembled by the Conn Music Company of Chicago from county Farm Bureaus in southeastern Iowa along the Mississippi River. Willson's River City doesn't exist but the Farm Bureau band came from river towns like Muscatine and Ottumwa.

In June 1933, the entire band arrived in Chicago on special cars of the Burlington Railroad to perform at the Chicago World's Fair, "A Century of Progress." The band was a big news story because a farm revolution seemed more likely than farmers forming a marching band. "Iowa, scene of unrest, farmers' strikes and general foment among cornbelters is sending its 800 piece Southern Iowa Farm Bureau Band with its $50,000 worth of musical instruments to the World's Fair," reported the *Chicago Daily Tribune*.[30]

An additional 1,000 Farm Bureau members accompanied the band. It must have been quite a sight. Disembarking at Chicago's Union Station, the band members brought traffic to a standstill as they marched across the city's financial district waving green and yellow Farm Bureau flags. AFBF had been unable to provide financial support for the band, but O'Neal greeted band members as they arrived in the city.

The Farm Bureau band was reported to be the largest in the world with musicians from nineteen Iowa counties ranging in age from 10 to 67. They played two performances before a packed house at the fair's Court of States. "It [the band] played merrily and with altogether commendable exactness," wrote a *Tribune* reviewer. "Music for the full band was mostly of popular character, marches, waltzes, well-known melodies, played energetically and with good tone." The big band did not get top billing in the music review that day. The honor went to a piano virtuoso who gave a recital of his own music, the incomparable George Gershwin.[31]

Is it possible that Meredith Willson heard or read about the Iowa band and recalled the story in writing "The Music Man"? There are a few coincidences to ponder between the real story and his highly acclaimed musical. The Southern Iowa Farm Bureau Band came to Chicago with 70 trombones (not 76, but close), 200 cornets, 300 woodwinds, and a couple hundred other instruments. The conductor was Mayo Williams, not Harold Hill, of course, but when Willson wrote the musical the Iowa Farm Bureau president was a farmer named Howard Hill.

Even without the coincidences, the Farm Bureau band is a remarkable story in itself. One can only imagine the sacrifices these farm families had to make in the middle of the Depression to rent musical instruments, take lessons, and learn to play well enough to be invited to a world's fair. When they got off the train and marched proudly across Chicago, they embodied the spirit of Farm Bureau.

Endnotes

1. Galbraith, *The Great Crash 1929*, 17.
2. "Text of Hoover's Speech at St. Louis," *New York Times*, November 3, 1928.
3. "Hoover Signs the Farm Relief Bill," *New York Times*, June 16, 1929.
4. "Thompson Sees New Farm Era in Relief Law," *Chicago Tribune*, June 16, 1929.
5. "Legge For Farm Aid By Organization," *New York Times*, March 24, 1930.
6. "Says He Inspired Coolidge 'Straddle,'" *New York Times*, February 27, 1930.
7. "Hyde Challenges Farm Board Critics," *New York Times*, July 29, 1932.
8. "Urges 'War' on Foes of the Farm Board," *New York Times*, May 12, 1930.
9. "Hyde Says Farmers Must Cut Output," *New York Times*, January 28, 1930.
10. Transcript, AFBF Annual Meeting, December 5–10, 1930, Boston, Massachusetts.
11. "U.S. Ends Buying of Wheat; Loss is $90,000,000," *Chicago Tribune*, May 1930.
12. "The Federal Farm Board Has Had a Stormy Life," *New York Times*, September 11, 1932.
13. *AFBF Policy Resolutions for 1933*.
14. *Twenty Years with the American Farm Bureau Federation*.

15. *Yearbook of Agriculture 1940*, 314.

16. "On Farm Problems," *Vital Speeches,* 2: 27, October 7, 1935.

17. USDA, *1940 Yearbook of Agriculture*, 139.

18. "Dust Storms Laid to Pacific Winds," *New York Times,* June 29, 1935.

19. "Huge Dust Cloud, Blown 1,500 Miles, Dims City Five Hours," *New York Times,* May 12, 1934.

20. "Thin Sheet of Dust Blown Out to Atlantic," *New York Times,* April 16, 1935.

21. Egan, *Worst Hard Time*, 227–228.

22. *AFBF Annual Report of 1931.*

23. Ibid.

24. Ibid.

25. Minutes, AFBF board of directors, 1932.

26. Ibid.

27. Minutes, AFBF board of directors, 1933.

28. Woell, *Farm Bureau Architects,* 24–26; www.gracyk.com/rodeheaver.shtml, accessed May 20, 2008.

29. The complete song is found at the back of this book. It was copyrighted in 1930 by the American Farm Bureau Federation.

30. "Iowa Farm Band of 800 Pieces to Visit the Fair," *Chicago Tribune,* June 11, 1933.

31. "George Gershwin to be Soloist for Concert Tonight," *Chicago Tribune,* June 14, 1933.

8 | The New Deal

THERE ARE SOME WHO SAY THE AMERICAN FARM BUREAU FEDERATION WROTE THE New Deal farm legislation, but that is a bit of an exaggeration. The fact of the matter is that the Agricultural Adjustment Act of 1933, landmark farm legislation and centerpiece of President Roosevelt's New Deal, was identical in principle to the farm relief program advocated by AFBF. Farm Bureau played a critical role in negotiations beforehand and in the program's acceptance by Congress and farmers afterwards.

"We were ready—ready with a carefully considered program and a trained leadership and powerful organization to support that program," recalled O'Neal at the 1933 AFBF annual meeting in Chicago. He drew on one of Christ's parables in the New Testament to describe the moment. "Like the ten wise virgins with their wicks trimmed and their lights burning, we were ready when our great opportunity came."[1] It was as if everything that had gone on before was a drill for these troubled times. This was the true test of Farm Bureau. Could a farm organization, conceived in good times, help farmers survive in the most perilous of times. If it couldn't, it would not be the Voice of Agriculture for very long.

Farm Bureau's future was on the line and so was the future of the family farm. Farmers could not survive another decade like the 1920s without some form of relief. The McNary-Haugen bills never made it into law and Hoover's Farm Board was buried under crop surpluses. By the 1928 AFBF annual meeting, the voting delegates realized that some form of "acreage regulation" was going to be necessary. The Farm Board came to the same conclusion toward the end of its life, but had no way to implement it. A plan to plow up one-third of the cotton crop was suggested but it was left up to the states. Half of the cotton state governors rejected the idea.

Louisiana's Gov. Huey Long called for a one-year moratorium on all cotton planting. The flamboyant Long said if his plan was adopted the South would see

20¢ cotton in three weeks.[2] Cotton prices in 1931 averaged 4¢ a pound, down from 20¢ a pound in 1927 and 40¢ a pound in 1920. Both cotton and wheat were in great surplus. Even Mussolini, Italy's self-proclaimed first farmer, became concerned about a worldwide wheat surplus and called a conference of producing nations attended by the United States.

Sixty rural economists and farm organization leaders, including AFBF Vice President Charles Hearst of Iowa, got together for three days of closed-door meetings at the University of Chicago to come up with a national farm policy. The economists were pessimistic about any improvement in the farm situation. One rumor coming out of the meeting was that USDA was studying dividing the country up into regions "for the specialized production of farm products."[3]

Perhaps the most unique idea for dealing with farm surpluses, particularly wheat, came from the Federal Bureau of Home Economics. It suggested a fashion change for women, a return to plumper Victorian styles of the previous century. "If we were eating bread today with the same gusto even as at the turn of the century, all those bushels would be nicely assimilated into our rounded figures, and there would be no farm problem," said *New York Times* staff writer Eunice Fuller Barnard.[4] The wartime food conservation campaign worked too well. Consumers ate less bread and continued eating less bread after the war.

AFBF convened a National Farm Conference at the beginning of 1932 in the nation's capital to enlist a united front on farm relief. The result was big news around the nation. AFBF, Grange, and Farmers Union agreed on a six-point legislative relief program. As reported in the newsletter, "It was the first time in the history of organized American agriculture that the 'big three' reached unanimous agreement on a project of such momentous significance to the industry."

Afterwards, one group of participants met with 100 members of Congress to convey results of the conference, while another group went to NBC studios in Washington for a national radio broadcast. The plan offered little in the way of new ideas, however. It still relied on marketing help through an equalization fee or export debenture. Other points included monetary reform, an end to short selling on commodity exchanges, and independence for the Philippine Islands. The latter was of interest chiefly because it would end the duty-free status of Philippine fats and oils.[5]

A few days later, the heads of the farm organizations testified at a special hearing of the House Agriculture Committee. O'Neal was the lead-off witness. He reminded committee members that they had often urged the farm organizations to get together on a single plan of farm relief, and now they had. He still supported the equalization fee concept, but there was an added element of production control. Nonproductive land would be taken out of production and no new marginal lands added. O'Neal also suggested that industrial uses be developed for wheat, corn, cotton, potatoes, rice, and other commodities. Using grain as a feed-stock for alcohol fuel was gaining interest.

Because 1932 was an election year, Congress could not agree on farm relief measures although it increased the capital stock of federal land banks and passed other measures to aid the banking industry. A last-ditch effort by Farm Bureau for a one-year emergency bill passed the Senate but died in the House. Speaker John Nance Garner (D-Texas) was blamed for postponing the legislation in hopes a Democratic administration could claim credit for farm relief.

While Farm Bureau worked on legislative remedies, there was a restlessness and feeling of despair out in the countryside. A few farmers began to think perhaps Farm Bureau wasn't an effective voice for them, especially if that voice needed to be a shout. They preferred direct action in the form of strikes and boycotts. These more radical elements in the Midwest coalesced in the Farmers' Holiday Association.

The strike movement was led by Farmers Union organizer Milo Reno of Des Moines. Reno had a simple plan to raise farm prices; farmers would not buy or sell anything for thirty days, the time he figured it would take to bring the local economy to its knees. He thought a widespread strike would force the federal government into at least guaranteeing farmers their cost of production. The Farmer's Holiday Association also wanted an end to farm foreclosures and showed up at auctions to keep legitimate bidders away. Their members bid a few cents on the dollar for property being auctioned off. After the "penny sale," the property was returned to the original owner.

A strike or holiday began in August 1932 on the western edge of Iowa around Sioux City and Council Bluffs. Strikers blockaded roads to stop trucks bringing produce, poultry, and eggs into the cities. It continued for a couple weeks until fourteen pickets were shot. "As a voluntary movement, the holiday was a dud," said one account. "For every farmer participating there are scores who are not and will not."[6] O'Neal sent a letter to county Farm Bureaus in Iowa with the approval of the state president urging county leaders to try to put an end to the violence and hysteria.

A Harrison County, Iowa, Farm Bureau member, Mrs. A. H. Beebee, took on the Holiday movement with her slogan, "Farm Bureau work doesn't stop for holidays." She also designed a Farm Bureau flag to put next to the American flag in the Farm Bureau office and dared the strikers to touch either one of them. The fearless farm woman became known as the "Betsy Ross" of Iowa.[7]

Roosevelt's defining speech on farm relief during the campaign was delivered in Topeka, Kansas, on September 14, 1932. He accused the Hoover administration of waiting for the perfect plan to deal with farm surpluses, and therefore doing nothing. He impressed farmers with his understanding of their problems.

"We have poverty and want in the midst of abundance. With incomparable natural wealth within the reach of these progressive farmers they struggle with poverty and unbelievably hard times. They try to hold on to their farms under conditions produced by corn, hogs, cotton, wool, cattle and wheat selling on the farm at prices as low as or lower than at any time in the history of the United States." He warned that the nation's farm families faced living under "the shadow of peasantry" if something wasn't done to help them.[8]

In October, Roosevelt and Henry Morgenthau met with O'Neal and Illinois Agricultural Association President Earl Smith in Chicago. Also present were Peek, Chester Davis, and Clifford Gregory, editor of *Prairie Farmer*. Peek thought the meeting was a good one and said that Roosevelt was "sound" on farm relief.[9] A Farm Bureau report said its leaders "interviewed" Roosevelt and were encouraged. "Gov. Roosevelt has shown a very sympathetic understanding of the whole farm problem," declared O'Neal.[10]

As the election neared, the domestic allotment plan developed by Montana State College economist M. L. Wilson and John D. Black, professor of economics at Harvard University, received attention. Farmers who signed contracts to limit production would receive certificates on the domestic portion of their crop. They could then sell these to processors. The farmer got the sale price of his crop plus the value of the certificate. Later the idea of an excise tax levied on processors was substituted for the certificates.[11]

Wilson worked hard to sell the allotment plan to Farm Bureau and Roosevelt. Some of his correspondence was sent out over the signature of W. L. Stockton, vice president of the Montana Farm Bureau, to imply Farm Bureau's approval, but that came later.[12] At the 1932 AFBF annual meeting, delegates adopted a policy resolution to restore to the producer "his pre-war purchasing power for the domestic quota of the most important cash crops."

Addressing the issue, O'Neal said, "Our plan for securing the advantage of the American market for American producers must contemplate as a fundamental step, an effort at controlling production. We, therefore, propose that in applying the principles set forth in this plan, allotments shall be made to states on the basis of average past production of the several crops . . . "[13] AFBF had no intention of retiring from the export market, but it realized a temporary solution must be found for farm surpluses.

Henry A. Wallace (who was mentioned in the press as the future secretary of agriculture) appeared at the same convention and reminded members of the importance of the Farm Bureau. "It is only through some general organization of this type that the power is generated whereby ideas originating in some individual's mind . . . can finally work out through the organization, through Congress and eventually into some scheme which we trust will be of great benefit to agriculture." Wallace received a long, loud applause, an indication of Farm Bureau's desire to see him in Roosevelt's Cabinet.[14]

AFBF went to work after the convention to develop a consensus on farm relief and to draft the main points of the legislation. There was a five-month waiting period for Roosevelt's inauguration. The Twentieth Amendment that moved the president's swearing-in to January came later. O'Neal presided over meetings that took place December 12–14, at the Harrington Hotel in Washington. The attendees included farm organization leaders and Roosevelt's economic advisers. It was here that agreement was reached on the main tenets of the New Deal farm program, rather than at the more celebrated meeting of agricultural leaders called by Wallace in March 1933.[15]

At the Harrington Hotel, Farm Bureau also let Roosevelt's advisers know that it preferred Wallace for secretary of agriculture. Roosevelt favored his good friend and fellow New Yorker Henry Morgenthau, a dairy and apple farmer. Morgenthau was the son of a respected banker and ambassador, but O'Neal spoke privately to Rex Tugwell and said Morgenthau wouldn't do. Roosevelt named Wallace secretary and put Morgenthau in charge of farm credit, the second most important agricultural post.[16] He later became treasury secretary.

The enigmatic Wallace was the scion of a respected farm publishing family. His father served as secretary of agriculture in the Harding administration and was an early supporter of the Farm Bureau movement. Henry A., a protégé of George Peek, was editor of *Wallaces' Farmer* and the first commercial producer of hybrid seed corn. Biographers Culver and Hyde described him as "high-minded and cerebral, reserved to the point of shyness." They said he did not make conversation easily, but when he did speak, it was with an earnestness that showed little emotion.[17]

O'Neal met with the president-elect on January 20, in Washington. Farm Bureau hoped to get the allotment and farm mortgage bills enacted even before Roosevelt took office, but a battle developed in Congress over which commodities to include in the allotments. Some congressmen wanted to limit them to wheat and cotton. O'Neal was adamant that tobacco, hogs, rice, peanuts, and dairy needed relief too. Corn price relief would come through marketing hogs. The House passed the Jones bill authored by the chairman of the House Agriculture Committee, Marvin Jones (D-Texas). It covered most of the commodities sought by Farm Bureau but the measure failed to pass.

The Farm Bureau president was so sure that a domestic allotment plan would pass once Roosevelt was in office that he moved on to another topic, Farm Bureau's call for an "honest dollar." A thirty-four page pamphlet entitled "Honest Money" was circulated by Farm Bureau to make the argument that the money supply should be inflated to raise the wholesale price of commodities. "We value wheat in dollars, but a dollar's worth of wheat varies greatly. A dollar would buy less than half a bushel of wheat in 1919, a bushel in 1929, and three bushels in the early summer of 1931." In Farm Bureau's opinion, the dollar was an inaccurate measuring stick of value.[18]

The commodity dollar or honest dollar idea originated with two Cornell University agricultural economists, George F. Warren and Frank A. Pearson, but was given wide circulation by Farm Bureau. John K. Galbraith credited the two economists with influencing Roosevelt and others around him in taking action to raise the price of gold and devalue the dollar. "It was an especially attractive policy for the farm belt, where prices, which farmers had linked since the days of William Jennings Bryan to the crucifying role of gold, were very bad," said Galbraith.[19]

In February 1933, a month before Roosevelt's inauguration, O'Neal warned on radio and before Congress that a revolt more serious and widespread than the farm strike was possible in farm country unless action was taken. On Farm Bureau's regularly scheduled radio broadcast over NBC, O'Neal said, "When I speak of revolt I refer to an economic revolt. We are in the midst of an economic revolution right now in this country." He called on Congress to adopt a farm allotment program and mortgage relief before farmers were driven to drastic measures. They are "losing their homes, their savings of a lifetime and all incentive for orderly living," said O'Neal on the air.[20]

Historian Arthur Schlesinger Jr. said O'Neal also warned a Senate committee around the same time, "Unless something is done for the American farmer we will have revolution in the countryside within less than twelve months."[21] Farm Bureau was not generally given to hyperbole, so one can assume that O'Neal meant what he said. Certainly Farm Bureau had a good handle on what was going on out in the country and the mood of farmers. Congress heeded the warning because it acted with unusual swiftness to pass the New Deal legislation, starting with agriculture.

A few months after the warning, several hundred strikers dragged a district court judge from his bench in LeMars, Iowa, for refusing to stop farm foreclosures while a moratorium was considered at the state house. With shouts of "Get a rope, let's hang him!" the mob took the judge to the edge of town and tied a noose around his neck. He was roughed up and humiliated, but not hanged. The governor called out the National Guard and declared martial law in several counties.[22]

When Wallace was sworn in as secretary of agriculture, O'Neal described him as "an ardent Farm Bureau member," and added, "We expect Wallace will make an outstanding secretary at a time when farmers face their biggest problems since the nation was founded." He also said that Wallace was "the farmer's right bower in the bureau's program," a reference to a trump card in a euchre hand.[23]

A special meeting of the AFBF board of directors was called right after March 4, 1933, the day Roosevelt was inaugurated and Wallace was sworn in as secretary of agriculture. From the meeting came a four-point emergency program: (1) a guarantee of new bank deposits and protection of rural banks equal to that given city banks; (2) monetary reform, a devaluation of the dollar or increase in the price of gold; (3) restoration of a price parity for agriculture with the products of industry; and (4) relief of mortgage indebtedness.[24]

Farm Bureau's four-point program was wired to Roosevelt, and O'Neal received a call from Wallace proposing a national conference of farm leaders. On March 10, leaders of Farm Bureau, the Grange, Farmers Union, national farmer cooperatives, and the farm press met in Wallace's office in Washington to thrash out a plan. There were fifty-five in the room, nine of whom were Farm Bureau leaders, including O'Neal and AFBF Vice President Hearst.

Near the end of the first day, agreement was reached to give the secretary of agriculture broad emergency powers to restore the parity price of agricultural products but not to guarantee farmers the cost of production. Roosevelt accepted the recommendations and ordered USDA to prepare the text of a bill. The job was given to AFBF special counsel Frederic P. Lee, who had been the Senate's legislative counsel for many years. Lee worked day and night for four days to complete the bill. On March 16, the president sent the bill to Congress with a note requesting urgent action.

Lee's work on the Agricultural Adjustment Act of 1933 is what led some to say that the American Farm Bureau Federation actually wrote the bill. Christina McFayden Campbell, author of *The Farm Bureau and the New Deal,* said Farm Bureau's role was a "crucial one." She gave Farm Bureau credit for being "a unifying agency within agriculture" and for bringing about sectional agreement between Midwestern and Southern farmers.[25] AFBF was the Voice of Agriculture that Roosevelt and his advisers listened to, that much is certain.

The farm relief bill sailed through Congress and was signed on May 12, by President Roosevelt in his White House office in front of a small group of men who had been involved in framing the legislation. They included O'Neal, Wallace, Tugwell, Peek, Wilson, Morgenthau, and four congressmen. L. J. Taber, Master of the National Grange, was the only other farm organization leader besides O'Neal.

Adjustment was the key word in the Agricultural Adjustment Act of 1933—to correct the imbalance between agriculture and the rest of the economy. This meant an adjustment in income, adjustment in credit, adjustment in production, and adjustment in land use. The other word that became part of the agriculture lexicon was *parity,* which not only was a measurement of a farmer's purchasing power, but a substitute for the older notion of equality for agriculture. Basically

they meant the same thing, but parity was more quantifiable. AFBF voting delegates first used the word in a policy resolution adopted at the 1932 annual
meeting—"The enactment of surplus control legislation to restore price parity to
agriculture with other groups."[26]

In a nationwide radio address over NBC, O'Neal could not have been more
exuberant. "Truly, it is a new day for agriculture and a great day of victory for the
American Farm Bureau Federation, which has stood at the forefront of agriculture
for so many years." As he watched the president's pen move on the paper, O'Neal
said he felt he was witnessing a new economic and social order in America. "It
meant the death knell of the Depression and the beginning of the restoration of
purchasing power of agriculture, employment for labor and prosperity for the
nation." To him, it was the greatest legislative victory ever achieved by organized
agriculture and the first fundamental farm relief measure advocated by agriculture
enacted into law.[27]

For the moment at least, Farm Bureau members forgot the troubles on their
farms and celebrated. AFBF historian Kile noted, "Congratulations rolled in upon
Chicago and Washington offices of the Farm Bureau from farm people everywhere. The Indiana Farm Bureau staged a statewide victory celebration."[28] Less
pleased were the packers, millers, and other processors who were taxed to fund the
adjustment program, although they could pass the cost on to consumers. Wallace
was not particularly worried about the impact on food prices. He thought consumers were paying only 60 percent of what they should be paying for food,
although he admitted it probably didn't seem like that to them.[29]

The Agricultural Adjustment Administration (AAA) was set up within USDA
to administer the programs aimed at raising the level of farm prices. George Peek,
Farm Bureau's ally in the early fight for equality, was the first administrator. The
Department of Agriculture quickly became an exciting place to work and the
largest branch of the government. New Dealers included future Democratic presidential candidate Adlai Stevenson, future Supreme Court Justice Abe Fortas, and
Alger Hiss, later accused of being a Communist spy by Richard Nixon.

With the same energy it had poured into securing passage of a farm relief bill,
AFBF went to work in rolling it out to the country. O'Neal spent several hours
with Roosevelt discussing the subject. He advised using the Extension Service,
farm organizations, and land grant colleges. The county agent was given the job
of setting up the local machinery, but where strong Farm Bureaus existed, they
literally took over the job of organizing local AAA committees and mobilizing
farmer participation and support. It was through the county production control
committees that allotments were made and compliance checked.[30]

The county agent already was identified with Farm Bureau and soon the
Agricultural Adjustment Administration became identified with it. Committee

members who weren't Farm Bureau members often felt compelled to join. This was a boon to Farm Bureau membership of course, but a lot hinged on the success of the adjustment program. Earl Smith, president of the Illinois Agricultural Association, said, "If it succeeds the administration will be credited with the success. If it fails, a good deal of the responsibility can be passed off on Farm Bureau and other farm organizations. Our organization must do everything it can to assure the success of the Agricultural Adjustment Act."[31]

An editorial in *Wallaces' Farmer* referred to "the Depression of Plenty" in America because farmers were sitting on enormous stocks of wheat and cotton, while eight million working men were unemployed.[32] The Agricultural Adjustment Act addressed the surplus problem through acreage reductions, production cutbacks, commodity loans, and marketing agreements. The Commodity Credit Corporation (CCC) made nonrecourse loans to farmers to set a floor price under commodities. Basic commodities included in the act were wheat, cotton, corn, hogs, rice, tobacco, milk, and its products. Added later were rye, flax, barley, grain sorghum, peanuts, cattle, sugarcane, sugar beets, and potatoes.

A cotton plow-up campaign was announced in June 1933, and by mid-July more than one million contracts were signed by cotton farmers who agreed to plow under a quarter to half of their crop. In 1934, the Bankhead Cotton Control Act made the voluntary program compulsory when two-thirds of the producers approved it in a referendum. Wheat farmers were not required to plow up any of the winter wheat crop in 1933 because of the drought.

The National Corn-Hog Producers Committee of Twenty-Five recommended immediate removal from marketing channels of four million baby pigs and one million sows about to farrow. This was by far the most controversial decision made in removing surpluses to raise prices. Three of five members on the executive board of the committee had Farm Bureau ties. Earl Smith of Illinois was chairman, O'Neal, and farm editor Clifford Gregory were members. Smith also secured a 45¢ loan rate for corn when the country price was only 23¢.[33]

Around 100 million pounds of pork products were distributed through food relief channels from the hog program, but food relief did not stop all the criticism. Secretary Wallace said farmers were entitled to limit their production just as industry was doing. "Times without number I have heard it said that there cannot be a surplus so long as there is a single hungry Chinaman. Fundamentally and eventually this may be true; but the same persons who weep that farmers should control production do not suggest that clothing factories go on producing without limit, regardless of effective demand for their merchandise, until every naked Chinaman is clothed," said Wallace. He also advocated an "ever-normal granary" that he attributed to Joseph in the Bible.[34] While good in theory, the build up of stores of grain in the good years, to await the occasional short crop, never worked very effectively as farm policy. It just depressed prices in the meantime.

The Farmers' Holiday Association was still stirring in the countryside after the New Deal farm program was announced. Its members were upset that Roosevelt's plan did not fix the price of farm commodities nor did it offer credit to producers at little or no interest. The strike movement also did not like how the New Deal elevated the Farm Bureau, and they were particularly upset that farmers paid more for goods like overalls and gasoline because of the National Recovery Act. "All this is food for the farm agitator who thrives on exploiting the farmer's troubles and leading him in revolt. The voice of Milo Reno is again heard on the land," said the *New York Times.*[35] As government checks started showing up in farmers' mailboxes, this strike movement faded off into history.

At the 1933 AFBF annual meeting in Chicago, O'Neal proclaimed the Agricultural Adjustment Act to be "Magna Charta of American agriculture" and part of an even bigger change. "We have entered upon a new era in American life—an era of national planning for agriculture, for industry, for labor, for finance, and for the nation generally." The mood of the meeting was upbeat; there was laughter when Dr. W. I. Myers, head of the Farm Credit Administration, told about a farmer who refinanced his debt and turned in bills to prove how the credit was used. Included was a $10 receipt for a lady's corset, which after some deliberation, was referred to the Agricultural Adjustment Administration as a surplus control matter.

Roosevelt sent a message to the convention thanking Farm Bureau for its "warm support," and adding, "Money is getting into the hands of people who need it; it is coming in the form of government checks for those cooperating producers who are willing to swap a hazardous present for immediate improvement and a stable future."[36]

Over the next two years, the government pumped a billion dollars into the farm economy. The Emergency Farm Mortgage Act of 1933 made emergency loans available to farmers at lower interest rates and expanded the activities of federal land banks. The Farm Credit Administration formed by executive order consolidated federal agencies dealing with agricultural credit into one unit. The Farm Credit Act of 1933 provided for the establishment of production credit associations to make short-term and intermediate term loans to farmers. The rescue effort saved literally hundreds of thousands of farm families from crushing indebtedness or foreclosure.

Farm Bureau's call for a guarantee of new bank deposits was handled by creation of the Federal Deposit Insurance Corporation in 1933. The Securities Act of 1933 and Securities Exchange Act of 1934 regulated the issuance and trading of securities. Farm Bureau had long been critical of speculation, primarily in the commodities market, but also on Wall Street.

Between 1932 and 1935, net farm income more than doubled, but the rug was pulled out from under the AAA in January 1936 when the Supreme Court ruled the Agricultural Adjustment Act unconstitutional because of the processing tax. One day later, O'Neal told Farm Bureau members, "The fight is on and this time all gloves are off." He said that the high court decision was a stunning blow to the national economic recovery and was perpetrated by those who want to keep farmers impoverished. The board of directors held a special meeting in Washington. Wallace and Chester Davis, who had taken the reins of the AAA from George Peek, were present. One option that was discussed was a constitutional amendment to give the federal government the authority to deal with farm problems.[37]

During January, Wallace called two major conferences of farm leaders to discuss various options. A statement from the first meeting said that the welfare of agriculture was vital to the general welfare of the nation as supported by the Constitution. After the second meeting, a decision was made not to budge from two main principles: (1) the right of American farmers to be given the machinery to adjust supply and demand, with safeguards for consumer welfare; and (2) the right of the farmer to receive prices to give him an average purchasing power equal to that he had in 1909–1914.[38]

The plan that emerged was to use the existing Soil Conservation Act to pay farmers to restore and maintain soil fertility by planting legumes and other soil-building crops. The idea doesn't appear to have originated with Farm Bureau, but O'Neal, Smith, general counsel Donald Kirkpatrick, and special counsel Fred Lee worked on it over several days and nights with Davis.[39]

By the end of February 1936, the Soil Conservation and Domestic Allotment Act zipped through Congress as a temporary expedient and received the president's signature. The emphasis of the farm bill shifted from acreage reduction to soil conservation but the results were the same—land was taken out of production. The processing tax was replaced with direct government appropriations. With soil conservation a goal and the Dust Bowl on people's minds, there was no urban backlash. Just to make sure, a major objective was stated to be, "the protection of consumers by assuring adequate supplies of food and fiber."[40]

Farm Bureau, however, did not like the farm outlook in 1937. Prices were starting to slide again and big crops were anticipated. When Congress adjourned in August without action on permanent legislation, AFBF persuaded President Roosevelt to call a special session in the fall. Its campaign on behalf of a new farm bill was documented in the 1937 AFBF annual report: "Fighting almost single-handed at times, daring to maintain its ground in the face of abusive criticism, refusing to compromise the future welfare and security of agriculture, holding out persistently for a constructive, fair and effective program, the American Farm Bureau Federation kept faith with the farmers of America."

The Agricultural Adjustment Act of 1938 included acreage allotments, commodity loans, and provision for mandatory marketing quotas if approved by two-thirds of the producers of a commodity in a referendum. Cotton and tobacco growers overwhelmingly endorsed marketing quotas, but O'Neal wondered if farmers really wanted such controls. "We will soon find out whether they meant what they said, or whether they wanted production controls only for the other fellow," he said.[41] Crop insurance also was made available to wheat growers.

New Deal farm legislation was a culmination of twelve years of hard work by the American Farm Bureau Federation to bring economic equality to agriculture and obtain farm relief from the depressed economy. Farm Bureau persevered despite its own flagging fortunes at the time. It never gave up hope, and hope was really what it was all about in the end. The restoration of hope was as powerful as any farm program.

Endnotes

1. Transcript, AFBF Annual Meeting, December 11–13, 1933, Chicago, Illinois.

2. White, *Kingfish, The Reign of Huey P. Long*, 127.

3. "60 Economists Seek A Remedy for Farm Ills," *New York Times,* September 8, 1931.

4. "New Styles in Diet As Well As Dress," *New York Times*, November 1, 1931.

5. *AFBF Official News Letter,* January 12, 1932.

6. "Farmer's Holiday Doomed to Failure," *New York Times*, August 21,1932.

7. "Iowa's 'Betsy Ross' Defies Enemies of Farm Bureau," *AFBF Official News Letter*, March 21, 1933.

8. "The Text of Gov. Roosevelt's Speech on Farm Relief at Topeka Yesterday," *New York Times,* September 15, 1932.

9. Fite, *George N. Peek and the Fight for Farm Parity*, 239.

10. "Farm Bureau Leaders Interview Roosevelt," *AFBF Official News Letter*, October 4, 1932.

11. *1940 Yearbook of Agriculture*, 316; Fite, *George N. Peek and the Fight for Farm Parity,* 231.

12. Fite, *George N. Peek and the Fight for Farm Parity*, 232.

13. Transcript, AFBF Annual Meeting, December 5–7, 1932, Chicago, Illinois.

14. Ibid.

15. McFayden Campbell, *The Farm Bureau and the New Deal*, 52.

16. Kile, *Farm Bureau Through Three Decades*, 194.

17. Culver and Hyde, *American Dreamer*, 73.

18. "Honest Money," American Farm Bureau Federation, January 7, 1932.

19. Galbraith, *A Journey Through Economic Time*, 89.

20. "O'Neal Points Out Dangers," *AFBF Official News Letter*, February 7, 1933.

21. Schlesinger, *The Coming of the New Deal*, 27.

22. "Recounts Threats to Kill Iowa Judge," *New York Times*, May 4, 1933.

23. "Hail Choice of Wallace," *New York Times,* February 27, 1933.

24. Kile, *Farm Bureau Through Three Decades*," 198.

25. McFayden Campbell, *The Farm Bureau and the New Deal*, 57.

26. Transcript, AFBF Annual Meeting of 1932.

27. "O'Neal Outlines New Deal Progress in NBC Speech," *AFBF Official News Letter,* May 16, 1933.

28. Kile, *The Farm Bureau Through Three Decades*, 103.

29. "The Purposes of the Farm Act Set out by Wallace," *New York Times,* June 4, 1933.

30. Ibid., 205.

31. Minutes, AFBF Board of Directors, August 1933.

32. "Ending the Depression of Plenty," editorial, *Wallaces' Farmer*, April 16, 1932.

33. McFayden Campbell, *The Farm Bureau and the New Deal*, 65.

34. "The Farm Situation," *Vital Speeches* 1: 47, December 3, 1934.

35. "Commodity Prices Alarm the Farmer," *New York Times*, September 10, 1933.

36. Transcript, AFBF Annual Meeting, December 11–13, 1933, Chicago, Illinois.

37. "AAA Is Gone," *AFBF Official News Letter*, January 7, 1936.

38. "New AAA Plan Indorsed," *New York Times,* January 18, 1936.

39. Kile, *The Farm Bureau Through Three Decades*, 228.

40. "History of Agricultural Price-Support and Adjustment Programs," 1933–1984, USDA.

41. "Do Farmers Want Production Controls," *AFBF Official News Letter*, March 29, 1938.

9 | Forward Again

Today, the American Farm Bureau Federation has 6.2 million member families, making it by far the largest farm organization. Not all of these members are farm families. They include rural residents who join Farm Bureau to take advantage of outstanding member services. But more farm families belong to Farm Bureau than any other single farm organization, and approximately four-fifths of farmers who join any farm organization belong to Farm Bureau.

The size and scope of Farm Bureau today would be totally incomprehensible to AFBF leaders of the 1930s. They believed in the dream that the founders had of an organization that would last a hundred years or more, but the Great Depression had a way of killing dreams. Economist Don Paarlberg noted that this economic downturn was unique in that it "often hurt good farmers more than poor ones." The good farmers, the more progressive ones, spent a lot for goods and services: farm machinery, fertilizer, fuel, etc. They had large and continuous debts to pay as farm receipts fell.[1] These same progressive farmers were the ones Farm Bureau appealed to most. When they got in trouble, so did Farm Bureau.

In 1933, there were only 163,246 dues-paying Farm Bureau members, roughly half what the national organization figured it needed to survive. Just as the organization hit rock bottom, an amazing thing happened. The New Deal raised farmers' hopes, and there was a renewed interest in Farm Bureau and an infusion of membership. Out in the country, Farm Bureau was getting credit for the New Deal farm programs, credit it gladly accepted.

A Farm Bureau membership poster proudly proclaimed, "Farm Bureau brings you a New Deal, join now, help finish the job." The message worked. By the end of 1934, AFBF reported "phenomenal growth." Total membership was 222,557, a 36 percent increase over 1933. Twenty-seven state Farm Bureaus reported gains, another three were unchanged and only seven states reported small declines.[2]

There were more than three million farmers participating in federal farm pro-grams, and they became "organization conscious" and exhibited a "greater spirit of unity." It was a perfect opportunity for building up the Farm Bureau. "There is a growing appreciation of the effectiveness with which the Farm Bureau organization can unify and speak for all types of farmers in shaping national policies and guiding their administration along sound lines," said an AFBF membership report.[3]

During the Farm Bureau Movement, some farmers had joined Farm Bureau because of all the excitement and to satisfy the neighbor who asked them to join. These members, however, slipped quietly out the back door when they became discouraged and dues seemed like an extravagance. Because Farm Bureau mem-bership was voluntary, the organization constantly had to reestablish its value to members.

The New Deal was another chance to mobilize a great membership and move forward again. Farmers recognized that, if they wanted to have a voice in federal farm programs, they had better join Farm Bureau. No one was in a better position to know that than Sen. John Bankhead, Jr. (D–Alabama), one of Farm Bureau's best friends on farm legislation. In a radio address over NBC's "National Farm and Home Hour," Bankhead praised Farm Bureau and added, "The farmers certainly need strong organizations to represent them and to express their will. They will never get what they are entitled to in the way of Federal legislation until they are organized in a way similar to the organizations of industrial workers."[4]

Out of the depths of the Depression, Farm Bureau's spirit soared. The 1935 annual meeting in Chicago was probably the greatest AFBF convention of all time. The first speaker on the morning of December 9, 1935, was President Roosevelt. He arrived by train at the Union Stockyards where more than 700 policemen and Secret Service agents were assigned to guard him. Two years earlier, Roosevelt narrowly escaped an assassin's bullets in Miami. Chicago Mayor Anton Cermak was wounded in that attack and later died.

A throng of people estimated at 19,000 was on hand at the convention to hear the president's address, making this the largest AFBF annual meeting audience ever. The International Amphitheatre seated 12,500 and was reserved for Farm Bureau members. Two wings of the building where the speech could be heard over loudspeakers were opened to the public.

"When President Roosevelt walked into the Amphitheatre on the arm of his military aid, the applause swelled into a roar," reported the *AFBF Official News Letter.* "As the President stood near the microphone with President O'Neal at his side, the great gathering arose, camera lights flashed, the applause became greater and greater and the United States Army Band from Fort Sheridan began to play 'America.' O'Neal introduced the President as the most distinguished member of the nationwide organization of thinking farmers."[5]

Five newsreel companies recorded the event and three radio networks carried the address live to the nation. Roosevelt was in fine form before an appreciative audience. He thumped the podium, a rare gesture for him, in defending the AAA and other New Deal programs and said that one of the greatest curses of American life was speculation, but not the speculation in stocks and bonds. "The kind of speculation I am talking about is the involuntary speculation of the farmer when he puts his crops into the ground. How can it be healthy for a country to have the price of crops vary 300 and 500 and 700 percent, all in less than a generation?"[6]

Before he left the stage, Roosevelt was awarded AFBF's highest honor, the Distinguished Service Medal. The award was a gold medallion. As he received the honor, Roosevelt said, "This makes me very, very happy. This has been a grand day in my life." The band played, the crowd sang, and Roosevelt waved goodbye.[7] Roosevelt was a Farm Bureau member in his home state, but also accepted an honorary membership in the McLean County, Illinois Farm Bureau, because it was the largest in the country.

With new-found success attracting members because of the New Deal, AFBF added regional organization directors or field staff starting in 1935. Vernon Vaniman, who first started on loan from the Illinois Farm Bureau, became director for the Midwest region. Thomas Buckman followed and became director for the West. Having a field staff took some of the pressure off top leadership. O'Neal typically visited twenty states, roughly half the member states, in a year. The vice president and board also filled in where needed. Not counting the president, AFBF had a staff of ten in 1935. In addition, there were probably five or six stenographers or secretaries who provided valuable assistance. The amount of work accomplished with a staff this size was truly amazing.

The task of building up the organization was an exciting one. New state and county Farm Bureaus were organized and existing ones were strengthened. Membership dues were raised in a number of states to keep pace with the amount of services being offered. Humboldt County, Nevada, blazed a trail for other county Farm Bureaus to follow. For a couple years in a row, 100 percent of the farmers and stockmen in Humboldt County joined the Farm Bureau. The fact that not a single recalcitrant farmer was found in the entire county was considered noteworthy.

Farm Bureau salesmanship or membership recruitment was taught at training schools around the country. Recruiters were reminded that the organization existed for the purpose of developing a program and not the other way around. Guideposts for recruiters were kept simple: (1) Membership is the lifeblood of the organization. (2) Leadership is developed by placing responsibility. (3) Farm Bureau membership must be sold. (4) When 10 or 20 percent of the people are kicking and finding fault with plans and policies, then conditions are normal. (5) Recruiters must have a definite membership goal.

Gradually, Farm Bureau built up confidence and membership numbers. Washington Farm Bureau went so far as to urge AFBF to help form a Farm Bureau in Alaska, which of course it did later. In 1937, AFBF membership was 409,766 and it passed the half-million mark for the first time in 1941, when there were 518,031 member families. Farm Bureau's recovery was well underway, but it would take a world war to restore the farm economy to health.

National preparedness was the dominant theme in 1941 as the United States armed and fed Britain, France, and Russia and shored up homeland defenses while hoping to stay out of the war. "We favor doing everything within our national power and honor to remain free from the present conflict abroad and can see no good purpose in entering the conflict now being pursued with other nations," said the policy resolution adopted at the December 1940 AFBF annual meeting in Baltimore.

The prewar years were not especially good for the economy. The country was in a recession, and farm prices were quite low. Large stocks of commodities were in Commodity Credit Corporation hands, and the export market for wheat, cotton, rice, tobacco, and lard shrank because of the rumblings of war. There were fears of another depression, but all that changed in 1941 as the United States edged closer to war. Thousands of workers were needed at defense plants. O'Neal noted that the wheel of fortune for agriculture made a complete spin for the first time since AFBF was born. Farmers received prices that were at or near parity.[8]

In January 1941, the AFBF executive committee met with President Roosevelt at the White House to assure him of ample food production to meet any emergency and to dismiss worries about the possibility of food scarcity. The crop surpluses accumulated by the government under Wallace's "ever-normal granary" had suddenly become an important wartime food reserve. Production controls were dropped over the next two years.

AFBF's major legislative success in 1941 was passage of a bill to raise the crop loan rate from 75 percent to 85 percent of parity for basic commodities. Dozens of Farm Bureau leaders made personal visits to Capitol Hill, sent telegrams, or contacted their members of Congress by phone over a five month period. Later the Steagall amendment gave the same price protection to nonbasic commodities vital to the war effort. They included milk, butterfat, chickens, hogs, eggs, and potatoes.

During the Depression, the chief concern was the disastrous deflation that struck agriculture the hardest and weakened the rest of the economy. But war brought another equally troublesome concern—inflation. "Inflation has always been the handmaiden of war, and World War II was no exception,"[9] said Paarlberg.

While AFBF and the administration agreed on how to end deflation during the Depression, they were not in agreement about inflation. AFBF wanted a ceiling on profits and wages and was willing to accept a reasonable price ceiling on commodities. The Roosevelt administration was chiefly worried about food prices and rents.

In April 1941, the Office of Price Administration (OPA) was established with Leon Henderson in charge. Initially, OPA had no price-fixing authority but relied on public opinion and indirect sanctions to get its way. At one point, Henderson tried to put a ceiling on combed yarn at 10¢ below the market price. He said the price had been driven up by speculation. The move incensed "Cotton Ed" Smith (D-South Carolina), the chairman of the Senate Agriculture Committee, who considered it an attack on cotton farmers. "Doggone the consumer," declared Smith at a hearing. "The farmers are so inflated now that they actually get enough to eat once a day." [10]

Farm Bureau accepted the inevitability of price controls on farm products but wanted to make sure that no ceiling was less than 110 percent of parity, a figure considered quite fair. State agricultural commissioners and some members of Congress advocated setting the ceilings at 120 percent. A number of other farm organizations and Agriculture Secretary Claude Wickard agreed with Farm Bureau. O'Neal also voiced the organization's interest in a ceiling on windfall profits and wages. "The farmer's prices represent his wage rates. The farmer cannot understand why his labor is not just as sacred as the labor of the man employed in the factory." [11] President Roosevelt, however, wanted to reserve authority over wages for himself.

On December 7, 1941, the day that Roosevelt said would "live in infamy," Farm Bureau members gathered in Chicago for what became known as the "war convention." They were shocked by news of the Japanese attack on Pearl Harbor. The convention's theme of "Patriotism and National Defense" turned out to be an appropriate one. Farmers were entering another challenging time in the nation's history.

The Associated Women were already meeting on Sunday afternoon and heard of the attack just as Mrs. William P. Hobby of the women's division of the War Department was getting ready to speak. She delivered her speech to a stunned and bewildered audience and closed by reminding farm women that "you are soft-hearted but never soft." Because of the sneak attack, Secretary Wickard and British ambassador Lord Halifax cancelled their appearances and remained in Washington. The secretary addressed the convention by radio and the chief of the British Food Mission took the ambassador's place in Chicago.

In his radio address, Wickard said that America had a great superiority in the number one material necessary for modern warfare—food. "This is the time to work together as if the United States were one big farm to produce just exactly what we need. We cannot afford to be careless in any way in our production efforts," he said. Farmers were urged to get all their farm machinery repaired and ready because metal parts would be scarce and subject to allocation. Women received special attention in the secretary's message. "Farm women will be called upon for additional sacrifices—in the form of harder work, longer hours, greater responsibility for helping to manage the farm business and farm contribution to our national production program."[12]

Delegates adopted a "mobilization for absolute victory" resolution that pledged farmers to keep up their end of the war effort. "We must devote renewed energies to the battle of production," said the resolution. "Any lagging by industry, by labor or agriculture will not be tolerated. We must recognize that modern warfare is waged by civilians as well as by men under arms."

The Emergency Price Control Act of 1942 with the 110 percent of parity price ceiling on agricultural products passed Congress and was signed by the president at the end of January. Later in the year, the president sought to lower the ceiling to 100 percent of parity and refused to make a definite commitment on wage control. AFBF, joined by the National Grange and National Council of Farmer Cooperatives, offered a counterproposal. They wanted the parity formula rewritten to include the cost of farm labor. Chairman Henry B. Steagall (D-Alabama) of the House Banking and Currency Committee introduced Farm Bureau's proposal. Not only was the cost of hired labor figured into the parity price, but the equivalent wages for the farmer and his family.

However, the president could not be deterred and intensified his effort to push back rising farm prices. In a September 1942 nationwide radio broadcast, he talked both about wages and food prices, and said, "If wages should be stabilized and farm prices be permitted to rise at any rate like the present rate, workers will have to bear the major part of the increase. This we cannot ask. The congress must realize that unless the existing control on farm prices is strengthened we must abandon our efforts to stabilize wages and salaries and the cost of living."[13]

The Big Three farm organizations then sent a letter to the Senate that drew a contrast between agriculture and labor. "Farmers are straining every effort to produce the greatest supply of food in the history of the country, working from seventy hours to as high as 100 hours per week, yet receiving the lowest pay of any group in the nation. At the same time factory workers on the average are working only forty-two hours a week with time and a half and double time for overtime, in addition to the highest wages in the history of the nation."[14]

The battle back and forth on wages and farm prices ended in October when Congress acceded to the president's wishes and lowered the ceiling on farm products to 100 percent of parity in the Stabilization Act of 1942. It was done in part because the president seemed to have the war powers to do it anyway. The bill also contained a loan rate revision that set the pattern for postwar price support legislation. The loan rate was set at 90 percent of parity and was extended for two years following a declaration of peace. This was to avoid any precipitous drop in farm prices after the war.

Roosevelt enlisted a new aide in controlling the wartime economy with the appointment of James F. Byrnes to head the Economic Stabilization Board. Byrnes had served as a Supreme Court justice for only a year and a half but gave up the lifetime appointment to help manage things on the home front. O'Neal joined the board as one of two representatives from agriculture. He received another appointment to the Management-Labor Policy Committee of the War Manpower Commission.

In 1943, President Roosevelt also issued a "hold-the-line" order that added to price controls and introduced consumer subsidies to keep a lid on the cost of living. Farm Bureau found consumer subsidies totally unnecessary. "Farmers simply cannot understand why, when wages are higher than they have ever been, labor leaders have any justification for demanding that part of the consumers' legitimate grocery bill be paid for by the government," said O'Neal in an address to the Alabama Farm Bureau.

One example was a $100 million subsidy fund maintained by the War Food Administration to pay dairy farmers an additional 25¢ to 50¢ per hundredweight on fluid milk to compensate for increased feed costs, while the retail price of milk was held unchanged. Farm Bureau feared that when the war was over and subsidies were withdrawn, the public would be unwilling to make up the difference in the price of food.[15]

It may seem as though Farm Bureau spent much of the war arguing with the administration and with labor about wages, prices, and price controls, while making its case in public and before a fairly receptive Congress. The disagreements should not take away from Farm Bureau's main story line during the war: farmers did a magnificent job, a miracle of production aided by favorable weather.

The mobilization of farmers that AFBF called for at its 1941 annual meeting occurred. They added sixteen million acres to production and boosted output by 30 percent over prewar levels. Farmers accomplished this despite shortages of farm machinery and labor. Around 1.5 million men left the farms to serve in the military. Another 365,000 or so were given draft deferments as agricultural workers under the Tydings Amendment of 1942. Farm Bureau had to intervene on their behalf late in the war as Selective Service tried to ignore the exemption.

President Roosevelt praised farmers' efforts in a nationwide radio address in November 1943. "While starvation has been the weapon used by the Axis resulting in disease, misery and death, the United Nations are using food as one of their most potent weapons to shorten the war and win a lasting peace," said Roosevelt.[16] Instead of making food sacrifices as had been done during the First World War, Americans actually ate more and better food than ever before. Farmers also fed eleven million men and women in the armed services, and some of them ate better than they had in civilian life.

"Rosie the Riveter" became a darling of the war on posters (and more recently on a postage stamp), but the farm woman was equally important to the defense effort. At a Farm Bureau conference in the Northeast, it was acknowledged that one of the chief problems facing farmers was losing the hired man to the war, but farm women stepped in. They went from being the "butter and egg woman" to the "handyman" on the farm. They drove tractors, milked cows, and did whatever else it took.[17]

In 1942, the United States and Mexico instituted the much-maligned Bracero program for Mexican workers to help with American crops. They were joined by workers from Jamaica and the Bahamas. High school students and city residents were enlisted for part-time farm work, and approximately 100,000 German and Italian prisoners of war worked on American farms and in rural communities. In Arizona, American soldiers were ordered out of the barracks to pick cotton and soldiers on furlough in New Jersey picked vegetable crops.

Food shortages were expected but they never occurred. Rationing was in effect for awhile for a number of consumer items, namely sugar, gasoline, meat, shoes, and tires. Families received ration coupon books and abided by a point system in making purchases. Workers had more money in their pockets because of high wages and overtime pay, but there was a shortage of durable goods for them to buy, so they spent more on nondurables like food. Meat and dairy consumption rose.

Farm Bureau adopted a policy during World War II that might seem out of character for the organization today. It lobbied for new taxes and higher personal income taxes to pay for the cost of the war. Between 1940 and 1945, federal expenditures rose from $8.5 billion to $70.6 billion. In the 1940s, Farm Bureau advocated a long-range policy by the federal government to gradually reduce the national debt, which today routinely stands at trillions of dollars.

By 1944, attention was turning to what the world would be like after the Nazis and Japan were defeated. "We must not repeat the mistakes made after World War I, when the nations of the world resorted to extreme nationalism and isolation to promote self-sufficiency and to secure selfish advantages through raising tariffs and trade barriers, through competitive manipulation of currencies and international exchange, through international cartels and other restrictive trade practices," warned an AFBF policy adopted at the 1944 annual meeting in Chicago. "In time of war prepare for peace" was Farm Bureau's admonition to farmers.

The postwar farm economy was to be cushioned by the 90 percent of parity price floor that was in place for two years after the war. At least there would be no sharp drop-off in farm income, but surplus buildup was an obvious concern unless foreign markets opened up. The old issue of equality for agriculture also had not completely gone away. The tremendous expansion in industrial plants and the power of labor unions were a concern to Farm Bureau leaders. "If business becomes concentrated into huge monopolies, and if labor unions attain even greater power with their monopolistic practices and theories of more pay for less work—what will that mean for the farmer? Farmers are fearful that they will be caught in a squeeze between," said O'Neal.[18]

At a time when industry, labor, and the federal government all expanded, there was a shift in manpower out of agriculture. More than seven million people left farms for the cities or to serve in the armed forces between 1940 and 1944. In a way, this made the American Farm Bureau Federation all the more important to farmers if they were to have a strong voice in national affairs. It also meant that the organization had to continue to build beyond its present strength and assume new and greater responsibilities. All these things were weighing on O'Neal and other Farm Bureau leaders as the war closed out.

The year 1944 also marked the twenty-fifth anniversary of the founding of AFBF in 1919. Membership had continued to climb during the war, reaching 687,499 in 1943. Another 140,987 families joined in 1944 bringing the total to an all-time high of 828,486. Delaware and South Carolina joined the federation as the forty-fifth and forty-sixth state Farm Bureaus.

Whatever doubts existed about the survival of the American Farm Bureau Federation a decade before were permanently erased. The first AFBF president, James R. Howard, was on hand for the 1944 convention and told the general session audience, "The Farm Bureau movement has certainly assumed a permanency, a place as one of the great American institutions."[19]

Farm Bureau recovered from the Depression and so had the farm economy, but the economic gains were due mostly to the war, not the New Deal. The governor of the Farm Credit Administration, Ivy W. Duggan, told Farm Bureau members, "In fact, since 1940, farmers have experienced a situation that does not usually come once in a lifetime. In addition to having a favorable growing season, record production, and almost unlimited markets, they have received good prices for what they produced." Farm assets grew from $54 billion in 1940 to $83 billion in 1944, largely due to an increase in farmland values. Farm income more than doubled in the same time frame.[20]

Farm Bureau was poised to take on the challenges of the postwar world, but it would be without the services of a promising agricultural economist. O'Neal had loaned John Kenneth Galbraith to the Office of Price Administration during the war where he became the chief deputy. He never got him back on staff. Galbraith's first book in 1952, *American Capitalism: The Concept of Countervailing Power,"* forecast an American economy managed by a triumvirate of labor, business, and an activist government.

Endnotes

1. Paarlberg, *American Farm Policy*, 18.

2. *AFBF Annual Report of 1934.*

3. "Unifying American Agriculture," *AFBF Annual Report of 1935.*

4. "Senator Bankhead Says Farmers Must Organize," *AFBF Official News Letter*, January 18, 1938.

5. "Greatest Meeting in History," *AFBF Official News Letter*, December 10 and 24, 1935 (as dated).

6. "Texts of President's Speeches Before Farmers and Notre Dame Students," *New York Times*, December 10, 1935.

7. "Roosevelt Elated," *AFBF Official News Letter*, December 10 and 24, 1935 (as dated).

8. *AFBF Annual Report of 1941.*

9. Paarlberg, *American Farm Policy,* 27.

10. "Senators Contest Price Authority," *New York Times,* May 30, 1941.

11. "Opposes Favoring Labor," *New York Times*, November 8, 1941.

12. *AFBF Official News Letter,* December 16, 1941.

13. "Rise in Farm Prices and Wages Saps the Nation's Economy," *New York Times,* September 8, 1942.

14. "Text of Letter of Farm Group Heads," *New York Times*, September 26, 1942.

15. "O'Neal Hits 'Consumer Subsidies,'" *New York Times,* November 3, 1943.

16. "Text of President's Message to Congress on Measures to Meet Our Food Needs," *New York Times*, November 2, 1943.

17. "Wife of Farmer Changed by War," *New York Times,* June 9, 1943.

18. "A Year of War," O'Neal address in *AFBF Annual Report of 1942.*

19. Official Transcript, AFBF Annual Meeting, December 12–14, 1944, Chicago, Illinois.

20. Ibid.

10 | Farm Bureau Insurance

THE STORY OF THE AMERICAN FARM BUREAU FEDERATION IS THE STORY OF ITS tremendous influence on agricultural policy and rural life. An equally impressive story is Farm Bureau's influence on the nation's insurance business. Farm Bureau insurance companies serve the needs of farm and other rural families with competitively priced financial products. The companies also reflect the values important to Farm Bureau families. Two of the largest insurers in the nation, State Farm and Nationwide, also trace their origins to Farm Bureau.

American Farm Bureau Federation's involvement with insurance began in the 1930s when it served as a clearinghouse of information for state Farm Bureaus wanting to organize mutual insurance companies. In 1945, a separate insurance department was formed for that purpose. In 1948, Farm Bureau fire and casualty companies along with AFBF formed a national reinsurance provider, the American Agricultural Insurance Company (AAIC). The company is headquartered in Schaumburg, Illinois, a suburb of Chicago.

Over the years, the success of Farm Bureau insurance companies helped fuel the growth of county and state Farm Bureaus, and consequently the American Farm Bureau Federation. Obtaining Farm Bureau insurance was another reason to join the Farm Bureau, and it cut down on the number of "free riders," people who liked what Farm Bureau stood for (and accomplished) but never got around to joining. Insurance products tailored to farm needs became a powerful incentive for a family to join Farm Bureau.

Once again, Farm Bureau benefited from a bit of good timing. The automobile gave farmers a new need for insurance. Few farmers carried car insurance at first, but an alarming rate of accidents changed that thinking. Fatal accidents numbered 15,000 in 1922 and jumped to over 32,000 in 1930. It got so bad that *Successful Farming* magazine suggested leaving the wrecks by the wayside as a warning to other drivers.[1]

Initially, farmers had few choices when shopping for auto insurance. The small farmer mutuals were organized mainly for fire protection, and big city insurance companies wanted to charge farmers the same high rates as city drivers. A man who saw an opportunity in this was George Mecherle, a successful farmer from Merna, Illinois. Mecherle was a member of the McLean County Farm Bureau and the founder of State Farm Insurance. He had retired early from farming to move to Florida for his wife's health. When the warm climate failed to improve her arthritis, the couple moved back to Illinois where Mecherle sold insurance and tractors.

In 1921, a company was formed by the Tazewell County Farm Bureau at Pekin, Illinois, to sell auto and property insurance to members at a cost-savings. There were nine directors, all of whom were Farm Bureau members, and two employees. Mecherle was thinking of forming an "honest insurance company" to serve farmers. He considered farmers to be a preferred risk and liked the business model of the Pekin Farmer's Insurance Company. However, he intended to sell his brand of auto insurance statewide.[2]

State Farm Mutual Auto Insurance Company was formed at Bloomington, Illinois, in 1922. State Farm had a loose sales arrangement with the Illinois Farm Bureau, but its big break came in November 1924, when the Indiana Farm Bureau signed a contract becoming the first state agent for State Farm. About 45,000 policies were sold through Indiana Farm Bureau by the end of 1930.[3]

Over time, Mecherle introduced a number of important features to automobile insurance. The first policies provided protection for loss or damage caused by fire, theft, or collision with a moving object. The policyholder was protected from liability stemming from injury to another person. Mecherle also established a deductible to avoid a lot of petty claims and to encourage safe driving. One idea that didn't last long was his restriction on collision claims. Mecherle understood how a farmer might hit another car at a country crossroads, but he was unsympathetic to the farmer who hit a tree or fencepost. He thought any driver who struck a stationary object shouldn't be behind the wheel in the first place.[4]

The relationship between State Farm and Farm Bureau was summarized by Mecherle biographer Karl Schriftgiesser. "At no time, of course, in any of the states did State Farm Mutual have anything to say about Farm Bureau policies or affairs—or vice versa. The association, from the beginning, did not extend beyond that of business contract between two parties for the single and simple purpose of mutual advantage."[5] State Farm Bureaus received a small fee or payment for each member policy and the policyholder was charged a better rate.

In 1925, Mecherle proposed a pact with the Ohio Farm Bureau similar to the one with Indiana. However, the state insurance director decided he would not grant State Farm a license as an out-of-state insurer. So instead Ohio Farm

Bureau formed its own company, Farm Bureau Mutual Automobile Insurance Company of Ohio. The insurer opened for business in 1926 with $10,000 in capital. Mecherle played a small part in the operation by supplying business forms and assisting in sales through his management company. By the end of 1926, there were 5,400 policies in force.[6]

The Farm Bureau Mutual Insurance Companies of Ohio took the name Nationwide Insurance in 1955. Today, Nationwide is the largest farm insurer and has a relationship with Farm Bureaus in a number of states. Its founder, Murray D. Lincoln, was a visionary and the man responsible for the success of Nationwide. He also served on the AFBF board of directors in place of the Ohio president, an anomaly no longer possible today.

Lincoln recalled what it was like to sell insurance in Ohio in the early years when Farm Bureau members were sent out to write policies for their neighbors. "If you were a Farm Bureau member you started out one rainy day when you couldn't work your fields and you stopped at those places where you knew the man was a good risk. If there was a neighbor you knew who was a fast driver, or a cantankerous type who yelled for money every time he collected another scratch, scrape or dent, you avoided him." Farm Bureau members didn't receive a dime in commissions but were glad to sign up policyholders because it was their company.[7]

A tall, imposing man, Lincoln was an advocate of cooperative endeavors to solve world problems. He was a founder of the Cooperative for American Relief Everywhere (CARE) in 1945 and served as the organization's first president and later its chairman. From 1941 until 1965, he was president of the Cooperative League of the U.S.A., now the National Cooperative Business Association. He was a vigorous proponent of expanding the farm-based cooperative movement to consumers, something that made him a controversial figure at the national level of Farm Bureau. The other leaders on the board felt no urgency to represent the nonfarm public and did not share Lincoln's vision of a gigantic cooperative involved in many different enterprises. They saw this as a distraction from Farm Bureau's mission.[8]

Lincoln blamed AFBF President O'Neal for the board's resistance to his ideas. He felt left out too because he was the only member who was not a president of his state Farm Bureau and a bona fide farmer. "The American Farm Bureau had listened to the dream music of legislation," said Lincoln in his autobiography. "All the farmer had to do was to let Uncle Sam fix everything for him. I wanted to see if the farmer couldn't do more to fix everything for himself by lessening his costs, bettering his markets, and saving money by purchasing and marketing cooperatively."[9] Lincoln overlooked AFBF's attempt at national cooperative marketing in the 1920s but was correct that farmers sought government farm relief as the economy worsened.

By 1935, State Farm was selling auto insurance in all but eleven states. The Farm Bureau Mutual Automobile Insurance Company of Ohio was operating in eight states. Independent Farm Bureau casualty companies also were entering the field. Illinois began in 1927, New Hampshire in 1928, and others followed. State Farm Bureaus formed their own insurance companies because they felt it was advantageous to control the board of directors and have a home office within the state.[10]

The Ohio insurance companies officially split from the Farm Bureau in 1948 under pressure from the Ohio insurance director. Lincoln regretted not putting up a fight. Instead, he resigned as executive secretary of the federation to head the insurance companies.[11] The split paved the way for the Ohio family of companies to expand beyond the thirteen states they were then doing business in, thus the choice of the name Nationwide. North Carolina Farm Bureau actually forced the name change so it could have exclusive use of the Farm Bureau name in the state. The North Carolina Farm Bureau Mutual Insurance Company began operation in 1954. The value and protection of the name "Farm Bureau" became increasingly important.

Critics have complained that the American Farm Bureau Federation is nothing but a big insurance company, a ridiculous charge, but the fact remains that it had a chance to be just that. Early on, Lincoln wanted AFBF's help in acquiring State Farm Insurance but was turned down.[12] Had AFBF followed Lincoln's advice, it might have veered off course as a farm organization. "Business . . . was the key to my feeling about the function of the Farm Bureau," Lincoln said. "The more businesses we got into, the happier I felt." Lincoln retired from Nationwide in 1964 after pursuing interests as diversified as broadcasting stations, housing developments, and Middle East oil refineries.[13]

The American Farm Bureau Federation wrote its own success story in the insurance business with the American Agricultural Insurance Company that celebrated its sixtieth anniversary in 2008. American Ag or AAIC was formed to provide stability to Farm Bureau insurance companies and help them grow. The combined assets of about twenty-five Farm Bureau property, casualty, and life insurance companies are over $50 billion. With the exception of the life insurance companies, most companies have a substantial portion of their reinsurance program with American Ag.

The AFBF affiliate began business with capital stock of $1 million in 1948. In the latest year, assets had grown to nearly $1.3 billion. AAIC is a stock insurance company. Ownership is held exclusively within Farm Bureau and primarily by the state Farm Bureau insurance companies. In other words, American Ag is owned by the companies it was formed to serve. The president and chairman of the board of American Ag is the president of the American Farm Bureau Federation (Bob Stallman, in 2008). The executive vice president is also the CEO (Virgil Applequist, in 2008). The board of directors is generally composed of state Farm Bureau presidents who are also presidents of Farm Bureau insurance companies.

American Ag has been a strong, steady reinsurer for the Farm Bureau companies but almost didn't make it past its twenty-fifth anniversary. The general manager at that time, William Pruett, got involved in questionable dealings with London reinsurance brokers, a situation that took several years and millions of dollars to straighten out. The American Farm Bureau Federation management team was caught by surprise when British creditors showed up right after Christmas 1973 with notes payable-on-demand in the amount of $20 million. American Ag had assumed a share of risk in the Cornhill Bank of London which got caught in the British financial crisis resulting from the Arab Oil Embargo.[14]

The reinsurance company had $48 million in assets and $19 million in surplus when faced with obligations of the failed bank. A few weeks later AFBF President Kuhfuss explained the "unfortunate experience" to Farm Bureau members at the 1974 annual meeting in Atlantic City. He said there had been a conspiracy to defraud the reinsurance company and legal action was underway in U.S. District Court.[15]

William H. Broderick came over from the federation side to become interim manager of the insurance company. Broderick and Allen Lauterbach, AFBF treasurer and general counsel, worked for two years to straighten out the mess and settle losses for $9 million. Farm Bureau insurance companies willingly subscribed to previously authorized but unissued shares, and the company was recapitalized and back on sound financial footing by 1976.[16]

The crisis underscored an important principle that still exists today. Almost every Farm Bureau insurance company at some point has had a time of need, due to insurance losses or some other circumstance. Sister companies were always willing to help in an appropriate manner with American Ag providing a leadership role.

In the early days, American Ag was primarily a pooling company for the state Farm Bureau insurance companies. Today, that is impractical because catastrophe exposures amount to between $2.5 and $3 billion. Therefore, much of the risk has to be placed with other reinsurers. American Ag, however, is able to consolidate reinsurance expertise in one place for the state Farm Bureau companies. A staff of ninety is deployed in underwriting, claims, actuarial, accounting, communications, and business development. The actuarial department has seen the most growth over the years because of the importance of computer modeling to forecast catastrophe losses.

The first billion-dollar event for the insurance industry was Hurricane Hugo that hit the Carolina coast in 1989. Hugo was four times greater than any previous storm loss. When Hurricane Andrew hit Florida and Louisiana in 1992 it was a $16 billion event for insurers. Hurricane Katrina was a $40 billion event on the Gulf Coast in 2005. American Ag has helped Farm Bureau companies and their policyholders recover from hurricanes, tornadoes, ice storms, and fires.

In 1995, American Ag and state Farm Bureau insurance companies formed American Farm Bureau Insurance Services, Inc. (AFBIS) to provide a central processing center for crop insurance, both multiperil (which is a federal program) and crop hail insurance. AFBIS offers state companies different levels of service ranging from data processing and training of agents to full service. In 2008, AFBIS processed over $500 million in premiums.

American Ag purchased Nationwide Mutual Insurance Company's reinsurance book of business in 1999. Applequist said the Nationwide reinsurance business was a good fit and had a Farm Bureau heritage. The Columbus, Ohio, operation with about twenty employees handles broker-assumed reinsurance from all over the world. American Ag serves only Farm Bureau insurance companies in the Schaumburg office.

Devastating losses from Hurricanes Katrina, Rita, and Wilma in 2005 shocked the reinsurance world and were felt by all. The Farm Bureau book of business fared better than the Columbus operation which had $140 million in losses. However, insurance rating service A.M. Best decided to change its criteria for rating companies, and American Ag needed an additional $100 million in capital to maintain an A-rating. Within two months, American Ag rounded up sufficient money from the state companies. Applequist said it reflected a partnership built on integrity and trust, a relationship important in light of the turmoil facing insurers and financial institutions in 2008.

In taking stock of the Farm Bureau insurance business today, roughly two-thirds of what the state companies write is auto insurance, about one-fourth is farm and homeowners insurance. If all the state Farm Bureau companies were put together they would be the tenth largest insurer in the United States, even though they don't write insurance in a number of the most populous states. According to A.M. Best, American Ag is on the list of the top thirty-five global reinsurers ranking twenty-ninth by premium for the year 2007. Obviously, it has a narrower market than most of the companies making the list. American Ag's combined ratio (loss ratio plus expense ratio) was 85.5 percent that year, an excellent result.

There is no question that American Agricultural Insurance Company and the state Farm Bureau insurance companies played a role in the success of the American Farm Bureau Federation. Farmer advocacy combined with member benefits and services have given the organization tremendous appeal in rural America.

Endnotes

1. "Auto Accidents," editorial, *Successful Farming,* vol. 21, no. 9, September 1922.

2. Schriftgeisser, *The Farmer from Merna,* 39–40.

3. Ibid., 89–90.

4. Ibid., 76.

5. Ibid., 116.

6. Franklin, *On Your Side,* 34.

7. Lincoln, *Vice President in Charge of Revolution,* 74.

8. Ibid., 102–103.

9. Ibid., 103–105.

10. Kile, *The Farm Bureau Through Three Decades,* 348.

11. Franklin, *On Your Side,* 69–72.

12. Ibid., 32.

13. Lincoln, *Vice President in Charge of Revolution,* 92.

14. Woell, *Farm Bureau Architects,* 128–129.

15. Transcript, AFBF Annual Meeting, January 14–17, 1974, Atlantic City, New Jersey.

16. Transcript, AFBF Annual Meeting, January 5–8, 1976, St. Louis, Missouri.

11 | No Deal

THE COMING OF THE NEW DEAL WAS AN IMPORTANT EVENT IN AMERICAN FARM Bureau Federation history. "The organization stands at the pinnacle of its power and influence," said W. R. Ogg, AFBF secretary and treasurer in his report to the board of directors in March 1934, an amazing turnaround in sentiment from two years earlier. But the euphoria wouldn't last. How could it?

The New Deal pumped up agriculture, but it pumped up organized labor even more. New Deal liberalism and centralization of power in the federal government proved to be too much for conservative Farm Bureau members. On top of that, accumulation of farm surpluses that plagued farmers before the New Deal continued until interrupted by the war and then resumed afterwards. Skepticism of the New Deal grew and extended to Harry Truman and the programs of his Fair Deal.

The *New York Times* described the three Rs of the New Deal as relief, recovery, and revolution.[1] Farm Bureau readily accepted relief and recovery but wasn't ready for the revolution advocated by the most liberal thinkers in the Roosevelt administration and first lady Eleanor Roosevelt. One of the trouble spots was the Farm Security Administration (FSA).

"What started out during the depression years as meritorious rural relief undertakings, or at least as interesting experiments, developed into one of the weirdest, more fantastic examples of government bureaucracy gone mad," wrote historian Kile.[2] The programs involved subsistence farming, relocation of farmers, and the organization of collective or cooperative farms by the federal government.

The idea of "subsistence homesteads" was first presented to Farm Bureau at the 1933 AFBF annual meeting in Chicago by M. L. Wilson, director of the Subsistence Homelands Division of the Department of Interior. Wilson was the Montana economist responsible for the domestic allotment plan. A small appropriation of $25 million was contained in the National Industrial Recovery Act to be administered by Wilson, but in 1935 the work was transferred to the Resettlement Administration headed by Rex Tugwell and later was absorbed into the FSA. One of the biggest supporters of government-subsidized communities was Eleanor Roosevelt.

Farm Bureau members listened politely to Wilson at the annual meeting as he outlined Roosevelt's plan for a new pattern of life known as "rural urban," which he described as a new class of citizenry living on small tracts of land in the country. Wilson assured the Farm Bureau audience of commercial farmers that new farmers attracted from the ranks of the urban unemployed would not compete with them. "In the first place, subsistence farmers will confine themselves principally to vegetable production. They will not produce the staples—wheat, corn, pork—and possibly in most cases will not produce dairy and meat products," he said.[3]

Farm Bureau believed in the Agrarian Creed tenet that anyone who wants to farm should be able to do so, but was not in favor of social experimentation in rural America. AFBF opposed the Resettlement Administration program to buy submarginal farmland on the Great Plains and relocate farmers at government expense or on government loans to collective farms, cooperative farms, or in some cases individual units. Farm Bureau believed in converting submarginal lands to soil-conserving uses but was not in favor of revamping rural America. Specifically, AFBF policy opposed: "experimentation in collective farming and other socialistic land policies, the purchase and long-time leasing of more and more land by the Federal Government, bureaucratic methods of administration and extreme regimentation of clients . . ."[4]

The most famous of all these projects was Arthurdale, West Virginia, where some of the buildings remain as a small, tourist attraction. Historian Arthur Schlesinger, Jr., referred to it as the "homestead *mystique*," a dream of "placid communities made up of small white houses with green shutters in which families stranded by urban or rural poverty would find shelter and peace, engaging in hand-weaving or woodworking or small manufacturing and growing their food in their own garden plots."[5]

Author John Steinbeck captured the Depression era interest in subsistence farming in his 1937 novel, *Of Mice and Men*. Two drifters, George and Lennie, dream of a little house and a couple of acres with a cow, some pigs, and rabbits. Lennie said they would go there someday "an' live off the fatta the lan.'"[6]

Mrs. Roosevelt saw Arthurdale as a chance for destitute people, in this case coal miners, to change their lives. She tried to bring light manufacturing to the community in addition to small-scale farming. There were twenty or more of these communities built or in the planning stages at one time, but nine years after it was started, Arthurdale was sold off at a small fraction of the more than $2 million invested in it. Roosevelt dismissed Arthurdale as a pet project of his wife. Congress, Farm Bureau, and even organized labor objected to subsidized community developments.

Farm Bureau played a major role in exposing the faults of New Deal resettlement programs and was sharply criticized for it. FSA personnel accused Farm Bureau leaders of being cruel, heartless, and interested only in commercial farmers, but Farm Bureau had good reason to be concerned. At least some in USDA had decided that the system of land ownership and owner-operated farms was to blame for agriculture's problems. "In large measure this failure grows out of the almost unlimited freedom of disposition of property that developed in this country," said the agency.[7] Central planners in the Roosevelt administration apparently felt that private property was an obstacle and not a virtue in the heartland of America.

The death of President Roosevelt was mourned by his friends in agriculture, especially Ed O'Neal. The AFBF president addressed the Farm Bureau family in a nationwide broadcast on April 14, 1945, only two days after the president's death. "Farm people in this country have reason to be grateful to a great man who championed their cause when their future seemed dark—at a time when chaos threatened the entire national economy." O'Neal took brief note of the differences between Farm Bureau and the administration in more recent years. "As in all human relationships, we differed at times as to methods for achieving the desired results, but he will be remembered by us all as a lover of the land and the man on the land."[8]

At first glance, the succession of Harry S. Truman to the presidency should have been a welcome event for the American Farm Bureau Federation. Not only was Truman a Farm Bureau member, as were many elected officials, but he had been actively involved in the Farm Bureau Movement.

In 1913, when he was 29 years old, Truman helped organize the Jackson County Missouri Farm Bureau. In 1914, he became president of the Washington Township Farm Bureau. Historian Richard Kirkendall said Truman's election to a Farm Bureau leadership position meant he was viewed as a good farmer because membership included the most progressive and successful farmers of the county.[9]

Farm Bureau wasted no time in offering its "hearty cooperation" to the president and former Farm Bureau leader. Obviously, Truman understood the importance of agriculture to the economy, the risks that farmers take to produce crops and livestock, and he held agrarian beliefs. "I spent the first ten years of my life on a farm," Truman fondly recalled. "A good agricultural background makes a safe republic, and when we cease to have a good agricultural background, we cease to have a republic."[10]

Truman's father was a livestock trader and Missouri farmer, but Harry spent much of his youth living in the town of Independence. After graduating high school in 1901, he took a job as a bank clerk. Five years later at age 22, he helped manage his grandmother's farm at Grandview.

If Farm Bureau expected smooth-sailing with one of its many early leaders at the helm in the White House, it was dead wrong. The Truman presidency is best remembered for the contentious fight with Secretary of Agriculture Charles Brannan during Truman's second term. It was one of the fiercest battles in Farm Bureau history and the stakes were high. The outcome determined whether the farmer's voice in his own affairs would be muted by the federal bureaucracy.

As World War II came to an end, Farm Bureau worried about a drop in demand for American farm products and a return of huge farm surpluses. Wartime demands had been met by farmers using more machinery, fertilizer, and a backlog of scientific knowledge that had gone untouched during depression years. Shutting down this revved-up farm production plant wasn't going to be easy without causing another farm depression. The defense plants had it easier; they shifted to producing automobiles, television sets, and other products for pent-up consumer demand.

Farmers continued to have a commodity price floor of 90 percent of parity through 1948, at which point price supports were to drop back to a range of 52 to 75 percent as mandated in the Agricultural Adjustment Act of 1938. At the December 1947 AFBF annual meeting in Chicago, delegates decided, "We do not believe an entirely new and revolutionary farm program should be written, but rather that we should confine our effort to refining and improving the present program." They also supported a revision of the parity formula to a ten-year moving average.

In January 1948, AFBF President Allan Kline asked the Senate and House Agriculture Committees to extend the current farm law for another year, but the Senate Agriculture Committee decided to work on a long-term program, and the AFBF board of directors had to know what to ask for. The board agreed on a flexible price support and an update of the parity formula. Senator George Aiken (R-Vermont) introduced a bill in the Eightieth Congress that was to Farm Bureau's liking. His bill replaced high, rigid price supports with flexible supports between 60 and 90 percent of parity based on supply and demand. The bill also had the Truman administration's support.

As Farm Bureau feared would happen once the war was over, there was a consumer backlash about food prices. "During recent months, some segments of city press have been attempting to convince public opinion that farmers are to blame for inflation," warned the *AFBF Official News Letter*. "Many city papers have used half-truths and innuendos to accomplish this objective. Their campaign now seems to be turning into an open attack against the whole farm program." AFBF reminded farmers that individually they were powerless against this kind of attack, but through Farm Bureau their response was widely heard.[11]

The House Agriculture Committee refused to go along with the Aiken bill and its flexible price supports. Instead, a bill introduced by Rep. Clarence Hope (R-Kansas) extended the 90 percent of parity loan rate on basic commodities until June 1950. Nonbasic commodities (the so-called Steagall commodities) were supported at no less than 60 percent of parity with the exception of dairy products at 90 percent. Hope's bill was intended as a stopgap measure, not a permanent farm program.

Thus, the Senate wanted to rewrite farm policy amid concerns about the cost of living and the cost drain of farm programs, while the House wanted to buy time and extend higher price supports. Republican Party leaders generally favored reducing government intervention in agriculture while Democratic leaders from the South and plains states wanted higher supports and were willing to accept tighter production controls.

With Congress ready to adjourn for the political conventions, a compromise deal was struck in a conference of the House and Senate. The Hope and Aiken bills were cobbled together in the Agricultural Adjustment Act of 1948. Price supports were frozen at 90 percent for another year, but then a 60 to 90 percent sliding scale went into effect. Senator Aiken credited Farm Bureau with influencing the outcome. "If it hadn't been for the support from the American Farm Bureau Federation we couldn't have put this price support program over," he said.[12] Truman signed the law but complained later about the "do-nothing" Eightieth Congress.

In his book, *An Opportunity Lost; The Truman Administration and the Farm Policy Debate,* Virgil Dean said the Hope-Aiken Act reflected the deep policy differences over postwar farm policy. He termed it unfortunate that permanent legislation was not passed earlier when some harmony still existed. "In 1948, though, it was the Republican Eightieth Congress that mishandled the farm policy ball and fumbled away a golden opportunity to write permanent agricultural legislation." After that, farm policy became "a political football."[13]

At about this same time, Secretary of Agriculture Clinton Anderson stepped aside to run for the Senate from New Mexico. Replacing him was Assistant Secretary Brannan, a lawyer and liberal New Dealer who had worked in the Farm Security Administration. If farm policy was becoming a political football then Brannan was like having Otto Graham, a football star of that era, on Truman's team. He knew how to play the game.

When Republicans attacked the president for keeping food prices high, Brannan turned the issue around. He accused the GOP of being anti-farmer and wanting to get rid of farm price supports altogether. It wasn't true, but some farmers believed it, especially after the Republicans stopped the CCC from adding new grain storage facilities when it was rechartered.

Truman survived an attempt by his own party to dump him as the presidential nominee and launched a vigorous election campaign in his famous "Give 'em hell, Harry" style. He wasn't given much of a chance of winning because the Democrats were splintered by the Dixiecrats and the Progressive Citizens of America party. Midwest farm states had returned to the Republican column during Roosevelt's presidency and were expected to stay there and vote for New York Governor Thomas E. Dewey.

If there was a turning point for Truman in winning the farm vote, it came in September at the Sixth National Plowing Contest in Dexter, Iowa. On a hot, sunny day, Truman stood before a throng of 60,000 to 80,000 farmers and accused his political opponents of having "stuck a pitchfork in the farmer's back." He said that Wall Street was raising enormous sums of money to elect a Republican administration that will listen to the "gluttons of privilege" first. But he expressed confidence that farmers had their eyes open and wouldn't be fooled. He promised a continuation of price supports and assured consumers that record farm production kept food prices down not up.[14] It was a masterful performance, and who were farmers to believe—Truman, who actually had been a farmer, or the urbane Dewey with his pencil-thin mustache that gave him the appearance of a comic strip villain?

AFBF remained neutral in the election campaign, encouraging members to work to get out the vote for "friends of agriculture." In one of the biggest presidential election upsets of history, Truman defeated Dewey with help from the farm states of Illinois, Iowa, Minnesota, Missouri, Ohio and Wisconsin. The Democrats also took over control of Congress.

A month after the election, AFBF met for its annual meeting in Atlantic City. Senator Aiken was the keynote speaker. Secretary Brannan was not invited but angrily demanded a spot on the program so delegates could hear both sides of the farm program debate. "Agriculture is at a crossroads," Aiken said, "and we can take one road with its cost-plus guarantees and easy money for perhaps two years more, with the certainty that controls, quotas, and penalties will then overtake us, or we can take the other road, which leads to a long period of agricultural prosperity for America at a somewhat lower level, with the assurance that the farmer will remain free to run his own farm without controls and penalties most of the time."[15]

Brannan spoke later, separated on the program from Sen. Aiken by awards and another speaker. Brannan labeled the 1948 Agricultural Adjustment Act a "political expedient" and called for a new farm program that would not make farmers the scapegoat of any future depression. "If there is to be any downward adjustment of the national economy we are not going to start with farmers," he added.

Earlier, Kline defended the 1948 Act. "It is based on the proposition that this great price system in America is a sound system, that the incentive system is a good system, that by and large it is not in the interests of the public to have prices administered by the public, by the government . . . " Kline also repeated a statement he had made earlier to the press. "It will certainly not be in the interests of the farmers of this country, or consistent with ideals of sound government, for us to invite a vast extension of regimentation and controls at a time of high prosperity and full-employment."[16]

According to *New York Times* reporter William M. Blair, "The American Farm Bureau Federation's annual meeting rocked today with rising disagreement among regional interests over high, rigid support prices for commodities."[17] Kline offered to resign and said he would make "a poor president" if the delegates decided for high mandatory price supports, a policy position that he in good conscience could not support.[18]

In the end, AFBF delegates failed to make up their minds. The policy they adopted stated, "We commend Congress for its recognition of the need for a long-range farm program in the enactment of the Agricultural Adjustment Act of 1948. We believe that the major provisions of this Act, which provide a modernized parity formula and variable price supports are sound and in the best interests of American agriculture."

The delegates expressed preference for a market-based farm economy. "We feel that compensatory income or price payments are not a desirable way of supporting farm prices or bringing income into agriculture." But they weren't willing to let loose of higher price supports. "We recommend that the Board of Directors give serious consideration to recommending that the price support for any basic commodity be at 90 percent of parity whenever marketing quotas are in effect on any such commodity."[19]

In early 1949, Secretary Brannan secretly worked on a scheme for a new farm program. He did not involve lawmakers or farm organizations which guaranteed a controversy, but the plan was radical and going to be disputed anyway. The dramatic introduction of the Brannan plan took place before a joint session of House and Senate Agriculture Committees in April 1949.

"Secretary Brannan proposed to let the price of food fall where it would be on a free market, while guaranteeing farmers a whopping cash income, no matter how cheaply their crops sold in the marketplace," reported *Time* magazine. Brannan used an example of eggs in explaining his plan. If the farm price for eggs was set at 45.8¢ a dozen but the market for eggs was only 35¢, the government would pay the farmer 10.8¢ for every dozen sold. The farmer would still get his price and the consumer would have cheap eggs. How much this would cost the government, Brannan wasn't prepared to say. "The powerful American Farm Bureau Federation thought it sounded pretty revolutionary," continued *Time,* while the National Farmers Union thought it was really wonderful and a "milestone" in farm policy.[20]

Brannan's proposal was to give ten basic farm commodities high government price supports through commodity loans or direct payments. In return, farmers would be subject to drastic controls on production and marketing. The loans were for storable commodities but covered only the first $25,000 of production. Perishable commodities were eligible for direct payments. In his election campaign the previous year, Truman had promised both high farm prices and a painless cost of living. Brannan concocted a plan to do both, or so it seemed.

AFBF President Kline termed the idea "dangerous" and said the "American farmer is not philosophically nor psychologically ready to go on a dole."[21] Kline emerged as the leading critic of the Brannan plan, but not the harshest. The governor of Nebraska called it "idiotic," and John Foster Dulles, Republican candidate for the Senate from New York, sarcastically described it as "the greatest miracle since the loaves and fishes."[22]

Writing in the *New York Times*, Arthur Krock said the plan was in conflict with the free enterprise system. "One of the most elaborate devices for a regulated national economy that has been sponsored by the Executive Department of a non-autocratic Government in the present age has now been presented to Congress by the Truman Administration." Krock picked up on the incalculable cost of the program. "No one could possibly estimate within hundreds of millions of what these payments to farmers would amount to at any time until the system has been established over a period."[23]

The *Chicago Tribune* accused Brannan of wanting to run the nation's farms by fiat from Washington. "Mr. Brannan and his socialist planners are arguing with epithets. They talk about industrialized farming as if it were an evil thing. Every good farm in the corn belt is an industrialized farm. If it weren't we'd be paying $2.50 a pound for steak and double the present price for bread." The newspaper said Brannan would limit every farm to around 250 acres in order to be eligible for price supports.[24]

In his memoirs, Truman said Brannan had warned him about the possible criticism, but Truman told him to go ahead anyway. The president dismissed Farm Bureau's objections as coming from "special interest farmers."[25] Truman conferred with Brannan several times a week and frequently had lunch with him.

In the summer of 1949, the Brannan plan was going nowhere in Congress and even a trial run involving just three commodities was soundly defeated. This didn't deter Brannan who figured that it might not pass Congress the first time through. Brannan staked a lot on the eventual outcome, however. He envisioned a farmer-labor coalition that would keep the Democrats in power for years. He also wanted to challenge AFBF's leadership on farm issues in Congress. "For me, it'll mean either a palace or a backhouse," Brannan was quoted in *Time*.[26]

Among Brannan's many critics was his predecessor, Senator Anderson, who was angered by the secretary's boldness in attempting to formulate farm policy without involving farm organizations and Congress. Anderson introduced a bill to raise the low end of flexible price supports from 60 to 75 percent. On the House side, Rep. Albert Gore (D-Tennessee) offered an extension at 90 percent for another year. A conference committee combined the bills into the Agricultural Adjustment Act of 1949. After a one-year freeze, price supports would be on a sliding scale.

At the 1949 AFBF annual meeting in December, there was solid delegate support for President Kline and the stand against the Brannan plan. Once again, the secretary wasn't invited to the convention, but he pleaded in a letter to Kline to let someone from USDA explain the Brannan plan to the delegates. Kline shot back, "The implication in your letter . . . that a group of free American citizens cannot objectively discuss both sides of questions of policies unless the discussion is guided by some federal appointee can hardly be made seriously." Kline assured him that Farm Bureau members were particularly well-informed.

As Kline got up to speak at the general session in Chicago's Stevens Hotel, the crowd of 3,500 farmers started a roaring cheer: "Two bits, four bits, six bits, a dollar! Everybody for the Farm Bureau stand up and holler!"[27] This time Farm Bureau policy was much clearer. "While farm programs should be directed toward the maintenance of parity, it is not the responsibility of the government to guarantee profitable prices to any economic group. Instead, we view farm price supports as an appropriate and necessary protection against unreasonable price declines." The delegates chided the Truman administration for the Brannan plan after both political parties had gone on record in favor of flexible price supports. AFBF policy listed seven main objections to the plan including the staggering cost and regimentation of agriculture.[28]

Senator Anderson was on the convention program with the topic "Who Shall Speak for Farmers?" Farm Bureau decided it would not be Charles Brannan, who came to Chicago anyway during the meeting. He may have expected a last minute summons to appear, but went Christmas shopping instead. Anderson told the Farm Bureau, "I want to see farm legislation developed by farmers through their own farm organizations in cooperation with members of Congress . . ."[29]

Brannan's political maneuvering certainly did not hurt Farm Bureau membership. AFBF reported a membership gain of 84,000 families to 1,409,795. Kline lost one fight at the convention, however. He wanted to move the organization's headquarters to Washington to be at the center of policymaking. He couldn't get his midwestern friends to listen to him and the general headquarters stayed in Chicago.[30]

Agriculture's performance during World War II had been something to celebrate, but mounting surpluses and the arguments over farm programs ended the celebration. The greatest embarrassment was in potatoes. "The potato program has given the whole farm program the blackest eye it ever had in the fourteen years we have had a farm program," said Sen. Majority Leader Scott Lucas (D–Illinois).[31]

In February 1950, the CCC was faced with taking over nearly seventy million bushels of potatoes. About two-thirds would go to school lunch programs and public institutions, but that still left twenty-five million bushels in government hands. The choices were to offer them free to alcohol plants, bring them to concentration points and burn them, or color them blue and turn the potatoes back over to farmers for use as fertilizer or livestock feed. The potatoes supported at $1.80 per hundredweight were resold to farmers for a penny per hundredweight. The only good thing about the potato surplus was that it spurred market development, especially for potato chips.[32]

In 1950, the government was storing seventy-three million pounds of dried eggs, equivalent of 219 million dozen fresh eggs, eighty-nine million pounds of butter, 198 million pounds of dry milk, and twenty-three million pounds of cheese. Farm surpluses became the subject of many jokes. *Business Week* reported, "We wound up sending so much honey and dry milk to West Germany that Washington began to describe the occupied territory as the land of milk and honey." As bad as these surpluses were, the feeling was that the Brannan plan might make matters worse. Representative Gore told a North Carolina Farm Bureau audience that the Brannan plan would make farm surpluses more mountainous, and in the case of potatoes, three or four times more costly.[33]

If there was one thing that could be counted on to change the farm outlook it was war. North Korean communist forces crossed the 38th parallel and attacked South Korea in late June 1950. After the North Koreans defied orders by the U.N. Security Council to end the aggression, the United States entered the conflict. Farm surpluses were viewed as a strategic stockpile once more. The Brannan plan that once seemed like a hot issue for the congressional elections was displaced by Korea and Communism. Republican candidates scored better than expected on these foreign policy and security issues, and Brannan's dream of a farmer-labor voter coalition never materialized.

One reason given for the defeat of the Brannan plan was its name. Brannan never wanted to name it after himself. That label was attached by AFBF's Roger Fleming and stuck even with members of Congress and the administration.[34] In the end, Charles Brannan never got the palace he was hoping for, and he probably had Farm Bureau to blame.

Endnotes

1. "Mr. Roosevelt's Recovery," *New York Times,* December 11, 1935.

2. Kile, *The Farm Bureau Through Three Decades*, 164.

3. Transcript of AFBF Annual Meeting, December 11–13, 1933, Chicago, Illinois.

4. AFBF Policy Resolutions, adopted December 10, 1942.

5. Schlesinger, *The Coming of the New Deal*, 364.

6. Steinbeck, John. *Of Mice and Men*. New York: Penguin Books (1993), 14.

7. USDA, Yearbook of Agriculture 1940, 404.

8. *AFBF Official News Letter*, April 17, 1945.

9. *AFBF Official News Letter*, May 1, 1945; "Harry S. Truman, A Missouri Farmer in the Golden Age," *Agricultural History*, vol. XLVIII, no. 4, October, 1974, 477. Kirkendall said Truman was active in Farm Bureau but did not help organize his county Farm Bureau. The AFBF newsletter attributed its claim that he was an organizer to the county agent at that time. Both newsletter and Kirkendall agreed Truman was a township officer; AFBF said he was president.

10. *AFBF Official News Letter*, May 1, 1945.

11. "This Is Your Fight," *AFBF Official News Letter*, September 29, 1948.

12. "Permanent Supports Passed," *AFBF Official News Letter*, June 23, 1948.

13. Dean, *An Opportunity Lost*, 77.

14. "Calls GOP 'Cunning,'" *New York Times*, September 19, 1948.

15. Transcript of AFBF Annual Meeting, December 14–16, 1948, Atlantic City, New Jersey.

16. Ibid.

17. "South's Farmers Urge Price Props," *New York Times*, December 14, 1948.

18. Woell, *Farm Bureau Architects*, 11.

19. AFBF Policy Resolutions, adopted December 16, 1948.

20. "Farm Pharmacy," *Time*, April 18, 1949.

21. "Brannan's Plan for Agriculture Assailed," *New York Times*, May 11, 1949.

22. Ibid.; "Something New," *Time*, November 7, 1949.

23. "Truman Farm Program Has Wide Implications," *New York Times*, April 10, 1949.

24. "A Blow at America's Breadbasket," *Chicago Tribune*, April 18, 1949.

25. Truman, *Memoirs by Harry S. Truman*, 267.

26. Hansen, *Gaining Access*, 120; "Take Your Choice," *Time*, June 27, 1949.

27. "Rustle in the Grass Roots," *Time*, December 26, 1949.

28. AFBF Policy Resolutions, adopted December 16, 1948.

29. "Let Farmers Speak, Anderson Insists," *New York Times*, December 15, 1949.

30. "New Rebuff Is Set for Brannan Plan," *New York Times*, December 10, 1949.

31. "Truman Scores Congress," *New York Times*, February 3, 1950.

32. "Brannan Orders Dumping 25 Million Bu. Of Potatoes," *New York Times*, February 4, 1950; "Plans to Spur Potato Chip Sales," *New York Times*, January 28, 1948.

33. "1950's Never Normal Granary," *Business Week*, March 4, 1950.

34. Woell, *Farm Bureau Architects*, 13; Dean, *An Opportunity Lost*, 226.

12 | Farm Politics and the Soil Bank

In the 1950s, AFBF proposed the soil bank that was the forerunner of today's Conservation Reserve Program (CRP). A land retirement plan was not terribly controversial, but it came up during a period of intense and sometimes bitter politicking for the farm vote. As AFBF President Kline noted, "There is no business in the whole country that has been so completely thrown into the arena of politics as farming."[1]

Truman's narrow victory in 1948 made both major political parties apprehensive of winning the farm vote. The balance of political power seemed to hinge on the farm states of Illinois, Indiana, Iowa, Kansas, Michigan, Minnesota, Nebraska, North and South Dakota, Ohio and Wisconsin. They had a history of falling into the Republican column until Roosevelt captured them. Truman won four of the farm states after barnstorming the country.[2]

The American Farm Bureau Federation scrupulously avoided telling members how to vote, but individual leaders were of course free to publicly back candidates of their choice. Illinois Farm Bureau leader Lester R. Stone was chairman of his state's agriculture committee for Dwight Eisenhower. Ike had a farm at Gettysburg, Pennsylvania, and liked to occasionally rub shoulders with Stone and other farmers.

Secretary Brannan, still smarting over defeat of his farm plan at the hands of Farm Bureau, accused Kline of promising to deliver the farm vote to Sen. Robert Taft (R-Ohio) in the 1952 GOP presidential primary. "He promised to deliver all the farmers to Taft, but I don't think farmers can be herded around like that," said Brannan at a news conference. He also alleged that Kline was Dewey's choice for secretary of agriculture.

"It is hard to believe that a responsible person such as the secretary of agriculture would make such statements," Kline responded. "They are not worthy of denial. They are simply complete falsehoods." The AFBF president denied any conversations about a Cabinet post with either Dewey or Taft, and said he would not accept such an offer.[3]

Delegates to the 1951 AFBF annual meeting in Chicago reaffirmed support for flexible price supports. The next summer at the Democratic National Convention in Chicago, Kline told a platform subcommittee what was wrong with guaranteeing farmers a high price. "Rigid high level supports promising seemingly profitable prices to farmers inevitably lead to an accumulation of surpluses and government controls which restrict the ability of farmers to earn a good income through high production."[4]

Not all Farm Bureau members agreed with national policy, and the organization made no pretenses. When Sen. Warren Magnuson (D-Washington) entered into the Congressional Record resolutions from several state Farm Bureaus that conflicted with national policy, Secretary-Treasurer Roger Fleming issued a rebuttal. Fleming said the purpose of the American Farm Bureau Federation was to speak for American agriculture, but the organization did not contend that each and every one of its members, who voluntarily paid dues to belong, supported every "single specific recommendation." Policies developed through a democratic process reflected the consensus of farmer thinking.[5]

The consensus in Farm Bureau was not to abandon farm programs but use them primarily as a safety net. "Farm price supports have become an accepted part of national life," said the *AFBF Official News Letter.* "Only a relatively small minority would argue against the desirability of government programs designed to provide farmers with justifiable protection against disastrous price declines."[6]

Governor Adlai Stevenson (D-Illinois) ran against Eisenhower for president in 1952, and Democrats used the same political strategy that worked on farmers in 1948. In a speech to Farmers Union, Truman warned about "reactionaries" who want to slash farm price supports and other measures to aid farmers.[7] Not much was known about Eisenhower's views on farm policy early in the race, but in a speech at Columbia, South Carolina, he said, "I believe wholeheartedly and without any 'ifs' or 'buts' in Federal programs to stabilize farm prices, including the present program insuring 90 percent of parity on all basic commodities."[8]

Ike's election did nothing to heal divisions over farm policy. As he did with other government policy areas, Eisenhower sought a "middle way." He accepted the high price supports until they ran out and then tried to turn agriculture on a free-market course.[9] He found capable allies in the American Farm Bureau Federation and his secretary of agriculture, Ezra Taft Benson.

Secretary Benson was even more controversial than his predecessor, but for entirely different reasons. He was as conservative as Brannan was liberal. Economist Don Paarlberg, who served on Benson's staff, described him as "an able economist, (who) saw that the prevailing policy of attractive price supports and ineffective production controls was a natural surplus breeder."[10] Benson was executive secretary of the National Council of Farm Cooperatives before becoming secretary of agriculture. Born on an Idaho farm and schooled in agriculture, Benson was an apostle in The Church of Jesus Christ of the Latter-day Saints, and took leave from the church's Council of Twelve to serve in government.

Benson served the entire two terms of the Eisenhower administration, remarkable for the fact that Democrats and even a coalition of Republican lawmakers called for his ouster. But he did not have to beg an invitation to AFBF annual meetings, where he was warmly received and given the Distinguished Service Award at the end of his years of service. Kline referred to him as "a very great American" in introducing him at the general session of the 1954 annual meeting in New York City. "Farming has a future in this country—a bright future," said Benson. "As I see it, American agriculture will come to full flower only under a system which respects the basic freedoms of the individual . . ."[11]

The Eisenhower administration's first success with its agricultural program was the Agricultural Act of 1954. Signed by the president in August, it reestablished the principle of flexible price supports. Eisenhower had gone on national television to appeal directly to farmers for support before the vote in Congress. He was the first president to be able to use the medium of TV. When he entered office, a little more than a third of the nation had TV sets, up from only 1 percent in 1948.

In 1954, $6 billion worth of farm products was sitting in government storage. School lunch programs and charitable organizations were the recipients of butter, milk, cheese, and other products. A plan suggested by Farm Bureau to remove surpluses from the market and donate them to needy countries was passed as P.L. 480. Of course, novel ways to empty the storage bins were proposed. A Washington, D.C., area research scientist experimented with pressing wheat into wall board to build houses and furniture. Stanley Reed said the wheat could be "puffed up" in the same way as breakfast cereal and made as strong as wood.[12]

Farm Bureau had another answer for the surplus problem: banking some of the land currently in production. "The agricultural plant in the United States is too big for effective demand at the moment. That is a statement of fact," said Kline.[13] Critics jumped on Kline's comment to suggest that he meant there were too many farmers and they needed to be weeded out. What Farm Bureau envisioned was a step away from specific crop controls to soil conservation on a section of a farmer's land. "By stockpiling fertility in the soil, we will build a 'soil fertility bank' as a reserve for use in national emergencies," said the resolution adopted at the New York convention.[14] Newspapers picked up on the idea and liked it.

At the end of the New York convention, Illinois farmer Charles B. Shuman was elected to replace Kline who retired for health reasons. Shuman and Kline were like-minded when it came to federal farm programs. At a Florida Farm Bureau meeting in Tallahassee, Shuman said, "More than a quarter century of experience with government controls in agriculture is behind us and that experience clearly indicates that government controls are not the whole answer to the surplus problem. In fact, there is plenty of evidence that controls have merely extended, instead of solving the problem."[15]

In the fall of 1955, Shuman asked state and county Farm Bureaus to study proposals to establish the Soil Bank. He also called a meeting in Chicago of 150 state Farm Bureau leaders, mostly presidents and organization directors. If Shuman thought the fall meeting of Farm Bureau leaders would head off any serious squabbles at the annual meeting, he was wrong. At the December meeting in Chicago, Charles Percy, president of Bell and Howell Company and future Illinois senator, quipped that he had witnessed fourteen murders on the same stage that year. Percy attended operas at the Civic Opera House where the Farm Bureau general session was held. There were no murders and no opera but plenty of drama at the convention.[16]

Angered by the resolutions committee's refusal to reconsider price supports at 90 percent of parity, H. L. "Tiny" Wingate, president of the Georgia Farm Bureau, threatened to pull his organization out of the federation. Other cotton-producing states also were upset because the cotton price support was scheduled to drop from 90 to 75 percent of parity, a level below their cost of production. At the end of the policy debate, the 163 members of the House of Delegates reaffirmed their belief in "the principle of variable price supports" but left some wiggle room for 90 percent of parity under certain circumstances.[17]

Farm Bureau's surplus reduction and Soil Bank plan called for farmers who participated in an acreage reserve to be compensated in certificates or cash. The certificates would be redeemable in commodities that farmers could use or sell on the open market. Farm Bureau urged Congress to make this its first order of business. The Soil Bank idea already appealed to Eisenhower who discussed it with Benson while the president was hospitalized in the fall, recovering from a heart attack. Eisenhower even considered a government buy-back of some of the land given farmers under the Homestead Act.

In his State of the Union message in January 1956, the president outlined his plan for a Soil Bank that would cost a half-billion dollars but would be less expensive than the current support program and the $1 million a day cost of buying and storing commodities. "This will include an acreage reserve to reduce current and accumulated surpluses of crops in most serious difficulty, and a conservation reserve to achieve other needed adjustments in the use of agricultural resources," said the president. The plan was very similar to Farm Bureau's.[18]

Farm Bureau's alliance with the Eisenhower administration strained its relationship with members of the House and Senate Agriculture Committees. House Agriculture Committee Chairman Harold Cooley (D–North Carolina) angered Farm Bureau by bringing Congress of Industrial Organizations (CIO) President Walter Reuther before his committee in support of rigid farm price supports. It was bad enough that Cooley sought out a labor leader for farm advice, but Cooley had the audacity to say that Reuther delivered one of the best farm testimonies he had ever heard. Fleming called the comment a "low blow."[19]

When Benson appeared before Cooley's committee in February 1956 to testify about the Soil Bank, it was another memorable event. The room was packed with Farmers Union members on a visit to Washington. Policemen stood by to keep order. Cooley chided Benson for taking partisan credit for the Soil Bank. Cropland retirement occurred under President Roosevelt and Democrats considered it their idea.

"Its sources probably go back to Joseph in Egypt," said Benson, conceding the point that Republicans hadn't thought of it first. Representative W. R. "Bob" Poage (D–Texas) said he didn't think Joseph was either a Democrat or Republican. This brought loud applause from the gallery. Benson smiled and offered an opinion that Joseph might have been a Republican. "Probably so," agreed Poage with a grin, "because there was some report of his taking golden vessels from the brethren."[20]

From a Korean War peak in 1951, farm prices had declined 28 percent by the end of 1955. Democrats and farm-state Republicans felt pressure to prop up prices in 1956. Therefore, the Senate Agriculture Committee sent a bill to the full Senate with the contradiction of the Soil Bank and high, rigid price supports. Chairman Allan Ellender (D–Louisiana) called the bill a bipartisan effort and said he could not support Benson's aims and still look farmers straight in the face.

Farm Bureau opposed the bill. "Those who favor a return to the rigid 90 percent price support program become unwitting advocates of socialism in agriculture," charged Shuman, "as the piling up of surpluses under a price fixing plan destroys normal markets and forces government controls and subsidies."[21] Farm Bureau assembled 10,000 members at Peoria, Illinois, for a rally where it accused Congress of crafting a vote-buying scheme with the farm bill and subverting the intention of the Soil Bank to reduce surpluses.[22]

When the farm bill reached Eisenhower's desk in April, he vetoed it with Farm Bureau's encouragement. Again, Eisenhower went on television to explain his veto to farmers and the rest of the public. A month later, Congress sent him a compromise measure shorn of the high price supports but with the Soil Bank provision. The Agricultural Act of 1956 authorized a three-year acreage reserve and a long-term conservation reserve designed to shift cropland more or less permanently to trees and other soil conserving uses.

In 1956, nearly 500,000 farmers participated in the first sign-up for the Soil Bank. Many more followed in the second year when twenty-one million acres were banked in the acreage reserve. The long-term conservation reservation reached a maximum level of 28.6 million acres in 1960 and was ended in 1972 when the last of its land was withdrawn.

The Soil Bank removed one-eighth of American farmland from production but failed to live up to expectations. Wheat is a good example. In 1957, 233,453 wheat farmers agreed to remove nearly thirteen million acres from production in return for $231 million in government payments. This should have cut production of wheat by around 20 percent from a year earlier. Instead, the crop was only about 4 percent smaller, and the yield was record-breaking. "One thing the soil bank once more proved was that barring police-state controls, farmers will always outsmart bureaucrats. This year for example, most farmers gave the soil bank their poorest acres," wrote *Time* magazine.[23]

It wasn't just that farmers outsmarted bureaucrats, they outsmarted everybody. On larger, more expertly managed farms, farm productivity had soared. In 1910–1914, the production of 100 bushels of corn required 135 man-hours of work. By 1950–1953, it took just thirty-four. Total farm output in 1955 was 48 percent above the pre-World War II years. The American farmer, who produced enough to feed ten other people in 1935–1939, managed to feed nineteen in 1955.[24]

At many farm gatherings, Benson's name was both cheered and booed. He was a catalyst for the formation of the National Farmers Organization or NFO. Started in southwest Iowa in the fall of 1955, the NFO was signing up members at $1 a head with the chief aim of sending a delegation of farmers to Washington to demand higher price supports. But at its meetings, the chief topic was starting a letter-writing campaign against Benson to force his resignation. The NFO was somewhat reminiscent of the Farmers' Holiday Association.[25]

Benson felt that Congress never gave the administration everything it needed to solve the farm problem, and he was not entirely sold on the Soil Bank. But Eisenhower wanted the Soil Bank as a transition from surpluses and government controls to a market-based economy that would strengthen the family farm. "Farm policy was the only area in which Eisenhower called for repudiation of the basic New Deal economic structure," wrote biographer Stephen E. Ambrose.[26] Eisenhower wasn't able to straighten out farm programs, but he had a lasting impact on rural America as the president responsible for the nation's interstate highway network.

Benson also is remembered by Farm Bureau for issuing Memorandum No. 1368 in November 1954 that separated Farm Bureaus from their sponsoring arrangement with the Extension Service. Complaints about Farm Bureau's relationship with Extension, USDA, and the land grant colleges had grown louder because of the Benson-Farm Bureau alliance on farm legislation.

The secretary's order prohibited Agriculture Department employees from advocating that any particular general or specialized farm organization was better adapted for carrying out the work of the department. Federal employees, including the county agents, could not accept salaries, office space, or other contributions from farm organizations, and they were expressly forbidden to assist in membership campaigns.

The greatest impact was on the Illinois and Iowa Farm Bureaus that provided significant financial support to Extension. Prior to Benson's announcement, the New York Farm Bureau went ahead and severed its ties. By this time, AFBF had joined the pro-separation forces because Extension ties remained in just a few states and separation would remove potential sources of embarrassment and conflict.[27]

The major push that Farm Bureau received from Extension was prior to the founding of AFBF, especially during the war. The growth of the organization after that was a result of its legislative successes and member services. Whatever Farm Bureau gained from Extension it more than gave back by providing a supportive group of farmers for the work of the county agent. After Benson's order, Farm Bureau continued to be the strongest supporter of adequate funding for the mission of the Extension Service.

Endnotes

1. Transcript, AFBF Annual Meeting, December 14–16, 1954, New York, New York.
2. Paarlberg, *American Farm Policy,* 112.
3. "Kline Sets the Record Straight," *AFBF Official News Letter,* March 17, 1952.
4. "Farm Blocs Split on High Price Pegs," *New York Times,* July 17, 1952.
5. "AFBF Policy Development Explained," *AFBF Official News Letter*, February 4, 1952.
6. "Price Supports Protect Farmers from Depression," *AFBF Official News Letter,* Aug. 25, 1952.
7. "Farmers of the Middle West Are Sitting On The Fence," *New York Times,* March 16, 1952.
8. Paarlberg, *American Farm Policy,* 111–113.
9. Wagner, *Eisenhower Republicanism*, 83.
10. Paarlberg, *American Farm Policy,* 159.
11. Transcript, AFBF Annual Meeting, December 14–16, 1954, New York, New York.
12. "He'd Puff U.S. Wheat Stocks into Houses," *Chicago Tribune*, March 4, 1954.
13. Ibid.
14. *1955 Policies of the American Farm Bureau Federation.*
15. *AFBF Official News Letter*, May 30, 1955.

16. Transcript, AFBF Annual Meeting, December 13–15, 1955, Chicago, Illinois.

17. "Farm Bureau Offered Plan for Soil Bank," *Chicago Tribune,* December 15, 1955.

18. Ambrose, *Eisenhower the President,* 277; "President Calls Farm Needs Too Vital," *Chicago Tribune,* January 6, 1956.

19. Woell, *Farm Bureau Architects,* 54.

20. "Benson Unshaken at Noisy Hearing," *New York Times,* February 22, 1956.

21. "Toward Socialized Farms," quoted in an editorial, *Chicago Tribune,* February 16, 1956.

22. "Ten Thousand Farmers Know What They Want," *Chicago Tribune,* February 22, 1956.

23. "A $700 Million Failure," *Time,* June 3, 1957.

24. "Revolution, Not Revolt," *Time,* May 7, 1956.

25. "New Farm Drive Spreads in West," *New York Times,* October 9, 1955.

26. Wagner, *Eisenhower Republicanism*, 63; Ambrose, *Eisenhower The President*, 293, 620.

27. "Orders County Agents to Quit Farm Bureau," *Chicago Tribune*, November 25, 1954; "Benson Aides Get A Code of Ethics," *The New York Times,* November 25, 1954; "Farm Agency Leaders Favor Ban on U.S. Aids," *Chicago Tribune*, November 26, 1954.

13 | Who Shall Speak for Farmers?

"Farmers have made an important decision to organize and join hands with their neighbors in a struggle for equality of opportunity for agriculture and the maintenance of freedom." This was the opening sentence in the 1952 AFBF policy resolutions book under the heading of "Who Shall Speak for Farmers?" The question became a new rallying cry for Farm Bureau in the 1950s and 1960s. [1]

When the American Farm Bureau Federation was formed, it was the answer to that same important question, "Who shall speak for farmers?" Business, labor, politicians, bureaucrats, and even clergy tried to speak for farmers, but Farm Bureau always made one thing abundantly clear: farmers should speak for farmers through their own general farm organization, namely Farm Bureau.

Of course, not everyone was happy with Farm Bureau's commanding position in agriculture and some attempted to dislodge it. Occasionally, battles erupted that grew bitter at times. Some of the charges made against Farm Bureau continue to circulate to this day whenever some group or individual decides to take on the organization. Farm Bureau's response to any attacks harkened back to something President Howard said at the very first convention. He said that Farm Bureau should be an organization that shoots straight from the shoulder.

The central thesis that the American Farm Bureau Federation is the Voice of Agriculture was a pretty big assertion. The legitimacy of Farm Bureau's claim was staked on being representative of agriculture throughout the United States. Farm Bureau had to overcome both "commodityism" and regionalism in order to deliver on that pledge. Also important to the claim—Farm Bureau was built from the grassroots up, not the top down, and its policy decisions were formulated in the same manner.

The Farm Bureau Movement caught other farm organizations and Congress off-guard at the start. It emerged suddenly after the war although the groundwork was laid over ten years of earlier development. Congress was startled by AFBF's bold moves. The Grange had a legislative program but focused on rituals and emphasized moral and spiritual values. Farmers Union tended to be more militant and aggressive in the manner of the old populist organizations and frequently aligned itself with the labor movement. "The Grange was lethargic and the Farmers Union suspicious," wrote Grant McConnell, who thought Farm Bureau took advantage of both groups' deficiencies.[2]

It took only a short while for jealousies to emerge after AFBF got started. Farmers Union publications attacked Farm Bureau and Extension for alleged alliances with the enemies of farmers. The Grange protested to every secretary of agriculture, beginning in 1921, instances of alleged discrimination in favor of Farm Bureau members.[3] Farm Bureau carried the mantle of the Voice of Agriculture, but it did not rest easily on its shoulders.

Many of the early complaints were about Farm Bureau's connection with Extension. AFBF tried to set the record straight by signing an agreement with Extension that made clear the duties of the farm adviser and kept them separate from membership activities. A delegate to the 1921 AFBF annual convention in Atlanta expressed the prevailing attitude. "We are backing up our county agents," he said, "but the Farm Bureau professes to do the work the county agent cannot do, should not do and we don't ask him to do."[4]

Nonetheless, Farm Bureau's connection to Extension continued as a trouble spot invariably seized upon by rival organizations. Usually the charges involved an overzealous county agent, as in the case of R. L. Griffin of Perry County, Alabama. In 1939, he mailed Extension-franked letters to farmers telling them that $1,532,780 in AAA benefit payments had been disbursed in the county since 1933. "The American Farm Bureau Federation is the largest farm organization in the world and only through this organization have you been able to receive these payments."[5]

While competing farm groups and politicians were the usual critics, urban liberals joined in attacking the Farm Bureau-Extension alliance once they found out that Farm Bureau was largely responsible for killing one of their pet social welfare agencies, the Farm Security Administration. Secretaries of agriculture and Extension officials issued memos to clarify the Farm Bureau relationship and finally a panel was appointed from USDA and the land grant colleges in 1948 to study the situation. Secretary Benson put the matter to rest with his separation order in 1954. Farm Bureaus could continue to give financial support to the work of the county agent, but the money had to go first to the university.

One of those who tried to discredit Farm Bureau and its connection to Extension was freelance writer Dale Kramer, author of a booklet, "The Truth About the Farm Bureau." According to Kramer, "Many farmers did not even know that the agent was paid out of government funds. They thought he was part of the Farm

Bureau service. In time some token expenses were paid in some cases from Farm Bureau dues—which probably the agent had collected in the first place. But smart tricks were used to confuse the Extension Service with the Farm Bureau in the minds of farmers and townspeople."[6]

There probably was some confusion, but it wasn't due to trickery. The relationship between Farm Bureau and Extension wasn't the same in every state. The Smith-Lever Act gave the states considerable latitude in administering the act. According to a 1930 survey, Farm Bureau was the chief cooperating organization in twenty-nine states, and in nineteen states the public wasn't always able to differentiate between Extension and Farm Bureau work.[7]

Kramer's anti–Farm Bureau material also appeared under the name of Sam B. Hall. The first copy was written in the 1930s and updated in 1964. Kramer's career as a freelance magazine writer was hailed in the 1964 booklet, but for someone purporting to reveal the truth about Farm Bureau, Kramer left out the truth about himself. He had been editor of *The Iowa Union Farmer* and *The Farm Holiday News*, the official organ of the Farmers' Holiday Association. After the death of Milo Reno in May 1936, Kramer became national secretary for the farm strike movement.[8] His booklet is still quoted by Farm Bureau critics today, as though written by an investigative journalist of that period, which of course he was not.

Farm Bureau's best defense against broad attacks and bogus charges was to strengthen the organization, particularly grassroots policy development, so there could be no question that Farm Bureau policies represented a consensus within agriculture. In the mid-1940s, the American Farm Bureau Federation also made some important additions to the staff which up until then was incredibly small for the breadth and scope of its work. It added W. E. "Gene" Hamilton, Allen Lauterbach, and Roger Fleming among others. Hamilton went on to become chief economist, Lauterbach, general counsel, and Fleming secretary-treasurer. All three played significant roles in the management and operation of the organization for more than three decades.

The first person to raise the question, "Who shall speak for farmers?" may have been Senator Anderson in his address to the 1949 AFBF annual meeting. Anderson warned Farm Bureau that others were trying to assume the role. "Probably most active in their efforts to speak for farmers are their elected Congressmen and U.S. Senators," he said. "Although the duly-elected farm organization leaders said one thing, many of the politicians insisted that these leaders didn't speak for farmers but, instead, the politicians themselves were the real reflectors of farm thinking."[9]

Bureaucrats thought they knew what farmers wanted or could find out without help from Farm Bureau. In 1951, Secretary Brannan organized a "Family Farm

Policy Review" and ordered county Production and Marketing Administration (PMA) committees to sample farmer opinions and get a "true reaction" on farm policy. Fleming, who was always good at turning a phrase, called it a "pay-roller's plebiscite."[10] Farmers received a voluminous report of USDA activities and recommendations along with a questionnaire for their responses. In Illinois, only 5,000 farmers out of nearly 200,000 responded to the poll and one-third of them were government employees.[11]

In 1952, *Successful Farming* magazine examined the whole issue of "Who shall speak for farmers?" and concluded, "You'd better stand up and be counted before you lose your God-given American privilege—freedom to speak for yourself." The writer of the article, Karl D. Butler, warned, "There are many who can speak *from the ranks* of agriculture, but to speak for the farmer is something else." He added farm business leaders and professional economists to the list of those who were trying to speak for farmers.[12]

"Practically everybody is willing to express an opinion on how the 19 percent of Americans on farms should be treated, how their economy should be adjusted, how they should conduct their business, and how government should treat agriculture," said AFBF in a brochure distributed to members in 1950.[13] Amazingly, not much has changed in this respect.

The whole issue of farmers speaking for farmers was enormously important to Farm Bureau. It was essential that Congress accept the policy positions of the American Farm Bureau Federation as an accurate expression of farmer opinion on national issues. Policy development continues to be emphasized today for the same reason.

"Farm Bureau's member-controlled grassroots policy development process is a point of pride, a true example of democracy in action. There is the give-and-take of spirited debate, followed by voter approval and acceptance of majority rule," said President Bob Stallman in an introduction to the organization's 2008 policy book.[14]

Stallman's description of the policy development process is essentially the same as a description by President Shuman forty years earlier. "The policies were developed through a program featuring individual member participation and including study, discussion and development of policy recommendations at local and state meetings. The resolutions . . . are the result of the considered judgment and mature consideration of these farmers," said Shuman.[15]

The first chain of events in the formation of Farm Bureau policy is as simple as two farmers talking about a common problem over the fence. In Shuman's time, the discussion might have continued with additional neighbors at a township Farm Bureau meeting. The township Farm Bureau was a subdivision of a county Farm Bureau. These neighborhood units generally have disappeared today.

American Farm Bureau Federation policies on national and international issues are developed from farmer opinions expressed through resolutions democratically developed at the county, state, and AFBF levels. The House of Delegates at the AFBF annual meeting resembles the U.S. House of Representatives because of its proportional membership. The size of a state Farm Bureau delegation to the house is determined by the total number of its members. At the 2008 AFBF annual meeting in New Orleans, there were 368 delegates representing all fifty states and Puerto Rico.

Every now and then, members of Congress questioned whether Farm Bureau policies were shaped by members or a few top leaders. Gene Hamilton remembered being at a Senate Agriculture Committee hearing in the late 1940s with AFBF Vice President Romeo Short. Senator Milton Young (R–North Dakota) who had survived a narrow reelection asked Short if the policies he was presenting to the committee were unanimously adopted at the AFBF annual meeting. "Mr. Short took off his glasses, looked straight at the Senator and said, 'I'm sure you would like to have the unanimous approval of your constituents at election time; but it is not always possible to get unanimity on questions of public policy.'" Short said the policies he came to talk about were the views of a substantial majority of Farm Bureau members. The senator smiled and the hearing continued.[16]

Orville Freeman, secretary of agriculture in the Kennedy administration, thought he found a way to bypass Farm Bureau as the chief spokesman for farmers. Freeman told an annual conference of the Extension Service that he wanted its 14,000 specialists to enter farm politics and help shape government farm policy. He recognized that this was an uncomfortable role for some "because it deals with matters that cannot be proved or diagnosed by chemical analysis or controlled experiments."[17] The use of ASCS (Agricultural Stabilization and Conservation Service) committeemen in the development of farm policy was part of the Cochrane-Freeman farm plan defeated by AFBF.

In attempts to chip away at the influence of the American Farm Bureau Federation, organized labor was often a willing accomplice. Union membership was only three million members in 1933, but by the end of the decade, union ranks swelled by another five million. Farm Bureau gave a dour assessment of the situation in a statement issued from a Midwest Farm Bureau Conference in 1944 in Milwaukee. "The people of this generation have witnessed a swing from the monopolistic practices of big business and sweatshops of industry, to an equally if not more serious abuse of power by certain leaders of labor."[18]

The American Farm Bureau Federation supported the right of working men and women to organize and bargain collectively, but often singled out labor leaders and union actions for sharp criticism. "Today, some labor leaders and their unions exercise tremendous power in total disregard of the rights and welfare of the general public," said AFBF President O'Neal before the House Labor Committee in 1947. Needless to say, union leaders bristled at public reprimands from Farm Bureau. In 1951, an American Federation of Labor (AFL) executive issued an attack on farm organizations saying that "farm bloc" representatives in Congress and state legislatures consistently voted against union measures.[19]

Labor unions made small, token attempts at unionizing farmers and harassing Farm Bureau. United Farmers of Illinois, an affiliate of United Mine Workers Union led by John L. Lewis, filed a lawsuit in 1944 to block public funds going to Extension because it claimed the county agents were part of the Illinois Farm Bureau. The lawsuit went nowhere. Organized labor generally found solace in supporting Farmers Union, the farm organization with policies closest to its own.

"Labor has a farm problem," reported the *New York Times* in 1956. "While factory earnings are setting new records, farm income is steadily falling. The farmer blames labor in part for his deteriorating economic status." There was certainly truth to that. Farm Bureau blamed featherbedding, jurisdictional conflicts, and boycotts for raising farmers' marketing costs. The *Times* writer, Joseph A. Loftus, said farmers were striking back by supporting state right-to-work laws and other anti-union measures.

There were occasional attempts to bridge the gaps between the American Farm Bureau Federation and organized labor, like when Labor Secretary Willard Wirtz attended the 1962 AFBF annual meeting in Atlanta. But Wirtz told President Shuman in front of the general session, "I was disturbed about your suggestion here on Monday that the position of organized labor is in your opinion antagonistic to the interests of American agriculture . . . with respect to basic issues of national concern." Wirtz did not have much success with the audience after that. He blamed agriculture for high unemployment because attrition of farm employment placed a burden on cities to provide jobs.[20]

Farm Bureau protected its status as the Voice of Agriculture and protected farmers from attempts by labor and other groups to muzzle them. AFBF leaders knew that efforts to silence Farm Bureau and challenge it were to be expected because the organization was big and influential, but even they were surprised by the bizarre attack launched by Rep. Joseph Y. Resnick (D-New York), chairman of the House Agriculture Committee's Rural Development Subcommittee.

His hearing took place in August 1967 and was described in the *New York Times* as "an unusual one-man inquiry into the nation's largest farm organization." Resnick's solo performance was not by choice; the other members of his subcommittee and the full House Agriculture Committee refused to have anything to do with it.[21]

Congressman Resnick was a New York industrialist who made millions of dollars with his brothers from the invention of the first preassembled television antenna. A pro-labor, liberal Democratic, Resnick entered the primary race for the Senate in 1968. His attack on Farm Bureau was probably an effort to enhance his reputation for the upcoming race. "Joe Resnick was not afraid to take on the establishment," said a fellow congressman. In Congress, however, he was seen as a rubber stamp for President Johnson.[22]

Resnick's vendetta against Farm Bureau was based on the same threadbare argument persisting over the years—that Farm Bureau was nothing more than a big insurance company masquerading as a farmer organization. If so, Resnick thought the organization should lose its tax-exempt status with the Internal Revenue Service (IRS). He also criticized Farm Bureau for allowing nonfarmers to become members.

Shuman said the inquiry was "100 percent political" and was linked to AFBF's criticism of farm programs and waste in the federal poverty program. But he said the organization welcomed a review and had nothing to hide. In fact, AFBF was routinely audited by the IRS and had gotten a clean bill of health only a couple years before. Shuman also readily confirmed that rural residents other than farmers frequently found membership worthwhile and joined their county Farm Bureau.[23]

Resnick took over a Federal courtroom for his hearing in Chicago where AFBF was headquartered. Hearings also were held in Omaha and Washington. The congressman used personal funds to run his investigation because the House Agriculture Committee by a vote of 27 to 1 disassociated itself "from charges" against the Farm Bureau or "any other general farm organization which carries on service programs for its membership."

The committee, chaired by Rep. Poage who often was at odds with Farm Bureau on farm programs, said it would not "endorse, condone or support the personal attack" by Resnick on Farm Bureau. A fellow New York congressman also defended Farm Bureau. Representative Samuel Stratton (D–New York) said of its members, "They are devoted to their profession and they take very conscientious interest not only in farm legislation but all kinds of legislation affecting our country."[24]

Despite the repudiation of fellow members of Congress, Resnick persisted in efforts to cut down Farm Bureau. His witness list included leaders of rival farm organizations, particularly Farmers Union. Shuman's name was dragged through the mud, which didn't bother him. He had a thick skin, and what one critic mockingly called a "Sunday school smile."

Shuman was denounced as "the king of all gentlemen farmers" by Resnick, when in fact he was a very modest, unpretentious man. Representative William Springer (R-Illinois) took offense at the characterization on the House floor. "Charles Shuman is a farmer," said Springer. "I would like to say for the record that I know of no person whose own personal integrity is thought more highly of in my entire congressional district than Charles Shuman." Farm Bureau boycotted the ad hoc hearings, but offered to appear before any responsibly conducted congressional hearing and gave information about its business affiliates to the press.[25]

Chicago Tribune's Richard Orr, respected for his thoroughness as a farm writer, reported that within the state Farm Bureaus there were twelve life insurance companies, twenty-seven casualty companies, thirty-one fire and allied companies, and twenty-one crop hail insurance companies. State Farm Bureaus also had an assortment of affiliated companies that were mainly cooperatives. Orr reported that AFBF had eight business enterprises including a reinsurance company and a service company operating through affiliates in thirty-three states.[26] If this information was a revelation to Resnick, it was because insurance services rarely had anything to do with the farmer advocacy work of the federation.

The Nation magazine praised Resnick for his "full-scale assault against the AFBF" which it described as the fifth-largest lobby in Washington and a patron of radical right-wing activities. The condemned activities included Farm Bureau citizenship programs for high school students and a program by Tennessee Farm Bureau women to put "Christ back into the U.S. Constitution."

The Nation also faulted AFBF for inviting conservative speakers to a number of annual meetings and other events and tried to link AFBF with the John Birch Society, a staunchly conservative, anti-communist group prominent in the 1960s. AFBF had no connection to the Birch Society. Individual Farm Bureau members were free to join other organizations, but the decision was up to them.[27]

Resnick never realized his goal of becoming a senator from New York. Whether his silly "exposé" of Farm Bureau had anything to do with that is hard to say. He lost the Democratic primary after his two opponents accused him of trying to buy the election with his family's wealth. The congressman passed away a short time later at the age of 45 while on a business trip. His campaign against Farm Bureau was later taken up by one of his political aides, Samuel R. Berger.

Sandy Berger updated anti-Farm Bureau material from the Resnick hearings in *Dollar Harvest,* a book he published in 1978. One of the items he rehashed was the expulsion of the Webster County Nebraska Farm Bureau in 1964. Webster County is located on the Kansas border in the south-central part of the state. In May 1963, Nebraska Farm Bureau President Charley Marshall received letters from two other county Farm Bureaus demanding that Webster County be disciplined for creating discord in the organization. The dispute centered on supply-management farm programs that Farm Bureau policy opposed. Policy dissents, while not encouraged outside the resolutions process, were tolerated. The leaders of this county Farm Bureau were openly critical of Farm Bureau principles, policies, and programs, and had been for some time. After a formal hearing, the state

Farm Bureau board of directors removed Webster County from the state federation and revoked the memberships of its key officers.[28]

The Webster County Farm Bureau dispute was an internal matter and a minor embarrassment. Berger suffered a much bigger public embarrassment himself in 2005 when he pleaded guilty to removing classified material from the National Archives. He was fined $50,000 and disbarred from the practice of law by the District of Columbia Court of Appeals in 2007. Berger's career peaked when he was National Security Advisor to President Bill Clinton. The documents he admitted taking involved the Clinton administration's response to terrorist activity before the September 11, 2001 attacks.[29]

Roger Fleming said there were several tests that could be applied for making sure that Farm Bureau did indeed speak for farmers. The first, of course, was that farmer members actually developed the policies. Not every farmer would take the time to participate but involvement was encouraged and the opportunity provided. The second test was that members participated in free elections to choose their leaders. The third test was that the organization was voluntary. Each year farm families must decide whether to become members or not. The fourth test was the long-term trend in membership. By all these standards, Farm Bureau was best qualified to speak for farmers.

Endnotes

1. *Resolutions of the American Farm Bureau Federation for 1952.*

2. McConnell, *The Decline of Agrarian Democracy*, 68–69.

3. Block, *Separation of Farm Bureau and the Extension Service*, 24.

4. Transcript, AFBF Annual Meeting, November 21–23, 1921, Atlanta, Georgia.

5. "Federation Fuss," *Newsweek*, June 12, 1939.

6. Kramer, "The Truth About Farm Bureau."

7. Baker, *The County Agent*, 128–129.

8. Robert A. McCown, "B. H. Shearer, Country Editor," *Books at Iowa 22*, University of Iowa, April 1975.

9. Transcript, AFBF Annual Meeting 1949.

10. Transcript, AFBF Annual Meeting, December 13–17, 1955, Chicago, Illinois.

11. "Claims U.S. Uses Tax Money to Rule Farmers," *Chicago Tribune,* November 16, 1951; "Brannan Quiz Is Ignored By Most Farmers," *Chicago Tribune,* October 24, 1951; Transcript, AFBF Annual Meeting, December 12–15, 1949, Chicago, Illinois.

12. "Who Shall Speak for Farmers," *Successful Farming*, November 1952.

13. "Who Shall Speak for Farmers?" AFBF brochure, August 1950.

14. *Farm Bureau Policies for 2008.*

15. *Farm Bureau Policies for 1966.*

16. "Working for Farm Bureau," unpublished memoirs of W. E. Hamilton, AFBF chief economist.

17. "Farm Units Shift to Politics Urged," *New York Times*, January 21, 1962.

18. "Midwest Farm Bureau Resolution," *AFBF Official News Letter*, June 27, 1944.

19. "Farmers Hostility Handicaps Labor," *New York Times*, January 9, 1956.

20. Transcript, AFBF Annual Meeting, December 10–13, 1962, Atlanta, Georgia.

21. "Inquiry Started on Farm Bureau," *New York Times*, August 5, 1967.

22. "A Fighting Politician," *New York Times*, November 15, 1967; "1,000 Attend Rites for Ex-Rep. Resnick," *New York Times*, October 9, 1969.

23. *Farm Bureau News*, July 17, 1967; "Raps Plan for IRS Farm Bureau Probe," July 11, 1967.

24. Congressional Quarterly, *Congress and the Nation*, vol. II, 576–577; *Farm Bureau News*, July 17, 1967.

25. "Springer, Findley, Arends Defend Shuman," July 17, 1967, *Farm Bureau News*; "Stratton Defends Farm Bureau," *Farm Bureau News*, July 3, 1967; "Harvest of a Scandal," *The Nation*, November 13, 1967, 205, 496–500.

26. "Farm Unit Grows Into a Giant," *Chicago Tribune*, August 7, 1967.

27. "Harvest of a Scandal," *The Nation*, November 13, 1967, 205, 496–500.

28. Woell, *Farm Bureau Architects*, 84, 94; Berger, *Dollar Harvest*, 133–136.

29. "Berger Is Disbarred After Archives Case," *The Washington Post*, June 8, 2007.

14 | Forward on International Trade

THE FIRST AFBF PRESIDENT, JAMES R. HOWARD, WONDERED WHAT IT WOULD BE LIKE if a ship could steam up to his back hog lots, and he and his Iowa neighbors could sell their surplus corn on world markets. There was an "unmovable mountain of corn" in 1922, and Howard contemplated how it could be made into mush to feed starving children in Russia.[1] Thoughts like this led Farm Bureau to become an early advocate of building the St. Lawrence Seaway, but Howard never would have been able to fathom the enormity of world trade today or its importance to American farmers.

Beginning in the last half of the twentieth century, nothing had been more important to the U.S. farm economy than exports and the expansion of foreign markets through fair and open trade. Granted, biofuels are important today as well, but without a thriving export market, U.S. farm production would have shrunk to fill domestic demand. The American farmer and rancher are the world's most reliable producers and have made a huge contribution to global food security and improved diets around the world.

The American Farm Bureau Federation adopted a worldview quite early in its history. The organization was barely four-years old in November 1923, when it sent a small delegation to Europe to study postwar conditions in agriculture. Dr. W. H. Walker, AFBF vice president from California, led a group that included Gray Silver, legislative director; Murray Lincoln, secretary of the Ohio Farm Bureau; and two others. The Farm Bureau leaders landed in Paris and traveled throughout Europe to investigate farming methods and markets.[2]

But U.S. trade policy of the 1920s and 1930s bore little resemblance to the more enlightened trade policy of today. Manufacturers insisted on high tariffs for the nation's young industries to protect them from cheaper European imports. Farmers generally preferred to see lower tariffs on manufactured products because they thought high duties raised the prices of things they had to buy. Failing in that, however, they wanted tariff treatment equal to that of industry. A popular view was that tariffs were necessary to maintain a high standard of living compared to foreign laborers and farmers.[3]

Tariff protection became the number two legislative priority for the American Farm Bureau Federation, second only to farm relief. The frontier of agriculture shifted after the war from America to Argentina, Australia, and Africa. On a few occasions, Argentina shipped corn to the United States even though it was in surplus here. The dairy industry was hurt by the importation of animal and vegetable fats and oils, and Cuban sugar posed a problem for domestic sugar producers. At the same time, overseas demand for American farm products was going down. The U.S. went from being a debtor to a creditor nation after the war and that decreased the buying power of European countries.

In 1929, with the U.S. entering a depression, AFBF lobbyists appeared eighteen times before the House Ways and Means Committee and the Senate Finance Committee armed with hundreds of pages of documents and statistical information to make the case for increasing duties on more than a hundred farm commodities. They got no argument from President Hoover, who said, "The first and most complete necessity is that the American farmer have the American market. That can be assured to him solely through the protective tariff."[4]

The Smoot–Hawley Act of 1930 raised tariffs by 30 to 60 percent on thousands of imported items, including farm goods. In response, protectionism rose to new levels around the world and choked off trade. U.S. farm exports dropped 66 percent between 1929 and 1932. The tariff spike did not cause the Great Depression, but it certainly made it worse. The Roosevelt administration changed course on trade policy. Secretary of State Cordell Hull became the champion of lower tariffs and expanded trade. He viewed trade as the path to economic recovery and a way to world peace. Historian Kile believed that Hull influenced his friend and fellow southerner, O'Neal, and other Farm Bureau leaders on the subject.[5]

Secretary of Agriculture Wallace expressed a similar view when he wrote a pamphlet in 1934 entitled "America Must Choose." Wallace said the choice was between sharply reducing the production of America's main crops, like wheat and cotton, or being competitive on the world market. That same year, Congress passed the Reciprocal Trade Agreements Act and gave the president authority to cut tariffs by as much as 50 percent and enter into trade agreements with other countries for up to three years. Senate ratification wasn't required. Fourteen agreements were signed by the end of 1935 and twice as many by 1945. Farm Bureau threw its support behind the reciprocal trade agreements.[6] The agreements were the forerunner of fast-track trade negotiating authority and established the "most favored nation" trade principle.

As World War II was nearing an end, AFBF delegates to the 1944 annual meeting in Chicago said, "Another war within twenty-five years cannot be tolerated." Farm Bureau members were weary of war and wanted peace and abundance for America. Abundance in food production was a foregone conclusion, and delegates to the convention struggled with how to deal with expected surpluses. In the end, they said farm output must become "a national blessing rather than a calamity," and the only way for that to happen was to find overseas markets.

AFBF Vice President Allan Kline attended the San Francisco peace conference, the founding conference of the United Nations (UN) in 1945 as a consultant on agricultural policy. Farm Bureau supported the newly created world organizations—the International Monetary Fund (IMF), the World Bank, the General Agreement on Tariffs and Trade (GATT), and the UN. The GATT created rules by which countries trade with one another. Farm Bureau's hopes for the United Nations faded, while the GATT became more important to agriculture as time went by.

In May 1946, world farm leaders met in London to finalize plans for an international farm organization. AFBF was represented by Kline; John Lacey, information director; and Tom Cowden, chief economist. Kline was enthusiastic about the possibilities. "We can do much in modifying old barriers to international trade and understanding," he said.[7] The United States delegation included the Grange, Farmers Union, and National Council of Farmer Cooperatives. Thirty-one nations sent observers to the meeting. Membership was limited to nongovernmental farm organizations.

The newly formed International Federation of Agricultural Producers (IFAP) held its first annual meeting the next year in The Netherlands. Farmer organizations from seventeen nations were charter members. This time Kline was less optimistic when he gave the AFBF board an appraisal. "After one has attended several of these conferences he can begin to see how negotiations break down and wars are started." At least it was a useful exchange of ideas with farmers of the world, he said.[8]

The American Farm Bureau Federation supported the Marshall Plan for the recovery of Europe after the war. "It will cost a lot of money [$13 billion], but the total cost will be small with the economic, social and moral cataclysm that would be the result of another war," said O'Neal at his final convention as president in 1947. Isolationists ridiculed the foreign aid plan, but farmers had become internationalists. Isolation offered them nothing. O'Neal also said it was high time that farmers made their voices heard at the world level and were consulted for advice by diplomats. He would have been gratified by Farm Bureau's reputation on world trade matters today.[9]

AFBF established a trade development department in the Washington office in 1948 directed by W. R. Ogg. The department arranged tours of farms in the United States for farmers visiting from Europe and elsewhere. At the request of the U.S. military government in Germany, leaders of three German farm organizations spent several months in 1949 touring farms and observing Farm Bureau meetings. The Danish government and State Department asked AFBF to facilitate year-long working visits by 100 young farmers from Denmark.

Ogg was struck by the good relations created by these Farm Bureau–arranged tours and work experiences. He told the board about Gayle Neal, a young Texas wheat farmer who had been a prisoner of war in Japan for nearly four years. Neal voluntarily selected as his personal guest for the day an official in the Japanese Ministry of Agriculture who was part of an IFAP group. "Mr. Owada was the natural guest for me," said Neal. "We are mighty happy to have him in the Panhandle." Neal's friendliness was typical of the Farm Bureau hospitality shown farmer representatives of Germany and Japan after the war.[10]

Farm Bureau's international trade policy of sixty years ago is remarkably similar to the policy of today in advocating fair and open trade. For 1949, the policy stated, "Our Nation should continue its leadership on a world-wide basis for the reduction of tariffs and import quotas . . . cartels, discriminatory practices and other barriers in order to facilitate expansion of international trade." Farm Bureau also noted that "the United States market is more freely available to the products of foreign countries than is any other major market in the world," and U.S. tariffs were at their lowest level since 1915.[11]

While serving as AFBF president, Allan Kline also became IFAP president in 1953 at the sixth annual meeting of the organization. Six years later, Charles Shuman, Kline's successor as Farm Bureau president, presided over AFBF's withdrawal from membership. Shuman acknowledged that contacts with world farm leaders were helpful but was dismayed by IFAP policies that supported a larger role for government in agriculture. In the years that followed, AFBF was in and out of IFAP several times.

The most important food export assistance program ever undertaken by the United States, Public Law 480 or Food for Peace, was developed with Farm Bureau support and signed into law in 1954. The idea originated with a young Army officer named Gwynn Garnett who commanded a tank company during the war in Europe and then served as director of the Food and Agricultural Division of the U.S. military government in the American zone of Germany. Garnett was in charge of procuring and distributing food to hungry German citizens. After his discharge from the military, he was on AFBF's trade staff from 1950 to 1955, where he advanced the idea of letting friendly nations pay for American farm products in local currencies. These soft-currencies were often practically worthless outside the country's own borders.[12]

AFBF's 1953 trade policy mirrored his plan. It emphasized trade over aid whenever possible, but said the U.S. should accept as payment for goods "the most convertible currencies in use in receiving countries." The soft-currency would be used for economic development projects within these countries or to purchase strategic materials for the United States and settle obligations arising from U.S. embassies and defense facilities abroad.[13]

The Mutual Security Act of 1953 incorporated some of this strategy, but P.L. 480 was much broader. The final bill had three titles. Title I allowed for the acceptance of foreign currencies for the purchase of farm commodities. Title II authorized the outright donation of food for famine relief and other emergencies. Title III was a catchall that covered CCC commodity donations both at home and abroad, as well as barter arrangements.

Sales under Title I were handled through commercial trade channels. The commodities included wheat, cotton, soybean oil, tobacco, and feed grains. Donations for humanitarian purposes under Title II were distributed by charitable organizations such as CARE, Church World Service, Catholic Welfare Service, and Jewish Joint Relief. Some barter arrangements under Title III were made for strategic metals like zinc and lead.

The Agricultural Trade Development and Assistance Act of 1954 or P.L. 480 was originally funded with $1 billion over a three-year period. Senator Spessard L. Holland (D-Florida) praised the export program at the 1954 AFBF annual meeting in New York City. He said that it would help end human suffering and turn back the tide of Communism. Turkey and Japan were first to sign deals to receive commodities.[14] P.L. 480 became a major instrument of U.S. foreign policy and a major component of farm export sales for many years. Between 1955 and 1964, the total value of U.S. farm exports was $44.8 billion. Of this amount, $12.2 billion or 27 percent of sales were attributed to donations, barter, or the soft-currency provisions of P.L. 480.

In addition to being a catalyst for P.L. 480 and trade expansion, AFBF strongly supported expanding the government's role in foreign market development and economic intelligence gathering. In March 1953, Secretary of Agriculture Ezra Taft Benson created the Foreign Agricultural Service (FAS) out of the old Office of Foreign Agricultural Relations (OFAR). This followed a Farm Bureau recommendation to the secretary.

The first administrator of FAS was former AFBF Vice President Romeo E. Short of Arkansas who resigned his position in 1953 to join USDA. A year later the Agricultural Trade Development and Assistance Act transferred agricultural attachés back to USDA from the State Department where they had been since 1939. Short was at FAS for only a short time before he passed away. Garnett then served as FAS administrator from 1955 to 1958.

In 1957, the AFBF delegate body authorized an agricultural trade office in Western Europe to expand sales of American farm products. H. H. "Herb" Alp, AFBF commodity director, went to the bustling trade center of Rotterdam and leased a small office in its trade mart, the *Groothandelsgebouw*. At the opening reception, 250 guests from nine European nations sampled American food products served by Dutch ladies in traditional dress. Chefs carved roast turkey for sandwiches garnished with Massachusetts cranberries. The sandwiches were a big hit because turkey was relatively unavailable in Europe at the time.

The trade office served both European importers of farm products and American exporters. It received a commission on sales it helped generate but was not engaged in buying or selling of the products it promoted. George Dietz, a former agricultural attaché, was the director. For a small subscription price, traders received valuable intelligence that included buying opportunities, commodity situation reports, market research, and technical data with conversions for grades, standards, weights and measures, and currencies. This was a lot for a small office to handle, including a promise to conduct business in all the languages used by the European Common Market.[15]

In 1960, the Rotterdam office held a reception to introduce Texas ruby red grapefruit. Dietz had to convince the guests that the red color was not the result of a freeze or artificial color as Europeans suspected. Later that year, AFBF formed the Farm Bureau Trade Development Corporation to "encourage, promote and facilitate the sale of agricultural products in the United States and abroad." The Rotterdam office became part of the new affiliate.[16]

Farm Bureau's experience with trade promotion convinced it that international trade would become an important part of the farmer's total market, not just bulk commodities, but also processed packaged foods which were relatively new in Europe. At the twenty-third Chicago World Trade Conference in 1960, President Charles Shuman said, "International trade is becoming less and less foreign and more like interstate trade in the United States." He cited better air and water transportation and an easing of trade restrictions for his optimism, and he added, "Agriculture's primary task in the export field is to develop dollar markets for its products on a permanent basis."[17]

AFBF battled the Kennedy administration on farm policy and labor matters but supported one of the president's key bills, the Trade Expansion Act of 1962 to replace the Reciprocal Trade Agreements Act. The administration mounted a campaign to secure passage with the theme of "trade or fade." Kennedy viewed trade as a way to unify Western nations against communist expansion and the Cold War. The bill gave the president new tariff-cutting authority that he hoped would lead to expanded trade with the six nations of the Common Market.[18]

During the 1970s, farmers were in the midst of a grain export boom, largely because of sales to the Soviet Union. The production of one acre out of three was exported and there were concerns that the world would run out of food. Farm Bureau discouraged calls for an international super-agency to store and distribute food supplies, a sort of global farm program. Instead, it said freer international trade would lead to an expansion of food supplies.

Allan Grant was elected AFBF president in 1976, during the middle of the Tokyo Round of GATT negotiations and served as a member of a U.S. agricultural policy advisory committee to the talks. Grant's philosophy on international relations was summed up in an article he wrote: "International trade, international travel help ease international tensions. Exchange of goods and services are important, but no substitute for a continuing exchange of people and ideas."[19]

America's most serious trade problems were with its two best customers at the time, Europe and Japan. Europe maintained high internal prices on farm products through a system of variable levies that Farm Bureau said were a dramatic example of nontariff trade restrictions. Japan imposed import quotas on farm products while running up a huge trade deficit with the United States. American cattlemen wanted access to a market where Japanese housewives were paying $20 a pound for beef. Grant thought one of the best ways to solve these problems was to meet face to face with farm leaders and politicians. He traveled to both Europe and Japan in his first year of office and stopped in Geneva to discuss the GATT negotiations with Director General Oliver Long.

In 1978, Congress passed an Agricultural Trade Act which was vigorously supported by Farm Bureau. It raised the diplomatic status of agricultural attachés in a number of countries and opened new trade offices. AFBF also sent a fifteen-member trade delegation to Geneva in mid-summer to review multilateral trade negotiations as the final stage of talks got underway. No other American farm organization monitored the talks as closely or gave as much input to the U.S. position as AFBF.

Just prior to the conclusion of the Tokyo Round of the GATT, Special U.S. Trade Representative Robert Strauss, a former chairman of the Democratic National Committee, complimented Farm Bureau for its persistence on trade matters. At the AFBF annual meeting in Houston, Strauss said, "My friends, agriculture in the previous round of negotiations, had been left completely out or put on the back burner, but it hasn't this time," said Strauss. "You are probably one of the—if not the—most sensible fair trade forces in the world, and you ought to take pride in it."[20]

The Tokyo Round concluded that April, five and half years after it began. As Strauss had said, the first six rounds of the GATT in the 1950s and 1960s virtually ignored agriculture. Tokyo ended that string. Otherwise, the accomplishments in agriculture were modest. The U.S. gained important market access for some of its farm products, including first-time access to Japan for beef and citrus, but there was no reform of weak rules governing agricultural trade and no reform of the dispute settlement process.

In 1982, AFBF President Bob Delano took a large delegation of more than twenty state presidents to Europe and a similar contingent to Japan. The U.S. Embassy in Tokyo said it was the first time that a group of American farmers visited Japan for the expressed purpose of gaining greater market access. The visit was extensively covered by the Japanese media and included a demonstration at the embassy gates by 8,000 Japanese farmers who held up a huge banner reading, "No more beef, orange or fruit juice to Japan."

Delano responded at a Farm Bureau-sponsored trade forum. "There is a relationship between the export of Japanese cars and television sets and imports of American beef and fruit . . . [both are] quality products, competitively priced." Delano's fair-trade remarks were not what the Japanese farmers wanted to hear. He later received mail from Japanese consumers who agreed with him. During the visit, Farm Bureau met with the minister of agriculture, members of the Diet (the Japanese parliament), and Japanese farm groups.[21]

The problem in Europe was not import quotas, but duty-free access (for soybeans and corn–gluten feed) and export subsidies. Europe was capturing markets from the United States at an alarming rate and depressing world prices. The Common Agricultural Policy was established in 1962 to assure self-sufficiency in food production for Europe, but its surpluses in wheat flour, sugar, poultry, and other farm products were spilling out all over the world.

In March 1984, Delano met French President Francois Mitterrand on the Illinois corn, soybeans, and hog farm of Secretary of Agriculture John Block. It was cold and muddy and a large contingent of reporters was present. Delano and the French president talked inside a machine shed. The AFBF president said the Common Agricultural Policy (CAP) to support farm prices was France's business, but when the Europeans were involved in the world market they should act as responsible traders.

Farm Bureau's trade policy called for a reduction in trade barriers and a vigorous export program for bulk commodities and value-added farm products to gain a greater share of the world market. U.S. farm exports peaked at $43.8 billion in 1981 before dropping to $26.3 billion in 1986 as the value of the dollar rose. Some farmers became discouraged and started thinking that mandatory production controls and marketing quotas with higher artificial prices were a better way to go, but AFBF stayed committed to expanding overseas markets.

Dean Kleckner was elected president of AFBF in 1986, eight months before the prelude to the next negotiating round, a GATT ministerial meeting at Punta del Este, Uruguay. Kleckner was invited by Special Trade Representative Clayton Yeutter to serve as one of twelve private-sector advisers to the U.S delegation at the meeting. "We were in favor of trade and trade agreements, but we wanted them to be fair," recalled Kleckner.[22] At the insistence of the United States, agricultural reform was the centerpiece of the multilateral trade talks—the first time this had happened.

Carla Hills became trade representative in the George H.W. Bush administration when Yeutter moved over to agriculture in the Cabinet. At the 1990 AFBF annual meeting in Orlando, Hills and Yeutter joined President Bush in addressing trade issues. "In the coming decade the American farmer must have a level playing field in the international trade arena . . . " said the president, who advocated phasing out export subsidies over five years and other trade-distorting practices by the end of the century. Hills later amplified the president's remarks. "Our agricultural proposal will require changes in all countries, including the United States. We must be prepared to put our own restrictions on the table. But we will not unilaterally disarm. When we say reform, we mean reform by all." Europe was spending over $9 billion in subsidies to export its growing surpluses while the U.S. countered with $1 billion spent on the Export Enhancement Program.[23]

The GATT negotiations were expected to finish in October 1990, but sharp differences remained between the U.S. and Europe over the steps countries could take to protect their farmers without distorting world trade. "Sovereign nations should have the right to support their farmers," agreed Paul Drazek, AFBF trade specialist. "But that support should not be on the backs of farmers in other nations."[24]

French farmers loved free trade in wine and the other high-value foods they produced, as much as they loved demonstrations against free trade. It was hard to figure, but a Farm Bureau delegation witnessed it in December 1990, when 30,000 angry farmers burned tires, and threw stones during a protest march in Brussels. A European magazine brushed off the unruly demonstration by saying there was a tradition of violent peasant revolt in Europe and the public was used to it.

President Bush again spoke to the AFBF annual meeting when it was held in 1992 at Kansas City, marking his second appearance in just two years. GATT was on the minds of the president and farmers in the audience. "Our administration will settle for nothing less than a GATT agreement that expands markets and increases opportunities for our exporters. We want free trade, and we want fair trade—and we want abundant trade," he said to loud applause from Farm Bureau members. The president noted in particular that for every $1 billion in farm exports, 25,000 American jobs were created. Unemployment was high and it was an election year.[25]

An AFBF delegation headed by Kleckner and Vice President Harry Bell of South Carolina met with Director General of the GATT Arthur Dunkel in May 1992. Dunkel warned that the talks were facing "tremendous dangers of fatigue," and the eighth round of the GATT could be the first to end in failure. He ultimately received much of the credit for breaking the stalemate with his own proposal. Farm Bureau never gave up on reaching an agreement. It met with the European Community (EC) Commission, the Cairns Group (a free-trade group led by Australia), and the trade counselor for Japan.[26]

In November 1992, one of the most contentious agricultural issues—EC oil-seed subsidy practices—was settled during a marathon negotiating session between U.S. and EC officials at Blair House, the White House guest quarters. The U.S. had lost more than $2 billion in soybean exports to the EC since the mid-1980s. The Europeans agreed to cut back oilseed production, a move that would help restore the lost markets. The Blair House Agreement smoothed the way for conclusion of the Uruguay Round in December 1993. By then, Bill Clinton was in the White House and Mickey Kantor was trade representative.

The American Farm Bureau Federation and other farm groups formed "Ag for GATT," a coalition to make sure Congress passed the agreement and the implementing legislation during a special session in November 1994. The multilateral trade agreement was approved despite last minute concerns about the World Trade Organization (WTO) that was going to be the successor to GATT. "It was unfortunate that all the hysteria about the World Trade Organization and U.S. sovereignty obscured the fact that the current playing field was tilted in favor of our competitors. The new trade agreement will rectify that," said Kleckner with relief.[27]

The Uruguay Round gave the United States first-time access to Japan's market for rice and improved access for pork. The U.S. also got improved global access for poultry and better access to the European market for almonds. The agreement included first-time limits on EC export subsidies, limits on trade distorting domestic subsidies, an improved dispute settlement system, elimination of nontariff measures (replacing them with tariff rate quotas), and an agreement on food safety and animal, plant health measures.

The American Farm Bureau Federation came a long way in its post-World War II efforts to expand agricultural trade opportunities for American farmers—from reaching out to foreign farmers after the war, initiating the Food for Peace program, opening a trade office in Rotterdam, confronting reluctant trading partners on their home turf, and representing American farmers at worldwide trade discussions. Globalization and the World Trade Organization opened a new chapter in trade.

Endnotes

1. Howard, James R. "We Want The Deep Blue Sea," *Wallaces' Farmer*, April 1922.

2. "Farm Bloc Heads Tour Europe To Study Situation," *Chicago Tribune*, November 4, 1923.

3. Benedict, *Farm Policies of the United States*, 121.

4. Kile, *Farm Bureau Through Three Decades*, 158.

5. Schlesinger, *The Coming of the New Deal*, 253; Kile, *The Farm Bureau Through Three Decades*, 312.

6. Culver and Hyde, *American Dreamer*, 150.

7. "Farmers Plan World-Wide Federation," *The Nation's Agriculture,* July–August 1946.

8. Minutes, AFBF board of directors, June 1947.

9. "O'Neal Warns of Limit on European Aid," *Chicago Tribune*, December 17, 1947; Transcript, AFBF Annual Meeting, December 16–18, 1947, Chicago, Illinois.

10. Minutes, AFBF board of directors, September 1949.

11. *Resolutions Adopted at the 30t^h Annual Convention* (for 1949).

12. "Fighting World Hunger: U.S. Food Aid Policy and the Food for Peace Program," *AgExporter,* USDA FAS publication, October 2004, 4–9; Allan Mustard, "An Unauthorized History of FAS," *Foreign Service Journal,* May 2003, 36–39.

13. *1953 Policies of the American Farm Bureau Federation*.

14. Transcript, AFBF Annual Meeting, December 14–16, 1954, New York, New York.

15. Woell, *Farm Bureau Architects,* 65.

16. "Trade Development Corporation," *AFBF Official News Letter,* July 4, 1960.

17. "International Trade Is Part of U.S. Farmer's Market," *Farm Bureau News*, March 21, 1960.

18. "Kennedy Drives for Trade Bill," *New York Times,* March 18, 1962; "Transcript of President's Speech," *New York Times,* May 5, 1962.

19. "Person-to-Person: Greatest Power for Positive Good," *Farm Bureau News,* June 7, 1976.

20. Transcript, AFBF Annual Meeting of 1979; "Moving Toward Freer Trade," *Time*, April 23, 1979; "23 Countries Agree to Ease Trade Limits," *Washington Post*, April 13, 1979.

21. "Delano Cites Progress from FB's Trade Mission," *Farm Bureau News*, May 3, 1982.

22. Interview with Dean Kleckner.

23. Transcript, AFBF Annual Meeting, January 7–11, 1990, Orlando, Florida.

24. "Sharp Trade Differences Exist between EC, World," *Farm Bureau News*, November 26, 1990.

25. Transcript, AFBF Annual Meeting, January 12–16, 1992, Kansas City, Missouri.

26. "GATT Round 'Best Opportunity' to Reform Trade Policies," *Farm Bureau News*, May 18, 1992.

27. "GATT Passes, Ending Eight-Year Wait," *Farm Bureau News,* December 5, 1994.

15 | The Wheat Referendum of 1963

REMEMBER THE WHEAT REFERENDUM! WHENEVER FARM BUREAU LEADERS AND STAFF faced a stiff challenge in the later part of the twentieth century, someone would always remind them of the Wheat Referendum of 1963. The battle over farm policy wasn't anything like the Alamo of 1836, but it had a few of the same elements. The American Farm Bureau Federation was outmanned and outgunned by a huge army—the federal bureaucracy. Farm Bureau staged a fight to the finish and overcame long odds to, in this case, win the battle.

The conflict was over two different farm policies and two likely courses for American agriculture. The choices were supply-management with tight government control over farmer decisions (what President Charles Shuman called "undisguised regimentation") or a more market-based farm economy with greater freedom for the individual farmer.[1] The epic battle had been building for at least fifteen years. First, Farm Bureau helped defeat the Brannan plan to regiment farmers during Truman's administration. Then President Eisenhower and Secretary Benson tried to swing farm policy in a free-market direction with lower price supports and less stringent production controls. With a Democratic administration taking office in 1961, the pendulum swung back in the other direction.

John F. Kennedy was admired by Farm Bureau members for the same reasons other Americans admired him and elected him president—his youthful vigor, leadership qualities, and his ability to inspire the nation. In 1956, Sen. Kennedy (D-Massachusetts) had been a speaker at the AFBF annual meeting in Miami Beach. It was true then that the organization generally heard from political speakers it liked at its biggest meeting of the year.

"You blessed the politician by inviting him," remembered Warren Newberry, former AFBF organization staffer and later Texas Farm Bureau administrator. Newberry had responsibilities for the general session program and recalled hearing a conversation backstage between the senator and Jack Lynn, AFBF's legislative director. "Jack, I won't ever be able to come and speak to your convention again, not for a long time anyway," said Kennedy. "What are you saying?" responded Lynn. "I want to be president," said Kennedy, "and the Democratic Party is controlled by organized labor, and the Farmers Union is their branch of agriculture. I can't be too closely associated with you fellows." Kennedy's speech on stage was rather short, but Newberry remembered that the crowd gave him its full attention.[2]

The conservative Shuman was a registered Democrat, which always surprised a lot of people. After Kennedy finished his speech and received generous applause, Shuman told the convention audience that he added Sen. Kennedy to the list of Democrats who best represented his own political philosophy. But true to the word he gave backstage at the AFBF convention, Kennedy distanced himself from the organization when he became president.[3]

Farm Bureau presented its "Platform for America" to both political conventions in the summer of 1960. At a meeting of the GOP platform committee in Chicago, Shuman said, "It is morally wrong" to delude farmers into thinking their best long-term interests lie in policies that provide bigger government farm program benefits. Of course, AFBF continued its policy of not endorsing a candidate, Nixon or Kennedy, for president. However, both party farm planks were printed in the newsletter, and AFBF said the choice was between a market system and compulsory supply control.[4]

Kentucky Farm Bureau's Chuck Fields also interviewed Henry A. Wallace just prior to the election for AFBF's radio program, "Across the Land." The old New Dealer surprised many people by saying that farmers won't like Kennedy's farm program because they will have to get a license to farm.[5]

JFK's choice of former Minnesota Gov. Orville Freeman as secretary of agriculture put Farm Bureau on alert. Freeman nominated Kennedy for president at the Democratic convention, but then lost his own reelection bid for a fourth term. Only forty-two years old, Freeman came from an important farm state but did not have impressive farm credentials. He was a founder of Minnesota's Democratic Farmer-Labor Party.

President-elect Kennedy and Secretary-designate Freeman invited farm organization leaders, including Shuman, to a conference in early January at New York City to discuss ways to "relieve the farm crisis." Whether there was a farm crisis was debatable. The biggest problem was that farm output was up 20 percent from the start of the Eisenhower administration on 6 percent fewer acres. Wheat stocks were at record levels.[6]

In March, Kennedy submitted a farm message to Congress in which he said "farm income could be gradually improved by a policy allowing farmers to write and adopt, subject to Congressional veto, new commodity-by-commodity marketing control programs . . . " Farmers Union and the Grange applauded the program. AFBF decided it was "a warmed-over version of the Brannan plan."[7]

University of Minnesota agricultural economist Dr. Willard Cochrane, who was Kennedy's farm adviser, described how Freeman viewed the situation. "He believed that farm incomes could be raised and the physical surplus problem eliminated through the vigorous intervention of government in the farm economy to control production." President Kennedy wanted to reduce the cost of government farm programs, so Cochrane said this "miracle" of higher farm prices and reduced government costs would have to be achieved through mandatory controls.[8] According to Cochrane, Kennedy understood that supply management meant farmers would have to give up some of their freedom to make production decisions, but he did not consider the sacrifice irrational or undesirable.[9] Farm Bureau did find it objectionable and labeled the idea the Cochrane-Freeman farm program.

In his first few months of office, Freeman hiked the soybean loan rate to draw acreage out of feed grains into oilseeds. Both the American Soybean Association and Farm Bureau objected. In a speech to 800 farmers at the McHenry County, Illinois, Farm Bureau, Shuman accused Freeman of sabotaging a sound market. He claimed the secretary was forming a "dictatorship" over farmers that would leave them at the "political whims of government controllers." Shuman complained that the agriculture department increased the number of employees by 20,000 since Kennedy took office to a total of 110,000."[10]

Battle lines in Congress over the Kennedy farm program were along party lines, a contrast to the old politics of agriculture. "For thirty years, congressional orientations toward the farm program had been dependably bipartisan; now they were partisan. For thirty years, congressional relations with the farm lobby had been universally solicitous; now they, too, were partisan," wrote John Mark Hansen.[11]

In the political bickering that followed, Farm Bureau was castigated by Rep. Poage for referring to the Cochrane-Freeman bill during testimony. The bill was introduced by Rep. Cooley, the chairman of the House Agriculture Committee, and Poage said it should properly be referred to by Cooley's name. Republicans accused Democrats of trying to buy election votes with a federal food stamp program. GOP congressmen also demanded a Justice Department investigation of charges that USDA officials threatened cotton warehouse operators with denial of a rate increase if the National Cotton Council testified against supply-management.

There were several attempts to dilute Farm Bureau's influence during this time. James G. Patton, president of Farmers Union, called for the formation of a federation of farm organizations. The Grange and National Council of

Farmer Cooperatives were invited to discuss an alliance; Farm Bureau was left out.[12] Secretary Freeman also announced plans for farmer advisory committees appointed from nominations made by Agricultural Stabilization and Conservation Service (ASCS) committee members. The committee members had a vested interest in continuing government farm programs, and Shuman called the advisers "window dressing." Freeman planned to appoint consumer representatives to the advisory panels from the ranks of organized labor. The House Agriculture Committee rejected the whole idea.

The Cochrane-Freeman proposal gave the secretary and executive branch unprecedented power over American agriculture and marginalized Congress. Dr. Kenneth Hood, AFBF commodity director, described it as a plan to "nationalize" American agriculture. As an agricultural economist, Hood was in demand as a speaker to explain farm program options to farmers. He got so comfortable making presentations that he later wrote a book with anecdotes, jokes, and other ways to enliven a talk.

In the book, Hood told about participating in a North Dakota farm meeting where sentiment was running strong for high price supports. A farmer asked him to write two different support prices for wheat on a blackboard, $2.38 and $1.81, and then tell him which one was larger. Hood knew the farmer was trying to corner him, and he noticed a young man sitting next to him. After ascertaining that the fellow was indeed the man's son, Hood explained that the $2.38 figure was higher for the father, but the $1.81 was a better number for the son's interests because it would build markets, expand usage, permit larger plantings, and lessen the problem of market-depressing surpluses.[13]

As originally proposed, the Cochrane-Freeman plan extended marketing quotas to all farm commodities. Therefore, farmers were restricted on the quantity marketed not just the acreage planted. Quotas or bases could be bought or sold which amounted to a licensing or franchising of farms and making entry to farming harder for young people. In a briefing for farm editors, Cochrane likened the idea to an automobile dealership. "You're also buying a certain and stable market. And hence the windfall of higher prices gets capitalized into farming and in a Chevrolet agency."[14]

AFBF led the opposition and was joined by livestock and poultry groups. Congressional allies included conservative southerners and Republicans who were ideologically opposed. Some urban congressmen also figured the plan would lead to higher food prices. Supporters of the farm program included the Grange, Farmers Union, National Farmers Organization, National Association of Wheat Growers, and National Federation of Grain Cooperatives.

The most objectionable features of the Cochrane-Freeman proposal were stripped from the Agricultural Act of 1961, and the farm press helped in the defeat.

Farm Bureau reprinted a number of the negative editorials in its newsletter. An editorial from *The Georgia Poultry Times* said, "The surrender by American producers to this socialistically inspired manifesto can lead to one conclusion—a comfortable peasant agriculture. If that be our choice then we deserve nothing better."[15]

During 1962, administration proposals for permanent production controls on feed grains, dairy products, and wheat were debated in Congress. AFBF opposed all three. Dairy and feed grains were defeated and wheat was amended before passage of the Food and Agriculture Act of 1962. However, the law set the stage for a showdown in the form of a wheat referendum.

Acreage diversion for wheat was mandatory in order to receive a price support, but then the farmer was given a choice. If approved by two-thirds of wheat producers voting in a referendum, producers would be issued marketing certificates for their share of wheat sold for domestic consumption and export. The wheat covered by marketing certificates would be eligible for a price support between 65 and 90 percent of parity, or $2.00 per bushel in 1964. The alternative, defeat of the referendum, would give farmers who complied with the allotment a price support of only 50 percent of parity.

Even urban dailies found the wheat referendum fascinating. "Without a doubt the wheat referendum campaign is the largest farm campaign ever waged," reported the *New York Times*. "Opponents contend the referendum will decide whether farmers will be 'free' or 'controlled' from Washington. Supporters cry 'Nonsense' and contend that the wheat plan will bolster farm income and end burdensome surpluses." Freeman praised USDA's data-processing capabilities to handle the program once farmers approved it. Shuman responded that the farmer was on his way to becoming a "faceless punch card."[16]

A warm-up to the big referendum was the administration's attempt at national marketing orders for turkeys and potatoes. Only the turkey order came to a vote of producers and it was defeated. Shuman termed the marketing order a "turkey birth control program" because the order placed quotas on hatcheries and controlled marketing. He wryly predicted "a national turkey watch" with federal agents assigned to count eggs on farms and police the poults.[17]

In April 1962, ASCS state chairmen and committeemen were brought to Washington at taxpayer expense. Both the secretary and president addressed them on the White House lawn. While acknowledging the fact that the group was prohibited by law from lobbying, the president dropped a hint. "We hope you also will see the members of Congress and acquaint them and the senators. We don't want them to be, as the secretary said, lonesome." ASCS committeemen also were required to sign a loyalty oath before taking office to support the programs they were called on to administer.[18]

At the 1962 AFBF annual meeting in Atlanta, Shuman told Farm Bureau members that USDA officials seemed "determined to either rule or ruin agriculture." At the business session later in the convention, the delegates declared, "In 1963 wheat producers have the responsibility to make the most important decision with respect to the future of the nation's farm business that any group of farmers has ever faced."[19]

Farm Bureau blasted the administration's hardball tactics but was powerless to stop them. In South Dakota, there was a report of an ASCS state-fair exhibit with a miniature railroad and a sidetrack with a train wreck. The sign on the exhibit read "Do not let Farm Program opponents sidetrack you onto a dead end," and "Free Enterprise Wrecked the Train." More than five million copies of seven different government pamphlets were mailed out, and radio and TV stations were encouraged to broadcast public service programs about it. Farmers Union and other groups urging a "Yes" vote ran their own campaigns. AFBF and state Farm Bureaus marshaled their public relations resources. "Freeman or Free Men?" was one campaign slogan. County Farm Bureaus in Kansas ran help-wanted ads in local papers that read, "Need farmers with character, resourcefulness and courage to help preserve the freedom to manage our own business. Vote No on the wheat referendum."[20]

Time magazine dubbed the referendum "The Wheat War" and observed, "The Agriculture Department has declared that it is not attempting to influence the outcome, but the department's publications explaining the wheat plan have made it abundantly clear to farmers that Freeman thinks they would be fools to vote against it."[21] ASCS personnel told farmers to get ready to accept $1 per bushel wheat if they voted "No." AFBF declared the issue was not the price of wheat but freedom to farm.

"Came the day of the referendum. The administration predicted it was in the bag, and most observers agreed. 'After all, you don't shoot Santa Claus,' said one." The results said otherwise. The Midwest was a solid "No" and Kansas, the largest wheat belt state, was 58 percent "No."[22] Nationwide, the referendum failed to get even half of the votes in a heavy turnout.

It could easily be said that the referendum lost because Farm Bureau opposed it. But the outcome showed that Farm Bureau spoke for farmers and accurately reflected their thinking. It appeared that farmers became suspicious of supply-management. Said one farmer, "What do I tell my old sow when she insists on farrowing 12 little pigs—when my quota is only 10?"[23]

Time magazine reported that Freeman got a phone call from President Kennedy after the results were in. "What happened?" asked the president coldly. Freeman's response was "I don't know." Of the more than one million votes cast in the referendum, 689,000 were "No" votes. The number in favor of the

Cochrane-Freeman program was just under 48 percent, far short of the two-thirds majority needed.[24]

Shuman felt that Secretary Freeman had deep and abiding distrust of the market price system and private enterprise framework. He recalled that Freeman had labeled it "the law of the jungle."[25] The AFBF president was excited about Farm Bureau's victory in the referendum. "This can be a turning point in the battle against Big Government," he said. It could have been, but of course it wasn't. The battle merely shifted to the regulatory front.

Orville Freeman's problems in office weren't confined to the Wheat Referendum. He was dragged into one of the biggest political scandals to beset the Kennedy administration when the agribusiness empire of Billie Sol Estes crumbled in 1962. The west Texas businessman had used political influence and shady practices to build an empire of grain elevators, warehouses, and fertilizer tanks in the South.

The scandal made headlines when state and federal authorities discovered that many of the fertilizer tanks mortgaged for millions of dollars didn't exist. Estes also used a scheme to obtain 3,000 acres of cotton allotments from farmers for which he was later fined a half million dollars. Several USDA employees were under fire for accepting gifts from Estes, and Freeman himself was accused of a cover-up. Republicans called for his ouster and Democrats accused him of giving the Kennedy administration a black-eye.

Shuman had warned that adoption of the Cochrane-Freeman farm program would multiply the opportunities for "fast-buck boys" like Billie Sol Estes and lead to more abuses like his transfer of cotton allotments. Shuman also said the case was not simply one of irresponsible wheeling and dealing. "It is an outgrowth of government programs which give government employees the power to make decisions that mean real money to farmers, warehousemen, and others."[26]

Farm Bureau's victory in the Wheat Referendum of 1963 eventually led to a more market-oriented government farm policy. The freedom of producers to manage their own farming operations was preserved.

Endnotes

1. "Administration Plans Complete Control," *Farm Bureau News*, February 19, 1962.

2. Interview with Warren Newberry.

3. Transcript, AFBF Annual Meeting, December 9–13, 1956, Miami Beach, Florida.

4. "FB's 'Platform for America' Presented to Both Parties," *Farm Bureau News*, July 25, 1960.

5. "Henry Wallace Says Farmers Won't Stand for Senator Kennedy's Farm Proposals," *Farm Bureau News*, October 31, 1960.

6. "Changes Mapped in Farm Program, *New York Times*, January 8, 1961.

7. "Kennedy Message in Brief," *New York Times*, March 17, 1961; *Farm Bureau News*, March 20, 1961.

8. Cochrane, *The Development of American Agriculture,* 146.

9. Cochrane and Ryan, *American Farm Policy 1948–1973,* 40.

10. "Farm Bureau Head Assails Dictatorship," *Chicago Tribune,* September 30, 1962.

11. Hansen, *Gaining Access,* 147–149.

12. "Farm Groups Seen In A New Dispute," *New York Times,* March 19, 1961.

13. Hood, *Spice for Speakers, Sports & Squares,* 18.

14. "Farming Franchise Is Newest Frontier," *Chicago Tribune,* June 19, 1962.

15. "Georgia Editor Says C-F Bill Leads to Peasantry," *Farm Bureau News,* May 15, 1961.

16. "Fight Over Vote on Wheat Controls Becoming Heated," *New York Times,* May 12, 1963.

17. Woell, *Farm Bureau Architects,* 86.

18. Ibid., 85, 92; "Shuman Raps Lobbying at U.S. Expense," *Chicago Tribune,* April 5, 1962.

19. "Get Off That Tiger," *Time,* December 21, 1962; *Farm Bureau Policies for 1963.*

20. "The Farmers Vote for Freedom," *The Reader's Digest,* vol. 83, September 1963, 95–99; "Fight Over Wheat Controls Becomes Heated," *New York Times,* May 12, 1963.

21. "The Wheat War," *Time,* May 17, 1963.

22. "The Farmers Vote for Freedom," *The Reader's Digest,* vol. 83, September 1963, 95–99.

23. Ibid.

24. "The Wheat Vote," *Time,* May 31, 1963; Congressional Quarterly, *Congress and the Nation,* vol. 1, 721.

25. "Administration Plans Complete Control," *Farm Bureau News,* February 19, 1962.

26. "The Taut Miles from Pecos," *Time,* May 11, 1962; "Estes Slapped with $554,162 U.S. Penalty," *Chicago Tribune,* May 10, 1962; "Wilson Asks Freeman To Resign," *Chicago Tribune,* July 2, 1962; "Tough Quiz for Freeman in Estes Case," *Chicago Tribune,* June 30, 1962; Woell, *Farm Bureau Architects,* 86; "Shuman Says Farm Bill Would 'Multiply Opportunities For the Fast-Buck Boys,'" *Farm Bureau News,* June 4, 1962.

16 | Defending Pesticide Use on Farms

SILENT SPRING, RACHEL CARSON'S BOOK ABOUT PESTICIDES PUBLISHED IN 1962, IS often considered the catalyst for the environmental movement in America. Carson characterized pesticides as "the elixirs of death" responsible for bird losses that could lead to a silent spring devoid of song birds. She introduced the fear of chemicals and doomsday environmentalism into American society. "For the first time in the history of the world, every human being is now subjected to contact with dangerous chemicals from the moment of conception until death," Carson wrote.[1]

Synthetic pesticides were developed during World War II to fight insect-borne diseases among military and civilian populations. DDT was the first of these modern pesticides. A persistent, broad-spectrum compound, it was hailed as the "miracle pesticide" and came into widespread agricultural and commercial usage in the late 1940s. The peak use of DDT was in 1959, just before Carson, a biologist, raised a public alarm about it.

The war had already given the world one new method of human extinction, the atomic bomb, and if Carson was to be believed, the pesticides developed during the war were making the Earth "unfit for all life." She said we lived in "a world filled with cancer-causing agents," that would become apparent in time. "The full maturing of whatever seeds of malignancy have been sown by chemicals is yet to come," she confidently predicted.[2]

AFBF's policy resolution on agricultural chemicals adopted the year *Silent Spring* was published (1962) said, "Modern agriculture could not provide adequate quantities of good quality food and fiber at a relatively low cost to consumers were it not for the continued safe use of agriculture chemicals and drugs." The delegates added that farmers had a responsibility to see that these products were properly used, and they deplored "the illusion" that there was widespread misuse of chemicals or that they posed a serious threat to public health.[3]

Carson's bestseller led to a nationwide ban on the general use of DDT in 1972, a ban opposed by the federation. Although DDT use already had declined substantially, it was still important for cotton, certain fruits, and vegetables. AFBF told the Environmental Protection Agency (EPA) that an objective study of DDT would show that the benefits outweighed the risks. USDA appealed the cancellation, and the World Health Organization (WHO) defended the pesticide. Dr. Norman Borlaug, who won the Nobel Peace Prize for launching the Green Revolution, warned that banning agricultural chemicals would lead to a world "doomed not by chemical poisoning but by starvation."[4]

DDT came into use about the same time as penicillin and saved hundreds of millions of lives from malaria, typhus, and other diseases. It was banned after being used to eradicate malaria in North America and Europe. In recent years, DDT has had a renaissance with the WHO endorsing its use in sub-Saharan Africa and other tropical regions where malaria still infects a half-billion people yearly, killing one million of them, mostly children.

Ironically, a few decades before Carson, farmers were told that unless they made greater use of chemicals, humankind would lose a battle for control of the Earth to insects. This was not in a science-fiction novel, but in a book by former USDA chief entomologist Dr. L. O. Howard. "They (insects) are our rivals here on earth, and probably the last living thing on the globe will be some active insect sitting on a dead lichen which will represent the last of the life of the plants." Howard urged greater use of airplanes to spray crops and offered mild encouragement that the human brain should be able to outsmart insects.[5]

Silent Spring put agriculture on the defensive, yet the cancer epidemic Carson predicted did not materialize, nor did the countryside become a deserted wasteland as she forecast was possible. The threat to birds from DDT was based on kills from direct contact or a softening of egg-shells affecting reproduction. Both claims appear to have been exaggerated, but there were some well-publicized fish kills from poorly directed spraying programs along rivers. Carson also claimed earthworms were transferring DDT to robins and other birds, but robins became the most abundant bird in North America during the DDT years.[6]

In the end, one of the pesticide's attributes became its curse—DDT did not break down quickly enough in the environment. In canceling its registration, EPA said DDT persisted in aquatic and terrestrial environments and built up in the tissues of animals and fishes.

In 1971 before the ban, DDT was withdrawn from use in the northeast against gypsy moths, and alternative sprays were not used. As a result, the moths stripped almost one million acres of trees and laid billions of eggs for future infestations. The chief of the bureau of insect control for Massachusetts said the gypsy moths sounded like "a gentle rain in summer" as millions of them chomped their way through the woods of Cape Cod.[7]

This was the kind of scene AFBF was trying to avoid for agriculture and the food supply. It warned the EPA that if no pesticides were used at all, crop yields would be cut by 50 percent, the cost of food would rise four to fivefold, and the quality would be unacceptable.

Farmers used the largest volume of pesticides, but about half of the registered products were for home, institutional, and industrial use. Pesticide was the general term for chemical pest killers that included insecticides, rodenticides, fungicides, miticides, and herbicides. Farm Bureau became the leading voice for farmers on pesticide issues and in 1965 created a natural resources department. Clifford McIntire was appointed director. A member of a committee that organized the Maine Farm Bureau Federation in 1950, McIntire was a seven-term congressman who had served on the House Agriculture Committee.

On April 22, 1970, millions of Americans participated in the first Earth Day held across the country to raise environmental awareness. The originator of the big public demonstration and teach-in was Sen. Gaylord Nelson (D-Wisconsin). Nelson had the idea for awhile, but the one thing that set it in motion was the fire on the polluted Cuyahoga River near Cleveland the year before. Flames shot up along the river from oil, grease, and debris. Nelson said he wanted to "tap into the environmental concerns of the general public and infuse the student anti-war energy into the environmental cause."[8]

Many future leaders of the environmental movement did emerge from the anti-war movement and became adversaries of mainstream agriculture. They already were strongly opposed to pesticides because of the use of Agent Orange during the war. The defoliant, a combination of two herbicides, 2-4-D and 2-4-5-T, was sprayed from the air by the U.S. military to remove enemy vegetative cover. Controversies about Agent Orange and health issues affecting Vietnam veterans remained long after the war.

The year 1970 was significant to environmentalism in another way. President Nixon created the EPA by executive order and named William D. Ruckelshaus as the administrator. Farm Bureau was instrumental in getting a special assistant for agriculture appointed to the new agency. Will Irwin, an Indiana farmer who had served with Ruckelshaus in the state legislature, advised him on farm issues and was in close contact with Farm Bureau. "You could almost smell the concern of the American farmers when they transferred the regulation of pesticides out of the Agriculture Department to the newly founded Environmental Protection Agency," recalled Ruckelshaus at the 1985 AFBF annual meeting.

Ruckelshaus shared some candid thoughts about environmental reporting at that meeting. He said the reporters who used to cover the EPA were told by

Walter Cronkite at CBS and his counterparts at the other two networks that it was easy to get a story on the evening news if it had an environmental twist to it. "This (television coverage) had an enormous impact on the public's awareness and concern about the problems of the environment, he said."[9]

AFBF increased its own outreach to the public on the environment and other issues with a daily radio commentary called *Insight* that was launched in 1970. The initial commentators included Jack Angell and Melvin Woell of the AFBF staff, Booth Wallentine of the Iowa Farm Bureau Federation, and Evan Hale of the California Farm Bureau Federation. The commentaries could be heard every evening in the West over KSL Radio, Salt Lake City, a 50,000 watt clear-channel station, and on dozens of other radio stations.

When Ruckelshaus spoke to AFBF in 1985, it was shortly after his second tour of duty as EPA administrator. His first term as agency chief was from 1970 to 1973. "The true environmentalist in this country is the farmer," said Ruckelshaus, "and not a shouting, screaming, hand-wringing, picketing type of environmentalist, but a practicing one whose economic well-being depends on an understanding and preserving of all elements of the environment."[10]

Earth Day ushered in the Environmental Decade. "The pollution that we were concerned about in those days was pollution that you could smell, touch and feel," said Ruckelshaus.[11] The Clean Air Act of 1970 superseded the mostly state-run efforts to curb air pollution in the Air Quality Act of 1967. The Clean Water Act of 1972 and the Endangered Species Act of 1973 followed. The National Environmental Policy Act (NEPA) of 1970 financed new municipal waste-treatment plants but also contained a provision that forced government agencies to incorporate environmental factors into their decision-making.

There were about a dozen major federal environmental initiatives in the 1970s, but pesticides became the first hot environmental issue for farmers and had led directly to the formation of EPA. The Federal Insecticide, Fungicide and Rodenticide Act of 1947 (FIFRA) was a pesticide labeling and registration law enforced by USDA. In 1972, Congress replaced it with an environmental protection statute requiring all pesticides to be registered with the EPA and divided them between general use and restricted use which required application by certified applicators. A few years later, Farm Bureau played a key role in the legislative process that led to the 1978 amendments to FIFRA. The changes enabled EPA to register products according to their chemical composition not their product name, thus speeding up agency approval. The states also were given significant power over use and misuse of pesticides.

The Wall Street Journal termed 1978 "the year of the insects" in an editorial that blamed a radical fringe of the environmental movement with wanting to give the nation back to the bugs—fire ants, gypsy moths, grasshoppers, Japanese beetles, and the ticks that spread Rocky Mountain spotted fever. The editorial credited the American Farm Bureau Federation with trying to restore balance to a struggle that seemed tipped in favor of bugs.[12] That year, AFBF intervened in a lawsuit filed by the Environmental Defense Fund (EDF) against EPA. AFBF sided with the agency in its decision to allow the state of Mississippi to use ferriamicide to fight fire ants.

Even when pesticides were used, insects threatened to gain the upper hand. A National Academy of Sciences study team reported that pests consumed 20 percent of all the world's harvests, and if post-harvest losses of stored foods were included, the toll amounted to 40 percent. The corn rootworm, tobacco budworm, and even the common housefly were developing resistance to the pesticides commonly used to control them.

A *Farm Bureau News* article in 1985 said farmers were being put on the spot over pesticides. "Whether it's watermelons or potatoes, the occasional misuse of pesticides and instances of contamination blamed on pesticides are increasing the public's awareness of the extensive use of chemicals in agriculture, and farmers and ranchers are the ones who could end up on the losing side of the debate." Also, migrant farm groups, environmentalists, and the AFL-CIO wanted to amend pesticide law so individuals could sue to stop alleged violations. "This could result in endless harassment of farmers in the course of normal agricultural production activities," said Mark Maslyn, AFBF environmental specialist on the national affairs staff.[13] AFBF successfully blocked the effort.

"Other than the weather, it seems to me that farm chemicals have the single greatest potential effect (for good or bad) on agriculture and farm income," wrote President Dean Kleckner in his column for *Farm Bureau News*. He cited the growing cost of farm chemicals, the public phobia about their use in food production, and the reluctance of Congress to clarify farm chemical standards and legal issues. Kleckner applauded the fact that most farmers were environmentally conscious.[14]

Public phobia about pesticides reached a high point with the Alar apple scare in February 1989. The alarm was triggered by a report from an environmental group, Natural Resources Defense Council (NRDC), on the health hazards to children from trace exposure to Alar (a trade name for the chemical daminozide used in orchards) on apples. The report first aired on CBS's *60 Minutes* news magazine.

The segment of the program opened with correspondent Ed Bradley seated in front of a graphic of a big red apple with a skull and cross bones on it. Bradley claimed Alar was the "most potent cancer-causing agent in our food supply" and said the cancer risk to children who eat apples and drink apple juice is "perilously high."[15] The chemical in question, daminozide, technically wasn't a pesticide. It was a growth regulator used to prevent pre-harvest fruit drop and to improve the color of red apples.

The apple scare came at the same time that two Chilean grapes were found to have been injected with cyanide, which prompted a halt to grape imports. "Fruit, the synonym for healthfulness, has turned into a food-safety nightmare. Apples and grapes, once simple snacks tossed into a lunch bag, have become Washington's latest political and economic crisis," wrote the *Washington Post*.[16] After the CBS broadcast, school boards in major cities pulled apples from cafeterias, and some supermarket chains refused to accept apples that had been treated with Alar. A supermarket executive defended the move by saying, "We are dealing with perceptions here; we're not dealing with reality."[17]

Parents became so hysterical that one mother sent state troopers to flag down a school bus after realizing she had sent her child to school with an apple for lunch. Apple sales fell and prices plummeted.[18] AFBF responded quickly to shore up public confidence in the nation's food supply. President Kleckner met with EPA Administrator John Moore in March and urged him to do something to dispel public fears about apples and apple products. Shortly after that, EPA, FDA, and USDA issued a joint statement dismissing the NRDC claims of cancer risks from eating apples. Moore called the environmental group's risk calculations "flat wrong," and said they used data previously rejected by a scientific peer review.[19]

The National Research Council of the National Academy of Sciences issued a 1,400 page report recommending Americans double their consumption of fruits and vegetables and said any small risk of cancer would be greatly outweighed by the health benefits of greater fruit and vegetable consumption. While the NRDC claimed that Alar could cause one case of cancer in every 4,200 preschoolers during their lifetime, AFBF countered with data from scientists showing that a forty-pound child would have to eat more than 20,000 apples a day for the rest of his or her life to ingest a dosage level equal to that given to laboratory rats.

Actress Meryl Streep took the stage for the NRDC as chairwoman of its newly formed group, Mothers and Others for Pesticide Limits. In television and newspaper interviews she urged parents to buy organic produce, and in dramatic testimony before the Senate, she said the government's failure to take Alar off the market amounted to little more than a laboratory experiment on the nation's children. In an op-ed piece in the *Chicago Tribune*, Kleckner said he didn't doubt that Streep entered the spotlight because she was a concerned mother, but he added, "Our society has a problem when views of a movie star are considered more credible than those of scientists and regulators of the Food and Drug Administration, the Environmental Protection Agency and the National Academy of Sciences."[20]

The apple scare was the work of a small Washington, D.C., public relations firm hired by the NRDC. A deal was made for *60 Minutes* to have exclusive access to the NRDC findings for the show's thirty million viewers. The plan was to strike first in the electronic media and then use newspapers to echo the story in headlines and news stories. The goal was to have so many repetitions of the message about apples and children that the average American consumer could not avoid hearing it. "Through an environmental group's adroit use of imagery to manipulate the media, the nation was stirred to frenzy," concluded the *Chicago Tribune*.[21]

Many scientists stepped forward to quell the fears. An ad hoc group of fourteen prominent scientific organizations representing 100,000 microbiologists, toxicologists, veterinarians, and food scientists called health risks from approved farm chemicals "negligible or nonexistent."[22] Dr. Bruce Ames, University of California microbiologist (and inventor of the Ames test, used to determine if certain chemicals cause mutations in bacteria or possibly cancer in humans), was one of the respected scientists who thought the pesticide link to cancer was overblown. Ames argued that many fruits contain natural carcinogens in concentrations 1,000 times greater than synthetic chemicals like Alar.[23]

Uniroyal, the major manufacturer of Alar, pulled the chemical off the market in response to the controversy. Nearly two years later, a group of Washington state apple growers filed a class action lawsuit against CBS, *60 Minutes*, NRDC, and the PR firm. The growers charged that they lost $130 million as a result of the false and deceptive acts of the plaintiffs in the widely discredited Alar report. AFBF horticulture director Scott Rawlins said the industry as a whole lost $300 million.[24] After the apple panic was exposed, a number of states enacted so-called anti-disparagement laws protecting agricultural products from false and malicious statements.

Another major battle over pesticides was the "Big Green" ballot initiative before California voters in 1990. If passed, Big Green would have given the state's farmers until 1996 to phase out pesticides shown to cause cancer in lab animals. "Big Green scared us," recalled California Farm Bureau Federation President Bob Vice. "Big Green basically would have taken about 60 to 70 percent of all the pesticides used on food crops away from us. We said this initiative is not going to fly; people are going to see through this because we couldn't raise food for them. But, about three months out from the election it was polling that 60 percent of the people were going to vote for it, so we got organized to tell our side of it."[25]

California was already known as "the environmental proving ground" by the time Big Green made it on the ballot, so farmers in other states were worried, not only for themselves but consumers who would be hit by produce shortages and higher prices. The challenge was a good example of how the Farm Bureau family worked. Farm Bureau leaders and staff from other parts of the country came to California and walked door-to-door to talk to consumers. The initiative reinforced the fact that farmers have to tell their story to the public. On election day, Big Green lost by a margin of almost 2 to 1.

A nationwide threat to continued use of pesticides developed in 1992 when a federal court in San Francisco ruled that EPA had to strictly enforce the outdated Delaney Clause that set a zero-tolerance for potential cancer-causing chemicals in processed foods. When the Delaney Clause was written in 1958, pesticide residues were detectable in parts per million. By 1996, scientists were able to detect pesticides in parts per billion and even parts per trillion. These traces might not pose any risk at all, but the Delaney clause said no level of concentration, no matter how miniscule, was acceptable. EPA wanted to substitute a "negligible risk" standard instead, meaning the chances of getting cancer in a lifetime were one in a million. The Delaney Clause also permitted older pesticides to stay on the market while it blocked the use of newer, safer ones. It was clearly obsolete, but environmental groups and the AFL-CIO took the issue to court and won.

After the court decision, one of AFBF's top priorities was finding a legislative fix for the Delaney Clause before EPA was forced to cancel the use of many important and necessary pesticides. In addition to testimony on Capitol Hill, AFBF publicized the effect on farmers and consumers in both *Farm Bureau News* and "Ag Feed," a television newsfeed distributed by satellite and tape. Ben Gramling, a South Carolina Farm Bureau member, lost 15 percent of his apple trees to alternaria leaf blotch because he was unable to use the fungicide that would protect them.[26]

In the spring of 1996, EPA was beginning the cancellation of a number of critically needed agricultural pesticides. Testifying before the Senate Agriculture Committee in June, President Kleckner warned, "The long-awaited Delaney disaster has begun." He emphasized that farmers in virtually every state were victims of unwarranted cancellations, including producers of California grapes, Indiana soybeans, Kansas wheat, Alabama peanuts, Florida tomatoes, and Vermont apples. Kleckner said the goal of the Delaney Clause—to prevent cancer-causing agents from entering the food supply—was admirable but the science on which it was based was no longer the best available.[27]

The Delaney Clause was the hang-up to rewriting workable pesticide regulations, with Farm Bureau and its allies on one side of the debate and environmental groups on the other. A breakthrough finally came in July when the House Commerce Committee chaired by William J. Bliley (R-Virginia) reached a compromise. The committee had partial jurisdiction over the bill because the Delaney Clause was in the Food, Drug, and Cosmetic Act. White House Chief of Staff Leon Panetta briefed state Farm Bureau presidents at the White House about the administration's position around the same time and said, "If we can get Delaney reformed, we are all for it."[28]

Before the month was out, the Food Quality Protection Act passed the House by a remarkable vote of 417 to 0. The Senate made its bill identical to the House and passed it by voice vote. President Clinton signed the act into law in August 1996 at a White House ceremony. In the past, environmental groups had won pesticide battles with messages alone, while AFBF often won the scientific debate. This time Farm Bureau prevailed with both science and messages. It was a major victory for farmers.

The Food Quality Protection Act (FQPA) substituted a "safe" standard for pesticide residues in both raw and processed foods. Safe was defined as "reasonable certainty of no harm." More than fifty crop protection chemicals were on their way to being banned before the law was passed, and in testimony before the first meeting of EPA's food safety advisory committee, Kleckner conceded that he was not expecting EPA to eliminate all restrictions or cancellations of agricultural pesticides. However, he expected decisions to be made on sound science and actual risks, and no longer on an obsolete standard. He also praised the new law for streamlining the registration of "minor crop" chemicals important to growers of fruits and vegetables and other low-acreage crops.

In August 2006, EPA completed a ten-year review of pesticides under FQPA. It took that long to assess nearly 10,000 tolerances or maximum pesticide residues in food. EPA Administrator Stephen L. Johnson concluded that "Americans can now be assured the pesticides used in the U.S. meet the highest health standards in the world." AFBF President Bob Stallman also was pleased with the review. "The EPA clearly recognizes the benefits of pesticide use in food production while establishing that products being used have a wide margin of safety that effectively protects both human health and the environment." While AFBF did not agree with all the decisions made in the assessment process, it noted that continued use was allowed of some important pesticides, such as atrazine, a widely used weed killer. On balance, good science ultimately ruled the day on pesticides.

Endnotes

1. Carson, *Silent Spring*, 15.
2. Ibid., 7–8, 226, 241.
3. *Farm Bureau Policies for 1963*.
4. "Who's for DDT?" *Time*, November 22, 1971.
5. "Calls Man To War on Insect Menace," *New York Times*, September 30, 1931.
6. Whelan, *Toxic Terror*, 107.
7. "A Plague of Moths," *Time*, July 26, 1971.
8. Nelson, *Beyond Earth Day*, 6–7.
9. Transcript, AFBF Annual Meeting, January 7–10, 1985, Honolulu, Hawaii.
10. Ibid.
11. Ibid.

12. "The Year of the Insects," *Wall Street Journal*, August 15, 1978.

13. Ibid.

14. "Farm Chemical Use," *Farm Bureau News*, February 1, 1988.

15. "A Is for Apple," *60 Minutes*, CBS–TV broadcast, February 26, 1989.

16. "Bad Apples, Sour Grapes? Learning from the Fruit Scares," *Washington Post*, March 22, 1989.

17. "Some Fear Bad Precedent in Alar Alarm," *Washington Post*, April 19, 1989.

18. Whelan, *Toxic Terror*, 185.

19. "3 U.S. Agencies to Allay Public's Fears, Declare Apples Safe," *New York Times*, March 17, 1989.

20. "America Tackles the Pesticide Crisis," *New York Times*, October 8, 1989; "Apples Are OK; Keep Meryl Away," *Chicago Tribune*, March 27, 1989.

21. Whelan, *Toxic Terror*, 186; "How 'Media Stampede' Spread Apple Panic," *Chicago Tribune*, March 26, 1989.

22. "Some Fear Bad Precedent," *Washington Post*, April 19, 1989.

23. "Endangered Earth Update Now Wait Just a Minute," *Time*, December 18, 1989.

24. "Apple Growers File Suit over Alar Report," *Farm Bureau News*, December 10, 1990.

25. Interview with Bob Vice.

26. "Farmers Feeling the Pinch of Delaney Enforcement," *Farm Bureau News*, May 6, 1996.

27. "Loss of Safe Crop Protection Concerns Farm Bureau," *Farm Bureau News*, June 17, 1996.

28. "FB Hails Breakthrough on Pesticide Reform Measure," *Farm Bureau News*, July 22, 1996.

17 | A New Paradigm of Food Supply-Demand

For the first fifty years, American Farm Bureau Federation farm policy was directed at removing farm surpluses and dealing with agriculture's excess capacity. These priority issues were related to improving farm prices and income and only ceased to be issues when interrupted by war. Beginning in the 1960s, however, the food supply-demand paradigm of chronic excess capacity in this country, farm surpluses, and low food prices was starting to change. Export embargoes, consumerism, and world food security popped up as new issues for Farm Bureau. The supply-demand paradigm was changing because of world population growth, growing affluence, and rising food prices.

Perhaps the changes started with a stop in Iowa by a portly, balding man on his first visit to the United States. When Soviet Premier Nikita Khrushchev visited Coon Rapids in September 1959, he was served a dinner of baked sugar-cured ham, fried chicken, and barbequed pork ribs. For dessert he had corn pudding and apple pie with cheese. A reporter noticed that Khrushchev smiled a lot during this visit to the farm of Roswell Garst to which the premier replied, "When a man smiles he is in good health."[1]

The visit was an eye-opener for Khrushchev because he saw for himself that Soviet collective farms could not compete with American family farms. The proof was found in farm fields, orchards, dairy barns, livestock pens, and the food on the table. A recent book about the Soviet leader said his pride was bruised by the farm visit. He bragged on the car ride back to Des Moines about a new Soviet turbojet airplane that could land on dirt fields like ones he saw from the car. It was his way of shifting the conversation to something the Soviets were more competitive at—building military hardware.[2]

The Soviet Union had vast acreages of fertile soil, suitable growing climate, and far more people engaged in agriculture than the United States, and yet its agricultural system was a failure by comparison. "It is no secret that Khrushchev has been unhappy with the steady deterioration of Russian agriculture under its system of state controlled and operated farms," said AFBF President Shuman in 1963. "He has tried to apply U.S. agricultural technology to the land of his country, but has left out the main ingredient of our private enterprise system and that is the profit incentive."[3]

On October 10, 1963, President Kennedy approved a grain deal with the Soviet Union—150 million bushels of wheat sold to the USSR through private commercial channels at a value of $250 million. The Soviets had made a $500 million deal with the Canadian government a month earlier. The deals were striking in that Russia used to be a grain exporter not an importer. Organized labor criticized the sale to a communist nation, but President Kennedy pledged that the Russian people would learn through broadcasts over the Voice of America that the wheat came from the United States.[4]

The 1963 sale was a prelude to much larger sales during the seventies. At the AFBF annual meeting that year in Chicago, Sen. Hubert Humphrey (D-Minnesota) made a prescient observation that "agriculture is in the forefront for the struggle for a better world. It's not a laggard. It's not a burden. It's not what is holding America back—it is what is putting America ahead." The loquacious Humphrey added, "We know of Sputnik; we know of the astronauts and the cosmonauts, but I want to say that despite all the genius of the Soviet technology and industry, they've never been able to operate a family farm."[5] Humphrey made it known during his political career that he was in favor of selling the Russians anything they could not shoot back at us—especially grain.

The consumer movement in America was spawned by 1960s activism and consumer crusader Ralph Nader who championed automobile safety and other consumer product issues. One of Nader's crusades was against the fat content of hotdogs.

Consumerism implied discontent, usually with the quality of the product, although rising inflation also made consumers mad about prices. In the past, organized labor occasionally voiced complaints by industrial workers about food prices. Consumers really didn't have a separate organization or voice.

Truth be known, families who lived through the Depression were happy to have three square meals a day. Food was not yet taken for granted. Many urban families were only a generation removed from the farm and had an appreciation for what it took to produce food. They were happy even though grocery bills took a big bite out of their paycheck. In 1929, the first year for which official statistics are available, Americans spent nearly 24 percent of their disposable income on food. By 1970, they were spending only around 15 percent; today it is closer to 10 percent.

A flash point for consumer activists came in 1965 when meat consumption was rising fast and vegetable crops were hurt by bad weather. Food prices advanced almost 6 percent in a one-year time frame ending in the third quarter of 1966. For the first half of the decade, food prices had risen on average only 2 percent a year. A group called Housewives Eager for Lower Prices (HELP) picketed supermarkets in nearly 100 cities coast to coast and organized boycotts in the fall of 1966. The housewives weren't sure who or what to blame for food price increases, but a Kansas City leader identified "games, gimmicks and fancy packaging." Supermarkets used trading stamps and promotional giveaways to attract customers. Meat cutters and other retail food workers feared the housewives' boycott would lead to layoffs, but supermarkets responded by marking down shelf prices.[6]

The American Farm Bureau Federation briefly considered purchasing a supermarket chain as a way to improve farm marketing. A study committee headed by Vice President Walter Randolph of Alabama held four meetings in 1965. Former supermarket chain executives and economists were called in as consultants. The idea occurred at the same time AFBF was adding another affiliated company, Safemark, to sell tires and batteries. The addition of a supermarket operation probably carried too much financial risk, and the committee's recommendation was to give greater emphasis to foreign trade instead.[7]

As inflationary pressures grew in the 1960s, AFBF President Shuman blamed President Johnson for making farmers the "whipping boy" for inflation instead of rightly blaming Johnson's War on Poverty and the Vietnam War. Farm Bureau also publicized the fact that the Defense Department had quietly cut the military's pork ration, especially bacon. *Farm Bureau News* ran the headline, "Shuman Charges Administration Uses Diet of GIs To Control Farm Prices." The military also got less canned fruits, tomatoes, and corn.[8]

President Johnson handed the Vietnam War and the inflation baton off to President Nixon after Sen. Humphrey was defeated in the 1968 election. Both the president and Vice President Spiro Agnew spoke to the 1969 AFBF annual meeting in Washington, their first year in office and AFBF's fiftieth anniversary. Nixon had spoken to AFBF before as vice president and was warmly received at the general session. It can be said that Nixon never forgot a friend or an enemy during his political career, and Farm Bureau was remembered as a friend. After he lost to Kennedy in 1960 and was defeated for governor of California in 1962, Nixon was invited to speak at the 1966 AFBF convention in Las Vegas. The president remembered it on stage at the fiftieth anniversary, and said he appreciated that last invitation most of all.

In 1971, the American Farm Bureau Federation decided that inflation control should be a major economic goal. "Inflation is a serious threat to economic stability. Excessive government spending is the basic cause of our current problem of inflation. Deficit spending by the federal government and policies which expand the supply of money and credit faster than production clearly lead to inflation," stated the policy resolution.[9]

In August 1971, President Nixon ordered a ninety-day freeze on wages, prices, salaries, and rents. Farm Bureau thought the freeze might have helpful "short-term psychological effects" but would do little about the root causes of the problem.[10] After the ninety-day freeze, Nixon rolled out a Cost of Living Council, Pay Board, and Price Commission to oversee a price stabilization program. AFBF was represented on the Cost of Living Council and organized labor on the Pay Board until it walked out in protest.

The AFL–CIO complained loudly about retail food prices and said the American public was being gouged at the supermarket and squeezed in the paycheck. Farm Bureau beat back any ideas that farmers were responsible for high food prices, as did Nixon himself. He said it would be a mistake to "make the farmer the scapegoat for high meat and food prices" and cited a Cost of Living Council survey that found a widening of the farm-to-retail price spread. Treasury Secretary John Connally summoned supermarket executives to Washington to explain why.

Nixon wage and price controls went through four phases and nearly 1,000 days before they were lifted for the most part in April 1974. Price controls were placed on a number of food products (beef, pork, and lamb included) but after the first point of sale. Thus the controls applied after the producer sold the product, affecting markups and profit margins for processors, wholesalers, and supermarkets. Of course, farmers figured price controls would work their way back to them anyway in the form of lower prices. AFBF held news conferences in New York and other major metropolitan areas where President Bill Kuhfuss warned that price ceilings on meat could lead to empty supermarket meat counters and black markets. AFL–CIO leader George Meany wasn't happy with just price ceilings; he wanted meat prices rolled back.

Price ceilings on meat also failed to quell a consumer revolt. Food prices rose at an annual rate of 8.8 percent from 1970 to 1975. This time the revolt was louder and more widespread than the one in the mid-1960s. A group called FIT (Fight Inflation Together) was organized in 1973 by three Los Angeles women. Before long it had affiliates in forty-six states. "Deplete Meat Until Prices We Beat" was their awkward slogan. Other groups were SCRIMP (Save Cash, Reduce Immediately Meat Prices) in Delaware, and LAMP (Ladies Against Meat Prices) in Boston.

AFBF responded with an "Operation Food Price Facts," a public-information campaign at all levels of the organization. Farm Bureau spokesmen were on the air waves across the country reassuring upset housewives.[11] At a Chicago news conference, Harold Steele, president of the Illinois Farm Bureau, said, "The homemaker will get better meat and better prices if she is willing to let the competitive enterprise system work."[12]

Farm Bureau also sampled public opinion about food prices in 1973, its first public polling effort. The survey by Leo J. Shapiro and Associates confirmed that the public was not blaming farmers for higher food bills. Two-thirds of those surveyed wanted supermarket profits limited. In contrast, more than two-thirds opposed the same treatment for farmers. Shapiro discovered that one reason consumers complained so much about food prices was that they usually bought food daily and paid cash.[13]

The Soviet Union had its own consumer problems in the early 1970s. Russian food production fell short of five-year plans, and food riots in Poland around the Christmas of 1970 shook Soviet leaders who worried about the restiveness of Russian consumers. In the spring of 1971, AFBF chief economist Gene Hamilton visited farms in the Soviet Union while attending a conference of agricultural economists at Minsk. Russian economists argued that collective farms were necessary to move the Soviet republic from a peasant-type of agriculture to a modern, mechanized, scientific agriculture. Hamilton got to visit a few of the farms with fellow economists, but the Russians wouldn't let him wander around. He reported seeing "non-descript cattle" and fields where grain and flax were still shocked by hand.[14]

The USSR entered the U.S. grain market in 1971 to purchase feed grains. They had waited so long because of cargo preference requirements attached to the 1963 purchase. Fifty percent of the grain had to be shipped on U.S. flag vessels, a costly means of transportation. AFBF asked President Nixon to stop the maritime unions from interfering with commercial exports and making foreign policy. The president finally cut a deal to revitalize the nation's merchant marine in return for labor's agreement to load the grain.

The 1971 sale of two million tons of corn, 600,000 tons of barley, and 300,000 tons of oats was the first of a series of Soviet grain purchases over the next decade to expand meat production and make up for harvest shortfalls caused by drought, winter freeze, or other problems. Later that year there was a changing of the guard at USDA. Clifford Hardin retired and was replaced by Dr. Earl Butz, perhaps the most colorful and outspoken champion of American agriculture ever to hold the Cabinet post.

Butz' appointment was solidly endorsed by the AFBF board of directors, and his first major address was at the 1971 AFBF annual meeting in Chicago. The former Purdue University dean and agricultural economist spoke for little more than a half hour to the general session of 6,700 farmers, who interrupted him twenty times for applause. "I am for farmers, and I want to state that without equivocation. We've got a great story to tell and we're going to tell it," said Butz.[15]

In July 1972, a blockbuster grain deal with the Soviet Union was announced by Nixon press secretary Ron Ziegler at the Western White House in San Clemente, California. In the largest, long-term grain sale ever negotiated between two countries, the Soviet Union agreed to purchase twenty million tons of grain valued at $750 million over three years starting in August. Credit terms were offered for purchases of wheat, corn, barley, sorghum, rye, and oats. President Nixon termed the sale "very important" in establishing commercial relations between Washington and Moscow.[16]

Nixon made historic visits to both Moscow and Peking in 1972, and Butz later confirmed that U.S. farm exports helped thaw relations with America's two powerful adversaries as the Vietnam War was ending. "At that point of course, he [Nixon] was fully aware that the Russians were going to be needing grain and the Chinese were going to be needing grain and one of the reasons we have the new détente with those countries is that they need us. One of the things they need is food," said Butz, who also visited the Soviet Union and held a lengthy meeting with party leader Leonid Brezhnev.[17]

In the summer of 1973, however, the Nixon administration did what up until then was the unthinkable—it clamped export controls on soybeans which had tripled in price from a year earlier to $12 a bushel. The action was taken because of fears that the United States would run out of soybeans before the next harvest began in September. Japanese and European customers were infuriated. The export embargo or moratorium didn't last long but cast doubts on the United States as a reliable supplier; it was later credited with giving rise to the South American soybean industry, which took export sales away from American producers.

At the 1974 AFBF annual meeting in Atlantic City, President Kuhfuss noted a mostly positive balance sheet for agriculture—record net farm income of $25.5 billion and record exports of $17.4 billion. "The new record in U.S. farm exports occurred as the marketplace took over from the political planners world-wide and the needs and demands of overseas consumers and customers were expressed at the market counter," he said.[18]

Around the time of President Nixon's resignation because of the Watergate scandal, Democrats in Congress became convinced that they had found another conspiracy and reviewed the Soviet grain sales. The Senate Permanent Investigations subcommittee headed by Sen. Henry Jackson (D-Washington) skewered Butz for what Jackson termed the "great American grain robbery" pulled off by the Russians and grain export firms. A General Accounting Office (GAO) report, however, found no evidence of excessive profits by any of the grain merchants. USDA's export sales reporting system resulted from the inquiry.[19]

Generally, the Russian grain deals were a blessing to American agriculture and the general economy. They helped balance our nation's trade deficit and relieved perennial farm problems of planting controls, surplus accumulation, and lackluster exports. Rarely though does every sector of the farm economy benefit at the same time. Dairy, poultry, and livestock producers were hurt by soaring feed prices.

But Nixon's moratorium on soybean exports had set a bad precedent for farm policy. Price no longer was the only acceptable way to ration supplies in peacetime. Instead, the government could jump in unexpectedly to halt sales and put a lid on commodity prices. In both 1974 and 1975, President Ford imposed supply–related embargoes on the Soviet Union. In the first instance, sales of 125 million bushels of wheat and corn valued at $500 million were held up pending an evaluation of U.S. crops hurt by a summer drought and early frost. A smaller deal was later concluded, and the Soviet Union made a concession by liberalizing its emigration policy.[20]

The International Longshoremen's Association (ILA) called for a ban on loading grain destined for Soviet ports in the summer of 1975 because of food prices. Their action prompted a sharp retort from Kuhfuss who accused the labor leaders of "dictatorial arrogance" and sabotaging American trade policy. "In denying U.S. farmers access to world markets for their bumper 1975 crops because of a fear of an increase in domestic prices, the AFL-CIO leaders are seeking to divert attention from the higher labor costs which are a major factor in retail food costs," said Kuhfuss. He met with Labor Secretary George Dunlop to get him to use his influence with the unions.[21]

The blunt-talking Meany backed the ILA action and called Soviet grain sales a "rip off" of consumers to achieve a "phony" détente with the Russians. Farm Bureau responded that the ban was a "thinly disguised effort to get special privileges for highly subsidized maritime unions through cargo preference requirements." Major dailies and business journals sided with AFBF. A *Wall Street Journal* editorial accused ILA president Thomas Gleason of piracy and said he should wear an eye-patch and carry a cutlass. On nightly news shows, Kuhfuss labeled the unions' contention that the ILA was protecting consumers "a cruel hoax."[22]

In August, Secretary Butz also called for grain exporters to temporarily hold off on further sales to the Soviet Union to appease labor leaders and buy time for the United States to determine the full extent of Soviet grain requirements. On August 18, the ILA stopped work on several ships in the Gulf of Mexico, but they were quickly ordered back to work by a U.S. District Court judge at Corpus Christi, Texas. AFBF also filed a complaint with the National Labor Relations Board claiming the action was a secondary boycott not permitted under the Taft-Hartley Act.

President Ford extended the temporary embargo until mid–October while a new grain agreement was worked out. The president met with Kuhfuss, but the AFBF leader termed the session "disappointing" in front of reporters at the National Press Club. Farmers did not like the government interference. "It's simply a case of government doing business with other people's property, and we don't like it," said Morris Bowman, Arkansas Farm Bureau president. "The government has no grain. The White House has no grain. The State Department has no grain, and the labor leaders have no grain. Farmers have the grain. It belongs to them. This is clear confiscation."[23]

President Ford was not afraid of public reaction to his pardon of Richard Nixon, nor was he afraid to face Farm Bureau members upset with his embargoes at the 1976 AFBF annual meeting. It was his third appearance at an AFBF annual meeting—as congressman, vice president, and now president, and he was always well-received. As vice president, Ford vigorously defended Nixon at the 1974 annual meeting in Atlantic City. The speech was written for him by Patrick Buchanan.

At the meeting in St. Louis, he defended his own actions. "On two occasions since I became president the government was forced to temporarily restrain farm exports. I recognize that these actions resulted in confusion and concern among farmers." But Ford told Farm Bureau members it could have been worse; that he withstood pressure from Congress to put all agricultural exports in the hands of a government management and control board, an action which he opposed.[24] Ford's appearance had no effect on the anti-embargo policy adopted by AFBF delegates. The resolution simply read, "We oppose any proposal to limit or control exports of U.S. agricultural commodities."[25]

The embargoes of the 1970s were supply embargoes; what came next was a foreign policy-related embargo. President Jimmy Carter embargoed sales of grain to the Soviet Union in January 1980, because of its invasion of Afghanistan. It was labeled a partial embargo because shipments already in the pipeline were allowed to pass through.

Carter's decision caught Farm Bureau leaders by surprise at the AFBF annual meeting in Phoenix. They were informed just before it became public know-ledge. The delegates to the convention adopted an emergency policy and sent it to the White House. "All segments of our nation must share in carrying the brunt of the sacrifices necessary to deal with the current crisis. We urge the president to take the necessary steps to end all cultural and economic contacts with the USSR." Basically, AFBF did not want farmers singled out by the use of food as a weapon.[26]

Couched in terms of national security, the grain embargo was difficult if not impossible for AFBF to oppose. Trade Representative Reuben Askew happened to be a speaker at the convention and appealed to the patriotism of the 8,000 Farm Bureau members in attendance. "Are the sacrifices we are being asked to make too high a price to pay for our national security? Is this too high a price to pay for the preservation of freedom?" Askew asked. He also promised that President Carter would "indemnify" farmers for any losses they would suffer from the suspension of sales. However, President Allan Grant expressed concern that American farmers were asked to bear the brunt of the action.[27]

Robert B. Delano, AFBF vice president from Virginia, was elected president at the Phoenix meeting to replace the retiring Grant. Delano anticipated leaving the convention as president but not with a big problem hanging over his head. The embargo was a particularly bad way to start a new decade in American agriculture. Inflation and tight credit already were impacting farmers and the embargo affecting seventeen million tons of grain took the steam right out of the farm economy.

The Commodity Futures Trading Commission (CFTC), the federal agency that regulates futures trading, ordered the exchanges closed for two days after the embargo announcement. When trading resumed, wheat, corn, and soybean prices all plunged. A key backer of the embargo was Zbigniew Brzezinski, Carter's national security adviser. In private White House discussions, Agriculture Secretary Bob Bergland had opposed it.[28]

AFBF put together a seven-point plan to mitigate the effects of the grain embargo, and the administration was amenable on most points but not the call for a diversion program of eleven million acres, land sufficient to reduce crops by the amount of grain embargoed. Farm Bureau also demanded tough sanctions across the board. Glenn Tussey, assistant director of AFBF's national affairs division, told a Senate subcommittee, "Farm Bureau stresses that an embargo on grain and high technology items and restrictions on fishing rights appears to be an insufficient response to the threat to our national security."[29]

President Carter invited Delano and John Datt, AFBF secretary-administrator, to the White House in February to discuss the embargo. Delano struck up a friendly conversation. He reminded Carter that they were both southerners and farmers—Carter a peanut farmer from Georgia and Delano a corn and soybean farmer from Virginia. Delano had better access to the president than his predecessor Grant who publicly had indicated a preference for Ford.[30]

At the end of March 1980, Delano asked Carter to withdraw the grain embargo. It was proving ineffective against the Soviets who bought at least six million tons of grain elsewhere, and the administration failed to adequately lessen the impact on farmers. Secretary Bergland, got the unenviable job of playing down the Russian market that U.S. farmers were missing. Carter himself telephoned a Farm Bureau meeting in April at Bloomington, Illinois, to talk about administration farm proposals. He said he had sent his "farm wife," Rosalyn, around the country to listen to farmers.[31]

One positive footnote to the embargo was passage of the Biomass Energy and Alcohol Fuels Act of 1980 which sought to open a new outlet for some embargoed grain—the energy market. Delano hailed the agreement for providing incentives and research long needed to direct America toward energy independence and away from dependence on OPEC countries. In 1980, there were over 2,000 service stations selling "gasohol" or ethanol-blended gasoline. Delano visited the Archer Daniels Midland Company's plant in Decatur, Illinois, to support the use of corn-based energy.[32]

Jimmy Carter did not get a chance at a second term, nor did he end his grain embargo. Just before leaving office, he quietly signed the papers to extend it for the next year. High interest rates and the Iranian hostage crisis cost him the election, but in farm country the embargo was a big factor. Delano said Congress and not Carter seemed to be making the decisions and providing the leadership near the end of his term.

Before the election, Carter and his successor Ronald Reagan were given a chance in *Farm Bureau News* to explain their views on export restrictions. Carter said, "We believe a suspension of grain sales is justified only when urgent matters of national security and foreign policy are at stake," which he said was the case with Afghanistan.

Reagan answered, "The Carter embargo on grain and oilseed exports to the Soviet Union has failed to deter Soviet aggression in Afghanistan. This ineffective embargo has damaged the credibility of American farmers as reliable suppliers." On the campaign trail he promised to end the embargo.[33]

Shortly after Reagan was inaugurated, AFBF went to work to get the embargo removed. For a time it looked as though Secretary of State Alexander Haig was standing in the way, and when an article came out in the *Washington Post* saying Reagan was not going to lift the embargo, Delano called James Baker, the White House Chief of Staff. Baker suggested Delano talk to press secretary James Brady who was with the president for a speech at the Washington Hilton Hotel. The date was March 30, 1981, the day the president was shot and Brady seriously wounded by a would-be assassin outside the hotel. Baker later promised Delano that the president would act on the embargo as soon as he got out of the hospital.[34]

In April, at the first meeting with his Cabinet since the attempt on his life, President Reagan announced his decision to lift the embargo which he termed ineffective and harmful to American farmers. The fifteen-month long embargo cost farmers at least $1 billion by AFBF's estimate and undermined the world's trust in America as a food supplier.

Today, farmers are still concerned about embargoes and similar restrictions, such as supply-related stoppages or the use of food as a weapon of diplomacy. AFBF policy in 2008 stated, "The threat of unilateral sanctions or other restrictions adversely affects markets and is an inappropriate tool in the implementation of foreign policy." Delegates also decided that "an embargo should not be declared without the consent of Congress."[35]

Besides the Soviet grain sales, embargoes, and consumerism, the American Farm Bureau Federation faced another issue for the first time in the 1970s: growing concern about the world running out of food. The issue wasn't exactly new. It was the major thesis of English economist and demographer Thomas Robert Malthus in the early nineteenth century. Malthus thought the number of people in the world was limited only by the number that can be fed and any increase in food supply would bring an increase in population. The result was a world always pushing the limits of the food supply and living on the edge of starvation.

Malthusianism returned with books such as *The Population Bomb* by Paul R. Ehrlich in 1968 and the less well-known *Famine 1975* by William and Paul Paddock in 1967. On the eve of the World Food Conference in Rome in 1974, the *New York Times* warned in a headline, "World Food Crisis: Basic Ways of Life Face Upheaval." *Time* magazine drew on the Gospel of Mark for the Rome meeting, starting with, "For nation shall rise against nation . . . and there shall be famines and troubles; these are the beginning of sorrows—Mark 13:8." About the same time, The Club of Rome, a global society and think-tank, published its view on the predicament in *The Limits to Growth*.[36]

The Club of Rome concluded that the limits to growth would be reached within a hundred years unless economic growth and population were brought into global equilibrium, meaning we all got by with less. The Paddocks weren't sure we would get that far. "The timetable of food shortages will vary from nation to nation, but by 1975 sufficiently serious food crises will have broken out in certain of the afflicted countries so the problem will be in full view. The Time of Famines will have begun."[37]

Reflecting the very nature of farmers, the American Farm Bureau Federation was always far more positive about the ability of the world to feed itself. Agriculture was such a miracle that farmers had a tendency to be optimistic about life on this planet. AFBF spread the good news of the Green Revolution and later biotechnology and other signs of hope. After the Rome meeting, AFBF opposed a worldwide grain reserve in a policy resolution adopted at the 1974 annual meeting in Atlantic City. "The best food reserve for America and for the people of the world is the productive capacity of our land and the ability of the American farmer," said the delegates. Instead of a grain reserve, Farm Bureau proposed an international food fund established by affluent countries. They would buy food on the open market and distribute it to needy countries.[38]

Before the Rome food conference, a subcommittee of the House Agriculture Committee issued a portentous statement: "Unless present trends in population growth and food production are significantly altered, a food crisis that will have the potential to affect everyone from every walk of life will hit with more impact than the energy crisis of 1973–74." The demand for food would skyrocket, the statement continued.[39] With a dire warning like that from a credible source, no wonder American farmers bought more land and machinery and began to expand production . . . which set the stage for the worst farm crisis since the Great Depression.

Endnotes

1. "Khrushchev's Iowa Farm Hosts Made Sure He Didn't Go Hungry," *New York Times*, September 24, 1959.

2. Fursenko and Naftali, *Khrushchev's Cold War*, 237.

3. "Soviet Agriculture Is in Virtual Collapse," *Farm Bureau News*, October 21, 1963.

4. "Aid to Peace Seen," *New York Times*, October 10, 1963; Morgan, *Merchants of Grain*, 120.

5. Transcript, AFBF Annual Meeting, December 9–12, 1963, Chicago, Illinois.

6. "Food Boycotts Peril Jobs, Workers Say," *Chicago Tribune*, October 29, 1966.

7. Minutes, AFBF board of directors, September 1965.

8. "Administration Is Making Farmer 'Whipping Boy,'" *Farm Bureau News*, April 18, 1966.

9. *Farm Bureau Policies for 1971*.

10. "Nixon's New Economic Proposals," *Farm Bureau News*, August 23, 1971.

11. "Operation Food Price Facts," *Farm Bureau News*, April 30, 1973.

12. "Steele Explains High Meat Prices," *Farm Bureau News*, March 13, 1972.

13. "What Do Consumers Think," *Farm Bureau News*, December 2, 1974.

14. "Soviet Collectivism," *Farm Bureau News*, June 7, 1971.

15. "Butz Speech to Farm Bureau Brings Cheers," *Chicago Tribune*, December 7, 1971.

16. "U.S., Russia Sign Deal for $750 Million in Grain," *Chicago Tribune*, July 9, 1972.

17. "Butz Links U.S. Grain Sales to Détente With Russia, China," *Chicago Tribune*, April 23, 1973.

18. Transcript, AFBF Annual Meeting, December 14-17, 1974, Atlantic City, New Jersey.

19. "Soviet Wheat Sale Ineptly Managed," *New York Times*, July 29, 1974; "U.S. Agency Finds No Excessive Profit in Soviet Grain Deal," *New York Times*, February 13, 1974.

20. "U.S. Halts 2 Grain Shipments to Soviets," *New York Times*, October 5, 1974; "Soviet Grain Deal Of Smaller Size Approved by U.S.," *New York Times*, October 20, 1974.

21. "Unions' Action to Ban Loading Grain," *Farm Bureau News*, August 11, 1975.

22. "Maritime Unions' Boycott Tactic," *Farm Bureau News*, August 25, 1975.

23. "U.S. Soviet Grain Agreement," *Farm Bureau News*, September 8, 1975; "FBs React," *Farm Bureau News*, October 27, 1975.

24. Transcript, AFBF Annual Meeting, January 5-8, 1976, St. Louis, Missouri.

25. *Farm Bureau Policies for 1977*.

26. "Emergency FB Police for 1980," *Farm Bureau News*, January 14, 1980.

27. Ibid.

28. "How Carter Reached Grain Plan," *Chicago Tribune*, January 9, 1980.

29. "Tougher Sanctions Against Soviets, FB Says," *Farm Bureau News*, January 28, 1980.

30. Interview with Robert B. Delano.

31. "Carter Switches His Tactics as Pressure Builds," *Chicago Tribune,* April 20, 1980.

32. "ADM 'Full Steam Ahead' on Gasohol," *Farm Bureau News*, June 2, 1980.

33. "Carter and Reagan Answer FB Questions," *Farm Bureau News*, October 20, 1980.

34. Interview with Robert B. Delano.

35. *Farm Bureau Policies for 2008.*

36. "World Food Crisis: Basic Ways of Life Face Upheaval," *New York Times,* November 5, 1974; "World Food Crisis," *New York Times,* November 11, 1974.

37. The Club of Rome, *The Limits to Growth,* 24; William and Paul Paddock, *Famine 1975,* 205.

38. "Seek Long Range Solutions to Food Problems," *Farm Bureau News*, September 9, 1974.

39. "House Unit Sees World Famine; Asks Food and Population Action," *New York Times,* October 20, 1974.

18 | The Grape Boycott

"WE USED TO OWN OUR SLAVES, NOW WE RENT THEM," INTONED NEWSMAN EDWARD R. Murrow near the beginning of the CBS News documentary about migrant farm labor, *CBS Reports:* "Harvest of Shame." He attributed the comment to an unnamed grower. First broadcast before Thanksgiving 1960, the documentary was a hatchet job on fruit and vegetable growers who relied on migrant labor at harvest. Interviewed sitting in front of a camera in coat and tie, AFBF President Charles Shuman appeared out of touch with the impoverished lives of the workers shown in the documentary.[1]

AFBF found more than a dozen factual errors, omissions, and biases, but the damage was done. "Harvest of Shame" became one of the most famous documentaries in all of television history, and from then on network television revisited the subject every five or ten years, hoping to find that nothing had changed and portraying field labor as one of the worst jobs imaginable. Ironically, pick-your-own fruit and vegetable operations became popular later, and city people decided it was fun to work in an orchard or field—for a couple hours anyway.

Shuman charged that "Harvest of Shame" was "rigged," and it was. The documentary was the American Farm Bureau Federation's first big brush with "advocacy journalism." The documentary was written and produced to make a case for federal regulation of migratory labor. AFBF supported state regulation of farm labor camps. "Harvest of Shame" also advocated unionization of migrant workers. Murrow supervised the post-production and narrated the documentary but barely left the studio for the filming. David Lowe was the field producer. Shuman admitted he "got took" by CBS, but predicted his bad experience would be of future value in working with the media.

Ed Murrow had grown up on a small farm in the state of Washington near the Canadian border. He apparently did not like farm life and was strongly in favor of labor unions, a combination that did not bode well for his treatment of Farm

Bureau. In *Murrow: His Life and Times,* biographer A. M. Sperber said Murrow was once asked why he was so pro-union and shot back, "Because I hoed corn in a blazing sun."[2]

The migrant workers interviewed by Lowe in the documentary had large families to support with few skills and little education. Unfortunately, they would have been poor under almost any circumstances. The filming took place mostly around Belle Glade, Florida, and along the east coast. At Belle Glade, newly arrived Haitians looking for any kind of work were part of the milieu of the film.[3]

Shuman acknowledged a migrant problem in America, but said it was primarily a social one, and only secondarily a worker-employer relationship problem. AFBF took issue with the wages reported in the documentary. A woman who insisted she earned $1 a day picking beans should have been making 60¢ per hamper and been able to pick two or more hampers an hour.

"Harvest of Shame" left the impression that few regulations governed employment, housing, and transportation of the workers, but Shuman later told a Senate Migratory Labor Subcommittee that twenty-eight states, or almost all the states employing substantial numbers of migrants, had appointed governors' committees to push legislation, appropriations, and administrative actions, and the ICC regulated migrant transportation.[4]

Farm Bureau opposed compulsory unionization of workers and in 1961 warned California farmers that the AFL-CIO was trying to build a base there among farm workers before moving into other states. Unions were a big threat to farmers because unlike a factory that could build up inventory and lock out workers or ride out a strike, a farm could not be closed, especially at harvest time. Farms were incredibly vulnerable to work stoppages. One year later in 1962, Cesar Chavez held the first convention of the National Farm Workers Association (NFWA) at Fresno, California. This was the beginning for Farm Bureau of a long fight to protect growers from unreasonable demands, work stoppages, consumer boycotts, violence, and vandalism that threatened farm businesses.

As leader of the United Farm Workers Union of America (UFW), Chavez became a cultural icon, compared by some to civil rights leader Dr. Martin Luther King, Jr., or India's Mahatma Gandhi. After he died in 1993, he was awarded the Medal of Freedom, the nation's highest civilian honor. Ten years later, the U.S. Postal Service issued a commemorative stamp to "introduce a new generation of Americans to his vital legacy."[5] California declared his birthday, March 31, a state holiday. Hollywood celebrities are spearheading a drive for a national holiday.

The legend of Cesar Chavez—humble leader of Mexican-American farm workers in a struggle for dignity and justice—is secure. One biographer viewed him as a "saintly revolutionary" rather than a union organizer, and new biographies are still being published. There is nothing to be gained from trying to change this image of Chavez as a hero of the Chicano civil rights movement, but Jack Angell, former NBC newsman who was AFBF's communications director for labor issues, has a decidedly different view about Chavez the labor leader. Angell claims he was a failure as an organizer of farm workers, but "a grand success in immortalizing Cesar Chavez." Angell is not alone in his thinking.[6]

Frank Bardacke writing for *The Nation* at the time of Chavez's death in 1993, described the UFW as no longer primarily a farm workers' union, but a fundraising operation run by members of the Chavez family "and using as its political capital Cesar's legend and the warm memories of millions of aging boycotters." Bardacke was a Watsonville, California, community activist and worked for seven years as a lettuce cutter in the Salinas Valley. He faulted Chavez for spending more time on consumer boycotts and publicity gimmicks than organizing farm workers.

Bardacke recalled how Chavez manipulated farm workers to gain public support for the boycotts. In one instance, young, piece-rate lettuce cutters were recruited to spend a weekend in Los Angeles organizing support for the union. They earned good money in the fields and liked to spend it on clothes and cars, but they were told that when they appeared at a press conference they had to wear their work clothes. "The union officials didn't want farm workers to appear as regular working people appealing for solidarity. They had to be poor, suffering, hats in hand, asking for charity. It may have made a good press conference, but the people who told the story were angered and shamed."[7]

From the time the first grape boycott started in 1967 until the last one faded away unnoticed years later, the American Farm Bureau Federation acted as a truth squad to counter propaganda by Chavez and his supporters. It wasn't an easy task. Chavez was a skilled manipulator of public opinion and had a diverse group of powerful friends—Big Labor, Democratic party leaders, Catholic and Protestant clergy, Black Panthers, Students for a Democratic Society (SDS), entertainers, liberal journalists, and others. To top it off, Chavez learned about community organizing and social protest from Fred Ross, a disciple of the master, Saul Alinsky. He was dedicated to the task and very well trained.

There were so many misconceptions about farm labor that Farm Bureau barely knew where to begin. California's farm labor force in the mid-1960s was largely residential; that is they weren't migrants at all. "Most of them were Hispanic, some Filipino. Most of them had families and lived in homes," said Angell. "They sent their kids to high school and in many cases college. Wages in terms of hourly production and piece rates were comparable with business and nonfarm income. They were part of the commerce and public life in places like Delano and Bakersfield and Porterville."[8]

Farmers were exempt from the National Labor Relations Act (NLRA) and therefore not required to recognize and bargain with farm labor unions for the reason stated earlier—they were more vulnerable to work interruptions than any other business. The NLRA, however, prohibited secondary boycotts and provided for secret ballot elections. Chavez made good use of the secondary boycott and abhorred secret ballot elections so the labor act exclusion actually benefited him.

"The cry of *Huelga* went up in 1965 from Mexican-Americans walking off the hot, flat, pesticide-clouded fields around Delano ... " wrote a reporter for the *San Francisco Chronicle*.[9] It was a vivid image if in fact it were true. The strike (*huelga* in Spanish) was not a strike of Mexican-American farm workers. When the NFWA struck Central Valley grape growers at Delano, pickets were brought in from nearby cities. The vast majority of farm workers did not walk off the job despite constant harassment from union sympathizers at the edge of the fields. Organizers also showed up at the homes of farm workers in town and taunted them using bullhorns.[10]

Chavez had little hope of getting the grape pickers to pay dues to join his union because they didn't see a reason for it. Most workers liked the freedom they had to choose where and when to work; they weren't interested in a closed shop or union hiring halls, which they saw as an effort to corral them. The strategy for Chavez and his associates was to compel the growers to sign contracts even if the workers didn't want them, and the way to do this was to bring outside pressure. This led to consumer boycotts of table grapes and lettuce in cities across the country.

The grape boycott was several months old when the 1968 AFBF annual meeting was held in Kansas City, Missouri. Jose Mendoza, leader of the Agricultural Workers Freedom to Work Movement, addressed the crowd of 5,000 and told them that Cesar Chavez was a "phony," who was more interested in organizing a powerful union than helping farm workers. Mendoza led well-attended rallies of grape pickers opposed to the strike in Delano and Bakersfield. After his address, seven California county Farm Bureaus passed out containers of table grapes.[11]

The United Farm Workers Organizing Committee (UFWOC) picketed the Municipal Auditorium where the AFBF convention was held and handed out boycott information. UFWOC was formed in 1966 from a merger of NFWA and the Agricultural Workers Organizing Committee of the AFL-CIO; later it became the UFW. In the convention hall lobby, AFBF passed out anti-boycott literature. Shuman called the anti-boycott campaign a "beef'n," to get the attention of Kansas City news media in a city known for its beefsteaks. A steer was paraded outside the auditorium with a sign on its flank that read, "Grapes Today, Beef Tomorrow." Shuman said farmers were "beefing" about the grape boycott, because if a tiny group can control grapes, then any commodity was vulnerable, including beef, oranges, or pecans.[12]

The consumer boycott was no more a boycott led by consumers than the strike was a strike by farm workers. It was "a political boycott—if indeed it was a boycott at all," said Angell at a horticulture meeting in Washington, D.C., in 1971. He quoted United Auto Workers Union leader Walter Reuther as saying, "We will see that nobody eats grapes in America; we will drive grapes off every table in America." California table grapes were plentiful despite the strike, but consumers weren't always able to buy them. Supermarket chain executives were harassed into taking California grapes off produce counters.[13]

One large Chicago supermarket chain told its customers it was removing table grapes "out of concern for the safety of our customers . . . in the face of threatened disorders." The president of the National Association of Food Chains complained of "accidents" at food warehouses causing destruction of table grape shipments and threats by local union leaders. In some stores on the west coast, the notorious Black Panthers intimidated customers, and the SDS staged sit-ins and threw bleach on grapes. Another tactic was to fill up a shopping cart, leave it at checkout, and walk out.[14]

Representative Bob Mathias (D-California), a U.S. Olympic decathlon champion, was a sharp critic of the boycott. "At stake is the right of the housewife to purchase products she wants, the right of the farmer to market his crop, and the right of the farm worker through secret ballot, to decide for himself whether he wants to join a union." Mathias charged in a letter to the chairman of the House Agriculture Committee that the farm workers union was seeking to destroy these rights.[15]

Farm Bureau worked with the major wholesale produce markets to keep the flow of table grapes moving. In 1970, Farm Bureau also held a sweepstakes for Farm Bureau members who either submitted a grocery receipt for the purchase of grapes or sent in the name of a grocery store where grapes were sold. State Farm Bureaus awarded prizes and winners became eligible for the national grand prize, a Ford pickup truck. This was small potatoes compared to Chavez who received a quarter million dollar grant from the Ford Foundation and thousands of dollars a month from the AFL-CIO. During the grape boycott, one in eight Americans reportedly stopped buying and eating California grapes leading to a 24 percent reduction in per capita consumption.[16]

The boycott was the primary tactic used by Chavez to gain national recognition, but he also went on fasts and organized marches or pilgrimages as he called them. In March 1966, he led a small band of sixty or so strikers on a 340-mile pilgrimage from Delano to the steps of the state capitol in Sacramento. By the time they reached their destination, few of the original strikers were left, but more than a thousand students and other sympathizers joined the procession. Chavez also went on a much-publicized twenty-five-day fast in 1968 to rededicate his movement to nonviolence.

Cesar Chavez preached nonviolence, but at times grape pickers were beaten by union thugs, packing sheds burned, and grapevines destroyed. Cecil Miller,

AFBF vice president from Arizona, accused the farm workers' union of pouring sugar into the fuel tanks of his tractors and trying to kidnap his son.[17] An AFBF staffer was beaten up after leaving a hearing where he testified against the union. Another staffer recalled being followed by a car as he left a farm after dark. He and others had helped the farm family pick grapes.

Chavez came up with a scare campaign to stop the public from buying grapes in the summer of 1969. He claimed that field workers referred to the pesticides used on grapes as "the walking death" and that thousands of farm worker children received medical treatment for illness or skin irritations linked to pesticides. UFWOC told a Senate labor subcommittee in August that two bunches of grapes purchased in Washington, D.C., tested 180 times the allowable limits for the pesticide aldrin.

The next month, another Senate hearing produced a clash between Chavez and Food and Drug Administrator Herbert Ley, Jr., who said grapes tested from the same chain store had no pesticide residues that exceeded safe tolerances. The FDA official raised serious doubts about the original grapes. Senator George Murphy (R–California) accused Chavez of duplicity and trying to frighten the American public.[18]

In 1970, most table-grape growers signed contracts with the UFWOC because of the union's disruption of marketing and its efforts to drive them into bankruptcy. In the fall, Chavez called a national boycott of all iceberg lettuce unless the wrapper carried the union's black Aztec eagle on the wrapper. He sent "a straggling group of field workers" to New York City to press shoppers in Manhattan grocery stores not to buy lettuce. The *New York Times* found it curious that they waved homemade flags sewn in a luxury apartment overlooking Central Park, the field workers' temporary headquarters, the newspaper said.[19] AFBF said the lettuce boycott cost the jobs of thousands of farm workers who already were making $5 to $7 an hour. The boycott was misleading in that most lettuce was grown under union contracts belonging to the International Brotherhood of Teamsters not UFW.

American Farm Bureau Federation along with twelve Arizona grape growers filed an anti-trust suit in 1971. The suit charged that the farm workers union conspired with the AFL-CIO unions representing butchers and retail clerks to deprive Arizona growers of markets for their grapes. Damages of $10 million were sought.

In May 1972, a group of fifteen young pickets representing the UFW picketed outside the AFBF headquarters in Park Ridge, Illinois. Their signs read, "Farm Bureau HATES Farm Workers." Of course, this was not true. Farmers relied on farm workers to harvest crops, and consumers would have less to eat without their labor. Farm Bureau was not anti-union, but it was anti-boycott.

In the same year, AFBF produced its own film about the grape boycott, *The Road to Delano*. Producer Jack Angell wanted the story told in the words of farm workers themselves. A busload of workers from Watsonville was driven to Delano where they talked to grape pickers on camera. The conversations in the film were revealing. Wages were substantially lower in Delano because employers cut back piece rates to meet costs assessed by the union; jobs were harder to find too because growers had turned to crops that required less hand labor, and the workers didn't like the heavy-handedness of the union hiring hall.[20]

At the December 1972 annual meeting in Los Angeles, one of the most unlikely speakers ever to appear at an AFBF convention took the stage, Frank E. Fitzsimmons, the president of the Teamsters Union. The successor to Jimmy Hoffa, Fitzsimmons was inside the convention hall and UFW pickets were outside. Fitzsimmons said that the clergy and do-gooders who promote boycotts at the drop of a hat were actually impeding the farm worker's bid for economic justice and job dignity.[21] In 1973, when the three-year labor contracts with the UFW expired, grape growers signed with the Teamsters, sparking a jurisdictional battle.

In 1975, California enacted a farm labor law to allow farm workers to choose a union or no union through a secret ballot election. Allan Grant, president of the California Farm Bureau, and soon to be AFBF president, hoped it would bring order to unionization and an era of peace to the state's farm fields which had gone through ten years of turmoil. The law also placed a limitation on secondary boycotts.

"Beleaguered U.S. taxpayers are being taken for a ride on a federal gravy train set in motion to provide massive sums of money to Cesar Chavez's United Farm Workers (UFW)," revealed a *Farm Bureau News* story in 1978. Farm Bureau was on to something big. The Community Services Administration (CSA) granted $600,000 to the union to finance a microwave relay system linking twenty UFW field installations with the union headquarters. This grant was made only weeks after the Comprehensive Employment and Training Act (CETA) awarded grants of $805,000 to the union to train microwave technicians. There also was another grant to bolster the UFW credit union. "Mr. Chavez is the first union leader we have heard of who had to have federal funds to build his union," said President Grant who promised AFBF would investigate the circumstances of the government largesse.[22]

The UFW struck vegetable growers in the Imperial Valley in January 1979. Chavez called it a "dream strike" because it was the union's first strike for higher wages and work rule changes, not a strike to win union recognition. For growers it was a nightmare. California Farm Bureau member Jon Vessey lost over $700,000 on lettuce left in the fields and was unable to plant crops of watermelon, sweet corn, and wheat. His total losses were over $1 million.

The strike also became increasingly violent as Chavez's prediction of a quick end proved wrong. Much of the violence was aimed at workers who went back to work or refused to picket. They were terrorized and beaten. Vessey pointed out that the issue was not poverty; Chavez wanted an increase in the base minimum wage but workers already were making $9 to $14 an hour piece rate.[23]

Having had enough of UFW strikes and boycotts, AFBF exercised its own economic leverage. In the summer of 1979, the organization announced it was pulling its scheduled 1982 convention out of San Francisco. The decision was made after the city's board of supervisors voted to support a boycott of iceberg lettuce and Chiquita brand bananas. Chiquita and Sun Harvest lettuce operations had the same parent company. "We regret that we cannot take thousands of farmers, their families and friends to the beautiful city of San Francisco," said President Grant who farmed in northern California.[24] Several years later, Kansas City council members reversed support of a grape boycott under pressure from AFBF.

In 1980, a little more than a year after the revelation of federal grants to the UFW for its microwave relay system, a suit was filed in Washington by a group of farmers and farm workers against three federal agencies to put an end to the unwarranted use of taxpayer funds. The Labor Department, Health, Education and Welfare (HEW) Department, and the CSA were named as defendants. AFBF, California Farm Bureau Federation, and Kern County Farm Bureau joined the suit. AFBF President Delano also asked the secretary of labor to investigate why federal funding of around $235,000 had resulted in the enrollment of only a single member of Chavez's union in an apprenticeship program. Two years later, two affiliates of the UFW were ordered by the Department of Health and Human Services (formerly HEW) to return $423,551 in improperly spent federal grant monies. An additional $255,452 was owed the Department of Labor in disallowed grants.

The Grape Boycott and UFW strikes led by Cesar Chavez were a challenge for Farm Bureau. Chavez had well-connected friends and wealthy contributors. He had a lot of help from clergy who saw him as a devout, humble man, unlike Hoffa, Reuther, or Meany. In his top leadership were savvy lawyers and organizers. American Farm Bureau Federation had to do more than speak for farmers. It had to *speak up* for farmers who were often cast as the bad guys. Perhaps there is justice in the fact that UFW is now just a shell of what it once was, while AFBF is a stronger organization today than it was during the Grape Boycott.

As for migrant workers in Florida, the setting for "Harvest of Shame," the hurricanes that battered the Gulf Coast in 2005 left many of them without work for awhile. There were no sugarcane, vegetables, or citrus to harvest. Migrant camps also were severely damaged. Florida growers, Redlands Christian Migrant

Association, and local communities pitched in to assist several hundred families with groceries and other necessities, and Florida Farm Bureau directed a large portion of money collected through its Hurricane Ag fund to migrant families.[25]

Endnotes

1. *CBS Reports*: "Harvest of Shame," 1960 (DVD), New Video Group, 2005.

2. Sperber, *Murrow: His Life And Times,* 595.

3. Interview with Jack Angell.

4. "AFBF Board Calls Farm Labor Telecast 'Rigged,'" *Farm Bureau News,* January 9, 1961.

5. "Civil Rights Leader Cesar E. Chavez to Be Honored on U.S. Postage Stamp," United States Postal Service news release, March 24, 2003.

6. Interview with Jack Angell.

7. "Cesar's Ghost: Decline and Fall of the U.F.W.," *The Nation,* July 26, 1993.

8. Interview with Jack Angell. Average wages for a migrant farm family in the mid-1960s to early 1970s was around $8,500 according to several sources.

9. Power, Keith (*San Francisco Chronicle* staff), "The Way of Chavez," *Chicago Tribune,* June 7, 1970.

10. de Toledano, *Little Cesar,* 25–30.

11. "Grape Pickers Don't Want Union," *Farm Bureau News,* December 12, 1968.

12. "Farm Leaders Enter Grape Boycott Fight," *Chicago Tribune,* December 9, 1968.

13. "Angell Calls Grape Boycott Political," *Farm Bureau News,* January 5, 1970.

14. "Threatened Disorders in Grape Boycott," *Chicago Tribune,* January 21, 1969; "Shuman Calls on Food Trade to 'Resist' Grape Boycott," *Farm Bureau News,* September 2, 1968.

15. "Mathias Says Jewel 'Combines' with Union in Grape Boycott," *Farm Bureau News,* May 25, 1971.

16. La Botz, *Cesar Chavez and la Causa,* 89.

17. Interview with Cecil Miller, Jr.

18. "Danger of Pesticides of Grapes Disputed," *Chicago Tribune,* September 30, 1969.

19. "Here to Spur Boycott of Lettuce, Farm Workers Urge: Remember the Grape," *New York Times,* October 9, 1970.

20. "Farm Labor Laws," *Chicago Tribune,* February 16, 1972.

21. "Lettuce Boycott Is a Fraud Says Union Leader Fitzsimmons," *Farm Bureau News,* December 18, 1972.

22. "$1.8 Million in Public Funds Granted to Farmworker Union," *Farm Bureau News,* October 23, 1978.

23. "Issue Isn't Poverty!" *Farm Bureau News,* March 5, 1979.

24. "S.F. Dropped as '82 Convention Site," *Farm Bureau News,* September 3, 1979.

25. "Fla. FB Aids Migrants after Hurricanes," *Farm Bureau News,* January 9, 2006.

19 | Big Government

"BIG GOVERNMENT MEANS SMALLER PEOPLE," SAID ALLAN B. KLINE, AFBF'S FIFTH president. No truer words were ever spoken in describing American Farm Bureau Federation feelings about the growth of the federal bureaucracy in the last sixty years of the organization's history. Today, about 20 percent of the labor force in the United States is employed by some level of government, vastly outnumbering the less than 2 percent of the population engaged in agriculture. Farmers needed a voice more than ever as the government assumed a bigger role over their lives and livelihoods.

The American presidents most admired by Farm Bureau during their presidencies were Franklin D. Roosevelt and Ronald Reagan. This may seem strange in a way. While both men were considered great leaders and superb communicators, they shared very different views on the role and responsibilities of the federal government. Perhaps the best way to explain this is that they were both right for their times, at least Farm Bureau thought so. Reagan himself was an admirer of FDR.

The American Farm Bureau Federation decided the New Deal was necessary during the Depression. The help needed to save capitalism and prevent a revolt in farm country was clearly beyond the capacity of the states. But big government proved incompatible with federalism, conservative values, and the entrepreneurial spirit cherished by farmers. Those hopes were manifested later in the Reagan Revolution.

New Deal liberalism was wearing thin on farmers before the end of World War II. In 1942, President Ed O'Neal was a speaker at a Farm Bureau training school in the northeast where the theme was "federal bureaucracy as a menace to agriculture." Farmers said they were "buried" under an avalanche of regulations. Federal spending, taxes and government waste were mounting concerns.[1]

A policy resolution adopted at the 1945 AFBF annual meeting in Chicago called for greater efficiency in government. "Economy in the spending of public money should be emphasized. Only so far as government expenditures are reduced can taxes be reduced over a long period. Now is the time to discontinue unnecessary government agencies and release employees that were added through the necessities of war." Farm Bureau proposed establishment of a bipartisan commission to make recommendations on federal spending and taxes.[2]

As Farm Bureau leaders became more worried about the extent of government control over agriculture and the general economy, *The Road to Serfdom* by economist F. A. Hayek, later a Nobel laureate, was published in 1944. Hayek warned that government central planning leads to the loss of individual freedom. Originally published in Europe, the book became widely acclaimed in this country, especially after *Reader's Digest* printed a condensation that sold 600,000 copies. "When it becomes dominated by a collectivist creed, democracy will inevitably destroy itself," wrote Hayek. "The clash between central planning and democracy arises simply from the fact that the latter is an obstacle to the suppression of freedom which the direction of economic activity requires." He also believed that private property (so important to farmers and ranchers) was a guarantee of liberty for everyone, not just property owners.[3]

Hayek's line of thinking about individual liberty and free-market capitalism versus government authority and socialism influenced Farm Bureau leaders in the Kline-Shuman era and beyond. "The bigger the government gets the more difficult it is for the people to be important, because the government is important," said Kline in his annual address at the 1952 AFBF annual meeting in Seattle. "The more the government takes care of the things that the individual has to do, the less the individual does himself. He just passes over his money. Big Government means smaller people," added Kline. Farm Bureau policy called for greater "self-government," meaning state and local government.[4]

Over the years, Farm Bureau mounted a number of successful attention-getting campaigns to curb federal spending, stop inflation, eliminate estate taxes, and obtain regulatory relief. One of the earliest ones happened sort of by accident. In March 1952, the California Farm Bureau secretary-treasurer, Don McColly, was giving a talk in Santa Clara County on the economy and federal government. "They are taxing the shirts right off our backs and I for one am going to send them mine," said an animated McColly.

The farmers listening to him agreed and said they too would take off their shirts and send them to Washington. The idea was picked up across the West when a bunch of shirtless Farm Bureau men gathered at a radio station to be interviewed on the air. Shirts with letters tucked inside started arriving by mail on Capitol Hill. One letter read, "You are taxing away everything but my shirt now. If you don't stop spending you'll get my shirt too. So here it is, take it now."[5] Typical of many Farm Bureau campaigns, it started at the grassroots level.

Although concerned about a drift toward socialism, American Farm Bureau Federation was not caught up in McCarthyism and the witch hunts for communists in government service during the 1950s. Farm Bureau was suspicious of any politician or leader who resorted to demagoguery or bullying tactics. The organization heard from a number of anti-communist speakers, however. One of the most interesting was Max Eastman, an American supporter of the Bolshevik Revolution who journeyed to Moscow in 1922 and became good friends with Leon Trotsky. He regarded socialism as an experiment to be tried in the United States, but later became an avowed anti-communist because of Stalin's purges, slave labor camps, and the famine in the Ukraine.

Farm Bureau members at the 1955 AFBF annual meeting in Chicago were fascinated by Eastman's insight into communism. He hoped for the day when the Russian people would rise up and overthrow the "Red Empire," sparing the world a terrible, costly war. His writings also influenced a certain Hollywood actor, Ronald Reagan. Eastman was one of the major figures portrayed in the 1981 movie *Reds*.[6]

Deflation had been a chief concern of farmers during the Depression, but in the 1950s, Farm Bureau viewed inflation as a greater enemy. "Historically, farmers have often favored inflationary policies," said AFBF Secretary-Treasurer Roger Fleming to a session of the Joint Economic Committee of the House and Senate, "but the thinking farmer of today knows that policies which destroy the value of the dollar are bad for agriculture."[7] Post-Korean War inflation also led President Shuman to observe, "Many people do not understand, that runaway inflation may result in economic hardships as great as those that come during prolonged deflation." Shuman's words proved prophetic in the decades just ahead.[8]

In Farm Bureau's view, government spending had to be paid for by higher taxes or inflation. Delegates to the 1958 AFBF annual meeting in Washington, D.C., took a firm stand on a balanced budget despite the Russian launch of Sputnik in 1957 and testing of atomic weapons. "It is apparent that current events in the realm of atomic weapons and space experimentation will be used as an excuse for extravagant appropriations and wasteful methods in government," said a policy resolution.[9]

When Dwight Eisenhower ran for president, he had campaigned on the platform of a balanced budget and a reduced role for the federal government, but even the Supreme Allied Commander who engineered D-Day at Normandy couldn't bring that about. President Lyndon Johnson's Great Society and War on Poverty greatly expanded the social welfare role of government, and Richard Nixon followed with environmental laws that resulted in a costly regulatory labyrinth.

By the 1970s, the fears that Farm Bureau held for years about big government were coming true. "The government has become so huge and domineering and we have turned to it so often for the solution of our problems that we have forgotten how much can be accomplished by private enterprise and by men and women who are free to determine their own destinies," said William Simon at the 1975 AFBF annual meeting in New Orleans.[10]

Simon, a former treasury secretary, wrote *A Time for Truth*, a few years later. The book was popular in Farm Bureau circles. In it, Simon warned about the dangerous path the country was headed down. "A nation that decreases its economic freedom *must* be less politically free. And because freedom is a precondition for economic creativity and wealth, that nation *must* grow poorer."[11]

In celebrating the nation's Bicentennial at the 1976 annual meeting in St. Louis, Farm Bureau delegates approved a "new declaration of freedom." They praised the small band of farmers who ignited the spark that led to the Declaration of Independence and reemphasized the belief that government should serve the needs of the people, not be its master. "We have concentrated too much power in the hands of our national government. This concentration of power has led to corruption and abuse, to inefficiency, and to widespread loss of confidence in our representative form of government," read the AFBF declaration.[12]

At the 1978 AFBF annual meeting in Houston, Allan Grant was looking for a dramatic way to illustrate the growth of federal regulations for his annual address to Farm Bureau members. Mel Woell, a public relations staffer and Chuck Fields, from the national affairs staff, came up with the idea of placing two stacks of the *Federal Register* on stage. The *Federal Register* is a daily compilation of proposed and final federal regulations and other regulatory changes and actions.

"Just 15 years ago, in 1963, the total output for the *Federal Register* for that year was about 15,000 pages," said Grant pointing to a stack of documents on the stage floor. He then turned to a larger stack that Woell and Fields were trying to keep from toppling over on them. The stack was balanced against Fields who stood at least 6 foot 6 inches tall. Woell added a few more reams of paper to the stack and it was over Fields' head. Grant went on, "This past year, during 1977, the *Federal Register* published about 65,000 pages. This is more than four times as much as 15 years ago."[13] The *Federal Register* has continued to grow to around 80,000 pages, and Grant, who had a good sense of humor, would today probably call for fewer federal regulations or taller staff members.

An AFBF policy resolution adopted at the 1978 annual meeting said, "The growing number, cost, and power of regulatory agencies is a major threat to the economic well-being and future growth of the country." Farm Bureau labeled federal regulations the fastest growing industry in the United States and took particular aim at agencies like the Occupational Safety and Health Administration (OSHA), which Farm Bureau said was given sweeping mandates and broad authority to pro-tect us from ourselves. Later that year, the Supreme Court ruled that OSHA must stop making safety inspections of farms and businesses without a search warrant. AFBF filed a friend of the court brief in the case that involved a small business.

An OSHA brochure on "Safety with Beef Cattle" was ridiculed by Farm Bureau for assuming farmers and ranchers lacked common sense. Under the heading of "Slippery Floors," the brochure said, "When floors are wet and slip-pery with manure, you can have a bad fall." Under the caption of "Don't Fall," the warning was, "Be careful that you do not fall into manure pits. Put up signs and fences to keep people away. These pits are dangerous."[14] Farm Bureau was instrumental in getting OSHA requirements waived for farms with only a few employees.

Ronald Reagan was not the biggest attraction at the 1979 AFBF annual meeting in Miami Beach; it was Ringling Bros. and Barnum & Bailey Circus. President Grant rode in on an elephant during the circus performance, much to everyone's surprise. Reagan was the convention's keynoter. He lost his 1976 run against Ford for the GOP nomination and was turning sixty-nine-years old in less than a month. He came to the AFBF convention as an ex-actor, former governor, syndicated columnist, and radio commentator—and a terrific public speaker.

The genial Reagan mixed humor—"A government program once started is the nearest thing to eternal life we'll ever see on this earth," with serious commen-tary about the direction of the nation—"Through the bribery inherent in federal grants and regulations spawned by bureaucrats who formed a fourth branch of government . . . we're governed by government employees, who actually deter-mine power to a greater extent than do our elected representatives."[15] Ten months later he announced his run for president.

Ronald Reagan won the support of farmers and ranchers during his eight years in office because he was determined to get the government off their backs. It certainly wasn't because of the farm economy. Although Reagan lifted Carter's grain embargo at Farm Bureau's behest, the farm debt crisis of the 1980s, a strong dollar that retarded farm exports, and a major drought near the end of Reagan's second term were very hard on farmers. But much like FDR, Reagan restored hope to America's farm families that things would get better.

The president outlined his economic recovery plan before a national television audience in February 1981. At its March meeting, the AFBF board of directors solidly endorsed the program, and President Delano told Farm Bureau leaders, "Let's get with it." In an urgent appeal, Delano said, "For two decades, Farm Bureau has said that inflation is our number one problem. Now you have an opportunity to do something about it." The president's proposals to cut personal income tax, accelerate depreciation in business investment, reduce regulation and federal spending, and work with the Federal Reserve Board to stabilize the money supply—all were Farm Bureau goals.[16]

Farm Bureau leaders did "get with it." They sent letters to the president, senators, and congressmen and made phone calls and personal contacts. There was an all-out effort to pass the president's economic recovery plan in Congress. Farm Bureau's "new declaration of freedom" expressed a few years before during the Bicentennial was manifested in the Reagan Revolution. The *New York Times* noted the change taking place. "In 190 days President Reagan has not only wrought a dramatic conservative shift in the nation's economic policies and the role of the Federal Government in American life but has swept to a political mastery of Congress not seen since Lyndon B. Johnson."[17]

Besides reducing tax rates, the 1981 Economic Recovery Act eliminated estate taxes for surviving spouses—the so-called widow's tax. The exemption on estates passing to other heirs was increased from roughly $175,000 to $600,000. Farm Bureau was disappointed that it was not eliminated altogether. President Reagan also fired 11,000 air-traffic controllers in 1981 for an illegal strike, a major blow to the power of labor unions. AFBF wanted to outlaw strikes by vital public servants, including those in the transportation field.

Spending on farm programs rose dramatically during the Reagan years from $11.3 billion in 1981 to $31 billion in 1988, reflecting the farm crisis. Farm Bureau realized it was hypocritical to propose spending cuts for others without agriculture accepting a fair share of cuts. Therefore, it advocated across-the-board cuts or federal budget freezes. Farm Bureau also supported the drive for a Constitutional amendment requiring Congress to operate on a balanced budget each year without deficit spending or increased taxes, except for waivers in extreme emergencies; and it supported an amendment to limit federal spending to a certain percentage of the gross domestic product (GDP).

The early 1980s saw a number of votes in the House and Senate on balanced budget amendments. An amendment introduced by Sen. Strom Thurmond (R–South Carolina) passed the Senate 69 to 31, two votes more than the necessary two-thirds majority. The House vote was 236 to 187, 46 votes short. At the same time, there was a drive to get two-thirds of the states to call for a national convention to amend the Constitution. "This could be our most important farm and ranch project of the decade," said Delano. Farm Bureau members played key roles in a number of states, and by 1984, thirty-two states called for the constitutional convention, just two short of the required number.[18]

AFBF also supported balanced budget legislation proposed by Sen. Phil Gramm (R–Texas), Warren Rudman (R–New Hampshire) and Ernest Hollings (D–South Carolina) in 1985. Signed into law at the end of the year, Gramm-Rudman, as it was known, had a goal of eliminating deficits by the end of the decade, but the deadline was later stretched out.

As far as Farm Bureau was concerned, President Reagan's biggest economic achievement was staying the course on inflation until it was brought under control. Tax cuts advocated by "supply-side" economists also led to economic growth. Reagan was not successful in getting government off people's backs, although he made some progress. Reminiscent of Kline's comments years earlier, Ronald Reagan made government seem a little smaller and citizens a little larger.

Deficit reduction also eluded the Reagan administration. Tax cuts and defense spending outweighed nondefense spending cuts and led to higher annual deficits. AFBF called for a "freeze and fix" as Congress wrestled with the budget at the end of 1987. Tax revenue between 1980 and 1987 had increased 63 percent. Yet, at the same time, federal spending increased 72 percent. President Kleckner attended White House briefings, was active on Capitol Hill, and in meetings with state Farm Bureau presidents to push Farm Bureau's budget plan.

Farm Bureau's outspokenness on the federal budget problem probably helped land it a spot on the National Economic Commission (NEC), a blue-ribbon, bipartisan panel appointed at the end of Reagan's term to study federal deficits during the election year, and to arrive at a solution for the next president. Kleckner joined the prestigious fourteen-member panel that included Washington heavyweights Robert Strauss, Caspar Weinberger, Donald Rumsfeld, Chrysler chairman Lee Iacocca, investment banker Felix Rohatyn, and AFL-CIO president Lane Kirkland. Several congressmen and senators joined them. *Time* magazine labeled the NEC, "Commission Impossible," because its task was to come up with a sound fiscal blueprint for the next administration.[19] In the end that was a pretty accurate description.

Kleckner said it was a relief when his duties on the NEC were over. In all, the commissioners heard testimony from eighty-five witnesses. "I was repeatedly criticized for being 'unreal' in not supporting any of the dozens of tax ideas that were floated," said Kleckner who believed that new taxes would only serve to check economic growth. He also objected to the commission operating in secrecy. No miracle cure was expected from the NEC and none was found after eleven months of work.[20]

President George H. W. Bush made his famous campaign pledge at the 1988 Republican National Convention, and he repeated it in a message sent to the 1989 AFBF annual meeting in San Antonio, Texas. "The leadership shown by your president, Dean Kleckner, and your organization on the no-tax pledge gives me great comfort in knowing that I am not alone when I say, 'Read My Lips, No New Taxes.'" AFBF voting delegates made their own pledge: "We urge the president and Congress to oppose any tax increase as a way to reduce the deficit and balance the budget."[21] Following the convention, Farm Bureau members sent thousands of letters to Congress with the message "No To More Taxes."

President Bush unveiled his legislative program for 1990 at the AFBF annual meeting in Orlando, Florida. He promised 7,000 Farm Bureau members, "Passage of our capital gains proposal, which would apply to the sale of farmland, will be one of our top priorities in this legislative year." He also paid farmers a compliment for having survived the drought and economic hardship of the 1980s. "But you have worked with your minds and your hands with a kind of can-do commitment that's been the hallmark of American farming for generations."[22]

By the end of the year, Bush dropped the fight to cut capital gains taxes and compromised with Democrats in Congress on spending reductions and tax hikes. Included was an increase in the gasoline tax which fell hardest on rural residents who typically drove longer distances. AFBF was skeptical that increased federal revenues would be used to reduce budget deficits. Associate director of the Washington office, Grace Ellen Rice, said, "There is a pattern of congressional history that shows for every dollar that comes in to the Treasury as revenue, Congress spends $1.58."[23]

In 1990, AFBF Executive Director John C. Datt introduced the National Legislative Action Program (NLAP) to enhance the power and influence of AFBF's nearly four million members. NLAP was designed to build upon Farm Bureau's classic grassroots structure that stressed involvement and action. Thousands of Farm Bureau members were enlisted to make effective contacts with members of Congress after receiving NLAP alerts that help was needed. Members were kept informed of the issues through *Farm Bureau News* and telephone hotline updates from the Washington office.

AFBF also began satellite broadcasts of its National Leadership Conferences in the spring of every other year from its television studio in the Park Ridge, Illinois, headquarters. State Farm Bureaus arranged small-dish (Ku-band) television downlinks at restaurants, community colleges, hotels, and members' homes. Satellite broadcasts were infrequent, but Farm Bureau leaders were well-informed through "knees-under-the-table" meetings, *Farm Bureau News*, and Speedline (a Farm Bureau precursor to email).

Bill Clinton was elected president in 1992 and one-fourth of the members of Congress were new. "We might be pleasantly surprised," said Kleckner at the 1993 AFBF annual meeting in Anaheim, California. "We've just completed 12 years under the most philosophically attuned presidents possible, and look where that's gotten us. Congress was a monkey wrench to many of our policy goals." With the administration and majority in Congress from the same party, Farm Bureau looked forward to an end to political gridlock.

Representative Charles Stenholm (D-Texas), a fiscally conservative "Blue Dog Democrat," was a leading advocate for amending the Constitution to balance the budget. Stenholm offered amendments that narrowly failed in 1990 and 1992. He told Farm Bureau at the Anaheim convention that he accepted his role reluctantly because Congress couldn't find the courage "and therefore we need a gun to our head to force us to do that which in our hearts we know we should do."[24]

Farm Bureau made a balanced budget amendment its top legislative priority for the early part of 1994. Representative Stenholm again introduced an amendment in the House with Bob Smith (R-Texas). On the Senate side were Sen. Paul Simon (D-Illinois) and Orrin Hatch (R-Utah). The amendment called for federal spending to be in line with revenues unless a three-fifths vote of the entire Congress agreed on more spending. The same was true for raising the national debt ceiling. The amendment was opposed by President Clinton and fell short by four votes in the Senate and twelve in the House.

Big government had been born in the 73rd Congress and the First Hundred Days of the Roosevelt administration, so Republicans decided to use the first hundred days of the 104th Congress in a dramatic bid to return power to the states and revitalize federalism. Their agenda was the Contract with America authored by Rep. Newt Gingrich (R-Georgia). In the fall of 1994, GOP representatives and congressional candidates assembled on the steps of the Capitol to introduce the contract. The main items were a balanced budget, tax cuts, welfare reform, and term limits for lawmakers. In the November election, Republicans swept to power winning the House for the first time in forty years and taking back the Senate. Gingrich became Speaker of the House.

The American Farm Bureau Federation did not sign on to the Contract with America but supported it on an issue-by-issue basis. The 1995 AFBF annual meeting in St. Louis reflected many of the same themes. Senate Majority Leader Bob Dole (R-Kansas) told the general session audience, "Federalism has given way to paternalism and the results have been disastrous. We're going to dust off the 10th Amendment. What we need to do, regardless of party, is to return power to states and the people." Dole wanted the Senate to address the issue of "unfunded federal mandates."

"An unfunded mandate is quite simply this: a federal or state order for you, or we in the cities, to do something—with the state taxpayers or you the members of the agricultural elite of America paying the bill," said another speaker on the program, Gregory Lashutka, mayor of Columbus, Ohio.

Farm Bureau members were surprised to find someone in the mainstream media who agreed with them on costly government regulations. ABC News "20/20" correspondent John Stossel said reporters were sometimes guilty of sensationalizing problems and calling for extreme solutions like the Superfund law and

Endangered Species Act, which he said were "wasting huge amounts of money on the wrong things and taking your freedom away."[25] By Farm Bureau's calculation, federal regulations were imposing $20 billion a year of costs on farmers.

Approximately one hundred days into the 104th Congress, another rally was held by Republicans to celebrate the Contract with America. Of the ten items on the agenda, two had already passed Congress and were signed into law. One of them was a limit on unfunded mandates. A major tax cut measure also was approved in the House prompting the chairman of the House Ways and Means Committee, Rep. Bill Archer (R-Texas), to declare, "The days of tax and spend are over. The days of smaller government and less taxes are at hand."[26]

Farm Bureau welcomed what it called "new thinking" in Washington. "What is the government's role in solving a particular problem? What level of government is best suited to deal with it? And, who is going to pay for it?" That's what exemplified the new thinking according to Mark Maslyn, deputy director of AFBF's Washington office. The new thinking was not new for Farm Bureau, however. "I think the fact that Farm Bureau members have been promoting our ideas on these issues for the last 20 years or so has a great deal to do with the activity we've seen," said Dick Newpher, executive director of the Washington office.[27]

Of course, slowing the expansion of the federal government was a little like bringing a speeding train to a stop; it takes a lot of track. Farm Bureau hammered hard on tax relief and reform of the tax system and federal entitlements. Success on estate taxes came in 1997 with an increase in the exemption to $1 million. A special family business exemption would raise it to $1.3 million for farmers. The capital gains tax rate also was cut. Farm Bureau also was interested in fundamental tax reform. In testimony before the Senate Small Business Committee, Missouri Farm Bureau President Charles Kruse said, "Farmers and ranchers want a tax system that is easy to comply with, does not distort day-to-day and long term business decisions, and encourages saving and investing."[28]

Farm Bureau's influence in Washington on issues beyond the realm of traditional farm programs undoubtedly was a factor in it being named to *Fortune* magazine's "Power 25," a list of the nation's most powerful lobbying groups. Farm Bureau was ranked seventeenth out of twenty-five and the only agricultural group to make the list in 1997. "When there are 10,000 registered lobbying groups and we're in the top 25, that's pretty good," said Newpher.[29]

In the spring of 2001, over thirty state Farm Bureaus and 3,000 Farm Bureau leaders visited the nation's capital. Many more participated in Farm Bureau's Agricultural Contact Team (FBACT), a successor to NLAP, to express grassroots concern to members of Congress, the White House, and federal agencies. One of the issues they pressed the hardest was total elimination of estate taxes. That June, AFBF won a major victory with passage of a ten-year $1.35 trillion tax cut package that included a phase-out of death taxes over ten years with full repeal in 2010. AFBF President Bob Stallman called it the end of a twenty-five-year battle. He thanked President George W. Bush and said it could not have happened without the efforts of a working farmer in Congress, Sen. Charles Grassley (R–Iowa). Grassley and Sen. Max Baucus (D–Montana) teamed up to write a bipartisan bill. The battle over death taxes was won but the war is not entirely over.

Under current law, estate taxes return to the pre-2002 level in 2011, an exemption of $1 million. Farm Bureau has continued working hard for permanent repeal. "Death should not be a taxable event, and farm heirs should not have to sell land, buildings and equipment to pay this unfair tax, which can be almost half the value of the estate," said Stallman.[30]

The year 2001 will always be a dreadful year in the minds of all Americans; the most shocking occurrence of the new century was the terrorist attacks on September 11 that killed 2,974 people. Obviously, many of the hopes for a smaller, less-obtrusive federal government were dashed over homeland security and the war with Iraq that followed. The federal budget, balanced for a few years under President Clinton, took a big hit with emergency spending for disaster recovery and the war on terrorism. At the 2002 AFBF annual meeting in Reno, Nevada, Stallman paid tribute to two Farm Bureau families who lost loved ones in the terrorist attacks. John Ogonowski of Massachusetts was a pilot and farmer and captained one of the hijacked airliners. Al Marchand of New Mexico was a steward on one of the planes that struck the World Trade Center.[31]

Fortune magazine selected a new "Power 25" in 2001, and AFBF moved up the list to fifteenth among powerful lobbies in Washington. President Stallman gave credit to volunteer members who form the grassroots of the organization. He said that members' abilities to explain Farm Bureau policies and legislative goals frequently trumped campaigns supported by heavily financed opposition. He also praised professional staff for training, informing, and motivating members.[32]

AFBF fiscal policy for 2008 supported a balanced federal budget except in time of war, national emergencies, and natural disasters and called for economic policies that encourage stability, growth, and a high degree of economic prosperity. It also supported fundamental reform in federal entitlement programs and cost-of-living adjustments. Farm Bureau has supported long-term reform of Social Security, the so-called "third rail" of politics, giving Americans a choice of government or private retirement systems.

One of the most prominent economists of the twentieth century, Nobel laureate Milton Friedman, shared the same view of big government as Farm Bureau. The University of Chicago economist was admired and often quoted by Farm Bureau, especially from his book *Freedom to Choose* published in 1980. "Our society is what we make it," said Friedman, who encouraged Americans to choose a society that "preserves and expands human freedom, that keeps government in its place, keeping it our servant and not letting it become our master."[33]

Endnotes

1. "Bureaucracy Seen as Farm Menace," *New York Times*, August 28, 1942.
2. *Resolutions Adopted at 27th Annual Convention* (for 1946).
3. Hayek, *The Road to Serfdom*, 1992 (reprint), 78, 115.
4. Transcript, AFBF Annual Meeting of 1952, Seattle, Washington.
5. "Californians Send Shirts to Congress," *Farm Bureau News,* March 17, 1952.
6. Diggins, *Ronald Reagan: Fate, Freedom and the Making of History*, 95, 107; Transcript, AFBF Annual Meeting, December 13–15, 1955, Chicago, Illinois.
7. "Fleming Tells Congress Why Farmers Fear Inflation," *Farm Bureau News*, February 16, 1959.
8. "'Halt Inflation'—Shuman," *Farm Bureau News*, February 18, 1957.
9. "'Balanced Budget Is Essential,' AFBF Says," *Farm Bureau News*, February 3, 1958.
10. "Simon Denounces Controls in AFBF Speech," *Farm Bureau News*, January 13, 1975.
11. Simon, *A Time for Truth,* 32.
12. "Saluting the Past—Securing the Future; A New Declaration of Freedom," *Farm Bureau News*, January 18, 1976.
13. Transcript, AFBF Annual Meeting, January 9–12, 1978, Houston, Texas.
14. "Pearls of Wisdom from 'Mother' OSHA," *Farm Bureau News*, June 28, 1976.
15. Transcript, AFBF Annual Meeting of 1979, Miami Beach, Florida.
16. "Urgent Message to Farm Bureau Leadership," *Farm Bureau News*, March 23, 1981.
17. "The President Attains Mastery at the Capitol," *New York Times*, July 29, 1981.
18. "States Forcing Congress on Balanced Budget Plan," *Farm Bureau News*, February 22, 1982.
19. "Commission Impossible," *Time*, March 14, 1988.
20. "What the NEC Taught Me," *Farm Bureau News*, April 3, 1989.
21. "Delegates Reaffirm Opposition to Any Tax Increase," *Farm Bureau News*, January 16, 1989; Message From President-Elect Bush," *Farm Bureau News*, January 16, 1989.
22. "Bush Calls Capital Gains Tax Cut 'Top Priority' for 1990," *Farm Bureau News*, January 15, 1990.
23. "Congress Adjourns, Enacts Farm Cuts, New Taxes," *Farm Bureau News*, November 5, 1990.
24. Transcript, AFBF Annual Meeting, January 10–14, 1993, Anaheim, California.
25. "Dole Says New Congress Offers Hope for Farmers, Reporter Says Regulations Hurt More Than They Help," *Farm Bureau News*, January 16, 1995; "Columbus Mayor: Unfunded Mandates Harmful to All," *Farm Bureau News*, January 23, 1995.
26. "Tax-Cutters Finish First," *New York Times*, April 6, 1995.
27. "Regulatory Reform Pendulum Swings," and "Legislative Gains Made in Congress," *Farm Bureau News*, April 17, 1995.

28. "AFBF: Tax Code Still Needs Reform," *Farm Bureau News*, October 27, 1997.

29. "FB Among 'Most Powerful,'" *Farm Bureau News*, December 8, 1997.

30. "Senate Rejects Full Death Tax Repeal," *Farm Bureau News*, June 12, 2006.

31. "Stallman Calls For Farm Bureau Strength, Unity," *Farm Bureau News*, January 21, 2002.

32. "FB Moves Up in Magazine's 'Power 25' Survey," *Farm Bureau News*, June 4, 2001.

33. Milton and Rose Friedman, *Free To Choose*, 37.

One of the first local Farm Bureau meetings in Broome County, New York, was held at the home of county Farm Bureau President James Quinn (on right). County agent John Barron (on left) led a discussion of bovine tuberculosis. (Courtesy of the Division of Rare and Manuscript Collections, Cornell University Library)

"All persons interested in the agricultural prosperity of Broome County" were invited to a big Farm Bureau meeting in 1913, around the time the Broome County Farm Bureau separated from its sponsor, the Binghamton Chamber of Commerce. (Courtesy of the Division of Rare and Manuscript Collections, Cornell University Library)

The first annual meeting of the American Farm Bureau Federation began on November 12, 1919, at the LaSalle Hotel in Chicago.

Automobile pioneer Henry Ford stands alongside a Fordson tractor. Ford had Farm Bureau's support to lease the munitions plants at Muscle Shoals, Alabama, for fertilizer production and hydroelectric power.

President Franklin D. Roosevelt addressed the 1935 AFBF Annual Meeting at the International Amphitheatre in Chicago. A crowd of 19,000 cheered the president for restoring hope to farmers after the Great Depression.

Chicago's opulent Civic Opera House was one of several venues for AFBF conventions in Chicago. The city was the location for more than 30 of 90 AFBF annual meetings starting in 1919.

ALWAYS AT YOUR SERVICE

(Mats of this cut available at $1.00.)

Cartoons by award-winning editorial cartoonist Ferd Himme appeared in the *American Farm Bureau Official News Letter* for several decades; this one in 1938.

Another award-winning cartoonist, Art Wood, created this cartoon for *Farm Bureau News* in 1993. Wood's collection of cartoons and caricatures is housed in the Library of Congress.

Presidents of the American Farm Bureau Federation

James R. Howard, 1919–1922
Marshall County, Iowa

Oscar E. Bradfute, 1922–1925
Green County, Ohio

Sam H. Thompson, 1925–1931
Adams County, Illinois

Edward A. O'Neal, 1931–1947
Lauderdale County, Alabama

Allan B. Kline, 1947–1954
Benton County, Iowa

Charles B. Shuman, 1954–1970
Moultrie County, Illinois

William J. Kuhfuss, 1970–1976
Tazewell County, Illinois

Allan Grant, 1976–1980
Tulare County, California

Robert B. Delano, 1980–1986
Richmond County, Virginia

Dean R. Kleckner, 1986–2000
Floyd County, Iowa

Bob Stallman, 2000–
Colorado County, Texas

American Farm
Board of Directo

American Farm Bureau Federation Board of Directors

Front Row, left to right:

Townsend Kyser, YFR Chair; Terry Gilbert, AFB Women's Leadership
Committee Chair; Barry Bushue, AFBF Vice President, ORFBF; Bob Stalln
AFBF President; Richard Newpher, Executive Vice President; Julie Anna Po
General Counsel and Secretary; C. David Mayfield, Deputy General Cou
Corporate Secretary

2nd Row, left to right:

Philip Nelson, ILFB; Alex Dowse, MAFBF; Mike Spradling, OKFB; David
Winkles, SCFBF; Jerry Newby, ALFF; Alan Foutz, COFB; Wayne Pryor, VA
David Waide, MSFBF; Zippy Duvall, GAFBF

u Federation
icers 2008

ow, left to right:

ie Anderson, LAFBF ; Carl Shaffer, PAFB; Marshall Coyle, KYFB;
ael White, NMFLB; Charles Kruse, MOFBF; Leland Hogan,
F; Keith Olsen, NEFBF; Steve Baccus, KSFB; Kevin Rogers,
F; Richard Nieuwenhuis, NJFB; John Lincoln, NYFB

ow, left to right:

Hoblick, FLFBF; Larry Wooten, NCFBF; Scott VanderWal,
F; Stanley Reed, ARFBF; Lacy Upchurch, TNFBF; Kenneth
chke, TXFB; Doug Mosebar, CFBF; Craig Lang, IAFBF; Bob
son, OHFB

President John F. Kennedy seated in his favorite rocking chair at the White House with AFBF President Charles Shuman (center) and Secretary-Treasurer Roger Fleming (right). They agreed to disagree on government farm policies.

A beaming President Richard M. Nixon helped the American Farm Bureau Federation celebrate its 50th anniversary in Washington D.C. "If I were a farmer in America today, I would be proud of it...and proud because of what you add to America in terms of character and strength," said the president.

President Gerald Ford met backstage with the AFBF board of directors at the St. Louis annual meeting in 1976. Ford addressed the Farm Bureau general session three times—first as Michigan congressman, then as vice president, and finally as president of the United States.

FEDERAL REGISTER
1963...15,000 Pages
1977...65,000 Pages
Up 4 times in 15 years

Farmers were buried under federal regulations starting in the 1970s. To illustrate this point during his annual address in 1978, AFBF President Allan Grant had the tallest member of the staff, 6' 6" Chuck Fields, balance a stack of regulations printed in the *Federal Register*.

President Ronald Reagan and Agriculture Secretary John Block sit on stage at the 1983 AFBF annual meeting in Dallas. Reagan added a little humor to a gloomy outlook for agriculture. He said Block was aging faster than the cheese in government warehouses because of the farm crisis.

"Open markets are the key to our economic future, both for American agriculture and business," said President George H.W. Bush at the 1992 AFBF annual meeting in Kansas City. Bush said he wanted American farmers to get a "fair shot" at trade around the world.

AFBF President Bob Stallman (right) led state Farm Bureau presidents at a White House meeting with President George W. Bush, Agriculture Secretary Ann Veneman, and U.S. Trade Representative Robert Zoellick in July 2001.

The American Farm Bureau Federation is headquartered in Washington D.C. at the Capitol Gallery, 600 Maryland Avenue, S.W. It occupies the top two floors on the right.

A Texas cattle and rice producer, Bob Stallman became the first AFBF president of the 21st century in 2000.

American Farm Bureau Federation officers and department managers for 2009. (left to right) Bob Young; Chief Economist & Director of Economic Analysis; Mark Maslyn, Executive Director Public Policy; Don Lipton, Director, Public Relations; David Conover, Director, Administrative Services; Richard Newpher, Executive Vice President & Treasurer; Bob Stallman, President; Julie Anna Potts, General Counsel & Secretary; Brad Eckart, Director, Organization; C. David Mayfield, Deputy General Counsel & Corporate Secretary; Christy Lilja, Director, Accounting Operations.

Sen. Blanche Lincoln (D-Ark.) received the AFBF Golden Plow Award in 2008 from Arkansas FB President Stanley Reed (left) and Director of Public Policy Mark Maslyn (right). Rep. Kenny Hulshof (R-Mo.) also received a Golden Plow that year, the highest AFBF honor presented to members of Congress for their advocacy on behalf of farmers and ranchers.

Missouri delegates to the 2002 AFBF annual meeting at Reno, Nevada, joined delegates from 49 other states and Puerto Rico in deciding AFBF priorities and policies for the year ahead.

2006 winners of the YF&R Achievement Award, Matt and Kellie Muller of Oklahoma, received the keys to a Dodge truck from Robbyn Shulman of Dodge. They are pictured here with their four children.

AFB Women's Chair Terry Gilbert, Ronald McDonald, and President Stallman passed along food cartons during a national Food Check-Out Day event at New Orleans in 2003. Food and cash donations were made to Ronald McDonald House Charities by Farm Bureaus across the nation.

20 | Sagebrush Rebellion and Endangered Species Act

ONE OF THE BIGGEST CHALLENGES FOR THE AMERICAN FARM BUREAU FEDERATION has been the relentless assault by the government, courts, and activist groups on private property rights. The problem became acute through greater federal regulatory control over farms and businesses and the rise of the environmental movement. Regulations to protect endangered species, wetlands, and coastal zone areas were greatly expanded by loose interpretations of the law, overzealous bureaucrats, and the prodding of environmental groups.

The Sagebrush Rebellion, a 1970s revolt against public lands policy in the West, also was closely associated with the loss of property rights. Federal bureaucrats and environmental activists often showed little regard for the concept of private property. The words of John Adams seemed all but forgotten. "The moment the idea is admitted into society that property is not as sacred as the laws of God, and that there is not a force of law and public justice to protect it, anarchy and tyranny commence."[1]

There are no greater defenders of private property rights than farmers and ranchers, and the organization that speaks for them, the American Farm Bureau Federation. Farmers spend a lifetime building a farm or ranch business, improving the land and conserving natural resources to pass on to the next generation. This is the essence of the family farm system in America, and a loss of property rights is probably the biggest threat to its existence. Private property is a core belief of the AFBF, simply stated as, "Property rights are among the human rights essential to the preservation of individual freedom."[2]

At the time AFBF was formed in 1919, communists in America and Europe wanted to overthrow capitalism and abolish private property, but they never got far with that agenda in this country. During the hard times of the 1920s and 1930s, many farmers lost farms to foreclosure and bankruptcy. Therefore, the struggle to hold on to property became deeply ingrained in modern American farm and ranch families.

After World War II, AFBF voting delegates complained about land acquisitions by the federal government. "The largest possible proportion of the land of the Nation should be held in private ownership and operated by private individuals," said a policy resolution for 1952. "In many cases, the Defense Department has acquired fertile agricultural land when adequate supplies of poor quality land, frequently already owned by the Federal Government, are available," added the resolution.

In addition to the Defense Department, the U.S. Forest Service, U.S. Fish and Wildlife Service, National Park Service, and the Bureau of Land Management (BLM) controlled hundreds of millions of acres in the western United States. In total, the U.S. government's domain amounted to around 726 million acres or one-third of America's 2.315 billion acres, most of it west of the Mississippi River. More than half of the land in the eleven most western states was under federal jurisdiction. In Nevada, the figure was 86 percent, in Idaho and Utah 64 percent.[3]

Livestock grazing had been classified as the "dominant use" on public lands until the early 1960s when the Interior Secretary Stewart Udall in the Kennedy administration introduced the multiple-use concept. Farm Bureau had no problem with giving full consideration to recreation and other uses. AFBF policy in the early 1960s stated unequivocally, "We favor multiple-use of federal lands."[4] Farm Bureau saw a bigger threat to livestock grazing from enactment of the Wilderness Act of 1964. The act contained the poetic description of wilderness as "an area where the earth and community of life are untrammeled by man, where man himself is a visitor who does not remain." Farm Bureau thought the wilderness designation should apply to mountain tops and remote forests and feared that it could be misapplied in the future to get around the multiple-use concept.

Thirty-three state Farm Bureaus were represented by the 145 leaders at an AFBF natural resources conference in March 1964 at Wichita, Kansas. Roger Fleming, AFBF secretary-treasurer, told the group to gear up for natural resource issues with strong state Farm Bureau programs to serve as a "backfire" against the "little step by little step" control by the federal government. Representative Wayne Aspinall (D-Colorado), chairman of the House Interior Committee, also addressed the meeting. He advocated putting some public land on the tax rolls by selling it to private interests.[5]

Aspinall, a powerful member of Congress, felt that conservation was equated with wise use, but President Johnson saw it differently. In a special message to Congress in 1965, the president called for a "new conservation" based on preservation of beauty.[6]

Johnson focused on blight, pollution, and congestion which essentially were eastern problems. Preservation, instead of traditional conservation, raised red flags among commodity users in the West, because it was interpreted to mean virtually no use of public lands. The West was interested in resource development and economic growth.

The preservation concept brought back bad memories of nineteenth century sectionalism when wealthy eastern interests plotted to overturn the grazing and water rights of the small stockmen and lock up natural resources for themselves in the forest reserves. Even the Homestead Act with its small 160 acre parcels of land had been shaped by eastern congressmen who did not want homesteaders to acquire so much land that they would become politically or economically powerful.[7]

The redefinition of conservation to include preservation and the ascendancy of the environmental movement spelled trouble. They meant that preservation values would receive greater attention by federal land managers. In addition, a 1974 court decision in a lawsuit brought by the Natural Resources Defense Council (NRDC) ordered the BLM to prepare a series of environmental impact statements reviewing the whole grazing program. No matter how long their families had been on the range, ranchers sensed a danger of being pushed off.[8]

Allan Grant became the first westerner to serve as president of the American Farm Bureau in 1976, which by coincidence was near the start of the Sagebrush Rebellion, a revolt by those states west of the 100th meridian against federal domination of land and water resources. Ranchers were among the leaders of the rebellion that included miners, loggers, and other traditional users.

"Suddenly, the Old West has become the Angry West, a region racked by an increasingly bitter sense of isolation and political alienation," said *Newsweek* magazine which made the Sagebrush Rebellion its cover story. "More and more, Westerners complain that a powerful absentee landlord, the Federal government is regulating them to death, that a Congress dominated by Eastern interests is riding roughshod over their views on land and water."[9]

In 1976, Congress passed the National Forest Management Act to strengthen the authority of the Forest Service over the national forests. The Federal Land Policy Management Act (FLMPA) also was passed by Congress the same year to give the BLM a formal mandate for the multiple-use concept of land management. The law was a result of a bipartisan review of public land policy that began in 1964.

FLMPA also declared that public domain lands would remain in federal ownership unless disposal of a particular parcel was in the public interest. This decision provided impetus for the Sagebrush Rebellion and was contrary to Farm Bureau's own policy adopted for 1976. "The public land states are, in effect, owned in part by the federal government. The federal government should grant the public land states equality of statehood by transferring ownership of all lands under the current management of the Bureau of Land Management to the states in which such lands are located."[10]

Not only was the West not about to get its land back, but its water was in dispute too. A federal appeals court in San Francisco ordered the Interior Department to enforce the Reclamation Act of 1902. The law authorized the building of irrigation projects to develop the West but stipulated that farms receiving the water be limited to 160 acres per family member, and the family had to live on the land. These provisions aided settlement but were quickly forgotten and not enforced. A small acreage was no longer suitable for irrigated farming, and AFBF and the California Farm Bureau filed suit in November 1977 to stop the breakup of farms required by the court ruling. The issue made its way to the Supreme Court while Congress worked to change the original law.

When Jimmy Carter became president in 1977, western anger boiled over. Carter had a hit list of water projects that he considered pork barrel spending, while at the same time he wanted to extract energy from the West through synthetic-fuels development. He also wanted to locate the MX intercontinental ballistic missile system in a couple of the western states. The gigantic project would have placed missiles on a circular railroad track and moved them to escape Soviet detection. There were mixed opinions on what this would do to the West besides making it a bigger target. Carter also imposed a fifty-five mile-per-hour speed limit on the nation's highways to conserve gasoline, which more severely impacted rural states with long stretches of open road.

Starting in 1971, the Forest Service began a study of roadless areas within its purview for further additions to the nation's wilderness inventory. The first Roadless Area Review and Evaluation (RARE) became embroiled in a lawsuit brought by the Sierra Club. RARE II, begun during the Carter administration, considered the fate of sixty million acres of land and pitted environmentalists against multiple-use advocates that included the Farm Bureau. In February 1979, AFBF held meetings in Denver and Washington to plan strategy to oppose further wilderness lock-ups.

The cavalier treatment accorded the public lands states by the Carter administration and Congress touched off the Sagebrush Rebellion. According to R. McGregor Cawley, author of *Federal Land Western Anger*, the first rebel shot was a bill in the Nevada legislature in 1979 asserting the state's authority over forty-eight million acres of land managed by the BLM, roughly 80 percent of Nevada. Wyoming went a step further and also laid claim to Forest Service lands within its borders. Other states considered or took similar action.[11] The rest of the nation had no idea that the federal government controlled so much land in western states, a unique situation forced on them by Congress in return for statehood.

Don Rawlins, director of the AFBF Natural and Environmental Resources Division, thought the Sagebrush Rebellion was an idea whose time had come. "Transferring public lands to the states and preventing the unnecessary purchase of land by the federal government will place the control of vast natural resources closer to the people who are best able to manage and develop them," he said.[12] That was a key and compelling argument, that public lands should be managed by state and local government, not Washington bureaucrats.

The Sagebrush Rebellion became less rebellious after Ronald Reagan became president in 1981. The former California governor declared that he too was a Sagebrush rebel and slowed the pace of wilderness legislation. Reagan appointed James G. Watt as Secretary of the Interior, a key member of his crusade against onerous government regulation. Watt had founded Mountain States Legal Foundation, a public interest law firm involved in property rights and public lands cases.

Watt quickly became a lightning rod for criticism from environmental groups who considered him pro-development. The secretary did not deny the fact, but called it "orderly development." He told the AFBF national affairs conference in May that the western states contained 50 percent of the nation's coal reserves, 90 percent of uranium reserves, and unknown quantities of oil and gas reserves in the Overthrust Belt of the Rocky Mountain states. He wanted to make more off-shore oil and gas drilling leases available, a move he said that would avert a crash program sometime in the future.[13]

AFBF President Robert Delano praised Watt's idea of "sensible" resource management and said, "I can assure you that Jim Watt does not want to destroy the beauty of America." Watt also had a favorable view of predator control, a big problem for western ranchers.[14] AFBF sued USDA and the Department of Interior in 1980 to force control of coyotes that were decimating the sheep industry. Eight to 10 percent of the lambs were lost each year, mostly to coyotes. President Reagan revoked a ban on the poison Compound 1080 in 1982, and EPA permitted limited use of the coyote killer in sheep collars in 1985.

When state Farm Bureau presidents got together in the summer 1981 for the Council of Presidents meeting, they informally endorsed Watt's call for orderly development and conservation, but James Watt did not last long in the Reagan administration. Watt said a number of things that caused controversy, but his departure was due in part to his entertainment preferences. Watt did not like the Beach Boys and thought the California singing group would attract undesirable fans to the Washington Mall Fourth of July concert. As Interior Secretary, he cancelled the Beach Boys and substituted Las Vegas entertainer Wayne Newton instead. His action was unforgivable to at least one Beach Boys fan, Nancy Reagan.

In 1987, a public lands advisory committee was appointed to advise the AFBF board of directors. All of the members used public lands in their farming and ranching operations. The committee looked at ways to boost the multiple-use concept and educate the public about grazing permits and range management. Environmental hardliners countered with a slogan of "Cattle Free in '93," a goal of removing livestock from the range completely.

The Sagebrush Rebellion was fought to a draw. The western states did not get their land back, and the deep ecologists and other preservationists weren't entirely successful either. Farm Bureau fought hard to keep ranchers on the land. The public relations department produced several documentaries about the value of livestock grazing with help from the Forest Service and BLM. "Keeping the West Wild," "In Harmony with the Range," and "I Belong to the Land" told the rancher's story and countered the philosophy that man was an unwelcome interloper in Nature's plan.

In fact, most of the damage from overgrazing had occurred long ago around the turn of the century. Rangeland science has since made great advancements, and ranchers were able to use scientifically developed grazing systems to manage forage for livestock and wildlife. Farm Bureau helped broaden the public image of the rancher from cowboy to knowledgeable resource manager. In Washington, Farm Bureau thwarted a number of attempts to raise grazing fees to unaffordable levels, and AFBF's Natural and Environmental Resources Department worked closely with the land management agencies to implement new dispute resolution processes.

The Endangered Species Act (ESA) was never meant to apply only to the West, although at times it seemed like that. Nor was it ever meant to be such a nightmare for private property owners. When Richard Nixon signed the law in 1973 it didn't seem like a big deal. He signed a number of bills that day near the end of the year. A job-training bill received most of the attention. The *New York Times* placed the ESA so far down in its story that it was beneath the Lyndon Baines Johnson Memorial grove of trees.[15]

Almost everyone agreed it was a noble cause to protect the American bald eagle, grizzly bear, whooping crane, alligator, and other prominent species from harm and extinction. The eighty-nation International Conference on Endangered Species that met in Washington in 1973 likewise focused on whales, leopards, cheetahs, sea turtles, gorillas—all very recognizable species.

"What they failed to take into account," wrote Rep. Richard Pombo (R-California) of the sponsors of the Endangered Species Act, "was that there were millions of species in the world, including thirty million species of insects, a million and a half of fungi and tens of millions of bacteria."[16] To some environmentalists at least, the underlying goal of the ESA was clearly this: "Save every species, no matter what the cost."[17] If scientific justification was needed it was found in the concept of biodiversity. The philosophical argument was ecocentrism, or the notion that no single organism is any more important than another.

The U.S. Fish and Wildlife Service (USFWS) is given the authority under the law to protect plant and animal species, while marine species such as whales and salmon are the responsibility of the National Marine Fisheries Service. Once a species is listed as "endangered" or "threatened" it cannot be hunted or harassed and its critical habitat cannot be modified. One thing the law accomplished was giving celebrity status to little known species of plants and animals. The first to gain notoriety was the snail darter, a three-inch species of perch that blocked completion of the Tellico Dam project on the Little Tennessee River.

The snail darter made it all the way to the U.S. Supreme Court, which ruled 6 to 3 in favor of the fish in 1978. Chief Justice Warren Burger wrote, "The plain intent of Congress was to halt and reverse the trend toward extinction." In a dissenting opinion, Justice Lewis Powell said the decision meant that federal projects would have to be cancelled if they "threaten some endangered cockroach." The dam was completed, but only after an exemption was made by Congress.[18]

In 1978, AFBF's policy on the Endangered Species Act recommended that listings be based on the actual threat of extinction, not because a particular species was rare or rarely seen. The delegates also said, "The law shall not encroach upon economic agricultural or silvicultural [forestry] practices."[19] Under the law, however, economic factors were not considered when it came to saving a plant or animal.

Later that year when the law was up for renewal in Congress, there was strong debate. Senator Howard Baker (R–Tennessee) pleaded for an infusion of common sense, and Sen. William Scott (R–Virginia) wanted "to have the welfare of man considered along with the welfare of lower animals." Critics agreed with Farm Bureau that the act was focusing on "obscure" species, which was not the original intent. The only significant reform, however, was creation of a cabinet-level committee that could override restrictions on federal projects. It was dubbed the "God Squad" for its presumed power over species.[20]

The "God Squad" was almost never used except in 1992 during the Bush administration when it overrode the northern spotted owl listing allowing federal timber sales on 1,700 acres of old growth forest in the Northwest. Environmental groups took the issue to court to halt the logging, and in 1993, President Clinton permanently put those acres off limits. A billion dollars was earmarked to retrain loggers and help their economically devastated communities. The spotted owl became the poster-child for the Endangered Species Act. Years later, it was discovered that the chain saw may not have been the main threat to the spotted owl after all. A rival, the barred owl, was suspected of attacking spotted owls and driving them off their nests.[21]

While it did not have all the cachet of the spotted owl, the Stephens kangaroo rat, a small, chipmunk-like rodent with an elongated tail, received plenty of media attention. The primary habitat for the endangered rat was an agriculturally rich part of Riverside County, California. The county Farm Bureau hired an environmental manager to sort out the red-tape this created for Farm Bureau members, and an AFBF video crew visited one of the ranching families, Andy and Cindy Domenigoni, to report on their experience.

The U.S. Fish and Wildlife Service ordered the Domenigonis to stop farming approximately 370 acres after kangaroo rat burrows were found on fallow ground that was part of a crop rotation. The fourth-generation farm couple grew wheat, oats, and alfalfa. They told AFBF video producer Mike Orso that the listing cost them $75,000 a year in lost crop revenue, and they still had to pay taxes on the property. Also, a large portion of the farm was placed in a kangaroo rat "study area" by the county government. A USFWS spokesperson acknowledged that harassing or harming the kangaroo rat or its habitat could be punishable by a fine of up to $100,000. By highlighting the kangaroo rat and other examples, like the fairy shrimp in western vernal pools (puddles), AFBF wanted to show lawmakers and the public that the cost of endangered species law should be shared by all the people, not just property owners who happen to have them on their land.[22]

Idaho, rich in fish, wildlife, and agriculture, had one of the most-publicized battles over endangered species, but the creatures caught in the middle of the fight were not any of the majestic ones associated with the West. "You could easily mistake them for pieces of grit, gravel or even grains of sand. It's hard to believe something so small could create such big problems. But some tiny snails are posing a potentially gigantic problem for agriculture in Idaho," wrote Julie Brown for *Farm Bureau News*.[23]

The Fish and Wildlife Service planned to cut off water rights to more than fifty farms and ranches, half of the economic activity in the area, to avoid lowering the level of hot springs where the snails were found. Farmers argued that the springs already were being replenished after a drought. *The Wall Street Journal* said, "It sure would be great if our laws against say, murder and assault, were enforced with the same zeal as the Endangered Species Act." Even long-time supporters of the act in Congress found its enforcement absurd.[24]

The Bruneau snail became such a cause celebré that even Richard Nixon mentioned it in a book he wrote shortly before his death in 1994. The former president who had signed the landmark endangered species law in 1973 recognized that "measures designed to protect endangered species such as bears, wolves and bald eagles are now being used to force Idaho farmers off their land for the sake of the thumbnail-size Bruneau hot springsnail."[25] Clearly, he did not agree.

Farm Bureau and other litigants scored a first-of-its-kind victory in 1994 when a federal judge overturned the listing of the Bruneau snail. Judge Harold Ryan criticized the USFWS for withholding scientific data and having its mind made up about listing the snail from the very beginning. "One of the problems with the Endangered Species Act is the lack of minimum scientific criteria in decision-making," said AFBF assistant counsel Rick Krause. "Species are listed on the basis of little or no scientific evidence." Government studies were usually done by those interested in listing a species, and Farm Bureau believed the results were slanted.[26]

The Endangered Species Act became known as the "pit bull" of environmental law. It had many unintended and adverse consequences and turned rural landowners against habitat preservation in the 1990s. "Cone's Folly" was one of the examples often referred to by Farm Bureau. In the 1930s, Ben Cone, Sr., purchased 7,200 acres of deforested wasteland in North Carolina. His friends did not think much of the purchase and labeled it "Cone's Folly." But the elder Cone and his son, Ben, Jr., applied the best silviculture practices to bring the land back as a well-managed tree farm. Cone's stewardship attracted deer, wild turkeys, and many bird species, including the red-cockaded woodpecker, an endangered species. In 1991, the Fish and Wildlife Service stopped Cone from harvesting trees on 1,560 acres of the property inhabited by twenty-nine woodpeckers. He received no compensation for the property and had to continue paying taxes on it. "Cone's Folly" took on a new meaning.[27]

One of the biggest cases the American Farm Bureau Federation got involved with was the government's introduction of gray wolves to the Yellowstone area. Although wolves have been called "nature's street gangs," their image had been recast by wildlife publications and documentaries. To the armchair naturalist in the East, the introduction of the wolf in somebody else's backyard seemed like a great idea. Pro-wolf forces argued that wolves were almost like dogs, but farmers and ranchers knew better. They had legitimate concerns about livestock depredation. The coyote already was a problem for cattlemen and sheep herders, but wolves are larger, more cunning and fierce.

At a Fish and Wildlife Service hearing on a draft plan for wolf relocation in October 1993, AFBF director of governmental relations, Jon Doggett, argued that the wolves had little to do with the Endangered Species Act or extinction. The wolf was not threatened with survival; there were tens of thousands of them in Canada, and thousands more in Alaska and across the northern United States. A few wolves already ranged into Montana. But Doggett argued that the gray wolf was not the same wolf that once inhabited Yellowstone, and there was nothing in the ESA to allow introduction of a listed species into an area outside of its historic range. He also pointed out that less than half of the people in the states affected wanted wolves; opposition was even stronger in the areas most affected.[28]

Nevertheless, the final rules for introducing wolves to Yellowstone and central Idaho were published in the *Federal Register* in November 1994. A few days later the American Farm Bureau Federation and the Farm Bureaus of Montana, Wyoming, and Idaho filed suit. In January 1995, a judge denied the request for a preliminary injunction to halt the relocation of thirty Canadian wolves. Senator Conrad Burns (R–Montana) asked Interior Secretary Bruce Babbitt to hold off until the legal issues could be settled, but Babbitt ignored his letter.[29]

As the wolves were being transported, however, Farm Bureau won a temporary stay from an appellate court, and they had to remain in their transportation crates until the order was lifted. Babbitt was furious. He accused Farm Bureau of trying to confine them to their "coffins." AFBF fired back that the Interior Department knew of the court action and should not have loaded the wolves.[30] Babbitt, who later sought the Democratic nomination for president, did not want to miss a great publicity opportunity. Later he recalled, "I was there on that day, knee-deep in the snow, because I had been given the honor of carrying the first wolves back into that landscape . . . I was there to restore the natural cycle."[31]

Arrayed against Farm Bureau in the fight were the Defenders of Wildlife, the Wolf Fund, National Wildlife Federation, and other wolf, wildlife, and environmental groups. In writing about the pro-wolf movement, author Thomas McNamee said it had "the romantic mass appeal of the civil rights and anti-war days of the sixties and early seventies. It was chic, it was exciting, it was time, it was *right*."[32]

It also was wrong. The Gray Wolf Reintroduction Program was declared illegal in December 1997 by district court Judge William Downes at Cheyenne, Wyoming, and he ordered the wolves' removal. The introduction of an experimental/nonresident population of wolves came under an amendment to the Endangered Species Act, but the judge ruled that the imported wolves could not be placed where they might endanger naturally occurring wolves already in the area.

Wildlife groups immediately raised public alarm about the fate of the wolves that the government so hurriedly brought in. The pro-wolf forces claimed the wolves would have to be rounded up and killed, but that was never Farm Bureau's intention. AFBF wanted them returned to Canada. The judge later clarified his order; the wolves were to be humanely captured and removed from the Yellowstone area.

Defenders of Wildlife brought a tamed wolf to Albuquerque, New Mexico, during the 1999 AFBF annual meeting and held a news conference at a local hotel. Admittedly, Farm Bureau's effort to keep wolves out of Yellowstone was a great fund-raising opportunity for Defenders of Wildlife, the National Wildlife Federation, and other groups. The *Wall Street Journal* labeled the ESA "The Emotional Species Act," and that was certainly true.[33] AFBF received a lot of negative mail about the wolf case but felt it had to stand up for the interests of its rancher members.

The 10th Circuit Court of Appeals in Denver overruled the eviction notice of the Wyoming judge in 2000, and the wolves got to stay. The gray wolf population in Idaho, Montana, and Wyoming reached over 1,500 in 2008. They have greatly reduced the elk and deer population in addition to killing livestock. Their diet has consisted of elk, coyotes, and livestock. Ranchers are reimbursed by wildlife groups for sheep and cattle losses if they are well-documented.

In 2002, the Forest Service admitted that several of its employees, including three biologists, working in northwest Washington "planted" false samples of fur from the threatened Canadian lynx. The false samples were submitted as part of an ESA survey affecting a number of states. This and other incidents have undermined farmer and rancher confidence in ESA data and land use restrictions resulting from them. Even if the evidence had not been tampered with, the conclusions often were suspect. "If all you had was a masters student, for example, saying a species was declining because he hasn't seen it where it normally is, that could be the best science available to make a listing," said Richard Krause, AFBF senior director of regulatory relations.[34]

Reforming the Endangered Species Act has been a priority of the American Farm Bureau Federation. A bipartisan House bill supported by Farm Bureau was passed in 2005, but went no further. "The current federal ESA must be amended and updated to accommodate the needs of both endangered and threatened species and humans with complete respect for private property rights within the framework of the United States Constitution," stated Farm Bureau policy in 2008.[35]

AFBF has long believed that incentives to private landowners and public land users will work better in protecting threatened and endangered species than restrictions and penalties and the good news is that environmental groups and the federal bureaucracy are coming around to this point of view. In the West, the Sagebrush Rebellion rode off, but its mark of good stewardship and multiple-use of public lands remains.

Endnotes

1. Adams, *Defence of the Constitutions of the Government of the United States,* text available online, www.constitution.org/jadams/john_adams.htm.
2. *Farm Bureau Policies for 2008.*
3. Pombo and Farah, *This Land Is Our Land,* 79.
4. *Farm Bureau Policies for 1963.*
5. "33 State FBs Are Represented at Natural Resources Conference," *Farm Bureau News,* March 30, 1964.
6. "Johnson Calls for Beautiful America," *Chicago Tribune,* February 9, 1965.
7. Hage, *Storm Over Rangelands,* 53–69.
8. Cawley, *Federal Land Western Anger,* 33.

9. "The Angry West vs. The Rest," *Newsweek*, September 17, 1979.

10. AFBF Policy Resolutions for 1976, adopted January 8, 1976 at St. Louis, Missouri.

11. Ibid., 1.

12. "An Idea Whose Time Is Now," *Farm Bureau News*, July 20, 1981.

13. "Watt: Orderly Resource Development Now," *Farm Bureau News*, May 25, 1981.

14. "Watt's Policies Called 'Sensible' Resource Management," *Farm Bureau News*, August 24, 1981.

15. "President Signs Manpower Bill," *New York Times*, December 29, 1973.

16. Pombo and Farah, *This Land Is Our Land*, 34–35.

17. Mann and Plummer, *Noah's Choice*, 215.

18. "Fishy Reprieve," *Time*, June 26, 1978.

19. AFBF Policy Resolutions for 1978.

20. "Endangered Species Measure Survives Attack in Senate, *Washington Post*, July 19, 1978; "Senate Defeats Drastic Changes in the Endangered Species Law," *New York Times*, July 19, 1978.

21. "One for the Loggers," *Time*, May 25, 1992; "The Owl and the Forest," *New York Times*, August 5, 2007.

22. "Species Law Ties Farm and Ranch Families in Red Tape," *Farm Bureau News*, July 27, 1992.

23. "Tiny Snails Pose Big Problems for Idaho Agriculture," *Farm Bureau News*, January 11, 1993.

24. "The Emotional Species Act," *The Wall Street Journal*, November 2, 1993.

25. "Endangered Snails Still Declining," AP story in *Deseret News*, Salt Lake City, January 1, 2007.

26. "Tiny Snails Pose Big Problems," *Farm Bureau News*, January 11, 1993.

27. The Adverse Consequences of the ESA," *Seattle Times*, October 25, 1995; "Extremists Would Punish Farmers' Good Deeds," *Farm Bureau News*, July 26, 2004.

28. "Farm Bureau Urges Further Study on Wolf Introduction," *Farm Bureau News*, October 4, 1993.

29. McNamee, *The Return of the Wolf to Yellowstone*, 48; Phillips and Smith, *The Wolves of Yellowstone*, 21.

30. "FB Continues Legal Battle Over Wolf Introduction Plan," *Farm Bureau News*, January 23, 1995.

31. Phillips and Smith, *The Wolves of Yellowstone*, 52.

32. McNamee, *The Return of the Wolf to Yellowstone*, 39.

33. "The Emotional Species Act," *Wall Street Journal*, November 2, 1993.

34. Interview with Rick Krause.

35. *Farm Bureau Policies for 2008.*

21 | Wetlands and Eminent Domain

IF THE ENDANGERED SPECIES ACT HAD BEEN THE ONLY THREAT TO PRIVATE PROPERTY rights and a farmer's ability to use his land, it would have been trouble enough. But coupled with government regulations to save wetlands and an expansion of the powers of eminent domain for economic development, almost every farmer or rancher faced a taking of property which would diminish its use and value.

Under the Fifth Amendment to the Constitution and the eminent domain or "takings" clause, private property cannot be taken for public use without just compensation by the government. Environmental laws posed an additional problem; they resulted in regulatory takings. University of Chicago law professor, Richard A. Epstein, well-known expert on private property rights, described the difference this way: "A physical taking deprives an owner of the present or future occupation of his property. A regulatory taking leaves an owner's right to the possession of his property untouched, but restricts his ability to use or dispose of it, or both."[1]

The clash between the American Farm Bureau Federation and the environmental movement was not so much over a healthier, cleaner environment and the protection of plant and animal species. "Farm Bureau has a deep and abiding interest in protection of the environment based on philosophical beliefs and practical self-interest," stated a 1978 policy resolution.[2] The differences had more to do with private property rights, the free enterprise system, and the role of the federal government.

According to Walter Rosenbaum, author of *Environmental Politics and Policy,* a clash was inevitable. "In its cultural stance, environmentalism sharply criticizes marketplace economics generally and capitalism particularly, and denigrates the growth ethic, unrestrained technological optimism, and the political structures supporting these cultural traits. Such an attitude places environmentalists on a collision course with dominant American values."[3]

Certainly, private property rights are one of America's most cherished values, and Farm Bureau is committed to defending them. "We oppose any governmental action that infringes on an individual's right to own and manage private property. Any erosion of that right weakens all other rights guaranteed to individuals by the Constitution," declared the AFBF delegate body in 1978.[4] Farm Bureau believed, as did James Madison, that property owners have a natural, fundamental right to use and develop the land so long as there is no harm to others. Obviously, this view clashed with regulatory or partial takings of property, and particularly with ambiguous wetlands regulations and enforcement actions.

From the earliest days, Farm Bureau members were the most progressive, enlightened, and successful farmers. However, soil and water conservation were a learning process for the entire nation. In the mid-nineteenth century, a series of Swamp Land Acts awarded federal land to more than a dozen states that promised to drain it. In the early part of the twentieth century, an organization known as the National Drainage Association promoted draining "swamps and overflowed lands" from Maine to Texas as a stimulus to the economy. Swamps and overflowed lands later became known as wetlands.[5]

Where the White House stands was once a malaria-infested swamp known as "Foggy Bottom." The very thought of draining wetlands today, even for a building housing the chief executive, would bring a collective gasp from a public that once thought it was a pretty good idea. Back then, swamps, marshes, and bogs were considered breeding grounds for disease-carrying mosquitoes. Even in literature, swamps were dark, foreboding places. Today, there is a much better understanding of the functions of true wetlands as natural filters, recharge for aquifers, and habitat for plant and animal species.

The first federal wetlands protection occurred in 1903 when President Teddy Roosevelt established the three-acre Pelican Island Bird Refuge in Florida. In the 1920s, Florida began to protect hundreds of thousands of acres of sawgrass flats, mangrove swamps, and other features of the Florida Everglades. Beginning in the 1930s, the federal government acquired other wetlands that were breeding grounds for migratory birds and waterfowl.

There was no wetlands controversy until after the Clean Water Act (CWA) was passed in 1972. The CWA regulated point-sources of pollution in the waters of the United States with a goal of cleaning up polluted waters by 1985. The law did not even mention wetlands, but Section 404 of the act regulated the discharge of dredged or fill material and created a permitting process administered by the Army Corps of Engineers. The Army Corps confined its application of Section 404 to "navigable" waters, the waters a boat could travel. However, a district court in Washington ruled in 1975 that the Army Corps had to apply its permitting process to the digging-out or filling-in of coastal waters, lakes, streams, wetlands, and flood plains.[6]

The Corps alerted farmers to the implications when it said that federal permits may be required for any farmer "who wants to deepen an irrigation ditch or plow a field" or "the rancher who wants to enlarge his stock pond." The Corps went on to say that millions of people could be subject to enforcement action and harsh penalties. EPA Administrator Russell Train accused the Corps of making false assertions and deliberately confusing farmers.[7] What appeared to be a gross exaggeration really was not.

Farm Bureau hoped to clear up any confusion with a rewrite of the law in 1977. The House passed a version supported by AFBF that limited the Corps' dredge and fill jurisdiction to waters used for interstate and foreign commerce and adjacent wetlands. Senator Lloyd Bentsen (D-Texas) agreed that the permitting process was leading to "federal over-regulation, over-control, cumbersome bureaucratic procedures and a general lack of realism." Senator Ed Muskie (D-Maine) opposed changing the law and said he was tired of picking up newspapers that were critical of Congress' protection of the environment.[8]

A year earlier Muskie, who helped draft the original law, admitted that the Corps created a "permit system we never envisaged, covering activities we never had in mind." This included farming.[9] The Clean Water Act of 1977 did nothing to ease farmers' concerns, and Farm Bureau continued to press for Congress to limit the authority of the Army Corps to the original intent of the law.

A "Swampbuster" provision to the 1985 Farm Bill denied farm program benefits to any farmer who drained a wetland for planting crops. "Sodbuster" similarly prevented the cultivation of highly erodible land. Farm Bureau supported the 1985 Farm Bill which was signed into law at the end of that year. Swampbuster only led to more confusion and differences, particularly in the upper Midwest where retreating glaciers long ago left behind so-called prairie potholes. Some of the indentations on the land, the smallest were around an acre, were unrecognizable from the ground and could only be noticed by flying overhead. Federal jurisdiction over isolated wetlands is still debated today.

Property rights figured in an unprecedented decision by the American Farm Bureau Federation in 1987. William Rehnquist, an advocate of property rights, was nominated by President Reagan to be Chief Justice of the Supreme Court and was affirmed by a vote of the Senate. Antonin Scalia replaced him on the bench. The president then nominated Judge Robert Bork to fill another vacancy on the high court. For the first time ever, the AFBF board of directors endorsed a judicial nominee in Bork, but he was rejected a month later after a fierce battle over his nomination in the Senate.

The wetlands controversy heated up in the late 1980s and early 1990s. One reason was a campaign pledge made by Republican candidate, Vice President George H. W. Bush. "My position on wetlands is straightforward. All existing wetlands, no matter how small, should be preserved," he said.[10] This became interpreted as "no net loss" of wetlands. While Bush's position may have been straightforward, the actual definition of a wetland was anything but clear.

As Bush became president in 1989, a new wetlands delineation manual for use by the federal agencies was issued without public review. The manual conferred protection on land saturated for as little as seven days. It also allowed determination by a federal agency to be made on the basis of two out of three essential criteria—water, soil, and vegetation. The missing criterion could be assumed, whereas in the past, all three needed to be present. Even EPA Administrator William K. Reilly conceded the wetlands criteria were too broad and would interfere with the sale of farmland. One Missouri farmer went to court over a dispute that he said started when a federal agent inspected his property for a minor levee repair along a stream, and mistook heads of grain sorghum for cattails.[11]

In 1990, Farm Bureau testified before Congress, met with administration officials, and warned farmers and ranchers of the consequences of the new delineation manual. Normal farming activities such as plowing, seeding, harvesting, and minor drainage on prior-converted cropland were supposed to be exempt, but appeared to be in jeopardy. Farm Bureau complained that the new rule was "once a wetland always a wetland." The Soil Conservation Service estimated that sixty to seventy million acres of farm fields were subject to Section 404 regulation requiring permits and possible costly mitigation.

A significant victory occurred in September 1990, when the Army Corps notified its field offices that prior-converted cropland would not be subject to regulation. The Corps announcement said, "In most cases, because these areas only minimally meet the hydrology criteria for wetlands, they do not show important wetland values."[12] An SCS study of wetlands losses also revealed far less conversion than environmentalists had been claiming. Wetland losses were roughly 100,000 acres per year in the 1980s, not the 300,000 to 500,000 usually claimed. Of the actual amount, 44,000 acres were on rural land; and some of that had been lost to drought, not conversion to other uses. (In recent years, there has been a net gain in agricultural wetlands.)

The "War Over The Wetlands," as *Time* magazine termed it, was far from over.[13] At the 1991 AFBF annual meeting in Phoenix, wetlands were a major topic of discussion and a number of horror stories about bureaucratic overkill were circulating. Farmers were afraid to clean debris out of ditches for fear any one of four federal agencies with wetlands jurisdiction would find fault. They were the EPA, Army Corps of Engineers, Soil Conservation Service, and Fish and Wildlife Service.

"When a productive corn field, a roadside drainage ditch, or an irrigated semi-arid farm fall under government wetlands mandates, someone's logic has been skewed," said President Dean Kleckner in an op-ed piece for the *Chicago Tribune*. He gave the example of Michael and Torri Schrock, a farm couple from Corvalis,

Oregon, who invested their savings to buy a 116-acre farm. Before purchasing the farm, the SCS told them that two acres of the property were wetlands. Reasoning that they could farm around that, the Schrocks proceeded with their plans. After investing $30,000 in irrigation equipment, they were told by other regulators that the farm actually contained seventy acres of wetlands. Amazingly, the original two were not part of the 70 acres.[14]

"I've always been proud to be an American, but I never thought I would have to fight my government to farm my land," said Michael Schrock at a news conference held by AFBF in Washington. The Shrocks' ordeal was one of 425 similar cases collected by mail from Farm Bureau members. Kleckner and Montana Farm Bureau Federation President Dave McClure took the letters to Washington and delivered them to Sen. Max Baucus (D-Montana), chairman of a Senate subcommittee on environmental protection. Baucus had asked for proof earlier when Kleckner testified before his panel.[15]

After what was termed "months of infighting," the Bush administration reached an agreement in the summer of 1991 that a common sense definition of wetlands was needed. The turnaround was engineered by Vice President Dan Quayle who chaired the administration's Council on Competitiveness. Farm Bureau also was pursuing wetlands legislation. Representative Jimmy Hayes, (D-Louisiana) was one of the primary sponsors. "Federal wetlands law has now become the land management tool for anyone wanting to dictate development across the country," said Hayes.[16]

As soon as the Bush administration endorsed changes to the delineation manual by adding to the "wetness" requirement, a hue and cry went up from the environmental community that claimed millions of acres of wetlands would be lost. Farm Bureau contended that these were merely "paper wetlands" created by the 1989 manual. AFBF went before reporters in Washington to say that "no true wetlands" would be lost and criticized the current policy for creating a refuge around "every mudhole and backyard puddle."[17]

In an open letter to the president and Congress, AFBF urged them to: "Recognize and respect the rights of private citizens who own wetlands, and when those wetlands must be preserved for the public convenience, compensate the landowner as the Constitution requires."[18] Already under criticism for not keeping his tax pledge, President Bush was accused by environmental groups of ducking out on his wetlands pledge. He was in a tough spot and pulled back reluctantly on the decision to change the manual. "We cannot accept standards that are not based on sound science and we cannot shut down the lives of thousands of Americans by going to 'extremes' on environmental policy," he complained.[19]

Meanwhile, Farm Bureau continued to draw attention to silly, capricious and often conflicting rulings from federal agencies. Such was the case with Bill Ellen, a forty-seven-year old environmental consultant who landed in federal prison. "Most of his fellow inmates in the minimum security section are serving time for drug offenses and white collar crimes. Ellen wryly refers to himself as the only 'wetlands filler' among them," wrote *Farm Bureau News* editor Joan Waldoch, who visited Ellen behind bars.[20]

Ellen's conviction was for his involvement in the development of a 3,000 acre hunting preserve and wildlife habitat in Maryland, a place he called a "duck heaven." A lifelong conservationist, Ellen was enhancing the value of wetlands and still ran afoul of the rules and regulations. AFBF said the case represented the shortcomings of current law, with its vague definitions and overlapping regulatory responsibilities. It was the latter that got Ellen in trouble. He had been told one thing by one agency and another thing by a different agency and went ahead with his plans. Ellen served six months in prison and his case got nationwide attention.

Another case involved one of Farm Bureau's state presidents, William Stamp of Rhode Island. AFBF News Service editor Mace Thornton wrote, "A cross-stitched verse hangs from the kitchen wall of Bill and Carol Stamp's modern New England farm home . . . The verse implies: hard work yields rewards; private property extends security to its owner; land empowers the one who works it." Thornton said these truths were being challenged by wetlands regulations and a "merciless bureaucracy."[21] Stamp now grows sweet corn in the southern part of the state and has a retail nursery a few miles from the state capital. Facing urban encroachment, zoning changes, and tax pressures, the Stamps decided to develop one field of their farm. The regulatory tangle they got into over a small, intermittent brook originating from a man-made pond tied up their financial resources and threatened to bankrupt the family.

In 1993, newly elected President Bill Clinton attempted to resolve wetland conflicts. He announced that the SCS would be the lead agency for agricultural wetlands, a move endorsed by AFBF to eliminate the inconsistencies between agencies. Wetlands converted to agricultural use prior to 1985 were exempted from new regulations, and Clinton found a way around the most contentious issue of all, the wetlands delineation manual. His policy called for using the criteria in the original 1987 manual until the National Academy of Sciences reviewed the matter. Environmentalists were not happy with the outcome, except that Clinton also declared millions of acres in Alaska to be protected wetlands.

Whenever the Fifth Amendment comes up in news stories, it is often about someone under investigation invoking his right against self-incrimination, in other words "pleading the Fifth." But in the last twenty years or so there have been a number of property rights cases involving the Fifth Amendment that made headlines because they went all the way to the Supreme Court. In those cases, Farm

Bureau filed *amicus curiae* (friend of the court) briefs in support of the property owners.

One celebrated property rights case began in 1986 when David Lucas purchased two South Carolina beachfront lots for nearly a million dollars. He planned to build two homes, one to live in and the other to sell. Later, South Carolina passed a law banning any new building along the coast and refused to compensate Lucas who was devastated by the decision. Essentially he was left with two worthless lots.

AFBF filed a brief in *Lucas v. South Carolina Coastal Council*, and in 1992, the Supreme Court ruled six to three in his favor. Eventually the state settled with Lucas for his property and resold it after deciding that coastline erosion wasn't such a big problem after all. "The Lucas ruling is a good result," said AFBF General Counsel John Rademacher after the decision, "and gives Farm Bureau members confidence that in the future, government will have to think twice before imposing burdensome regulations on agricultural interests, the costs of which should more equitably be borne by the public."[22]

In 1994, AFBF came to the aid of Florence Dolan in the case of *Dolan v. the City of Tigard*, a classic case of a widow versus city hall. Dolan and her late husband owned a plumbing supply store in Tigard, Oregon, a suburb of Portland. They applied for a permit to double the size of the store and pave a parking lot. In exchange for the permit, city officials demanded the Dolans donate 10 percent of their property for a drainage area, bicycle path, and green space. The Dolans lost the first few rounds of the case in the Oregon courts, but Florence Dolan continued to fight for her land even after her husband lost a battle with cancer. "Tigard can have a bicycle path if they want, but I don't feel that my company should have to pay for the city's bicycle path," she said.[23]

Farm Bureau contended in its brief that a governmental body should not be allowed to evade its constitutional obligation to compensate a landowner when it required a portion of property be set aside as a condition for use of that property. In an editorial, AFBF alluded to the bike path forced upon the Dolans and said the Supreme Court should make the sanctity of property rights secure, "similar to a hardened-steel bike lock."[24]

In June 1994, the Supreme Court decided five to four that the public easement required by Tigard was not justified. Chief Justice Rehnquist wrote in the majority opinion that the requirement was unconstitutional unless the government could show a "rough proportionality" between the easement and harm posed by the development, like traffic congestion or storm runoff. In finding for Dolan, the high court also said, "We can see no reason why the Takings Clause of the Fifth Amendment, as much a part of the Bill of Rights as the First Amendment or the Fourth Amendment, should be relegated to the status of poor relation."[25]

AFBF also was involved in two more recent cases involving partial takings and diminished value of property, *Palazzolo v. Rhode Island* in 2001 and *Tahoe-Sierra Preservation Council, Inc. v. Tahoe Regional Planning Agency* in 2002. Both cases had similarities to the Lucas case. Farm Bureau hailed the Palazzolo decision for reaffirming that landowners are entitled to seek compensation when they are forbidden by government from realizing their property's full potential.

The question of federal jurisdiction over wetlands also came before the Supreme Court. In a 2001 decision involving an Illinois gravel pit that had a small pond at the bottom of it, the court ruled against federal regulation of isolated ponds and ditches. In a 2006 decision in the case of *Rapanos v. United States*, a divided court maintained that the federal government can enforce the Clean Water Act on wetlands within a state if a significant connection exists to a body of water that is actually navigable. An opinion written by Justice Antonin Scalia said the Corps had stretched its authority "beyond parody" by regulating land that contained nothing but storm sewers drainage ditches and "dry arroyos in the middle of the desert."[26]

Farm Bureau had been saying virtually the same thing as Justice Scalia, arguing for clarity and common sense. "The average person expects to see water in a protected wetland. It's a problem when farmers and ranchers have to consult or hire a 'wetland scientist' to determine if they've got a wetland," said Don Parrish, AFBF senior director of regulatory relations.

In June 2005, American Farm Bureau Federation went into high gear after a Supreme Court decision (*Kelo v. New London, Connecticut*). The Court ruled that local governments can seize private property for economic development. AFBF, eighteen state Farm Bureaus, and various other groups filed a friend of the court brief, saying that taking property away from one private landowner and giving it to another, in this case a developer, is not "public use" as required under the Constitution. The victim was homeowner Susette Kelo who bought a run-down Victorian cottage in 1997 and lovingly restored it. The city wanted to bulldoze her property and that of her neighbors to make way for a big commercial and residential development.

Farmers were used to having land condemned under eminent domain for roads, highways, schools, and genuine public use, but the Kelo case was frightening. In a dissent that echoed Farm Bureau's feelings, Justice Sandra Day O'Connor said, "The specter of condemnation hangs over all property. Nothing is to prevent the state from replacing Motel 6 with a Ritz-Carlton, any home with a shopping mall or any farm with a factory."[27]

Shortly after the Kelo decision, AFBF launched the Stop Taking Our Property or STOP campaign. State and county Farm Bureaus used brochures, talking points, and sample letters to the editor developed by AFBF to raise public awareness of the Supreme Court ruling and its impact on property owners. In just a little over a year's time, nine states passed ballot initiatives to limit government eminent domain authority and twenty-five state legislatures passed laws clarifying public use or prohibiting the use of eminent domain for economic development.

"Since the Supreme Court's ruling in *Kelo*, farmers have become vulnerable to the possibility of having their property taken for economic development and open space designations," said President Bob Stallman as AFBF filed a friend of the court brief in 2007. The case involved a New Jersey township that condemned private property for "open space" preservation without going through a public and deliberative process.[28]

No organization in agriculture has taken more action or been more vigilant about private property rights than Farm Bureau, and there is no sign that it can relax any time soon. The 150th anniversary of the Homestead Act of 1862 is very near, and there are proposals to reverse the land act and seize large chunks of private land on the Great Plains for a "Buffalo Commons," essentially a huge park for buffalo. This would take eminent domain to the next level or what proponents are calling a federal deprivatization program and the ultimate national park.

Endnotes

1. Epstein, *Supreme Neglect*, 97.
2. *Farm Bureau Policies for 1978.*
3. Rosenbaum, *Environmental Politics and Policy,* 40.
4. *Farm Bureau Policies for 1978.*
5. "Reclaiming Eastern Lands," *Chicago Tribune*, October 7, 1907.
6. "True to the Corps," *New York Times*, June 16, 1975.
7. Ibid.; "Army Criticized On Dredging Rule," *New York Times*, May 17, 1975.
8. "Dredge and Fill," *Farm Bureau News*, July 18, 1977; "Senate Votes for Retaining Controls on Waterways," *New York Times*, August 15, 1977; "Congress Votes Clean Water Rules," *New York Times*, December 16, 1977.
9. "Ford for Control of All U.S. Waters," *New York Times*, July 29, 1976.
10. "Wetlands Policy Shift," *Washington Post*, August 10, 1991.
11. "Millions of Acres May Lose Designation," *Washington Post,* August 2, 1991; "For Farmers, Wetlands Means a Legal Quagmire," *New York Times*, April 24, 1990.
12. "Cropland Exempted from 404 Wetlands Restrictions," *Farm Bureau News*, October 1, 1990.
13. "War Over the Wetlands," *Time*, August 26, 1991.
14. "Balance Property Rights, Wetland Value," *Chicago Tribune,* August 27, 1991.
15. "Evidence of Wetlands Confusion Presented to Senator," *Farm Bureau News*, July 22, 1991.
16. "FB-Backed Wetlands Bill," *Farm Bureau News*, March 11, 1991.
17. "Changes in Manual Won't Cause Wetlands Losses," *Farm Bureau News*, November 18, 1991.

18. "An Open Letter," *Farm Bureau News*, September 30, 1991.

19. "Bush Says He Seeks Balance on the Environment," *New York Times*, May 31, 1992.

20. "Ellen Case Shows Contentious Issues of Wetlands Debate," *Farm Bureau News*, May 10, 1993.

21. "Farmer in Quagmire of Federal Wetlands Regulations," *Farm Bureau News*, May 27, 1991.

22. "Supreme Court Ruling Favorable for Property Rights," *Farm Bureau News*, July 13, 1992.

23. "It's Oregon Woman vs. City Hall in Property Fight," *Farm Bureau News*, March 21, 1994.

24. "Pedaling away Property Rights," *Farm Bureau News*, February 21, 1994.

25. "Dolan v. City of Tigard; Another Step in the Right Direction," *Environmental Law*, January 1, 1995.

26. "Justices Divided on Protections over Wetlands," *New York Times*, June 20, 2006.

27. "Eminent Domain Project at Standstill Despite Ruling," *New York Times*, November 21, 2005.

28. "Farm Bureau Files Brief in Supreme Court Property Rights Case," AFBF news release, June 11, 2007.

22 | Farm Credit Crisis of the 1980s

Every now and then in the history of American agriculture the cry of "Save the Family Farm" goes up. At no time was this any more the case than during the farm credit crisis of the 1980s. Economic conditions for farmers started deteriorating in the late seventies. When times are good, government farm programs are vilified in the media and farmers themselves are criticized. When times are bad, the media coverage decries the loss of the family farm. The 1980s was the last time agriculture received such widespread media coverage, in good or bad times.

The theme of the 1978 AFBF annual meeting in Houston was "Farmers Speak Through Farm Bureau." Little did anyone in the organization realize that for the next eight or nine years, the American Farm Bureau Federation's role as the Voice of Agriculture would be challenged once more, this time by the American Agriculture Movement (AAM) and other populist groups that sprang up. Protest groups are an agrarian tradition of course, and AAM seemed particularly mindful of the words of the Farmers Alliance leader from Kansas, Mary E. Lease, who exhorted farmers to raise less corn and more hell.

American Agriculture, later the American Agricultural Movement, was spawned in the wheat fields and coffee shops around Springfield, Colorado, to protest rising production costs, low farm prices, and the level of price supports in the 1977 Farm Act. AAM wanted the government to set prices for all farm products at 100 percent of parity. By this time, parity was viewed by farm economists as an obsolete measurement of a farmer's buying power, but AAM found it a useful tool because it meant prices for wheat would have to double to reach full parity.

In his book *Private Interests, Public Policy And American Agriculture,* William Browne said AAM leaders thought the entire agricultural establishment of policymakers and Washington lobbyists was out of touch with conditions on the farm. "The single strategy for ensuring public responsiveness, as they saw politics, was to develop new farm representation through an organization that could express the anger of producers in some dramatic and attention-getting way."[1] The first attention-getting device was the old standard, a farm strike. If Congress did not agree to meet their demands by December 14, 1977, farmers would not plant any crops for 1978.

A farm strike was completely out of character for the American Farm Bureau Federation which took a dim view of any strike, whether by labor or farmers. Besides, withholding actions or strikes had been tried before by farm movements without success. AFBF Secretary-Treasurer Roger Fleming also cautioned Farm Bureau members about "crying poor-mouth." Fleming thought this sorrowful attitude was counter-productive and just gave the federal government an excuse to take away the farmer's freedom and replace it with bureaucratic decision-making.

An AAM flyer issued an ultimatum to farm groups, including Farm Bureau, to join their strike or else. "This proposal is being presented to all existing agricultural organizations in the United States. If these organizations do not endorse and support this proposal, we will cancel all memberships and insurance held in these organizations by the American Farmers and Stockmen."[2]

AFBF President Allan Grant responded that he and the board of directors could not support a strike without the approval of the voting delegates. He called the strike advocates "sincere but ineffective," and said moving more wheat and feed grains into export channels was a better solution. The Denver-based National Cattlemen's Association issued a statement saying cattlemen were advocates of the free enterprise system, not of parity. A dairy farmer in Defiance, Iowa, raised a question at a strike meeting: "What am I going to do? Dump my milk down the drain for 30 days?"[3]

The organizers knew there was little chance of a strike succeeding, but they thought it would give farmers a more militant image and cause the urban public to wake up to farmers' problems. Borrowing a page from truckers, AAM organized convoys of tractors. A tractorcade was worth more than a hundred news conferences in generating publicity, but it wasn't necessarily the kind of publicity most farmers wanted.

Around the December strike deadline, AAM organized tractorcades to Washington and a bunch of state capitals. The tractorcade to Atlanta on Interstate 75 was described by *Newsweek* as a five-mile long procession of expensive air-conditioned tractors and motor homes. A trucker who observed the passing vehicles said, "This is the richest-looking group of broke people I have ever seen." One of the riders on that tractorcade was Gloria Carter Spann, President Carter's sister.[4]

At the 1978 annual meeting, Secretary of Agriculture Bob Bergland said he had no quarrel with the farmers' right to strike and air their grievances, but about their demands he said, "We do not think that government's role is to guarantee full parity under all circumstances. To do that would entail a bureaucracy you wouldn't believe . . . You'd have federal agents all the time policing every sale . . . I don't think anyone is prepared to accept that kind of total government control over this great industry." Bergland praised Farm Bureau for its policies to expand markets overseas for farm products and added, "You are there with a voice everyone is going to appreciate, respect and honor."[5]

Whatever public sympathy the American Agricultural Movement garnered in the beginning dissipated quickly with a tractorcade in February 1979. This time AAM members ground up sod on the National Mall, drove a tractor into the Reflection Pool, and caused other damage for the benefit of television cameras. *Forbes* magazine said the tractorcade succeeded "only in portraying them [farmers] as manipulative zealots with a questionable grip on reality."[6] The *Washington Post* said, "Angry American farmers, brandishing pitchforks and hurling fresh-laid eggs used 2,000 lumbering tractors to tie up traffic and sow ill will among thousands of commuters Monday in the nation's capital."[7]

AFBF had a minor run-in with AAM demonstrators at its Washington office during the tractorcade. A group of 150 AAM members, some of whom probably also were Farm Bureau members, stopped by the office and demanded to be heard. Staff proposed that a representative body of eight come in to talk, but the whole group pushed its way in, accompanied by reporters and photographers. A reasonable discussion was difficult because of shouts, accusations, boos, and occasional cheers.

Before leaving, the visitors threw a twelve-inch pot containing a jade plant out of the window—a window on the seventh floor overlooking a busy street. Cigarette butts were stomped out on the carpet, bumper stickers placed on the walls and furnishings, tobacco juice expectorated on the carpet and tables, the front door lock jammed, and a stink bomb set off.[8]

When word of the AAM visit got around, Kansas Farm Bureau sent Grant a replacement plant with a parachute attached, a spittoon, and a cigarette-butt picker-upper. Grant was thoroughly amused by the gesture, but in a response to AAM he said, "This is an era when the problems of agriculture need our best minds and not our worst emotions."[9]

In 1984, Hollywood brought the problems of the nation's heartland to the screen in three movies. Jessica Lange and Sam Shepard starred in *Country*, the story of a Midwestern farm family facing foreclosure. Sissy Spacek and Mel Gibson starred in *The River*, another movie about a farm family facing hard times, and Jane Fonda starred in *The Dollmaker* about a Kentucky sharecropper.

The three leading ladies were thrust into new roles before an agricultural task force of the House Democratic Caucus. Lange, who played Jewell Ivy in *Country*, was the most outspoken of the three. She was directed in her role as a farm crisis spokesperson by Rev. David Ostendorf, Midwest director of Rural America. Lange described the farm economy as "1,000-fold worse than ever investigated by the press."[10]

"Crisis Sprouts Bumper Crop of Farm Groups," said a *Successful Farming* magazine headline in 1984. Rural America, Iowa Farm Unity Coalition, North American Farm Alliance, Groundswell, U.S. Solidarity, Prairiefire, and Farm Survival Committee were among the pop-up groups. The Farmers Home Administration (FmHA) was their chief target. In *Country*, FmHA gave Jewel Ivy and husband Gilbert thirty days to repay delinquent loans or face foreclosure. Populist leaders like Ostendorf also took plenty of swipes at AFBF. He likened the farm protest to the civil rights movement and said, "One never knows when the spark is going to hit the tinder. We're in the process of stoking it."[11]

In January 1985, the American Farm Bureau Federation held its annual meeting in one of the worst possible locations for the times—Honolulu, Hawaii. While Farm Bureau members enjoyed the tropical warmth and trade wind breezes along the hotels on Waikiki Beach, back home in farm country the financial crisis was getting a lot worse.

AFBF first went to Hawaii in 1977 and the convention was so popular that members could not wait to return. Therefore, Honolulu was put on the list after Phoenix, New Orleans, San Diego, Dallas, and Orlando. Decisions about convention locations had to be made four to six years in advance, in order to secure the convention center and required hotel space. When the AFBF board of directors decided on Hawaii, they had no idea that farm auctions would be all over the front pages of newspapers.

At his opening news conference in Honolulu, AFBF President Bob Delano was asked by *Des Moines Register* farm editor Don Muhm if he thought agriculture was in a crisis. "I said not all of agriculture," recalled Delano. "Part of it in the grain areas, yes, it is in a crisis, but these farmers paid all of this money for the land and all of a sudden it isn't worth it."[12]

Later in his annual address, Delano referred to the crisis as "this time of severe economic adjustment for farmers and ranchers," and added that "there must be national awareness of the harsh economic reality facing one farmer in three across the country." The other critical issue was the drafting of a 1985 farm bill, something AFBF had focused on for a full year. Farm Bureau delegates approved a farm policy that moved in the direction of a "market-oriented" agriculture, rather than government action to determine production and price, but they opposed any deadline for phasing out target price and deficiency payments. The delegates also opposed a moratorium on farm foreclosures, because they felt it would be unfair to those who made payments on time.[13]

Muhm's story in the *Register* headlined, "Farm Bureau Chief Downplays Ag 'Crisis,'" was just the beginning of a public relations nightmare. By the end of the week, the headline over the letters to the editor column read, "Farm Bureau Word from Sunny Hawaii: 'No Farm Crisis.'" On January 14, the paper published an editorial cartoon of Delano sitting on Waikiki Beach at a Farm Bureau luau sipping a tropical drink and watching a hula dancer perform. The balloon caption over his head said, "Crisis, What Crisis?"[14]

Muhm was one of the top farm writers in the nation and a veteran of many Farm Bureau conventions, so the attack was unexpected. The *Register* left the distinct impression that Farm Bureau was out of touch or didn't care. Readers and a few politicians angrily responded. Representative Cooper Evans (R–Iowa) said the "group's failure to recognize the farm debt crisis increases a view that the Farm Bureau is an organization of big, wealthy farmers." A reader suggested that the reality of the farm crisis was found in the "cry of the auctioneer and not the swish of grass skirts in a tropical paradise."[15]

Delano was not a wealthy farmer; he and his wife Martha owned a modest-sized Virginia grain farm. He was a working farmer and proud of it. A politician caught in the same jam as Delano might have wriggled out of it by saying he "misspoke." The AFBF president did not look for an escape route. When a political leader saw him in Washington later and suggested he had lost touch with his farm neighbors, Delano invited him down to his farm, just two hours from the nation's capital, to meet his neighbors.

He was basically correct in his analysis, if not his choice of words. What he said was that the farm debt crisis did not extend to all of agriculture. Later he defined the hotspots as the Midwest, Georgia, South Carolina, and parts of Texas. His comments, however, were not what farm activists and many politicians were saying. Representative Thomas Daschle (D–South Dakota) said, "I fear we could have an economic collapse in the next 18 months that could make the Depression look like a picnic."[16]

Iowa State University economist Dr. Neil Harl said later that the crisis was not uniform throughout agriculture. "Families were suffering in the midst of the relative prosperity enjoyed by those with no debt who were able to avoid the various factors that moved farmers into the window of vulnerability. The farm debt crisis of the 1980s was a little like a neutron bomb. Damage was done silently and almost invisibly."[17]

Like the farm depression of 1920, the crisis followed a real estate boom. The economic climate encouraged farmers to buy land. Abundant credit from a variety of sources was available to finance the expansion. The headlines about a world running out of food only seemed to confirm the need for expansion. Net farm income reached a record $34 billion in 1973. Farmers had no way of knowing it, but that was a high-water mark for a long time. Net farm income dipped to $14 billion in 1983, but recovered to $26 billion in 1984, before the Hawaii convention. Farm debt on the other hand kept going up from around $50 billion in 1971 to more than $200 billion in 1985.

Before the end of January, Delano appealed to President Reagan to expedite farm credit relief measures. FmHA was getting swamped with loan requests, and Reagan's farm debt plan announced in the fall of 1984 did not seem to be working yet. The plan called on bankers to write off 10 percent of the principal on farm loans in return for a federal guarantee on the other 90 percent, but the bankers preferred an interest rate writedown instead.

About this time, budget director David Stockman appeared before at a Senate Budget Committee hearing. When asked what relief the administration was going to extend to farmers, he responded, "For the life of me I cannot figure out why the taxpayers of this country have the responsibility to go in and refinance bad debt that [was] willingly incurred by consenting adults who went out and bought farmland when the price was going up and thought they could get rich, or went out and bought machinery and production assets because they made a business judgment that they could make money."

Time magazine dubbed Stockman, "the Administration's sayer-out-loud of the politically unthinkable," and Sen. Charles Grassley (R-Iowa) told him, "Please refrain from sermonizing on the free market, which seems most hypocritical from a government that has been the root cause of the current farm-economy crisis."[18]

In a *Farm Bureau News* column headlined, "Bankruptcy: A Personal Tragedy," Delano wrote a thoughtful column to assuage some of the guilt farmers felt about their predicament. "Hindsight makes it easy to see that escalating farmland values of the early 1970s were a trap for farmers and ranchers who were looking to expand because it was generally thought that land values would stay firm and perhaps even strengthen," he said. "Many of the financial signals sent out by the federal government, rural bankers and other branches of the farm credit system reinforced the belief. After learning to live with inflation, many people were convinced it was here to stay and that buying made more sense than renting."[19]

In the rearview mirror, the farm crisis was fairly predictable. Monetary policies designed to choke off double-digit inflation drove up interest rates. Export markets contracted because of the strong dollar and slow world growth, and farmland prices fell rapidly as inflation was tamed. Farmers were hung out to dry, unable to respond quickly to the economic changes—certainly not as quickly as the investor or businessman.

Ronald Reagan wanted the 1985 post-election year to be one of sweeping reform in farm policy, cutting farm spending from around $15 billion to the

$3–5 billion a year level of the 1970s. His timing wasn't any better than the AFBF convention in Hawaii. When the administration's farm bill proposal was presented in February 1985, AFBF was swift in its response. "Even those of us who want to see a reduction in government spending cannot support a farm program based solely on budget considerations . . . It cuts farm programs too far, too fast." The features AFBF *did* like were loan rates set at competitive world-market levels and elimination of the farmer-held grain reserve.

The federation soon unveiled its own farm bill proposal, the Farm Bureau Farm Bill or "FB/FB" as it was dubbed. At a Washington news conference, Delano said Farm Bureau had a moderate alternative to Reagan's plan. "By tying dairy price supports and commodity loans for major export crops to formulas that depend on average market prices rather than on arbitrary 'political' numbers, Farm Bureau's bill sets a market-related course for American agriculture—while also providing needed protection against financial disaster."[20]

In late February 1985, the National Farm Action Rally was held at the Hilton Coliseum in Ames, Iowa. A crowd of nearly 14,000 farmers was on hand to listen to a long list of speakers including Iowa Farm Bureau President Dean Kleckner who was booed and heckled. A large balloon was launched from the stands with "Farm Bureau Hot Air" written on it. This was not an easy time to be a Farm Bureau leader and a voice calling for reason.[21] The auctioneer's chant at a farm sale led off the evening news on many nights, and Farm Bureau leaders who appeared on television talk shows like *Donahue* during the crisis found hosts, guests and audiences stacked against them.

After Bergland left office with the Carter administration, John Block was given the unenviable job of restoring the farm economy. Block said the losses suffered by American agriculture amounted to $100 billion. "We can't change it. The government can't legislate against it. It occurred. We have to pick up the pieces and build it back," he said.[22] Reminiscent of Farm Bureau's Fleming, Block called on reporters to quit "poor mouthing" agriculture. At a meeting of the Newspaper Farm Editors of America, he said most farmers were getting the money they needed for spring planting. But he warned, "The mood of doom and gloom can become a self-fulfilling prophecy."[23]

Block was right about the rhetoric. Even some of the people allegedly trying to help farmers overcome despair and grief were fanning the flames of rural discontent. In December 1985, a Kansas family counselor told the *Denver Post*, "When farmers are out next March and April starting to plant—and others can't plant because they didn't get loans—then you'll see all hell break loose." He predicted that things could get "pretty bloody."[24]

Predictions of widespread rural violence never came true, but a year earlier in the fall of 1984, Nebraska farmer Arthur Kirk was killed by a state patrol SWAT team near his farm. Kirk, heavily armed and wearing a gas mask, opened fire first before being shot dead. A third generation farmer faced with losing his farm to the bank, he was initially viewed as a martyr of the farm crisis. However, Kirk had ties to Posse Comitatus and other right-wing extremist groups that were actively trying to recruit farmers.[25] Farmer suicide rates remained about the same despite financial problems and a steady diet of discouraging news. If there was a farmer suicide, however, it was in all the headlines.

In a few hotspots around the country, farm broadcasters criticized Farm Bureau and propagandized for AAM and similar groups. Their numbers were very small compared to the farm-radio industry as a whole. The dissatisfaction with Farm Bureau was as predictable as a hot summer in Kansas. Farm Bureau is a problem-solving organization; it tackles the root causes of the farm problems and refuses quick fixes that do more harm than good. Anger, confrontation, disruption, threats, and conspiracy theories never found a home in Farm Bureau.

AFBF leaders also refused to join the doom and gloom crowd, which would have been the easiest thing to do. "Agriculture is in an adjustment period. Don't let anyone tell you agriculture is going out of business," said Elton Smith, AFBF vice president at a meeting in Rochester, New York. "We thought inflation would keep on, and it didn't. We got carried away."[26] During the crisis, there were plenty of sympathizers. Civil rights leader Jesse Jackson donned a farmer's cap and hopped aboard a tractor for a 140-mile ride to the Minnesota state capitol. He also led a march to a county courthouse in protest of a farm foreclosure. "Save farms, Export Reagan," repeated the crowd in unison after him. In Ohio, the Girl Scouts raised money for farmers.[27]

The big event in 1985 was Farm Aid, a marathon country music and rock-and-roll concert, held at the University of Illinois football stadium in Champaign-Urbana. The event organized by musicians Willie Nelson, John Mellencamp, and Neil Young drew 78,000 fans. Nelson thought Farm Aid would raise $50 million to $70 million to aid family farms; he came up with $9 million instead. Most of the money was used for legal assistance, counseling, and to run a farmers' hotline.

Illinois Farm Bureau produced video spots on farm life to be televised during the concert, but Farm Bureau was disappointed that musicians politicized the event by plugging the "Save the Family Farm Act," a costly measure laden with government controls that Farm Bureau opposed. Nelson came back with another Farm Aid concert the next year in his native Texas, but the money raised was much smaller.[28]

The Farm Bureau Farm Bill was introduced by Sen. Mitch McConnell (R-Kentucky), who said, "Congress must act aggressively to give American farmers the tools they need to be competitive in the world marketplace and this farm bill does provide those tools." A unique feature of the Farm Bureau Farm

Bill was its Bonus Incentive Commodity Export Program (BICEP) which proposed to use a portion of government stockpiles as a bonus or incentive for foreign buyers of farm commodities. What the government spent on export bonuses would be recouped in savings on storage costs. BICEP came at just the right time. USDA was lowering export projections and the European Economic Community (EC) was taking American markets. France was balking at trade liberalization talks.

Senate Majority Leader Bob Dole (R–Kansas) convinced the administration to embrace the concept of BICEP for immediate use. In May, Block announced a three-year, $2 billion commodity bonus plan to meet competition from the Europeans. Block acknowledged that the plan was not good trade policy, but the United States could not sit idly by while other nations subsidized agricultural exports.

While the farm bill was under consideration in Congress, AFBF worked on farm credit relief. Delano appointed an AFBF Agricultural Credit Study Committee chaired by Vice President Smith that included Henry Voss, California Farm Bureau president; Harry Bell, South Carolina Farm Bureau president; Bryce Neidig, Nebraska Farm Bureau president; and Keith Eckel, Pennsylvania Farmers' Association president. The committee held a series of meetings with officials of the Farm Credit Council, Farm Credit Administration, American Bankers Association, Independent Bankers Association, and USDA credit officials.

Among their recommendations were a restructuring of the Farm Credit Administration and financial assistance to the Farm Credit System after its surplus was exhausted in covering bad loans. Delano said, "Farmers and lenders are partners and neither can succeed if the other fails. The changes we are urging will give lenders more flexibility in dealing with farmers with debt difficulties and allow debt restructuring in order to provide farmers the opportunity to work out their difficulties."[29] AFBF's analysis of the problem indicated that one-third of commercial farm operators held two-thirds of the commercial farm debt and as much as $50 billion of farm debt could not be serviced given the outlook for farm income. A reduction in interest rates and higher commodity prices would help some individuals but would not solve the overall problem.

Just before Christmas, President Reagan signed the new five-year omnibus farm bill. There had been seven different farm bills up for consideration in the Senate, including Farm Bureau's. Lawmakers tagged the final version "The Best We Can Do Act of 1985." AFBF supported the farm bill but expressed similar feelings. The major features of the Food Security Act of 1985 were a reduction in loan rates, a target price freeze, whole-herd dairy buyout, export bonus program, Conservation Reserve Program (CRP), and Sodbuster and Swampbuster. AFBF economist Ross Korves singled out the reduction in loan rates as a big step forward toward a market-oriented agriculture. "That's a clear and certain break with the politics of the past 50 years and one that will send economic shock waves from here to every grain-producing and consuming country in the world."[30]

Earlier in the year, AFBF dairy specialist Hollis Hatfield warned that heifer numbers were the highest in twenty years and milk output was about to jump. The final bill froze the dairy price support for 1986 and required the secretary to offer bids to producers willing to sell their entire dairy herd for slaughter or export and exit production for at least three to five years. More than 14,000 dairy farmers participated in the buyout over the eighteen-month period for bids.

The farm credit rescue that Delano termed "critical" in November also was signed by the president. A new Farm Credit Capital Corporation was set up by legislation to take over and restructure bad loans from the farm credit network and redistribute surplus funds among those banks and lending cooperatives in trouble. A provision for federal funds to shore up the system was included, but congressional appropriation was required first.

The 1986 AFBF annual meeting in Atlanta was the last for Bob Delano as president. Dean Kleckner was elected to succeed him. Farm Bureau had been on the defensive much of the time over the farm crisis, but Delano believed it strengthened Farm Bureau's resolve. "I see a growing competence and a greater aggressiveness as our members and leaders face up to leaner times and harder problems," he said in his annual address. "Proof of this has been demonstrated many times this past year, particularly in our work on farm credit and the farm bill."

At the same meeting, Sen. Dole expressed his opinion that the farm crisis was ending. "I happen to believe that 1986 is a watershed year for American agriculture" and that "many of us believe that we are starting to bottom out." It turns out he was right, but work still lay ahead.[31] One of the first things Kleckner did as president was to meet with Federal Reserve Chairman Paul Volcker, Treasury Secretary James Baker, and Agriculture Secretary-designate Richard Lyng.

Despite all the clamor and frustration in the late 1970s and early 1980s, Farm Bureau was still the organization that farmers looked to for a solution to the farm crisis, and one was found in the Two-Tier Debt Restructuring Program that Farm Bureau championed in 1986. The basic idea was to get farmers and lenders beyond the "one more year" syndrome and help those who could make things work out in the long run.

In the AFBF plan, Tier-1 debt was the amount of a farmer's debt which analysis showed the operator would be able to pay interest and principal on at expected commodity prices over the next five years. The prevailing interest rate would be paid on Tier-1 debt. Tier-2 debt was the amount of total debt not part of Tier-1. No principal payments would be required and the lender would charge a reduced interest rate. As the farming operation was able to reduce Tier-1 debt, equal amounts would shift over from Tier-2.

An internal report to the AFBF board indicated that 100,000 to 125,000 farm operators needed debt restructuring in order to avoid liquidation. Losing a substantial number of these farmers would cause a domino effect of failed banks, high interest rates to cover losses, and further declines in land values. The Farm Credit System was dumping troubled loans or forcing liquidations with little thought given to debt restructuring.

In the first use by AFBF of satellite video conferencing technology, Two-Tier Debt Restructuring was rolled out to state Farm Bureaus in a two hour live broadcast. Leaders in twenty-six states assembled at community colleges, local TV stations, homes, and wherever else they could find a satellite downlink to view the program. State Farm Bureaus then picked up the ball and met with Farm Credit System, Farmers Home Administration officials, and bankers. The Nebraska state legislature was so impressed that it passed a resolution in support of Farm Bureau's plan and commended the organization for it.[32]

Within a month of the AFBF plan, commercial banks had received the regulatory clearance they needed to work things out with farmers and practice forbearance, but AFBF said the Farm Credit System was still "a reluctant restructurer" even though in theory it is a cooperative system owned by the borrowers. "In practice, the system seems to want to flush out its troubled borrowers and be left with the cream of the crop of agricultural producers. The trouble is that many of today's distressed borrowers *were* yesterday's cream of the crop."[33]

Representative Lindsay Thomas (D–Georgia) was the sponsor of a Farm Bureau-backed resolution urging the Farm Credit System to practice forbearance. The vote of 407 to 0 left no doubt about where the House stood on loan restructuring. Bowing to pressure from Congress and Farm Bureau, the Farm Credit System implemented a nationwide loan restructuring program in May 1986. The plan did not eliminate foreclosures but made them a last resort after careful analysis of the alternatives.

AFBF lobbyist Mary Kay Thatcher remembered debt restructuring as Farm Bureau's biggest grassroots lobbying effort of the 1980s. In the end, the tractorcades, Farm Aid concerts, and sympathetic media coverage did not solve the farm crisis.

Hard work by Farm Bureau and a coalition of farm groups and action by Congress produced a solution.

Endnotes

1. Browne, *Private Interests, Public Policy And American Agriculture,* 66.
2. "Agricultural Strike," four page flyer of American Agriculture, Springfield, Colorado.
3. AFBF news release issued October 28, 1977; "Farm Strike Stirs 'So What' Attitude," *Chicago Tribune,* December 18, 1977; "They Rally in Defiance for Proposed Farm Strike . . .," *Des Moines Register,* November 20, 1977.
4. "The Tractor Rebellion," *Newsweek,* December 19, 1977.

5. Transcript, AFBF Annual Meeting, January 9–12, 1978, Houston, Texas.

6. "Welfare Tractors," *New Republic*, March 3, 1979; "Tractorcade Follies of 1979," *Forbes*, March 5, 1979.

7. "Farmer Protest Plows Through D.C.; Arrest 19," *Washington Post,* February 6, 1979.

8. "When Visitors Came!" *Farm Bureau News*, February 19, 1979.

9. Ibid.

10. "UPI News in Agriculture," Farm Editor Sonja Hillgren, May 5, 1985; "UPI on the Farm Front," Farm Editor Sonja Hillgren, October 3, 1984.

11. "Crisis Sprouts Bumper Crop of Farm Groups," *Successful Farming,* October 1984; "Protests Grow With Careful Cultivation," January 13, 1985.

12. Interview with Bob Delano.

13. Transcript, AFBF Annual Meeting, January 7–10, 1985, Honolulu, Hawaii.

14. "Farm Bureau Word from Sunny Hawaii, 'No Farm Crisis,'" *Des Moines Register*, January 13, 1985; editorial cartoon by Duffy, *Des Moines Register*, January 14, 1985.

15. "Farm Bureau Is 'Out Of Touch' Evans Charges," *Des Moines Register*, January 12, 1985.

16. "Farm-State Democrats Take Lead," *Washington Post*, February 9, 1985.

17. Harl, *The Farm Debt Crisis of the 1980s*, 221.

18. "Real Trouble on the Farm," *Time,* February 18, 1985.

19. "Bankruptcy: A Personal Tragedy," *Farm Bureau News*, March 4, 1985.

20. "Farm Group Breaks with Reagan on Aid," *Chicago Tribune,* March 14, 1985; "Our Farm Program Bill," *Farm Bureau News,* April 1, 1985.

21. "Farm Bureau's Kleckner Is Heckled," *Des Moines Register*, February 28, 1985.

22. UPI wire story by Farm Editor Sonja Hillgren, March 4, 1985.

23. "UPI News in Agriculture," Farm Editor Sonja Hillgren, April 23, 1985.

24. "Farm Crisis Increases Potential for Violence," *Denver Post*, December 15, 1985.

25. "Armed, Angry Farmer Killed By SWAT Team, A Martyr of Madman?" *Des Moines Register*, February 17, 1985; "Right-Wing Extremists Seek to Recruit Farmers," *New York Times,* September 30, 1985.

26. "Farmers See Bright Future," UPI regional wire story, December 4, 1985.

27. "News in Agriculture," UPI wire story, April 1, 1985.

28. "Farm Aid Cause Has a Tough Row to Hoe," *Chicago Tribune*, September 22, 1985; "Politicking at Farm Aid Furrows Some Brows," *Chicago Tribune*, September 28, 1985.

29. "FB Makes Recommendations to Ease Farm Credit Problems," *Farm Bureau News*, November 18, 1985.

30. "Working with the New Farm Bill," *Farm Bureau News*, January 13, 1986.

31. Transcript, AFBF Annual Meeting of 1986.

32. "FB Holds First-Ever Video Conference," *Farm Bureau News*, March 31, 1986; "State Farm Bureaus Tackle Debt Restructuring," *Farm Bureau News*, April 28, 1986.

33. "The Farm Credit System: A Reluctant Restructurer," *Farm Bureau News*, April 21, 1986.

23 | Globalization and Farm Bureau

THE WORLD TRADE ORGANIZATION (WTO), NORTH AMERICAN FREE TRADE AGREEMENT (NAFTA), and opening up of trade with China were part of the phenomenon known as globalization, the flatter, interrelated world that author Thomas L. Friedman brought to popular attention.[1] Globalization is an acceleration of internationalism, an integration of economies, cultures, communications, governmental policies, and political movements all over the world. Farm Bureau supported the ideals of internationalism after World War II and globalization in the new century.

Globalization spreads not only goods and services, but freedom and ideas around the world. It is an imperative for American farmers and Farm Bureau because approximately 96 percent of the world's people live outside the United States and represent a growing market for American producers.

American Farm Bureau Federation President Bob Stallman called globalization the "new frontier" in agriculture. The old frontier was the historic westward migration, free land, and expansion of agriculture on the continent. The twenty-first century frontier for agriculture is the expanded global marketplace and the technology and resources necessary to meet rising global demand for food, fiber, energy, and a healthy environment. Like the old frontier, the new frontier is full of opportunity but comes with daunting challenges.

Globalization first became a buzz word in the 1990s because of NAFTA and the WTO. AFBF already was thinking globally when it helped secure passage of the U.S.–Canada Free Trade Agreement in 1988 and worked to defeat the Gephardt amendment to the Trade Act of 1988. The amendment by Rep. Richard Gephardt (D-Missouri) required sweeping retaliation against countries that persisted in maintaining a large trade surplus with the United States. It would have been a step backward toward protectionism. That same year the AFBF board of directors authorized a trade advisory committee of state Farm Bureau presidents. Florida Farm Bureau President Carl Loop served as the first chairman in 1989.

At the January 1989 AFBF annual meeting in San Antonio, economist Dr. Barry Asmus described an emerging world economy in which markets have little relation to geographic territory. More and more we must think in terms of world markets and value-added products," he said. "At last we are learning that free trade is the way to go. And, as the world economy grows, countries of the world will eat better and demand more agricultural products."[2]

The North American Free Trade Agreement ratified by the United States in 1993 provided for the elimination of all tariffs between the U.S. and Mexico over fifteen years and extended the principles embodied in the U.S.-Canada Free Trade Agreement to the entire North American continent. AFBF policy approved the negotiating process, but reserved judgment on the trade deal itself until the ink was dry. After careful consideration, the board of directors approved the pact prior to President Bush signing it in December 1992. Bush's successor, Bill Clinton, supported NAFTA but wanted to hammer out a number of side-deals before submitting it to Congress.

During 1993, AFBF joined a coalition of 175 other farm groups and agribusinesses known as Ag for NAFTA. The coalition was necessary to counter strong opposition from labor and environmental groups. In *Farm Bureau News*, House Agriculture Committee Chairman, Rep. Kika de la Garza (D-Texas), termed NAFTA a once in a lifetime opportunity and Rep. Pat Roberts (R-Kansas), the ranking member of the committee, said, "NAFTA could be the most important Congressional vote affecting agriculture this decade."[3]

Farm Bureau went to bat for NAFTA with a solid informational effort to let members know what was at stake and how the trade agreement could affect their particular commodity interests. A Royerton, Indiana, Farm Bureau member, Joe Russell, cut a ten-acre crop-art message in his soybean field, "Yes, NAFTA." Other Farm Bureau members participated in a nationally televised rally for the trade agreement with President Clinton.

A few days before the historic vote, AFBF sent a letter to all members of Congress that said, "NAFTA is in our national interest. It will help us retain our pre-eminent position in the world economy; its defeat would stun the world and help to elevate other countries and blocs as major forces in world trade."[4] President Clinton expressed the same sentiments. "I tell you, my fellow Americans, that if we learned anything from the collapse of the Berlin Wall and the fall of the governments in Eastern Europe, even a totally controlled society cannot resist the winds of change that economics and technology and information flow have imposed in this world of ours."[5]

The NAFTA campaign made for some strange bedfellows, particularly on the opposing side. Consumer activist Ralph Nader, conservative Republican Patrick Buchanan, and Texas billionaire Ross Perot all were against NAFTA. Perot who ran unsuccessfully for president in 1992 had a quick wit and was good with one-liners. He said NAFTA would create a "giant sucking sound" as jobs left the United States for cheaper Mexican labor. Clinton and three former presidents, Carter, Ford, and Bush, made a joint appearance in favor of the trade pact.

Late on the night of November 17, 1993, the House passed NAFTA by a vote of 234 to 200. The Senate agreed a few days later by a more comfortable margin. The Ag for NAFTA coalition was absolutely crucial to passage. Overall it was a big victory for Farm Bureau trade policy, but not all farmers agreed. The Florida Farm Bureau dissented from official AFBF policy on NAFTA out of concern that Mexican tomatoes would drive Florida growers out of business. AFBF always tried hard to reach a consensus on policy issues, but once in a while it wasn't possible.

"Our people were very much opposed to NAFTA," recalled Carl Loop, former AFBF vice president who was a board member at the time. "What we were afraid would happen, actually happened. We went from 300 growers down to about 100 growers. Acreage didn't decrease; the big ones got bigger and they bought up a lot of that acreage and could produce it more efficiently."[6]

Three weeks after NAFTA was ratified by Congress, the Uruguay Round of the GATT concluded. In 1995, AFBF commissioned a trade study to help producers take advantage of trading opportunities under both agreements. From a trade standpoint, NAFTA has been a success. Between the years 1992 and 2007, U.S. farm and food product exports to Canada and Mexico grew by 156 percent, and they became the first and second largest export markets for the United States.

The World Trade Organization established in January 1995 after the Uruguay Round of the GATT is the international institution most associated with globalization. WTO was set up to administer agreed-upon rules of trade among member countries. The rules are set forth in the form of a contract. Members that join have an obligation to carry out the rules and can seek redress from members who fail to abide by them. A binding dispute settlement process was one of the big improvements over GATT. The 128 countries that belonged to the GATT at the end of the Uruguay Round joined the WTO, and new member countries were added.

The WTO ministerial meeting at Seattle in December 1999 was one of the most memorable, but for all the wrong reasons. "For trade negotiators, the name 'Seattle' will probably forever conjure up vivid images—of costumed or masked demonstrators, of police and national guardsmen in riot gear; of much delayed, all night and ultimately unsuccessful meetings," recalled international trade consultant and former AFBF staffer Paul Drazek.[7] The WTO meeting became known as the "Battle in Seattle" for the riots Drazek described. Black-clothed anarchists were joined by environmental protestors dressed as sea turtles. The anti-biotechnology crowd, labor movement, animal rights activists, consumer activists, and others were present that week. It was a far cry from the normally staid GATT meetings at Geneva.

Farm Bureau's delegation of state presidents could smell the tear gas in the air when they stepped outside the meeting rooms. The anti-globalization forces had a number of gripes, but generally thought that governments had "sold out" to multinational corporations. They ignored the fact that the WTO was a democratic organization that arrived at decisions by consensus, and if a vote occurred, it was one vote per member country.[8] Kleckner and the other Farm Bureau leaders met with Secretary of State Madeline Albright, state governors, China's foreign trade minister, Cuba's minister of foreign affairs, and farm organization leaders from around the world.

Late in 1999, China and the U.S. signed a bilateral trade agreement committing China to dramatically lowering tariffs on U.S. exports and allowing for more foreign investment. The agreement was a crucial step in China's accession to the WTO, and AFBF figured it was worth $3 billion per year in farm exports for the American farmers. The next step was for the United States to grant permanent normal trade relations (PNTR) to China.

Bill Clinton was in his last year of office in 2000, and Bob Stallman was in his first as AFBF president. Both said getting Congress to grant permanent normal trade relations was a top priority. The international trade resolution adopted by the voting delegates at the annual meeting in Houston read, "We support extending normal trade relations (NTR) (formerly referred to as Most-Favored Nation) to China and Vietnam to preserve and expand that agricultural market."

To implement the policy, Stallman encouraged Farm Bureau members to make contacts with Congress by letter, phone calls, and district office visits. "Many of this nation's farmers and ranchers stand at a crossroad. Generations-old farms stand on the brink of failure as dwindling market opportunities have taken their toll. China offers a huge opportunity for this nation's agricultural community," said Stallman in one of his first columns as AFBF president.[9]

"The Chinese market is opening," said House Speaker J. Dennis Hastert (R-Illinois) as House debate was ending in May 2000. "The question is who will be there when it opens?"[10] Farm Bureau expected that if PNTR was voted down, the European Union (EU) would take full advantage of the Chinese market for *its* farmers.

The timing of the vote was good for Farm Bureau. Numerous groups of state Farm Bureau leaders were in Washington during the spring to meet with their congressional delegations. The volunteer leaders lobbied hard for PNTR. Stallman made Farm Bureau's final push at a Capitol Hill news conference. Agriculture Secretary Dan Glickman, House Agriculture Committee Chairman Larry Combest (R-Texas), and the ranking minority member of the committee, Rep.

Charles Stenholm (D-Texas), also spoke, along with representatives of many commodity groups. The opposition to PNTR consisted of organized labor, environmental groups, human rights activists, and social conservatives.

President Clinton answered the critics when he said, "Opening trade with China will not in itself lead China to make all the choices we believe it should make, but clearly the more China opens its markets, the more it unleashes the power of economic freedom, the more likely it will be to fully liberate the human potential of its people."[11] The vote in the House was 237 to 197 in favor of PNTR. The Senate vote was never in doubt.

Stallman returned from meetings with WTO and foreign trade officials at Geneva in October 2000, and said at a news conference, "America's farmers and ranchers need fairer and freer trade. We also must make sure that agricultural trade is not ignored. That's our top concern." WTO Director-General Mike Moore assured Stallman that agriculture would have a place at the "head of the table" of future talks.[12]

President George W. Bush took office in 2001 with a bold agenda for trade that included a hemisphere-wide free-trade zone, a new WTO round, and fast-track or trade promotion authority. Trade promotion authority (TPA) was legislative authority given the president to strengthen his hand in trade negotiations. Congress still had the power to approve or reject trade agreements but could not tack on amendments that might scuttle a deal. Congress refused to renew TPA for President Clinton in 1994.

Farm Bureau was very eager to see fast-track restored. In its absence, other countries were moving forward on trade agreements while the United States was stalled. "We are danger of being left behind," said U.S. Trade Representative (USTR) Robert Zoellick before the House Ways and Means Committee in March. One thing holding up TPA was discussion about including labor and environmental concerns in future trade agreements. AFBF felt this was a big mistake. "The inclusion of labor and environmental concerns in trade negotiations has the potential of opening a 'Pandora's box,'" said Chris Garza, AFBF director of governmental relations. "Some countries see it as disguised protectionism and would refuse to negotiate with us while other countries with more stringent labor and environmental standards may see it as an opportunity to force their standards on the United States."[13]

Trade promotion authority passed the House near the end of 2001; the Senate passed it the following spring. Stallman said the renewal of TPA sent a clear message to our trading partners that the U.S. was ready to assume a leadership role in the negotiations and had the backing of Congress.

The Doha Round of trade negotiations was launched by the WTO at Doha, Qatar, in November 2001, after a two-year standstill caused by the Seattle failure.

There was a subdued atmosphere because of the terrorist attacks of 9/11 on the United States. China officially joined the WTO at this time ending a fifteen-year wait to get in. Agriculture was at the center of the new round of trade negotiations.

The Bush administration proposal for WTO negotiations in agriculture was released in Washington in July 2002. Stallman stood beside Zoellick and the top U.S. negotiators for agriculture at a USDA news conference and declared the plan "credible and aggressive." Zoellick also told state Farm Bureau presidents meeting in Washington that the proposal put together "with Farm Bureau's suggestions and help gives us an excellent jumping off point for a very good offense."[14]

The trade proposal was a two-phase process. First, export subsidies would be eliminated, and worldwide tariffs and domestic trade-distorting farm subsidies reduced. Second, all tariffs and trade-distorting support to farmers would be eliminated by a date to be determined in negotiations. AFBF was particularly interested in seeing that trade inequities were addressed. For example, U.S. farm exports faced global tariffs that averaged 62 percent, while U.S. tariffs averaged only 12 percent.

The European Union, with roughly the same value of agricultural production as the U.S., was providing $60 billion in support a year for its producers in so-called "amber" box payments. The United States was limited to $19 billion. The boxes were analogous to a stop light. Amber or yellow light were the most-trade distorting; green meant go-ahead. The EU also accounted for 87 percent of the world's export subsidies, which would be eliminated under the U.S. proposal.

In September 2002, Stallman went to the WTO headquarters in Geneva with two members of the AFBF trade advisory committee, Wisconsin Farm Bureau President Howard "Dan" Poulson and South Carolina Farm Bureau President David Winkles, to deliver the message that American farmers were standing solidly behind the Bush administration proposal. After meeting with representatives of the EU, Stallman said they were "not nearly as thrilled with our proposal as the Cairns Group," the free-trade group that included Australia and Canada.[15]

Hoping for a continuation of the "spirit of Doha" that initiated the talks, the WTO put forth an ambitious timetable to finish by January 2005. Within agriculture there were "three pillars" of the negotiations—market access, domestic support, and export competition or export subsidies. One controversy that showed up in these talks was described by AFBF trade economist Megan Provost as the battle between the "-eds" and the "-ings." There were thirty-two developed countries or "-eds" in the WTO; "ings" or developing countries made up the rest of the 147 members. The classification was self-determined so Brazil or South Korea could claim to be developing. The "-ings" felt that WTO rules on agriculture were written for the "-eds" and their domestic farm programs. There were other issues as well, including consumer concerns about food safety.[16]

The Bush administration also worked on a number of free trade agreements involving one or more countries. NAFTA was one such agreement; an even larger objective was the Free Trade of the Americas Agreement among thirty-four nations of the Western Hemisphere, first proposed during the Clinton administration. While FTAA was hopelessly stalled, the Bush administration began negotiating a series of bilateral agreements. These free trade agreements eliminated tariff and nontariff barriers between the members only. The U.S. wasn't alone in this; Canada and the EU also were signing up partners.

The American Farm Bureau Federation generally supported the bilateral trade pacts or free trade agreements; the first one with a South American country was reached with Chile in December 2002 after two years of negotiations. Stallman characterized the Chile FTA as a positive development that would improve market access for U.S. pork, wheat, feed grains, corn, soybeans and soybean meal, and other commodities. Chile was not a big market for American farmers, but Stallman thought a good precedent had been set for future FTAs. The pact included provisions for import-sensitive commodities to protect U.S. farmers from a sudden surge of imports from Chile.[17]

While negotiations over other FTAs continued in 2003, AFBF's top trade priority was the WTO negotiations. A ministerial meeting was held in September in Cancun, Mexico, marking the mid-way point of the Doha Round. Prior to the meeting, the U.S. and EU reached agreement to bridge the gaps in their initial proposals on agriculture. Cancun, a resort known for spring break revelry, drew free-trade protestors by the thousands, like Seattle. "It is both a festival of color and a repository for every grievance against today's world order," reported one news service in describing protestors ranging from Mexican peasant farmers to European anarchists to animal rights activists wearing dolphin-shaped hats.[18]

The multilateral trade talks at Cancun hit a roadblock and developing countries staged a walkout that ended negotiations. Agriculture was a source of friction, but did not lead directly to the breakdown which was over rules sought by the EU and Japan covering cross-border investment and anti-trust. "We had indicated our strong willingness to reduce domestic supports and to negotiate improved market access. The entire world, especially developing countries, would have greatly benefited from a successful round," said Stallman.[19] The *Washington Post* wondered if free trade had reached the end of its rope. "After decades of rapidly advancing globalization, do the nations of the world lack the stomach to open their borders further to trade and investment?"[20]

Shortly after the Cancun collapse, Trade Representative Zoellick announced plans to pursue FTAs with Panama, Colombia, and Peru under the umbrella of the Andean countries. Ecuador and Bolivia possibly could be included. Meanwhile, negotiations reached a successful conclusion in December 2003 on the

Central America Free Trade Agreement (CAFTA) between the U.S. and five Central American countries, Costa Rica, El Salvador, Guatemala, Honduras, and Nicaragua.

During the 2004 AFBF annual meeting, delegates debated CAFTA and its impact on the domestic sugar industry. At one point, Indiana Farm Bureau President Don Villwock was recognized to speak and said, "Bonjour, Mr. Chairman, We are turning into Europeans here today." Illinois Farm Bureau Federation President Ron Warfield agreed that if the United States was going to obtain market access overseas, it could not do it by denying access here.[21]

Under AFBF policy, the board of directors could analyze, review, debate and vote on all FTAs, whether regional or bilateral. In March, after careful study, the board voted to support both CAFTA and with certain conditions the Australia Free Trade Agreement. Under the CAFTA agreement, the Central American countries could export an additional 145,700 tons of sugar to the U.S., or about 1.5 percent of U.S. sugar production. After full implementation of CAFTA, tariffs on all U.S. agricultural products entering those countries would fall to zero. "Our analysis shows a strong gain for the whole of American agriculture," said Stallman of the agreement.[22]

In 2004, the Dominican Republic joined CAFTA so it was renamed DR-CAFTA. President Stallman told the Senate Agriculture Committee in June 2005 that the agreement "provides balance by giving U.S. agriculture the same duty-free access that DR-CAFTA nations already have to our markets." He was referring to the benefits these nations already received from the Caribbean Basin Initiative. Stallman cited AFBF's forecast of $1.5 billion in increased exports for U.S. producers of grains and oilseed products, livestock products, and cotton. Rob Portman who became USTR in April wrote in *Farm Bureau News*, "CAFTA is also a way for Americans to support freedom, democracy and economic reform in our own hemisphere."[23] CAFTA was approved by Congress in the summer of 2005, but only narrowly squeaked through in the House, 217 to 215.

An AFBF trade team that included President Stallman, Oklahoma Farm Bureau President Steve Kouplen, and Oregon Farm Bureau President Barry Bushue visited Geneva and the U.S. Mission, foreign embassies, and WTO staff in 2005. "The ambassadors and agricultural counselors we met with wanted to hear the thoughts and concerns of American agriculture directly from producers," said Stallman. They met with India, Brazil, Australia, New Zealand, Japan, European Union, Canada, China, Argentina, Egypt, Malaysia, Thailand, and Norway.[24]

Stallman served as a member of President Bush's advisory committee on trade policy and negotiations, an industry group that reviews trade negotiations and makes recommendations. "We [AFBF] have a close working relationship with the administration, USTR and our negotiators," he said. "We may not be sufficient to get a trade agreement passed, but we are necessary, because without agriculture's support for a trade agreement, I don't think it stands a chance of being passed." Farm Bureau's involvement included everything from assisting with economic analysis to public relations efforts to "heart to heart talks" with the trade ambassador.[25]

Stallman's *Farm Bureau News* column was headlined, "WTO: Let's Not Tap Dance Around the Issues," after the U.S. made a dramatic proposal for cutting domestic supports here and in the EU by 60 percent. "It takes two to tango and right now the United States is waiting for its dance partner," Stallman said, pointing out once again that Europe was outspending the United States 3-to-1 in domestic supports. "The United States will do its share to reduce domestic supports," he said, "but developed and developing countries must do their part in reforming and expanding market access opportunities."[26]

The U.S. proposal presented to American farmers what Stallman termed "significant short-term economic challenges for some commodities and specific farm types." He added, "We firmly believe, however, that in the long term U.S. agriculture will overcome any challenge through the expanded opportunity for exports created by specific and measurable improvements in market access."[27]

The United States had been instrumental in launching the Doha Round in 2001 and helped resuscitate the talks a number of times, but in July 2006, WTO Director-General Pascal Lamy declared an impasse and announced an indefinite suspension. The EU never did come to the dance in Farm Bureau's opinion and developing nations weren't ready to provide further market access either.

A last-ditch effort by Lamy to resume negotiations was made in the summer of 2008, but it too ended in failure after India and China asserted their rights to protect their poor farmers from imports and the uncertainties of world markets. Farm Bureau wasn't buying it. "It is regrettable that India and China were not prepared to negotiate improvements in agricultural trade for themselves and other developing countries," said Stallman in a statement.[28] China's position was particularly disappointing because AFBF supported China's admission to the WTO. Since that time, China's total exports quadrupled from $300 billion to $1.2 trillion, much of them going to this country.

The lack of a new WTO agreement has not hurt American farm exports—not yet anyway. They have doubled from $56 billion in 2003 to a projected $108.5 billion in 2008. "The ultimate outcome of this round in terms of agriculture will not lead to a lot more trade," said Stallman, and the WTO goals for agriculture (reducing domestic farm subsidies and lowering import tariff barriers) are being met at least temporarily. "This current situation we have with food commodity prices being high is accomplishing that better than the negotiations to a large extent. Domestic subsidies have been reduced because the prices are high, and countries are lowering their tariff barriers because they want and need the product."[29]

It may seem as though the grassroots advocacy takes a backseat in global trade because agreements are negotiated government to government or in the setting of the WTO. But foreign governments understand that AFBF has a lot of influence in trade decisions, not only in advising the administration but working with Congress to make sure trade agreements are acceptable.

Endnotes

1. Friedman, *The World Is Flat*.
2. "Economist Describes Emerging World Economy," *Farm Bureau News*, January 16, 1989.
3. "NAFTA: Good for Our Country and Our Farmers"; "The Most Important Vote Affecting Agriculture This Decade," op-ed. from *Special Farm Bureau News Supplement*, October 25, 1993.
4. "FB Urges 'Yea' Vote On NAFTA," *Farm Bureau News*, November 15, 1993.
5. Hamilton, *Bill Clinton, Mastering the Presidency*, 179.
6. Interview with Carl Loop.
7. "Post-Seattle Prospects For Agriculture," *Farm Bureau News*, January 10, 2000.
8. Hoekman and Kostecki, *The Political Economy of the World Trading System*, 70.
9. "Farmers Have Much Riding on PNTR Vote," *Farm Bureau News*, April 3, 2000.
10. "House Passes China Trade Bill," *The Washington Post*, May 25, 2000.
11. "A WTO Rescue Mission," *Newsweek*, October 23, 2000.
12. "Farm Leader Advocates Ag Trade Reforms," *Farm Bureau News*, October 20, 2000.
13. "USTR Outlines Bush Trade Agenda For Congress," *Farm Bureau News*, March 19, 2001.
14. "FB Applauds WTO Agriculture Package," and "Farm Bureau Presidents Discuss Farm Bill, Trade Policy," *Farm Bureau News*, July 29, 2002.
15. "FB Team Takes Trade Message To Geneva," *Farm Bureau News*, September 22, 2002.
16. "In Global Trade Talks, It's the 'eds' Versus the 'ings,'" *AFBF Trade Topics*, February 2005; "Key Issues in the World Trade Organization Negotiation on Agriculture," *American Journal of Agricultural Economics*, August 1, 2003.
17. "FB U.S.-Chile Agreement Is Positive," *Farm Bureau News*, December 16, 2002.
18. "Anti-WTO Protests Erupt," *Chicago Tribune* (Knight Ridder/Tribune Business News), September 11, 2003.
19. "Statement by Bob Stallman, President American Farm Bureau Federation Regarding the Conclusion of WTO Negotiations in Cancun," Washington, D.C., 2003.
20. "Walkout Shadows Free Trade's Future," *Washington Post*, September 16, 2003.
21. Transcript, AFBF Annual Meeting of 2004.
22. "Farm Bureau Supports Free Trade Agreements," *Farm Bureau News*, March 22, 2004.
23. "Stallman Urges Passage of DR-CAFTA," and "CAFTA Is a Win-Win for Trade and Democracy," by Rob Portman, *Farm Bureau News*, June 13, 2005.
24. "FB Leaders Meet with Trade Negotiators," *Farm Bureau News*, May 16, 2005.

25. Interview with Bob Stallman.

26. "WTO: Let's Not Tap Dance Around the Issues," *Farm Bureau News*, November 7, 2005.

27. "U.S., Other Countries Offer WTO Agriculture Proposals," *Farm Bureau News*, October 17, 2005.

28. "Statement by Bob Stallman . . . Regarding Lost Opportunity to Reform WTO Trade Rules," Washington, D.C., July 29, 2008.

29. Interview with Bob Stallman.

24 | Biofuels and Energy

At the 1974 AFBF annual meeting in Atlantic City, New Jersey, Vice President Gerald Ford made a prediction to Farm Bureau members that the United States would achieve "a self-sufficiency of energy by 1980, if not sooner." He based his prediction in part on American expertise—"the same technological brilliance that placed men on the moon is developing new energy resources," he said.[1] Today, America is still struggling to lessen dependence on foreign oil, and some politicians are calling for an energy program like the lunar space program. That much has not changed in thirty-five years.

Farm Bureau also was calling for a national energy program in the 1970s, and noted that the decline of the nation's railroads had made this country more dependent on truck and air transportation, which required greater amounts of energy. An AFBF energy resolution also included the line that "Farmers are in the energy business in a big way, converting solar energy into food energy." Today, that sentence is not complete, because farmers also are in the energy business in a "big way" by converting farm commodities to renewable fuels.[2]

The development of American agriculture in the twentieth century was inextricably linked to energy and cheap energy at that. Tractors, trucks, irrigation systems, fertilizers, and pesticides all relied on some form of petroleum. Rural electrification made chores easier around the farm and lit up rural homes. One could easily say that agriculture was transformed by energy. No longer were human backs, horses, mules and coal-generated steam the chief sources of power.

By the time Farm Bureau got underway at the county and state level, gasoline-powered tractors were available. The most popular of the tractors during the Farm Bureau Movement was the Farmall, a tricycle-type, row crop tractor, sold by International Harvester in 1923. Farmers had experimented with steam powered tractors, but they were slow, unsuited to farm work, and sparks from the boiler could set a dry field on fire. Gasoline-powered tractors were easier to start, more nimble, and could do a variety of jobs around the farm. Once again, the American Farm Bureau Federation benefited from good timing; the organization came into existence around the start of mechanized farming.

Except for rural electrification, energy was not a hot button issue. It was cheap and plentiful. However, Farm Bureau took an interest as far back as the 1930s in converting farm crops and crop waste to ethanol as a way to dispose of crop surpluses. Ironically, the corn surplus was the result of feeding fewer horses. One-fourth of corn acreage used to go to feed the horses that were replaced by gasoline-powered tractors.

Ethanol's potential as an octane booster failed to materialize at first because leaded gasoline hit the market in the 1920s. General Motors and Standard Oil of New Jersey jointly owned the Ethyl Gasoline Corporation, and it licensed refiners to add the anti-knock compound to gasoline. The dangers of tetraethyl lead were known by then, but scientists thought that auto exhaust emissions were not harmful.[3]

Prohibition also impeded ethanol's growth because alcohol was highly regulated. Henry Ford advocated turning breweries into distilleries to make fuel for cars, and there was a revival of interest during the Depression and after Prohibition. The *Bureau Farmer* carried an article under the headline, "Shall We Elevate the Depression with Ethyl Alcohol?" The author, Mrs. M. S. Campbell, talked about the "live-at-home movement" which encouraged farmers to get by on the farm without buying anything in town. "You stay at home these days because the gas costs money and all the buggies were junked long ago," she said.

Campbell was intrigued by a proposal to blend gasoline with 10 percent ethanol. She heard about it from her husband who attended an insurance meeting in Illinois. What today is called a "renewable fuels standard" was at the time referred to as "an alcohol-gasoline dilution plan." Corn, wheat, apples, sugar beets, and potatoes were considered feedstock. Campbell voiced some skepticism, however, and in her farm vernacular said, "I do not know how many bugs there are under that alcohol chip."[4] Doubts about ethanol were nothing new it seems.

Ethanol simmered on the back burner of energy policy because no one knew for sure how much crude oil was in the ground or how long it would last. Alcohol was seen as the most viable backup if oil supplies ran out. Interest was kept alive too by Farm Bureau and others who wanted to find industrial uses for farm crops. The term for this was "chemurgy," which seems to have been first coined by chemist William J. Hale. Chemurgy was the branch of applied science concerned with producing industrial products from raw farm materials.

Farm Bureau was a supporter of chemurgy and farm-based fuels in particular. An AFBF resolution adopted in the 1930s said, "Industrial alcohol blended with gasoline deserves further study as a means of using great quantities of grains, potatoes and other farm crops grown in all parts of our nation."[5] In 1933, a Farm Bureau committee was formed and a technical adviser from Iowa State University engaged to run tests on ethanol blended fuel. That same year, the Illinois Farm Bureau began test-marketing "Hi-Ball" gasoline which sold at a 2¢ to 3¢ premium from regular gasoline. Gasoline prices were especially volatile in 1933, almost doubling from 12¢ a gallon to 23¢. The 10 percent ethanol-blended Hi-Ball brand was popular with motorists who bought 54,000 gallons in two months from a Farm Bureau affiliated service company. Motorists overwhelmingly rated Hi-Ball "superior to motor fuel now available."[6]

USDA's first endorsement of ethanol also came in 1933 in response to a Senate request to consider its merits. The report said ethanol could "materially increase" the price of crops used for its production. Later, as part of the Agricultural Adjustment of 1938, USDA opened four regional laboratories to research a number of new uses for farm products.

In the same year at a meeting of the American Chemists Society in Milwaukee, Dr. Burke Jacobs, senior research chemist of the U.S. Bureau of Chemistry and Soils, threw cold water on ethanol. Jacobs said it was feasible but not practical until petroleum prices were considerably higher or feedstock could be purchased at lower prices. He recommended looking into producing fuel from corn stalks, cobs, and the leftovers of other crops.[7] A Farm Chemurgic Council also was formed in the 1930s, but it soon angered Farm Bureau and the Roosevelt administration by opposing the New Deal farm programs. The council believed chemurgy was farmers' ticket out of the Depression.

World War II cut off the supply of natural rubber to the U.S. and alcohol was needed to produce butadiene, a chemical base for synthetic rubber. With the end of the war in sight, Farm Bureau sought to keep interest in alcohol production alive. The resolutions committee to the 1945 AFBF annual meeting in Chicago recommended the board hire a "technical man in the fields of industrial alcohol and synthetic rubber." Instead the board of directors consulted with the director of research for Seagram's distilleries. The resolutions committee expressed hope for the future of farm grown fuels, saying that one day they could be an important part of crop usage.[8]

At the end of the war, AFBF President Ed O'Neal made one last attempt at keeping alive the interest in ethanol. O'Neal tried to persuade the government not to shut down the war plants that produced the alcohol for synthetic rubber. His appeal fell on deaf ears, perhaps because the oil industry wanted the plants shut down.[9] After that, no commercial ethanol was available in the United States until the late 1970s after the Organization of Arab Petroleum Exporting Countries (OPEC) briefly shut off oil to the United States because of the Yom Kippur War with Israel.

The oil embargo, high oil prices, and lines at the gas pumps made Americans realize that oil was an economic weapon and an energy crisis could become a permanent fixture of American life. The tiny flame still burning under ethanol was turned up, and the blend of 10 percent ethanol and 90 percent gasoline was given a new name—gasohol.

The 1977 Farm Bill had authorized money for gasohol research and construction of four pilot plants. The Energy Tax Act of 1978 established a 4¢ per gallon exemption on federal excise taxes on gasohol. This launched the modern era of biofuels.

"Almost anybody can grow corn and make alcohol. It can be almost a cottage industry," said an excited *Chicago Tribune* columnist, Jack Mabley, in 1978.[10] Gasohol was indeed viewed by some as a cottage industry with farmers building on-farm stills to produce alcohol from corn. AFBF publicized the feats of these ethanol pioneers who were real experimenters and *Successful Farming* said, "Yes, you can build or buy a still that will produce alcohol on your farm." All it took was $3,000 and a permit for experimental alcohol production.[11]

The picture in people's minds of patriotic American farmers foiling the plans of evil Arab oil sheiks was a topic worthy of discussion at the coffee shop. In Illinois, however, the largest producer of ethanol was not the farmer with a backyard still, but Archer Daniels Midland (ADM). ADM produced 15,000 gallons a day through its wet-milling plant at Decatur, Illinois.

AFBF elevated energy to "one of the most critical problems facing our nation" in its policy book and favored deregulation of oil and natural gas. A 1978 energy policy resolution called for the investment of government and private funds to research "coal gasification, the utilization of feedlot and other organic waste, shale oil extraction, utilization of grain alcohol as fuel, solar energy, wind energy, nuclear energy, wood, geothermal, and other sources of energy."[12]

In a 1979 *Farm Bureau News* article, the question was raised in a headline, "Gasohol: Alternative Energy Source?" No one was quite sure. "Let's reorganize the energy business and give some of that business to American farmers," suggested Richard Merritt of the National Gasohol Commission. AFBF and several state Farm Bureaus signed a contract with Battelle Laboratories in Columbus, Ohio, to investigate ethanol production. Battelle recommended using sweet sorghum instead of corn. When the American Petroleum Institute was contacted about gasohol by Farm Bureau, it responded, "If American farmers can produce an alternative energy source, more power to them."[13]

President Carter's answer to the nation's energy problem was a windfall profits tax on oil companies and a dose of energy conservation. He urged Americans to drive less and in smaller cars. "I'll give it to you straight," said the president. "Each of us will have to use less oil and pay more for it." Congress also approved his gigantic plan to develop synthetic fuels or "synfuels" to replace imported oil. This program focused on producing crude oil from coal, shale rock, and tar sands. President Reagan later closed it down.[14]

The American Farm Bureau Federation came up with a novel idea—why not barter U.S. food for Arab oil? The trading partner AFBF had in mind was the North African desert nation of Libya, which imported 65 percent of its food. Libya was a purchaser of American grain and interested in expanding its animal agriculture. Libyan oil amounted to 10 percent of all U.S. oil imports. It seemed like a perfect match, with just one problem—Libyan leader Muammar el-Qaddafi was a supporter of revolutionary movements around the world and had a reputation for practicing diplomacy in unorthodox ways.[15]

In a search for dry-land farm technology, Libyan officials were in contact with American companies, organizations, and universities, including the University of Idaho. An Iraqi-born professor arranged for a visit to Idaho and contacted Idaho Farm Bureau to help organize it. At some point, the Libyans expressed interest in purchasing wheat and AFBF was brought into the picture. A number of U.S. farm cooperatives were in the refining business so a swap of wheat for oil made sense.

This was just the sort of bold initiative that appealed to AFBF President Allan Grant. He was not afraid of a dialogue with anyone if it served the interests of American agriculture, and he firmly believed that agriculture served the interests of the whole nation. Grant desperately wanted to meet Qaddafi face-to-face. No doubt he would have told him to drop his ties to world terrorism and improve the lives of the Libyan people.

New York Times columnist William Safire theorized later in 1979 that Qaddafi had another reason to be interested in Idaho, besides its agriculture. Libya had purchased a number of C-130 air transports from the Lockheed Corporation, but the Nixon administration refused to grant export licenses for them. Qaddafi hoped to persuade Sen. Frank Church (D-Idaho), who was in line to become chairman of the Senate Foreign Relations Committee, to free up the planes.[16]

One of the most surprising events during an AFBF annual meeting occurred in 1979 at Miami, when as many as forty Libyan singer-dancers and diplomatic officials made an unannounced appearance at the general session. The colorfully robed singers and dancers wound through the audience to the stage accompanied by musicians on drum and flute. It was a complete surprise to Farm Bureau members and most staff. Grant informed the board in advance but only a small trade delegation was expected, not a dance troupe.

On stage, Ahmed el-Shahati, head of Libya's foreign liaison office and a personal representative of Qaddafi, delivered a lengthy greeting in Arabic and read a pledge of friendship. Ali el Houderi, newly appointed Libyan ambassador to the

United States, interpreted his remarks. The Libyans created more buzz than former California Governor Ronald Reagan, also on the program.

A dinner and talks with Libyan officials followed that evening in Miami. The Libyan diplomats asked the American Farm Bureau Federation to become the liaison between American agribusiness and the Libyan government to facilitate technology transfers and commodity sales.

In May 1979, Grant, his wife Irene, and several AFBF staff members went to Tripoli for meetings with oil, agricultural, and diplomatic officials. A visit with Qaddafi also was promised. Grant met first with Shahati at the foreign minister's office across the street from the palace of King Idris, who was overthrown by Qaddafi in 1969. Grant was told that Qaddafi favored an exchange of oil for grain and farm technology because it involved American farmers rather than the U.S. government. Over several days of meetings it was established that farm cooperatives could use in excess of 500,000 barrels per day of light Libyan crude oil. Shahati and his oil minister saw no problem in this and would make the oil available at below the world price. They suggested a starting date of February 1980.

The deal never materialized and neither did Qaddafi. The colonel proved elusive despite repeated promises that he would meet personally with Grant. The Farm Bureau group was kept busy in meetings with young agricultural students and farm organization members and a visit to ancient Phoenician ruins. Back at his hotel, Grant recognized an American and went over to chat with him. It was boxer Muhammad Ali who showed up later on Libyan television in a lively discussion with Qaddafi.

Why Qaddafi avoided the AFBF group was never known. Grant did visit the Libyan embassy in Washington later in the year and saw both Shahati and Houderi. They were still interested in swapping oil for grain, but this time it was AFBF that backed away. Qaddafi was sounding more out of control on news broadcasts, and Grant wanted nothing to do with him.[17]

In retrospect, the Libyan interest was part of a short-lived, but genuine effort to improve relations with the United States that started around 1976. The Libyans targeted a number of influential Americans for visits to Libya in 1978, including former Senate Foreign Relations Committee Chairman J. William Fulbright and President Carter's brother, Billy Carter, who visited Libya with a group of Georgia businessmen.[18]

By the 1980s, the term gasohol faded away, but ethanol was very much alive, primarily as an octane booster. A phase-out of unleaded gasoline caused ethanol production to increase by 40 percent in 1985 to 600 million gallons. The AFBF Natural and Environmental Resources Division reported "it would be ideal to reduce the grain surpluses and raise farm prices without arousing public ire about producing fuel instead of food." Farm Bureau also was in touch with researchers working on blending vegetable and plant oils with diesel fuel.[19]

But 1985 also brought a shake-out in the ethanol industry caused by a sharp drop in oil prices. Half of the commercial ethanol plants ceased production. Several major oil companies also conducted what Farm Bureau termed "well-advertised smear campaigns" against the product, and highway users groups lobbied to end tax exemptions for ethanol. "As farmers and ranchers we need to recognize a good product when we see it, and more importantly we need to use it ourselves and promote its use," said President Kleckner at the first-ever industry-wide conference in July 1988 in Nashville. The conference was sponsored jointly by AFBF, the National Corn Growers Association, *Successful Farming* magazine, and the Renewable Fuels Association.[20]

Ethanol was touted as an octane booster but its "green" environmental qualities were recognized in 1988 when the city of Denver mandated oxygenates like ethanol in gasoline to clear the city's air in the winter months. In 1990, the Clean Air Act's reformulated gasoline program gave ethanol a foot in the door nationwide. The law required the nine cities with the worst traffic-related air pollution to use oxygenates like MTBE (methyl tertiary butyl ether) or ethanol in gasoline by 1995.

However, EPA narrowly interpreted the rules and did not give ethanol enough credit for reducing exhaust emissions. Gasoline blenders wanted to use MTBE instead because it was a petroleum product and cheaper to mix with gasoline. At an EPA hearing in 1994, two members of the AFBF board of directors, Bryce Neidig of Nebraska and Merlin Plagge of Iowa, testified in favor of giving ethanol a 30 percent share of the oxygenate market.[21] In August of that year, in what was billed as "Big Oil against the farmer," the Senate by the narrowest of margins upheld President Clinton's order backing the 30 percent ethanol share. Vice President Al Gore cast a tie-breaking vote for the measure to pass, but refiners went to court to stop the mandate from taking effect.[22]

Time was running out on MTBE, however. By 1995, it started showing up in groundwater after leaking from underground gasoline storage tanks. Medical experts said it could cause cancer and other health problems. The largest single market for MTBE was California, and AFBF and other ethanol supporters were enthusiastic about the substitution of ethanol for MTBE. But the state responded by asking for a federal waiver to meet the auto emission standards without using any oxygenates. The debate flared up in 1999 when the farm economy was in bad shape and farmers desperately wanted to expand the ethanol market, which had reached 1.8 billion gallons.

One of the first actions of newly elected AFBF president Bob Stallman in 2000 was to assure the nation that ethanol could help meet the nation's energy needs. Stallman looked at it pragmatically—fuel consumption on farms, city streets, and highways was a fact of life. "The sad aspect, however, is that we are missing out on a wonderful opportunity to have America's farmers grow a greater percentage of our fuel at home."

Stallman noted the criticism of MTBE and said it was time to elevate ethanol as the clean, safe alternative.[23] A short time later in March 2000, EPA Administrator Carol Browner recommended the phase out of MTBE and replacement with safe biofuels. Major gasoline retailers in California began using ethanol in reformulated gasoline. Connecticut and New York banned MTBE leading to as surge in ethanol production.

Ethanol has a long history of support by Farm Bureau, but for different reasons—first as an outlet for crop surpluses, then an octane enhancer and oxygenate, and finally as a renewable fuel to reduce reliance on foreign oil. Recently EPA lifted the oxygenate requirement across the nation, but ethanol use was soaring anyway because of the renewable fuels standard (RFS). The RFS is the minimum annual level of renewable fuels blended in the nation's fuel supply. In 2002, AFBF played an important role in forging an agreement in the Senate to include a renewable fuels standard for the first time in the Senate energy bill. The agreement called for the use of five billion gallons of renewable fuels, ethanol, and biodiesel, by 2012.

The Energy Policy Act of 2005 contained a RFS of 7.5 billion gallons of ethanol and biodiesel by 2012. Earlier that year, President Bush visited a biodiesel refinery in Virginia. Biodiesel production increased from a half million gallons in 1999 to 30 million gallons by 2004, making it the fastest growing alternative fuel. Troy Bredenkamp, public policy specialist for AFBF, said the renewable fuels standard would result in a "technology bloom" with ethanol and biodiesel derived from cellulosic technology, such as corn biomass, straw, orchard prunings, and sugar commodities.

The RFS is a reflection of the nation's desire for energy independence and homeland security, and the ethanol industry with 175 plants in operation should have no trouble meeting the standards which were raised again at the end of 2007. The new standard is for 9 billion gallons of conventional biofuels in 2008 and up to 15 billion gallons in 2015. At that point the standard is capped, but advanced biofuels resulting from the technology bloom will bring America to at least 36 billion gallons of biofuels annually by 2022.

In 2008, American farmers harvested their second largest corn crop ever despite getting off to a terrible start with heavy spring rains that flooded fields. It was a sure sign that farmers were working hard to feed and fuel the nation, but as food prices rose during the year, the criticism of biofuels mounted. It was the "Food vs. Fuel" debate that Farm Bureau recognized could happen someday when ethanol was still in its infancy. Corn reached an all-time high of more than

$7 per bushel in 2008 triggering alarms that corn was to blame for higher retail food prices.

AFBF, Renewable Fuels Association, National Corn Growers Association, and others defended biofuels. "Condemning biofuels, yet failing to offer another path forward, relegates us to the status quo and further delays the hard work of diversifying our nation's energy future," said Stallman. One of the arguments in the debate has been that fuel would compete with food for land, but that isn't true. The AFBF president pointed out that in 2002, 324 million acres were cultivated for crops and ethanol production was one billion gallons. In 2008, there were 320 million acres of cropland, and ethanol production jumped to nine billion gallons.[24] Ethanol output from a bushel of corn also has been going up, and is about 2.8 gallons per bushel.

Energy Secretary Samuel Bodman and Agriculture Secretary Edward Schafer both said that crop production for biofuels was playing a small role in food price increases in 2008, approximately 3 to 5 percent of the overall increase.[25] "In fact, if you take away ethanol, you're going to drive up the cost of energy and food even more," said Sen. Charles Grassley (R–Iowa), one of ethanol's staunchest defenders in Congress.[26]

The oldest criticism in the book—that ethanol has no net gain in energy—has also been effectively disproved. Ethanol actually produces two-thirds more energy or 167% of the energy that goes into making it. Industry tax breaks have been another favorite target, but the breaks given the ethanol industry pale in comparison to the tax breaks for Big Oil.

There is one criticism within agriculture that Farm Bureau as a general farm organization must take seriously. "On the crop side, in particular for corn growers, ethanol is very positive," said Terry Francl, AFBF senior economist. "On the livestock side, there is no question it is driving up grain and feed prices higher than they would have been, so it is a plus and minus situation." But Francl pointed out that agriculture is a large user of energy, and all farmers have benefited from ethanol in at least one respect. Ethanol was estimated to have knocked 45¢ off the price of gasoline in 2008 when the pump prices topped $4 per gallon.[27]

Going forward, AFBF has joined with over 100 other organizations in endorsing the 25X'25 initiative for agriculture to produce 25 percent of the total energy consumed in the United States by 2025. "We can grow a wide variety of crops to produce ethanol and biodiesel. We can harvest the sun and wind to produce electricity," said President Stallman.[28] Farmers will still be converting the sun's energy into food of course, but the conversion of farm crops and crop waste into energy is an exciting dimension of farming, one that Farm Bureau first supported long ago.

Endnotes

1. Transcript, AFBF Annual Meeting, January 14–17, 1974, Atlantic City, New Jersey.

2. *Farm Bureau Policies for 1975; Farm Bureau Policies for 1976.*

3. "Ethyl, The 1920s Environmental Conflict Over Leaded Gasoline and Alternative Fuels," William Kovarik, Ph.D., Paper to the American Society for Environmental History, Annual Conference, March 2003. www.radford.edu/~wkovarik/papers/ethylconflict.html, accessed July 12, 2007; "Leaded Gasoline," *Time*, February 1, 1926.

4. Texas Farm Bureau edition, *Bureau Farmer*, April 1932.

5. *AFBF Policy Resolutions of 1934.*

6. "Further Reports Favor Alcohol Blended Gasoline," *AFBF Official News Letter*, May 2, 1933; "Downtown," *Time*, August 7, 1933.

7. "Alcohol Fuels Too Costly," *AFBF Official News Letter*, September 13, 1938.

8. Minutes, AFBF board of directors, December 1945.

9. "Should Not Scrap Alcohol Plants," *AFBF Official News Letter*, October 31, 1945.

10. "Politicians Leap on Gasohol Bandwagon," *Chicago Tribune*, October 16, 1978.

11. "More Energy Alternatives," *Successful Farming*, February 1980.

12. *Farm Policies for 1978.*

13. "Gasohol: Alternate Energy Source," *Farm Bureau News*, April 30, 1979.

14. "Carter to End Price Control on U.S. Oil," *New York Times,* April 6, 1979; "Synfuel Success," *Time,* June 2, 1980.

15. Woell, *Farm Bureau Architects*, 145–146; "Libya Says It Tries to Improve Relations, but U.S. Is Balking," *New York Times,* September 28, 1976.

16. William Safire, "Essay, Libya and Idaho," *New York Times,* February 15, 1979.

17. Woell, *Farm Bureau Architects*, 150–153.

18. "Billy Carter and the Bumpy Route of U.S.-Libyan Ties," *New York Times*, August 2, 1980.

19. "Ethanol and Vegetable Oil as Fuel," *Farm Bureau News*, September 20, 1982.

20. "With Back to Wall, Ethanol Industry Fights for Survival," *Farm Bureau News*, July 25, 1988.

21. "FB: Ethanol Would Help Environment, Economy," *Farm Bureau News*, January 24, 1994.

22. "Senate Narrowly Upholds EPA Ethanol Rule," *Chicago Tribune*, August 4, 1994; "Court Puts Off Ethanol Requirement," *Chicago Tribune*, September 14, 1994.

23. "Farmers Can Help Meet Energy Needs," *Farm Bureau News*, February 21, 2000.

24. Stallman, Bob, "Letter to the Editor," *Time*, April 2, 2008.

25. "Biofuel Plays Small Role in Food Prices," *Dow Jones Newswires*, June 11, 2008.

26. "Ethanol Has Unfairly Become Punching Bag," Federal Document Clearing House, Capitol Hill Press Releases, May 8, 2008.

27. Interview with Terry Francl.

28. "Big Three Automakers Endorse New Energy Vision," Energy Coalition news release, May 18, 2006.

25 | Farm Bureau Leadership

A SPECIAL GAVEL WAS PRESENTED BY THE INDIANA FARM BUREAU TO AFBF PRESIDENT James R. Howard during the second annual meeting in December 1920. The gavel was cut from a wooden flagstaff of Battery E of the Seventh U.S. Army Field Artillery. It had been shattered in the colossal Battle of the Argonne and was passed on to Farm Bureau by a U.S. Army major. The officer made one stipulation—the gavel should never be wielded in a selfish act against humanity.

The presidents of the American Farm Bureau Federation have been true to that pledge. They have led an organization dedicated to the high principles and sound policies of farmer members. There have been eleven presidents of the American Farm Bureau Federation. All were farmers or ranchers: three were from Iowa, three from Illinois; and one each from Alabama, California, Ohio, Texas, and Virginia. The AFBF president and vice president are elected separately by the voting delegates at the annual meeting for two-year terms. There are no term limits.

The AFBF president was considered the second most influential person in agriculture by *U.S. News and World Report*, which listed the secretary of agriculture first in a survey it used to publish. Every one of the presidents over the last ninety years recognized that high regard went with the position, not the person, and all were honored to serve Farm Bureau members.

The first president, James R. Howard, farmed 480 acres in Marshall County, Iowa. The corn-hog farm he grew up on was named Homelands. Howard held a degree in philosophy from the University of Chicago and worked as a bank cashier, school teacher, and college professor before deciding to make farming his career. He returned to Homelands with wife Anna and expanded the farm. Howard was the first president of the Marshall County Farm Bureau in 1916, and first president of the Iowa Farm Bureau in 1918.

Howard was forty-six-years old when he became the president of the American Farm Bureau Federation. He was tall, angular, and made a "veritable and convincing emissary of agriculture," according to historian Kile.[1] As president, he was invited to a dinner party in New York City given by prominent investment banker Otto Herman Kahn. Howard was astonished when he saw the guest list. It included the heads of railroads, insurance companies, banks, and newspaper chains. There were no speeches that evening other than Howard's talk about life on the farm and the problems of the twentieth-century farmer. The dinner marked Farm Bureau's acceptance by the nation's power brokers.[2]

Much of Howard's time in office was spent traveling by train between Chicago and Washington and testifying before Congress, a schedule which put a strain on his health. He was diagnosed with tuberculosis and retired in 1922. Howard's intuition and intelligence served the young organization well. He rejected an idea to form regional Farm Bureaus instead of a national federation and hoped that one day that Farm Bureau would be an international organization.[3]

The second president of the American Farm Bureau Federation, Oscar E. Bradfute of Ohio, easily could have been the first, but Bradfute looked more like a prosperous banker than a farmer. At the founding convention, few of the delegates knew anyone outside of their own state. Bradfute was a heavy, lethargic man, and his appearance mattered to the delegates. After they got to know him better, they elected him to replace Howard.[4]

On his farm near Xenia, Ohio, Bradfute raised purebred Aberdeen-Angus cattle. He was a leader in what was the forerunner of the American Angus Association and helped organize the International Livestock Association in 1899. Bradfute organized his county Farm Bureau and served as first president of the Ohio Farm Bureau. A graduate of Indiana University, Bradfute served many years as a trustee of The Ohio State University. Although handicapped by budget deficits and declining membership, he led AFBF through some troubled waters in cooperative marketing.

Sam H. Thompson, the third AFBF president, was tall, gray-haired, and slightly stooped. At age sixty-four, he was already a bit frail, but he had a sincere, almost religious conviction that won over people. The Illinois "dirt farmer" also had been a member of the state's general assembly and president of a bank. Thompson had a keen business sense that he brought to the Illinois Farm Bureau as president in 1923. The AFBF annual meeting where he was elected president in 1925 was the first one to call for a national farm policy, something Thompson believed in very much.

Thompson found the AFBF presidency far more demanding of his time than his state Farm Bureau position. He especially missed going home to farm. "When I left my home in Quincy on January 2, 1926, I little realized that during the next 36 months I should travel twice that many thousands of miles, that I should spend more than a hundred nights in sleepers, and that I should make more than two hundred public addresses."[5]

In the spring of 1931, Thompson turned the president's gavel over to Vice President Edward A. O'Neal III of Alabama in a nationwide radio broadcast. O'Neal was a southern planter with a 2,800 acre farm near Florence, Alabama. A tall man with thinning hair, O'Neal had a disarming, infectious smile, and a hearty laugh that ended with a cackle.[6] O'Neal's maternal great-grandfather, Gen. John Coffee, soldiered with Gen. Andrew Jackson during the War of 1812. His grandfather, Edward Asbury O'Neal I, was a brigadier general in the Confederate Army and served as governor of Alabama, as did an uncle. He seemed suited for a career in law or politics but a love of the land drew him back to farming after graduation from Washington & Lee University.

On the occasion of his twentieth year in Farm Bureau, President Roosevelt sent O'Neal a message that read, "I shall always gratefully remember your helpfulness to me at the most critical stages of the long struggle to set up an agricultural policy and program adjustable to changed conditions in a changing world." Senator Lister Hill (D-Alabama) described O'Neal as "one of the greatest agricultural statesmen in the history of our country."[7]

Franklin D. Roosevelt has been called the most consequential man of the twentieth century by some historians, and O'Neal can be considered the most consequential AFBF president of the century. They first met at the New York State Fair when Roosevelt was governor of New York. O'Neal gave a main-stage speech and toured the exhibits with Roosevelt who rode in a wheel chair. At the Indian exhibit, O'Neal was honored with a ceremonial robe, headdress, and an Indian name. He looked to Roosevelt for help on what the name meant. Roosevelt told him, "Big Wind," and roared with delight. They were friends from then on.[8]

After O'Neal retired, Iowa hog farmer Allan B. Kline was elected AFBF's fifth president in 1947. Born in Nebraska, Kline graduated from Morningside College at Sioux City, Iowa, and later received a B.S. degree in agriculture from Iowa State College at Ames. During the First World War he served as a sergeant in the Army medical corps. Kline and his wife Gladys rented a farm for a few years before purchasing a rundown piece of land near Vinton, Iowa. He built up the farm from 240 acres to 560 acres and was recognized as a Master Farmer.

Kline worked his way up in Farm Bureau starting as a director of his township Farm Bureau. He was county and state Farm Bureau president before becoming vice president of the American Farm Bureau Federation in 1945. A student of agricultural economics and international affairs, the astute Kline spent two months in Britain in 1944 on a mission for the Office of War Information, and represented AFBF as a consultant to the 1945 conference in San Francisco where the UN charter was drafted.

A tall, well-built man, Kline had bushy eyebrows and dark brown hair flecked with gray. He spoke with a strong, resonant voice and knew how to hold an audience. His election came at a time when the Midwest was eager to assume the presidency after O'Neal's long tenure ended in 1947. Although he was not in office long, Kline had a significant impact. He led AFBF in moving away from New Deal farm policies and what he considered socialized agriculture.[9]

Kline was an excellent debater and appeared frequently on "Meet the Press" and other public affairs programs on television where he used common sense developed on the farm to make his points. "I don't know much about economics, but I do know about pigs," he would say and then proceed to illustrate a complex economic issue in terms of hog production.[10] Kline was the first AFBF president to travel by airplane to Farm Bureau meetings, but air travel only served to expand an already busy schedule. He retired for health reasons in 1954, with a year remaining on his term.

Charles B. Shuman was an inspiration for many Farm Bureau leaders who rose through the ranks in the 1960s, 1970s, and 1980s. The Illinois leader was the only candidate nominated to replace Kline. Vice President Walter Randolph, an experienced and popular southerner, chose not to run. Born on a 375 acre grain farm near Sullivan that had been in the family since 1853, Shuman earned a master's degree in agronomy from the University of Illinois. He went from director of the Moultrie County Farm Bureau in 1932 to president of the Illinois Farm Bureau in 1945.

Shuman had wavy hair and spoke with gravely voice. He was the only AFBF president to appear on the cover of *Time* magazine. The September 3, 1965, cover was a drawing of him standing in a field. The headline read, "The Man Who Wants the Government To Get Off the Farm." The description was totally accurate; that was his personal belief, although he adhered to Farm Bureau policy which was not as explicit. According to *Time*'s article about him, Shuman and Farm Bureau wanted to restore the "lost prototype" of the farmer as "a sturdy pioneer who fed the nation's body and nourished its spirit with his fierce independence, his self-reliance, his courage."[11]

One time Shuman got carried away with his criticism of federal farm policy and claimed that it "denies the unmistakable pattern of God's law." The statement was too much for Farmers Union president James Patton who complained—"This is Shuman's arrogant attempt to make God a member of Farm Bureau."[12] Anyone who knew Shuman would not put that past him, but there was nothing arrogant about him. He was a humble, frugal man who never moved to Chicago but commuted by train so he could return to the farm on weekends. When in Chicago, Shuman stayed at the same hotel but always took whatever room was available, refusing to reserve a suite as suggested by AFBF staff. A widower, Shuman met his second wife Mabel on the train.

Two major affiliated companies began business during Shuman's sixteen years in office. The American Agricultural Marketing Association (AAMA) was incorporated in January 1960 to assist state Farm Bureau marketing associations and create a multistate marketing network. The American Farm Bureau Service Company was organized in June 1965 to coordinate group purchasing for tires, batteries, and other products sold under the Safemark private brand. Both programs were successful for a number of years and then phased out.

Shuman stepped down at the 1970 AFBF annual meeting in Houston with a year left on his term. The South failed to come up with a successor and William J. Kuhfuss, president of the Illinois Farm Bureau, was elected. Bill Kuhfuss raised Angus beef cattle with his brother and son on an 800 acre grain and livestock farm in Tazewell County. The tall, athletic-looking Kuhfuss was an All-American baseball player in college at Illinois State University in Normal where he graduated with a degree in education.

AFBF went through a major change under Kuhfuss' leadership. For the first time in its history, the general headquarters left the city of Chicago. It moved from the giant Merchandise Mart to a colonial-style building in the northwest suburb of Park Ridge, near O'Hare Airport. On September 4, 1974, Bill Kuhfuss sat at a telecommunications terminal in the Park Ridge office and typed a message to state Farm Bureaus. "Farm Bureau effort and action can be no better than the information backing the effort or action. This is using modern technology at its best for the greatest farm organization in the world." It was the first bulletin that went out to state Farm Bureaus on a new "Speedline" network designed for high-speed, two-way communication. AFBF entered the Information Age, well ahead of other organizations. [13]

The 1976 AFBF annual meeting at St. Louis where Kuhfuss was defeated for reelection was one of the worst in history. The temperature outside the Chase Park Plaza Hotel was below zero and there were several inches of snow on the ground when a woman drove her car through the hotel's front window. Members also had to stand outside waiting to go through a magnetometer before entering the convention for President Ford's speech. The delegates voted then and there to hold the annual meetings in warmer parts of the country, a decision that stood for many years.

California Farm Bureau President Allan Grant became the first westerner elected national president. Secretary-Treasurer Roger Fleming was asked to move from the Washington legislative office to the Chicago headquarters but retired instead after nearly forty years of Farm Bureau service. Grant brought in the California Farm Bureau administrator, Richard Owens, as secretary, and William H. Broderick was named treasurer. Grant was seventy-years old and looked the part of an elder statesman, but he had the stamina of a much younger person. He was especially proud of the hardships he endured to become a successful farmer and Farm Bureau leader.

The Grant family had no previous farming experience before young Allan decided to raise a calf as a 4-H project. He studied agricultural economics at Montana State College and the University of California at Los Angeles. The death of his father forced him to drop out and become the family breadwinner. He worked as an oil field roustabout and stevedore on a ship, before he sharecropped and joined Farm Bureau in 1930.

Grant and his wife Irene put together a 2,000 acre farming operation in Tulare and Madera counties and switched from dairying to raising Red Angus cattle, mules, and Belgian draft horses. He was first elected president of the California Farm Bureau in 1963 and named chairman of the California Board of Agriculture by Governor Ronald Reagan.

Faced with tight finances and having to cut a half-million dollars out of the budget, the AFBF board discontinued *The American Farmer* magazine in 1976. The magazine was the single most costly item because it was mailed to all two million member families. For fifty years, AFBF published a magazine first named *Bureau Farmer*, then *Nation's Agriculture* and finally *The American Farmer*, but rising postal rates, printing costs, and questions about the value of the publication made it expendable.

Grant's first annual meeting as president also was the first one ever held outside the continental United States. The convention at Honolulu in January 1977 was one of the most popular ever with 12,000 Farm Bureau members in attendance. Grant expanded AFBF's influence worldwide with trade trips to the European Economic Community, India, Japan, Mexico, Libya, Israel, the Soviet Union, and Peoples Republic of China.

At the 1980 annual meeting in Phoenix, Robert B. Delano of Virginia was elected to succeed Grant. AFBF membership was 3.3 million members and 1.8 million were from the South. Bob Delano had graduated from Virginia Polytechnic Institute with a bachelor's degree in animal husbandry. During World War II, he served in the U.S. Army Horse Calvary in the India-Burma area. A good-looking man with a pleasant smile and distinctive Virginia Tidewater accent, Delano helped reorganize the Richmond County Farm Bureau in 1955 and became its president. He was first elected president of Virginia Farm Bureau in 1962.

Bob and his wife Martha lived on a farm in Warsaw, Virginia, on a peninsula between the Potomac and Rappahannock Rivers. Although he raised livestock earlier in his farming career, Delano later grew corn, soybeans, wheat, and barley on 500 acres. The Delano family tree traced back to colonial America and an ancestor who arrived from Holland in 1621. Delano enjoyed farming and made it home on weekends whenever possible to do some fieldwork. His column in *Farm Bureau News* was appropriately titled, "Observations from the Tractor Seat."

Delano's management style and financial knowledge were suited to what he thought AFBF should do—get back to the basics. President Grant had concentrated so much on overseas missions that organizational matters needed more attention. Delano expanded the field staff to improve relations with state Farm Bureaus and engineered a dues increase. While he was president, AFBF introduced ACRES, a commodity market information and analysis program available by satellite and later over the Internet. When Grant Moffett retired as his administrative assistant, Delano named Dave Conover assistant to the president and Dave Mayfield became secretary.

Although president for just six years, Delano had more than his share of unexpected challenges, like the explosion of the Mount St. Helens volcano in 1980. The blast showered Washington and Idaho with ash that covered thousands of acres of farmland and infiltrated farm equipment. At the 1981 AFBF annual meeting in New Orleans, the Alabama Farm Bureau left the federation over an insurance dispute with neighboring states. Alabama was traditionally one of the strongest Farm Bureaus in the nation and the withdrawal was a deep loss. Determined efforts to settle the dispute failed. "You know it was their right," said Delano years later. "Being from Virginia and a background in the Civil War, I understood that states had the right to secede back then and states had the right to secede from AFBF."[14] Alabama reaffiliated with AFBF as the Alabama Farmers Federation in 2005.

Described as trim and youthful-looking with a wealth of jet black hair when he became the tenth AFBF president in 1986, Dean R. Kleckner was compared favorably to the last Iowan to head the federation, Kline. Both had corn-hog operations; Kline was a Master Farmer, and Kleckner received the state's Outstanding Young Farmer recognition. They also had a common interest in economics and international affairs.

First elected president of his Floyd County Farm Bureau at the age of 28, Kleckner served ten years as president of the Iowa Farm Bureau before being elected president of the American Farm Bureau Federation. Dean and wife Natalie lived on a 550 acre farm near Rudd where he grew corn, soybeans, and marketed hogs in a farrow-to-finish operation. He enjoyed small-town life, farming as a youth, and was a pitcher for his high school baseball team and center in basketball. After high school, he joined the Army and served in Germany.

As it had done for others, the AFBF presidency propelled Kleckner to a bigger stage than generally expected for someone coming from a small farming community. Nothing other than politics perhaps offered so much opportunity for leadership, service, and recognition. All the presidents recognized the role they had as chief spokesman for the federation, but Kleckner relished media opportunities more than most. He was naturally suited to radio and television at a time when media relations received more attention. During his presidency, AFBF installed a private satellite network and became a leader in corporate video communications.

Kleckner was the third longest-serving president; his fourteen years placed him behind O'Neal and Shuman. He was challenged for reelection by Vice President Harry Bell of South Carolina at one point. A natural rivalry existed between the South and Midwest largely because of the commodity interests—the South with peanuts, cotton, and tobacco and the Midwest with corn, soybeans, and wheat. Commodity differences and membership size, where the South gained a significant edge, separated the four regions. Bell did not consider this diversity a weakness, but one of Farm Bureau's strengths.[15]

The 2000 AFBF annual meeting at Houston was about change in the twenty-first century, and the delegates voted for a change at the top. Bob Stallman, president of the Texas Farm Bureau, and a third-generation cattle and rice producer from Columbus, succeeded Kleckner.

Anyone guessing Bob Stallman's occupation might venture to say head football coach because of his commanding presence and voice. In fact, the 6'3" Texan played both offensive tackle and middle linebacker for his high school team which needed him on both sides of the ball. Like a coach, Stallman is a motivator of leaders and staff. He presides over board meetings and policy resolutions in a way that one observer described as "masterful." Like his predecessors, Stallman is never far from an AFBF policy book. He has a copy in his desk and one stored on his laptop computer. He makes sure the AFBF game plan is consistent with the will of its members.

While he enjoys his role as one of the top leaders of agriculture in the world, Stallman did not anticipate making a career of it as a young person. "I left the farm in the summer of 1970 to go to the University of Texas, and I swore I was never coming back to farm. Five years later I was back," he recalled. Stallman assumed a lot of responsibilities on the farm as a teenager after his father was thrown from a horse and injured. The opportunity to escape to corporate America with his honors degree in computer science looked good but something was missing. "I missed the outdoors and all the dynamics of being able to grow a crop," he admitted. Stallman returned to the farm in time to go through the financial crisis of the 1980s, although the rice business wasn't hit as hard as some others. Today the family-owned farm still raises rice and cattle.[16]

Stallman's grandfather was a charter member of the Colorado County Farm Bureau and his father was the county's president. His own interest in Farm Bureau started because of a water issue. He was impressed by the way Farm Bureau went to bat for local producers on the matter. A Texas Farm Bureau fieldman invited Stallman to a Young Farmer and Rancher conference in Austin where he enjoyed meeting other young farmers. Stallman first served on his county Farm Bureau board as young farmer representative. By 1993 he was president of the Texas Farm Bureau and the following year was elected to the AFBF board of directors.

There are two prestigious advisory committees that he serves on: The White House Advisory Committee for Trade Policy and Negotiations (ACTPN) and the Advisory Committee on International Economic Policy (ACIEP), the State Department's principal advisory panel on international economics. Stallman is married to Stacie Lynn Bryan and has two daughters who reside in Texas.

Bob Stallman heads AFBF at a truly significant time in the history of American agriculture and has already led the organization through some dramatic changes. Leadership has not been a scarce commodity in Farm Bureau. "If there is one single contribution that I would say AFBF provides for our country, it is leadership. We always need leaders in Farm Bureau and our leadership programs are designed to help surface and train them," said Stallman.[17] Grassroots leadership is what Farm Bureau is all about. The federation's success has always been tied closely to farmer leaders who accepted the gavel and the responsibilities that go with it.

Endnotes

1. Kile, *The Farm Bureau Through Three Decades*, 58.

2. Ibid., 8.

3. Ibid., 106.

4. Ibid., 115.

5. Ibid., 140.

6. Ibid., 172–173.

7. Davis, *One Man, Edward Asbury O'Neal III,* 42–46.

8. "Reminiscences of Edward Asbury O'Neal," Columbia University, New York City, June 17, 1953: interview conducted by Dean Albertson, 74–76.

9. Transcript, AFBF Annual Meeting, December 14–16, 1954, New York, New York.

10. "Reflections on Freedom," Kline, lectures delivered May 3–5, 1965; Woell, *Farm Bureau Architects,* 30.

11. "Agriculture, How to Shoot Santa Claus," *Time,* September 3, 1965.

12. Ibid., 25.

13. Woell, *Farm Bureau Architects*, 124.

14. Interview with Bob Delano.

15. Interview with Harry Bell.

16. Interview with Bob Stallman.

17. Ibid.

26 | The Roles of Women and Young Farmers and Ranchers

IF THE AMERICAN FARM BUREAU FEDERATION HAD NEVER ACCOMPLISHED A SINGLE thing legislatively, it would still have been rated a success for improving the image of the farm family. In 1948, Louis Bromfield, the Pulitzer Prize winning author, conservationist and Ohio farmer, said, "Nothing more remarkable has happened in American life during the past generation than the rise in dignity and importance of the American farmer." Bromfield added that no organization played a greater role in this transformation than Farm Bureau.[1]

The most famous image of a farm couple of course is Grant Wood's painting, "American Gothic." Wood's sister posed as the wife and a local dentist as her husband. The dentist was given a hayfork to hold and the rest is history. The dour-faced man and stern woman created a storm of protest from farm women because they thought it was a parody of rural life. The painting suggested that farmers and small town residents were small-minded, judgmental, and grim.[2]

Wood painted "American Gothic" in 1930, but he could have painted a more accurate portrait of a rural couple by attending the AFBF annual meeting that year in Boston. Farm Bureau members made the trip their annual vacation. They traveled by train to Washington, Philadelphia, and New York, and visited historic sites before arriving in Boston. Those who got off in New York City were offered free passage to Boston on the S.S. Leviathan, a famous Victorian era steamship.

Rural families enjoyed the fellowship of Farm Bureau friends, and because Farm Bureau has always been a family organization, the programs and benefits of membership were not exclusively for the male head of the household. The important roles of women and young people in agriculture were recognized very early by Farm Bureau. Today, the AFB Women's Leadership Committee and the Young Farmer and Rancher Committee develop leaders, work on national policy issues, and promote agriculture to the nonfarm public.

There were three women present for the first AFBF annual meeting, the 1919 organizing convention. At the 1920 AFBF annual meeting in Indianapolis, two women spoke to the general session, and all the women in the audience were invited on stage. Mrs. Charles (Edna) Sewell of Indiana told Farm Bureau members, "There isn't a man here this evening, no matter how good a farmer he may be, or how capable a manager he may be, who is capable enough to manage and direct all the affairs of his farm and his homestead unless he has in close partnership and cooperation with him an up-to-date woman to help him."

With that, an Arizona male delegate jumped to his feet and offered a resolution in support of full-equality for women in Farm Bureau. During the business session, a formal resolution was passed that said in part, "The influence of this organization which is a potent factor in our national life will be materially extended and reflect itself over rural America in a more significant manner, by the admission of women to membership and they are invited into full participation . . ."[3]

Women's organizations known as "Home Bureaus" grew up alongside Farm Bureaus in a few states, and the first Women's Committee was appointed in 1921 to serve in an advisory capacity to the AFBF board of directors. The chair of the committee was Mrs. Charles Schuttler of Missouri. The initial program of work included community organization, recreation, rural libraries, conservation of time and human energy, intelligent use of leisure, rural schools, health and hygiene, raising home making to the status of a profession, and world peace.

"The most important social unit in America is the American farm home," said Frank Evans in 1926, when he served as AFBF's general marketing counsel. The improvement of farm homes and the advancement of rural life were two of Farm Bureau's important goals, and Evans said, "This particular phase of the Farm Bureau work will rest most safely in the hands of the Farm Women—to be carried out through the Farm Bureau." A Home and Community Department was established that year with Sewell as staff director.[4]

In time the Home and Community designation was too limiting because women also were interested in national and international issues. At the 1934 AFBF annual meeting in Nashville, delegates approved creation of the Associated Women of the American Farm Bureau Federation, an "affiliate member" of the federation. Women from state Farm Bureaus, Home Bureaus, home demonstration councils and similar organizations were accepted as members.

Sewell became director of the Associated Women and as a speaker was the equal of most men. In a national radio address to farm women, she said it was time to end self-pity and work aggressively on behalf of Farm Bureau policy. "Someone has said that farm women have unconsciously developed a 'Can't Have It' complex and have worked overtime trying to contrive ways and means to eke out the pitifully scanty income from the farming business that was always allotted to them. Isn't it about time to leave that complex along with the other, 'I'm just a farmer's wife,' and right–about face?"[5]

A farm woman's labor was worth $50,000 over thirty years, according to a Farm Credit Administration official who spoke at an Indiana women's conference in 1937. She based the value on the average number of garments mended, bread baked, fruit canned, etc. Any smart man would have avoided the issue entirely and declared his wife priceless, especially if she was within earshot.[6]

The first annual convention of the Associated Women was held in conjunction with the 1935 AFBF convention in Chicago. A speaking contest at the convention drew thirteen entrants. The winning speech was about the hard facts of farm life. "Farm homes want more than recovery, the return to a former state of misfortune. They want permanent security against misfortune for their livelihood, their culture, their happiness," said the winner, Carrie Smith Colby of Litchfield, New Hampshire.[7]

The Associated Women of Farm Bureau moved quickly to join the Associated Country Women of the World and gain recognition from other women's groups. At a national women's conference sponsored by the *Chicago Tribune* in March 1937, the chair of the Associated Women of Farm Bureau, Abbie Sargent of New Hampshire, was a featured speaker. "Rural women with their city sisters must be informed on matters pertaining to international relations. They must be firm in upholding the policy of representative government and the purity of the ballot, and of working for a living wage," she said.[8]

Nation's Agriculture, the AFBF magazine, gave regular attention to women's activities and encouraged women to round up new Farm Bureau members, especially the ones in their own family. "Bring up children so that they do not have to join Farm Bureau—they just grow into it," was one bit of advice. Sewell believed that Farm Bureau played a role in building a happy, contented farm home, and she seemed to be right about that. Mrs. Thomas Williams, a Kansas dairy farmer's wife and member of the Happy-Go-Lucky Farm Bureau Club of Logan County wrote, "This is a glorious age to be alive. I don't have to work 30 days 14 hours long to get enough money to buy a ticket to the opera. I can listen to it at night at home."[9]

At a meeting in Washington in 1949, Sewell heard from Dr. Jonas Salk, a research professor at the University of Pittsburgh, who discussed what little was known about infantile paralysis or polio. In 1955, after Dr. Salk perfected a vaccine to fight the crippling disease, Farm Bureau women were at the forefront of efforts to get rural residents vaccinated. Dr. Albert Sabin introduced an oral vaccine administered on a sugar cube in the early 1960s, and again Farm Bureau women made sure friends and neighbors went to community centers to receive the vaccine. Farm Bureau women played an important role in alerting rural America to polio and its prevention.[10]

Delegates to the 1954 AFBF annual meeting in New York City approved a major bylaws change that brought the Farm Bureau women's program into the mainstream of the organization. The Associated Women of Farm Bureau was dissolved and replaced with an American Farm Bureau Women's Committee that consisted of a chair, vice chair, and one Farm Bureau woman from each of the four regions, later expanded to two women from each region. For the first time, the women's chair served on the AFBF board of directors.

Virginia Smith of Nebraska became chair of the AFB Women's Committee in 1955, a position she held for the next eighteen years before leaving to enter politics. While she was committee chair, Smith issued a challenge to Farm Bureau women. "Know and understand the issues so you can discuss them knowledgeably, intelligently and easily." In 1964, she appeared before a House Judiciary Subcommittee to argue against the Supreme Court decision that removed prayer and Bible reading from public schools. "The vast majority of farmers and ranchers do not believe religion should be confined to one day of the week, or to church, or to home," she said.[11]

Smith was elected as a Republican to the House of Representatives in 1974 at the age of sixty-three, after she defeated seven men in the primary election for the district that covers the western two-thirds of Nebraska. The national Republican Party sent a twenty-two-year old student out to work on her campaign. He was Karl Rove, who later became deputy chief of staff to President George W. Bush. Smith was reelected every two years until she retired in 1991. When she died in 2006, a colleague remembered, "She was for agriculture all the way and she wasn't shy about it."[12]

Through most of the 1980s, Berta White of Mississippi was chair of the AFB Women's Committee. A former state legislator, White was a confident, articulate woman with southern charm. The biggest accomplishment during White's years of office was the beginning of the Agriculture in the Classroom Program (AITC), which has been enormously successful in teaching school children where food, natural-fiber clothes, and renewable fuel come from.

In May 1981, Agriculture Secretary John Block named a sixteen-member task force to come up with a strategy to provide schools with more relevant information about production agriculture. One of the original planners was AFBF staff member Marsha Purcell. Farm Bureau women were key players in implementing the strategy. By 1988, forty-seven state Farm Bureaus had staff coordinators for Agriculture in the Classroom. The original teaching included agricultural geography, basic economics, world agriculture, and careers in food production. At the local level, Farm Bureau women volunteered to be in the classroom, which was the first time many inner-city students got to meet a farmer and hear about farm life. At the national level, AFBF developed educational materials and training aids.

Farm Bureau women also were active in Farm-City Week, a fall event to increase understanding between rural and urban neighbors.

At a 1984 conference of state Farm Bureau Women's Committee leaders in Washington, Transportation Secretary Elizabeth Dole was the featured speaker. She told the women that a "quiet revolution" was taking place in American society. Women were increasingly entering politics and professions once dominated by men. Dole proved it herself by briefly running for the Republican presidential nomination in the 2000 election and getting elected to the Senate from North Carolina in 2002.[13]

Throughout the 1980s, Farm Bureau women were active in policy implementation. During the 1985 farm bill debate, they launched Project 51,000, a network of Farm Bureau women who could generate that many letters to senators and congressional representatives at critical times in the debate. White also led a group of women to Capitol Hill after a women's conference. In just a few hours, the forty-seven women made 134 legislative contacts.

Berta White stepped down as chair of the AFB Women's Committee at the 1993 annual meeting in Anaheim. The previous year had been declared the Year of the Woman because four women were elected to the Senate and House representation had also increased. "Farm women are needed more than ever, and not just in agriculture," said White, "but in issues influencing the spiritual, social and economic fiber of America."[14]

White's successor was Linda Reinhardt, a Kansas go-getter who raised cattle in southeastern Kansas. In the mid-1970s, Reinhardt was invited to serve as women's chair for Neosho County Farm Bureau. When she asked the board about her responsibilities she was told, "We would like for you to fix the coffee and bake the cookies for the meetings." Reinhardt graciously replied, "I'm glad to do that, but I want to get involved in policy."[15] Cookies they could always get, but in Reinhardt the county leaders found a person focused on women helping women, not only in this country but abroad.

Under her leadership, the AFB Women's Committee helped farm women in the former Soviet Union with income-generating projects. Reinhardt led a Farm Bureau women's delegation to Ukraine in 1994, sponsored by the Citizens Network for Foreign Affairs (CNFA). The delegation traveled to farms, visited schools, and talked to the Ukrainians about organizing and lobbying for legislation. Back home, they raised $30,000 to start a canning factory in the village of Velyki Luchky near the border with Hungary. The Ukrainian women had only rudimentary methods to preserve fruits and vegetables, and about half of the crop usually spoiled.

In 1997, the AFBF Women's Committee held the inaugural Food Check-Out Day on February 10. The promotional idea was brought to the committee by one of its members, Betty DeWitt of South Carolina. Food Check-Out Day was modeled after Tax Freedom Day, although it fell much earlier in the year. It was the date by which most Americans earned enough disposable income to pay for all the food they ate, at home or away, for the entire year. Reinhardt had the idea to link it with Ronald McDonald House Charities, so food and monetary donations collected for the celebration would go to help families with seriously ill children. A long-lasting relationship with McDonald's developed. The celebration was later renamed Food Check-Out Week. Starting in 2009 the emphasis is on stretching the food dollar with nutritious meal selections.

The first National Women's Conference was held by the federation in 2000. "American farm women have made significant contributions throughout our history to building Farm Bureau's record of accomplishments," said AFBF President Bob Stallman at the inaugural event in Colorado Springs, Colorado. Over 500 enthusiastic women from thirty-five states participated in the conference and workshops and left with ideas to energize their local and state programs.[16]

In 2002, Linda Reinhardt retired and Terry Gilbert, a cattle and tobacco producer from Danville, Kentucky, was elected chair of the AFB Women's Committee. The soft-spoken Gilbert is a strategic thinker with a passion for providing the tools and encouragement to women to make them successful leaders in agriculture. "My challenge to you as Farm Bureau Women leaders is to make your programs stronger than ever and help us make the AFBF program stronger than ever," she said.[17]

Regional women's multistate meetings were held in April 2002, where the White-Reinhardt Fund for Education was announced. Administered by the American Farm Bureau Foundation for Agriculture (AFBFA), the fund assists with Agriculture in the Classroom projects and awards scholarships to teachers to attend the National Agriculture in the Classroom annual conference.

The Women's Committee also played a leading role in a new and very different educational project for Farm Bureau. In 2003, Farm Bureau became an exhibitor at Innoventions, in Epcot at Walt Disney World Resort. The exhibit was titled "Beautiful Science" when Farm Bureau took it over from Monsanto Company. With funding from AFBFA, the exhibit was enhanced and renamed "The Great American Farm." The Farm Bureau exhibit introduced families visiting Epcot to the science and technology necessary to supply them with food. One of the featured attractions was the Great American Pizza Game, a game show about where food comes from.

In 2007, the Women's Committee adopted a new name—AFB Women's Leadership Committee. "Our committee is the only one that provides leadership opportunities specifically for women," said Gilbert in explaining the addition of "leadership" to the title. "When it comes to leadership opportunities it doesn't matter whether you are a man or a woman, what matters is passion, input and the ability to do it," she said. Through women's conferences, workshops, and seminars, Farm Bureau women are gaining a comfort level they might not develop otherwise, in Gilbert's view. In addition, a Women's Communications Boot Camp was added to the training mix to give a small group more intensive training as spokeswomen.[18]

Another National Women's Leadership Conference was held at Louisville in 2008 and 700 farm and ranch women attended this time. Stallman was there again and offered the women a challenge to "crash through the perception of Farm Bureau as a good ol' boys club." Many women are in fact serving as county Farm Bureau presidents and voting delegates to the AFBF annual meeting. AFBF's Home and Community Department was important in its day when the social aspects of farm life needed improving. Today, the AFB Women's Leadership Committee reflects the mission implied in its name, developing women leaders who speak out for agriculture.

The American Farm Bureau Federation long recognized the value of young people to the growth and vitality of the organization. An early report on Boys' and Girls' Club work noted, "It is a self-evident, yet startling fact that without youth as a potential part of our organization, the Farm Bureau would pass away with the passing of its present available members." But in 1927 after several years of a farm depression, the outlook for young people in agriculture was not promising. "A disturbing element in agriculture has been the fact that so many of our brightest boys and girls have become dissatisfied with country life," said a report to members.[19]

At that time there was a surplus of people involved in agriculture, but that's no longer the case. If young people are disillusioned about farming today, it would be a serious problem for a nation dependent on fewer farmers for food, fiber, and fuel. But the sixteenth annual survey of participants in AFBF's Young Farmer and Rancher Program (YF&R) conducted in 2008 is reassuring. The YF&R program is for farmers between the ages of eighteen and thirty-five. Despite facing some significant challenges, these young men and women are enthusiastic about the future of agriculture. A remarkable 92 percent of those surveyed see themselves remaining in farming for the rest of their lives, and 95 percent would like to see their children follow in their footsteps.[20]

For the last ninety years, AFBF has staked out a better future for each new generation of farmers and prepared them for leadership positions. Out of the ranks of young people in Farm Bureau came Secretary of Agriculture John Block, 1967 chairman of the AFBF Young Farmers and Ranchers Advisory Committee, AFBF, and state Farm Bureau presidents, elected officials, and agribusiness leaders.

In the early years, however, much of the emphasis was on supporting programs outside Farm Bureau—4-H Club, Future Farmers of America, and Boy Scouts.

The AFBF president had a seat on the board of directors of the National Committee on Boys' and Girls' Club Work. The committee was formed in 1921 to coordinate private support for 4-H type programs and had its offices at the AFBF headquarters in Chicago. County and local Farm Bureaus provided much of the leadership for 4-H, which had an enrollment of 640,000 members by 1928. The *Bureau Farmer* magazine also carried 4-H news to Farm Bureau members.

In a number of states, Junior Farm Bureaus or Rural Young People's Programs were formed to bridge the gap between 4-H, Future Farmers, and Farm Bureau adult membership. In 1935, the AFBF voting delegates asked the executives officers and board of directors to look into organizing a national youth program. Several years later, a planning committee recommended a program primarily for unmarried young people between the ages of eighteen and twenty-eight.

One of the key recommendations was that young people should be given responsibility to elect their own officers, formulate programs, and carry them out. AFBF Secretary R. W. Blackburn emphasized that leadership training was the cornerstone of the program. "The Farm Bureau needs youth, not to build Farm Bureau, not to shift the organization burdens to the young, not to provide parties and dancing for the young, not just for the sake of organizing, but rather so together we can work for the solution of the problems of the farm, the farm home and the rural community . . ."[21]

A National Rural Youth Committee, cosponsored by AFBF and Extension, was organized in 1944 and a Rural Youth Department followed in 1948. Carlysle De La Croix, an Indiana Farm Bureau youth leader, was named director. The National Rural Youth Committee of AFBF sponsored a National Talk Meet held at the annual convention and also conducted a national conference, leadership training school, and four regional conferences. By 1951, thirteen state Farm Bureaus had rural youth programs and Warren Newberry of Oklahoma was the national staff director. Newberry farmed a full section of land before President Allan Kline hired him to direct AFBF youth activities. He had experience in organizing a Junior Farm Bureau in Oklahoma.

The National Rural Youth Talk Meet was one of the popular events at the AFBF annual meeting and was the predecessor of today's YF&R Discussion Meet Finals, except the contest was a speech, not a roundtable discussion. Newberry remembered one particular talk meet that occurred when he was still working with Oklahoma Farm Bureau. An Indiana youth, Birch Bayh, came in second or third in the national contest won by a young lady from Enid, Oklahoma, named Marvella. When a celebration was held for her in Oklahoma, Newberry was surprised to find young Bayh present.

Bayh explained to Newberry that he met Marvella at the talk meet, fell in love with her, and wanted to get married. Birch Bayh, a talk meet runner-up, served

Indiana as Senator from 1963–1981. A Democrat, he was the principal architect of the Constitutional amendment to lower the voting age to eighteen, a notable advancement for all young Americans. His wife, Marvella Bayh, used her Farm Bureau speaking skills to become a leading cancer activist before she succumbed to the disease in 1979.[22]

One unique program in the early 1950s was the German High School Training Program conducted in cooperation with the State Department. Seventy-five German teenagers sponsored by Farm Bureau were living in American homes and learning "the true facts about America."[23] Around that time, AFBF's Rural Youth Program also changed its name to the Young People's Program, as it separated from Extension's youth work.

In the 1960s, AFBF was one of the principal sponsors of the annual National Youthpower Congress, an activity of the National Food Conference, which included farm industry groups and foods retailers. The event drew over 200 teenagers from twenty-one states to Chicago's Palmer House Hotel in 1963 when Miss America, Marilyn Van Derbur, was a featured speaker. The conference focused on how teens could adopt better eating habits and find careers after college in the food industry.

In 1967, the national program for young people took the Young Farmers and Ranchers Program name. There was not a lot of change during the 1970s and 1980s, except the plural form of the name was dropped. The program was open to singles and couples between the ages of eighteen and thirty. The chair of the YF&R Advisory Committee, elected by fellow committee members, sat on the AFBF board of directors for the one year of his or her term.

The YF&R conference held in late winter after the AFBF annual meeting attracted around 500 young leaders who especially enjoyed the opportunity to network with farmers their age from all over the country. Many lifelong friendships were formed. The Discussion Meet replaced the Talk Meet and an Outstanding Young Farmer award was given to three winners who were judged on the success of their farming operation, achievements in agriculture, and community service. Philip Nelson of Seneca, Illinois, won in 1984 and received free use of an Allis-Chalmers tractor for a year. He was elected president of the Illinois Farm Bureau in 2003.

In the 1990s, the Dodge Truck Division of Chrysler Corporation began awarding trucks to the winners of the Achievement Award contest and the Discussion Meet contest. The trucks weren't just any trucks either. In 1998, Daryl and Cheryl Brown of Tennessee won the Achievement Award and dashed off stage to hop into the cab of their Dodge Ram 3500 4X4 Club Cab, Cummins-powered pickup. Case IH gave the runners-up free use of a tractor for a year. The YF&R Awards Program became the most exciting event at the AFBF annual meetings.

The YF&R Committee started off the twenty-first century with a bang by hosting the World Congress of Young Farmers in February 2000 at Disney's Coronado Springs Resort in Orlando, Florida. More than 1,300 farmers from forty-three countries gathered for the conference, workshops, and farm tours that included a barbeque at a Florida cattle ranch and citrus grove. Mfoula Biyo'o, a young farmer from Cameroon, said, "It was an opportunity to develop new relationships with other farmers, and I believe those relationships will have positive results." Fawzi Hamad Al-Sultan, president of the International Fund for Agricultural Development (IFAD), addressed the group and commended the YF&R Committee for making the event happen.[24]

Competitive events were so popular with young farmers that AFBF added a new one, the Excellence in Agriculture Award, debuting at the 2003 AFBF annual meeting in Tampa, Florida. As with the other competitions, young farmers who won at the state level were eligible to compete for awards at the national level. Excellence in Agriculture recognizes young people who do not derive a majority of their income from an owned agricultural operation, but who actively contribute and grow through their involvement in Farm Bureau and agriculture. The first winners of the award were Matt and Andrea Lohr of Virginia. The Lohrs were recognized for their motivational speaking business, inspiring members and staff of agricultural organizations.

Over the years, the YF&R Program widened the age range for participation from eighteen to thirty-five-years old. Many of the young people it attracts are returning to the farm after completing college. "Most of them are looking for a professional organization to continue building their skills and I think they look towards Farm Bureau to do that through leadership development," said Dan Durheim, who directs the national program.[25] There are sixteen positions from the four regions on the YF&R Committee. They are occupied by a husband and wife or a single person for a two-year term. Officers are elected by the committee for one-year terms.

The explosive growth of the YF&R Program has continued recently through collegiate programs in more than twenty-five states. When Colorado Farm Bureau formed a chapter at Colorado State University in 2000, more than eighty students signed up during an initial membership drive. The chapters function much like a county Farm Bureau and give students the opportunity to research and discuss agricultural and natural resources issues. Collegiate Farm Bureaus also hold discussion meets.

In 2003, AFBF began an advanced leadership training program for a select group of young people. Partners in Agricultural Leadership (PAL), initially sponsored by Altria Group and later Monsanto Company and the Farm Credit Foundation, had ten participants in the first class who went through six months of training in media, crisis communications, public policy development, and global and emerging issues in agriculture.

The YF&R Program also added a service program that targeted hunger relief in 2003 with Harvest for All. The program was spearheaded by the YF&R Committee through America's Second Harvest, the nation's food bank network, and included Syngenta and the National Association of Farm Broadcasters as sponsors. In the first year, $80,000 was donated and 718,000 pounds of food collected for hungry Americans. The results were announced at the 2004 YF&R Conference in Salt Lake City, where members sorted through 30,000 pounds of food at the Utah Food Bank, 8,000 pounds of which was donated by Utah farmers. Harvest for All was a winner of the prestigious Summit Award from the American Society of Association Executives.

One thing noticeable among attendees at an AFBF annual meeting is the admiration that middle-aged and older farmers have for the younger generation of agricultural leaders. They marvel at their abilities and achievements in the YF&R competitive events. "Unlike many of us who took over the family farm that had remained basically unchanged for generations, these young folks are dealing with an ever-shifting slate of issues and challenges that have never before been experienced," said Stallman in his news column, "The Ag Agenda."[26]

Both the AFB Women's Leadership Program and Young Farmer and Rancher Program do not want to be considered islands or isolated programs. Today, they work to build the whole federation rather than their franchise in it. Without women and young farmers and ranchers, Farm Bureau would not have succeeded as a family farm organization; it would have become something less.

Endnotes

1. "The Rise of the Farmer," as reprinted in *AFBF Official News Letter*, September 15, 1948. Original article was in the *Ohio Farm Bureau News*. Bromfield's beautiful Malabar Farm is a popular tourist attraction today near Lucas, Ohio.

2. Biel, *American Gothic*, 46.

3. Transcript, AFBF annual meeting, December 6–8, 1920, Indianapolis, Indiana.

4. *Resume of the Work of the American Farm Bureau for 1926*.

5. *AFBF Official News Lett*er of March 3, 1934.

6. "Philosophy of a Farm Woman," *Nation's Agriculture*, September 1939; "Expert Computes Value of Farm Women's Labor," *Chicago Tribune*, March 21, 1937.

7. Ibid.

8. "Throngs Open Fourth Woman Congress Here," *Chicago Tribune,* March 11, 1937.

9. "Home and Community Workers Corner," *Nation's Agriculture*, September 1939.

10. Woell, *Farm Bureau Architects*, 248.

11. "When First Ladies Get Together," *Nation's Agriculture*, January 1970; *Farm Bureau News*, June 8, 1964.

12. "Smith Impressed Many with Her Skills," *Grand Island Independent*, January 26, 2006.

13. "FB Women Get Involved in Issues, Image and Influence," *Farm Bureau News*, April 16, 1984.

14. "White Delivers Final Address As AFB Women's Chair," *Farm Bureau News*, January 18, 1993.

15. Interview with Linda Reinhardt.

16. "Women's Conference a Resounding Success," *Farm Bureau News*, May 22, 2000.

17. "Gilbert Strives to Further Build Women's Program," *Farm Bureau News*, January 21, 2002.

18. Interview with Terry Gilbert.

19. *Resume of the Work of the American Farm Bureau Federation for 1926; The American Farm Bureau Federation in 1927.*

20. "Young Farmers and Ranchers Anticipate Bright Future," AFBF news release, March 18, 2008.

21. Minutes, AFBF Board of Directors Meeting, March 1941.

22. Interview with Warren Newberry.

23. "Rural Youth Work in Farm Bureau Has Continued," *AFBF Official News Letter*, December 10, 1951.

24. "World Congress of Young Farmers," *Farm Bureau News*, March 6, 2000.

25. Interview with Dan Durheim.

26. "Young Farmers and Ranchers: The Future of Agriculture," *Farm Bureau News*, February 6, 2006.

27 | Farm Bureau in the Twenty-first Century

At the January 2000 AFBF annual meeting in Houston, Farm Bureau members breathed a sigh of relief with the rest of the world because the anticipated Y2K computer meltdown did not occur as clocks ticked over to the next millennium. Farming had been going on for around 10,000 years, the American Farm Bureau Federation for eighty-one years, and both were advancing to a new century and a new millennium.

"Agriculture Beyond 2000" was the title of an AFBF documentary that premiered during the convention's general session. What would food and agriculture be like in the next century? Would farmers and ranchers be living in concrete domed homes and driving sky cars instead of pickup trucks—the dust trails on a country road a thing of the past? The more down-to-earth predictions involved biotechnology, biofuels, precision farming, and robotic tractors. Global climate change was a wild card not just for agriculture, but for the planet.

The founders of the American Farm Bureau Federation wanted an organization that would last at least 100 years. The sand in the hourglass would run out in 2019, and there was little doubt that Farm Bureau would be around long after that. But it was time to take stock of American agriculture and the organization that had reached a total of 4,952,244 member families that year.

The first program of work written in 1920 summed up the reason for Farm Bureau: "To develop a completely unified national organization to act as spokesman for the farmer and to adequately represent the farmer and the farmer's interests on all occasions."[1] Farm Bureau successfully became that Voice of Agriculture. Would it continue in that role in the next century? What would the organization look like? What needed to change? What ties to the past should stay intact? What were the emerging issues that would impact American agriculture?

Farm Bureau had a keen interest in assessing the future. Near the end of 1999, 200 Farm Bureau staff leaders from twenty-four states participated in a teleconference to explore strategies for involving "Generation Me," anyone born in the 1970s, 1980s, or 1990s. "Generation Me" supposedly puts the individual first. How would this play out in Farm Bureau where success was the result of cooperative action?[2]

The outlook for the agriculture industry heading into 2000 was not good. The biofuels boom was still a little ways off. On the livestock side, hog prices plunged as low as $8 per hundredweight in some Midwestern markets in 1999. Net farm income was projected to hit a five-year low. USDA chief economist Keith Collins told Farm Bureau that 14 percent of farmers would experience serious debt problems.

The farm economy and future were on the minds of the AFBF delegate body when they elected forty-seven-year old Bob Stallman to be the first president in the twenty-first century. Jack Laurie of Michigan was elected vice president. There had not been a change of president since 1986. Kleckner would have liked one more term, but the delegates were ready to move forward. In assessing the road ahead, Stallman said the time had come for farmers and ranchers who understand "down-home, dirt farm economics" to communicate to Congress and the administration the needs of agriculture.[3]

Dick Harris, who had been the top staff executive of the Iowa Farm Bureau, was brought in as chief administrative officer and secretary-treasurer of the American Farm Bureau Federation shortly after Stallman's election. Dave Mayfield became corporate secretary and Dave Conover was named director of administrative services. Dick Newpher continued as executive director of the Washington office.

One of the issues that confronted Stallman and the board was whether to retain two separate offices. For the entire history of the organization, all of the lobbyists and approximately half of the public relations staff had been in Washington. Stallman thought that bringing the offices together would result in better staff interaction, and he felt that some Farm Bureau members did not even realize there was an office in the Chicago area. They had come to think of Washington as the headquarters.[4]

In January 2002, the voting delegates considered an increase in dues payable to AFBF from state Farm Bureaus. Without a dues increase, a move to Washington probably could not happen because federation finances had deteriorated. State Farm Bureaus were paying AFBF $3.50 for each membership in a county Farm Bureau. An amendment to the bylaws was proposed to raise the amount.

"I guess at the end of the day we want to make sure we have a very, very strong American Farm Bureau," said Terry McClure, president of the Ohio Farm Bureau during debate. "My father had a strong American Farm Bureau fighting for him. I have a strong American Farm Bureau fighting for me. I want a strong American

Farm Bureau for my son in the future." That was the prevailing sentiment of the delegates who voted by the necessary two-thirds majority to raise dues to $4.00.[5]

With that hurdle cleared, the directors voted unanimously at the October 2002 meeting to relocate the general headquarters to Washington in the next year. The office on the eighth floor of the Capitol Gallery building at 600 Maryland Avenue, SW, was remodeled and expanded. Additional space also was found on another floor. At the end of September 2003, AFBF kicked off three days of events to celebrate the opening of the new headquarters. Agriculture Secretary Ann Veneman, members of Congress, foreign embassy officials, state Farm Bureau presidents, and others in the agricultural community toured the new facilities.

One of the distinguished guests was Sen. Craig Thomas (R-Wyoming), who was AFBF's natural resources director from 1971 to 1975, and also a former executive with the Wyoming Farm Bureau. The three-term Senator worked closely with Farm Bureau on public lands and rural health care issues. He died of leukemia a few years later in 2007.

Not long after AFBF settled in, an unexpected opportunity came along to move to a newly constructed "west wing" of the Capitol Gallery. The office space on the ninth and tenth floors offered more conference space and was less spread out. In the summer of 2006, the move was completed. The décor of the office is contemporary, but there are traces of history. The fiftieth anniversary plaque that adorned the front of the old LaSalle Hotel in Chicago where AFBF was founded is on a conference room wall. An interior stairway was constructed to resemble a farm silo. Wood trim around the stairway and in the lobby looks like old barn wood. The office has a striking view of the Capitol and there is a rooftop patio.

"I think we are positioned as well as we can be with facilities and office space now as any organization here in Washington, D.C.," said Stallman. "We have a hotel right across the street for members to use. We are within walking distance of Congress, USDA, and the Mall for those who want to see it. I can't imagine any better set up for a grassroots organization," he added.[6]

The move to Washington sparked a small concern that AFBF would develop an "inside-the-beltway mentality," but Stallman made it clear that the grassroots policy nature of Farm Bureau and its mission would not change. "Our mission remains the same, and that's to improve the economic well-being of farmers and ranchers . . . as well as the quality of rural life," he said. "That mission and the policies that go along with it are developed by our grassroots membership . . . our home has changed but our mission has not."[7]

Having coordinated the move to Washington, Dick Harris retired and Dick Newpher became the chief staff person. As of October 2008, the officers were President Stallman, Vice President Barry Bushue of Oregon, Executive Vice President and Treasurer Newpher, and General Counsel and Secretary Julie Anna Potts.

There are approximately 100 staff and support staff positions at AFBF. The American Agricultural Insurance Company, the reinsurance affiliate, remained in the Chicago area in new office space.

In 1920, the work was organized by divisions: Legislation, Cooperation (cooperative marketing), Transportation, Economics and Statistics, Trade Relations, Education and Publicity, and Organization. At present the staff is grouped by departments: General Counsel (legal), Economic Analysis, Organization, Public Policy (legislation and regulation), Public Relations, Administrative Services, and Accounting.

The consolidation was a major change and helped answer the question about what Farm Bureau would look like in the foreseeable future. The intention, however, was not to cut back programs and services. All departments were retooled to respond better to the needs of state Farm Bureaus.

For example, in 2006, the AFBF Legal Advocacy Program was adopted by the board with a reserve for litigation. "We are putting a budget toward policy work in the judiciary just like we do in the legislative branch or the executive branch of government," said General Counsel Potts. An advisory committee of state Farm Bureau general counsels, administrators, and national affairs coordinators was set up to advise her office.

The American Farm Bureau Foundation for Agriculture (AFBFA) became part of an enlarged Organization Department and is reaching millions of students a year with popular education programs about agriculture, including one that addresses common misconceptions about science and farming.

Trade issues that were handled during the GATT rounds by one person now command the attention of five trade policy specialists in the Public Policy Department. Economic Analysis and Public Relations fine-tuned their efforts in economic forecasting and issues management respectively. "There isn't any other organization that has as many competent people to do the work of volunteer leaders in Washington," said Newpher. "And there aren't many, maybe less than ten organizations of any kind, that have the depth and the abilities that farm Bureau has."[8]

Unlike other large associations that bear little resemblance to their roots, Farm Bureau has never lost sight of its grassroots character. The federation structure of county, state, and national Farm Bureau with control resting in elected farmer leaders is unchanged. The programs and activities that helped define Farm Bureau in the early years are still there—grassroots policy development and lobbying, annual meeting, awards and recognition, leadership training, women and young farmer and rancher programs, and member service benefits. Membership remains the lifeblood of the organization.

If a Farm Bureau leader from the 1919 convention could return to visit the 2009 AFBF annual meeting at San Antonio, Texas, he would still recognize the organization. His hat might be blown off by the size and strength of the federation, but he would understand this was the same Farm Bureau he helped start. And the issues confronting farmers would probably leave him speechless.

The problems and opportunities for farmers in this century are far more complex and on a much bigger scale. In 1920, Farm Bureau was trying to decide what to do about imported seed corn from Italy that turned out to be of poor quality. Today, acceptance of biotech seeds is a critical factor in feeding a growing world population. In the early years, Farm Bureau asked for more information about crop yields in Argentina and other grain exporting countries. Now farmers want to know about global climate change and the market for sequestering carbon on farms. Ironically, one issue has remained pretty much the same—dissatisfaction with the nation's tax system. In 1920, Farm Bureau proposed a study of England's income tax methods to see if they were any better. In 2008, delegates were calling for replacing the current federal income tax system.

One of the biggest tasks lately has been defending farm program spending, which Farm Bureau views as an investment by the public in American agriculture. Yes, it is true that President Shuman was famous for his statement about wanting to get the government out of agriculture, but there were different circumstances in the 1960s. That was before the European Union and Japan spent so much money to subsidize their farmers and limit market access. In 2001, Japan supported its farmers to the tune of $3,960 per acre, the European Community $320 per acre and the United States provided just $49 per acre.[9]

In Shuman's time, Farm Bureau policy was to get the government out of programs that "fix prices and control production" and into programs that "more effectively serve the interests of farmers at a greatly reduced cost to taxpayers."[10] That policy is consistent with the way farm programs have evolved. The old programs of paying farmers not to farm are a thing of the past. They were replaced by programs that give farmers more planting flexibility and allow them to respond to signals in the marketplace. As a percentage of the total federal budget, the cost of farm programs has come down from 3 percent in 1965, during Shuman's tenure, to less than one-half of 1 percent today.

One of the first things Farm Bureau did in 2000 was to prepare for the next farm bill in 2002. The previous bill, the 1996 Federal Agricultural Improvement and Reform Act (FAIR Act), was a big departure from the past. Farm Bureau and the agriculture community were stunned by the plan when it was first offered by House Agriculture Committee Chairman Pat Roberts (R-Kansas), but AFBF supported its market-oriented direction. Farm payments were decoupled from production decisions. The old supply control was replaced by freedom to farm. "This measure is the best possible outcome," said President Kleckner at the time. "Farmers will have greater flexibility to compete for markets and there will be an orderly seven year phase-down of government payments for farmers."[11]

Freedom to Farm, as the law became known, was soon derisively labeled "Freedom to Fail" after commodity prices tanked and energy prices soared, driving up the cost of farm production. There just was not enough of a safety net for a farming industry that is capital intensive, risky, and very dependent on the weather. Farm Bureau did not blame the FAIR Act for low commodity prices; and it opposed abandoning the market-based concepts, but Stallman reminded the House Agriculture Committee in 2000 that the entire bargain had not been kept. "Congress gave farmers their word regarding access to additional foreign markets through trade policy reforms, relief from overburdensome regulations, additional and improved risk management tools, and tax reforms for their support of the FAIR Act," he said.

The FAIR Act also called for appointing a commission to study farm programs. In 2001, the Commission on 21st Century Production Agriculture made its report. There were eleven members of the commission, which included Kansas State University agricultural economist Barry Flinchbaugh as chairman. Three state Farm Bureau presidents were appointed commissioners: Stallman, Texas; Charles Kruse, Missouri; and Don Villwock, Indiana. The commission suggested that lawmakers continue with fixed Agricultural Market Transition Act (AMTA) payments, loan deficiency payments and marketing loans, and cited the need for a countercyclical income support program.

Farm Bureau grassroots action was critical in getting both the 2002 and 2008 Farm Bills passed. There are twenty-five farm groups and hundreds of agribusiness organizations located in Washington, but Farm Bureau is still the Voice of Agriculture. John Keeling, former AFBF lobbyist and executive vice president and CEO of the National Potato Council, said the others look to the American Farm Bureau Federation for the broad overview. "I think in terms of that 40,000 foot level of establishing the overall direction we are going . . . in the pure farm policy side of things at that 40,000 foot level where the basic sideboards are being set, I think what they [AFBF] bring to the table is incredibly invaluable." Keeling also gave Farm Bureau high marks for leading on trade issues.[12]

The 2002 Farm Bill was roundly criticized in the media for supposedly raising farm spending by 70 percent, but the charge was misleading. Money spent on ad hoc income disaster payments over the past few years was rolled into the new bill. "As I said many times before, the farm bill continues with roughly the same amount of support as we have been providing our farm sector over the past four years . . . ," responded Secretary Veneman at a USDA news conference.[13] Besides experiencing income disaster, farmers faced plenty of weather disasters in 2001–2002. Drought, flooding, and hard freezes hit so many places that almost 90 percent of

U.S. counties were declared disaster areas. Farm Bureau joined with thirty-one farm and lending organizations to press the case for emergency disaster aid.

Halfway through 2002, Farm Bureau leaders from thirty-six states had already traveled to Washington (and nine states made the trip twice) to lobby for farm legislation. The Public Policy staff updated Farm Bureau leaders, many of whom were county presidents, on pending legislation before they went to the Hill. Almost 2,400 leaders personally lobbied members of Congress in just six months. In "The Ag Agenda," his *Farm Bureau News* column, Stallman likened grassroots lobbying to a proverb he found in a fortune cookie. It read, "None of the strategies for success will work, unless you do."[14]

The 2008 Farm Bill that should have been finished in 2007 was particularly frustrating to Stallman. It moved a lot slower on the Senate side than in the House, plus the federal budget was tight. A commodity price rise fueled by energy prices slowed the momentum for Congressional action. The Environmental Working Group tried to undermine support for the bill by publishing lists of farmers who received farm payments and how much. "Our goal as an organization as opposed to maybe other organizations has been to have a productive agricultural industry," said Stallman. "Not to talk about a certain farm size as being the correct farm size. Not to talk about a certain income level for a farmer being the appropriate income level. We support agriculture as an industry."[15]

Farm Bureau earned its title as the Voice of Agriculture during the Farm Bill debate when so many editorial writers and pundits were against farmers. They thought farmers had it too good and were responsible for high food prices, as was written in the *Wall Street Journal*. The paper called farmers "the most undeserving welfare recipients in American history."[16] Stallman found a basic lack of understanding in these editorials and responded to them. Of the entire $300 billion package, only $35 billion "goes to funding a basic, no frills safety net for America's farmers," he said. Most editorials missed the fact that the Farm Bill provided food assistance and nutrition programs for the needy, conservation of natural resources, food safety, and rural development.[17]

The 2008 Farm Bill was another big victory for the American Farm Bureau Federation. President Bush vetoed the bill, but his veto was overridden twice in a manner of speaking. A clerical error left out the Trade Title, one of fifteen titles in the legislation, and it had to be passed separately. In signing the 2002 Farm Bill, the president had said, "It helps America's farmers, and therefore it helps America," but this time around, he considered it wasteful spending. House Speaker Nancy Pelosi (D-California) disagreed. She said the Farm Bill contained significant reforms in farm programs and termed the nutrition money vitally important.[18]

High farm income and commodity prices made passage of the Farm Bill more difficult than usual, but AFBF was pleased that it was able to maintain a national farm policy that works. "That was the unbelievable thing given all of the budget pressures. We in essence were able to maintain farm policy as is, and there were huge increases in conservation funding," said AFBF Public Policy Director Mary Kay Thatcher.[19] Other than the oil industry perhaps, no industry over time has been more cyclical than agriculture.

During World War I, the American public recognized the value of a strong agriculture, but that was a long time ago. At the 2003 AFBF annual meeting in Tampa, Stallman called for a campaign to emphasize the importance of agriculture to the fabric and security of the nation. The terrorist attacks on 9/11 made Americans take stock of the nation's strengths and vulnerabilities. Farmers took steps to guard against bioterrorism. Then the nation was rocked in 2008 by the energy crisis and meltdown of financial markets. This kind of instability cannot be allowed to happen in food and agriculture, which is one of the reasons Farm Bureau believes the Farm Bill is a prudent investment.

In 2003, the American Farm Bureau Federation undertook a very comprehensive project managed by the Economic Analysis Department to determine where agriculture was going to be when that hourglass ran out of sand, in 2019. The board created the Making American Agriculture Productive and Profitable (MAAPP) Committee to develop a vision and policy recommendations for consideration by the board and voting delegates. The 156-page report was presented by the committee of twenty-three Farm Bureau members at the 2006 AFBF annual meeting in Nashville.

"Education, training and technology are going to be even more important for the next generation of farmers and ranchers," said MAAPP Committee Chairman William Sprague, former president of the Kentucky Farm Bureau. "Technology used to change every 15 to 20 years; now it changes in just two or three years." Another finding that surprised many was that farmers will be more dependent on rural communities for the quality of life they want to enjoy, but these communities will be less dependent on agriculture for their economic stability.[20]

Farm Bureau is giving added attention to rural development, a subject that admittedly was not a priority in the past when a prosperous agriculture was generally equated with a prosperous rural America. "Look at Kansas and look at how the countryside of Kansas is undergoing absolute irreversible changes," said Newpher. There is an out-migration that hasn't been seen since the Dust Bowl days. Somehow for the good of agriculture, rural America and the country generally, we need to find ways to sustain an economic base in those rural areas, he added."[21] A staff position for rural development was added in the AFBF Public Policy Department.

When the MAAPP Committee took a look at farm cash receipts, it found that farm income was roughly split between livestock and crops. Cattle and calf receipts accounted for 40 percent of the cash generated by the livestock sector. Dairy was in second place. The beef cow, sheep, and lamb inventory was held by a more diverse set of producers than hogs and poultry which tended to be concentrated in larger operations. What they all shared in common was a renewed attack by animal rights activists.

Animal rights first became an issue for Farm Bureau in the early 1980s when the veal industry came to AFBF for help. In 1982, AFBF bused a group of Chicago area businessmen, educators, and news people to a Wisconsin veal farm to acquaint them with the way veal calves were raised and treated. This was in response to a campaign by the Humane Society of the United States against veal production.

The Humane Society wanted consumers to stop eating veal, particularly milk-fed veal served in fine restaurants. Farm Bureau responded with a full-page ad in the *New York Times* to separate the myths from the facts. The core message was "No one has greater concern for the care of farm animals than the farmer or rancher who raises them." That same year, Dr. Hugh Johnson, a poultry specialist in the Commodity Division, was named to head AFBF's animal welfare activities.

Farm Bureau disavowed the notion that farm animals had "rights" equal to human rights, and sought to better inform the nonfarm public about animal care on the farm. "It isn't surprising that agriculture has not developed a tradition of explaining itself to the public. For so long *it was the public*," said Dick McGuire, New York Commissioner of Agriculture, speaking at a 1989 animal rights conference in Albany. McGuire was a former president of the New York Farm Bureau. His point was that in the past the majority of Americans had milked a cow, gathered eggs, and cared for a horse. The "whys and hows" of agriculture were no mystery to them.[22]

Thirty years after AFBF first defended poultry and livestock producers, animal rights remains an important challenge. Confined animal feeding operations (CAFOS) are the main target. PETA (People for the Ethical Treatment of Animals) has been going after fast-food chains to get them to adopt PETA guidelines for livestock production. Farm Bureau believes the real objective is to eliminate food production from animals all together.

Stallman warned Farm Bureau members that "animal warfare" was coming to their state after Arizona's Proposition 204 passed in 2006. Activists spent millions on the ballot initiative to essentially shut down one hog operation in the state. He also pointed to the move by Smithfield Foods and Maple Leaf Foods to switch from gestation crates to group housing because of marketing pressure, not animal health reasons. The AFBF president urged farmers to be a proactive voice for animal agriculture and be ready to combat animal warfare propaganda.[23]

The proactive approach to livestock issues led AFBF to launch the "Conversations on Animal Care" initiative in the summer of 2008. The initiative supports farmers and ranchers who are eager to engage consumers in a positive dialogue about animal care. "This program helps farm families like mine tell the truth about how important animal welfare is to us," said Chris Chinn, a pork producer from Clarence, Missouri, who is a past chair of the YF&R Committee.

Farm Bureau set up a website for consumers with farmer testimonials, an open forum, and other information about animal care. Public Relations Director Don Lipton believes consumers appreciate hearing directly from farmers. "We live in a world of spin. It has become pretty commonplace that nobody wants to hear that much from paid representatives of an organization. They lack authenticity."[24]

A major component of the Farm Bureau initiative is to teach farmers to share their stories effectively and help them find an audience to amplify their message. Although it uses sophisticated public relations tools and web technology, "Conversations on Animal Care" is just a modern example of farmers speaking through Farm Bureau.

Going forward there is a plateful of challenges (not just animal rights or farm program spending) facing agriculture at this milestone in AFBF history. After nine decades, it is worth pausing to consider that the founding of the American Farm Bureau Federation was one of the great events in the history of American agriculture. It marked what farmers did for themselves to meet the challenges they faced. "Forward! Farm Bureau" was a rallying cry to build the organization long ago, but it resounds today in the drive and determination that characterizes Farm Bureau members.

Endnotes

  1. *American Farm Bureau Federation Annual Report*, March 4, 1920–December 3, 1920.
  2. "Audio Conference a Farm Bureau 'First,'" *Farm Bureau News*, January 10, 2000.
  3. "Stallman: Ag Must Be a U.S. priority," *Farm Bureau News*, January 24, 2000.
  4. Interview with Bob Stallman.
  5. Transcript, AFBF Annual Meeting, January 8–9, 2002, Reno, Nevada.
  6. Interview with Bob Stallman.
  7. "New Home, Same Mission for AFBF," *Farm Bureau News*, October 20, 2003.
  8. Interview with Dick Newpher.
  9. "Farm Bill Critics Are Telling Only Part of the Story," *Farm Bureau News*, August 25, 2003.
 10. *Farm Bureau Policies for 1962*.
 11. "Clinton Signs Farm Bill," *Farm Bureau News*, April 8, 1996.
 12. Interview with John Keeling.
 13. "Administration Begins Farm Bill Implementation," *Farm Bureau News*, May 27, 2002.
 14. "Implementing Farm Bureau Strategies For Success," *Farm Bureau News*, June 10, 2002.
 15. Interview with Bob Stallman.

16. "Who Wants to Be a Millionaire," *Wall Street Journal*, May 14, 2008.

17. "Stallman Defends Farm Bill in Letters to Editor," *AFBF Executive News Watch*, May 16, 2008.

18. "President Signs Farm Bill," White House Office of the Press Secretary release, May 13, 2002; "Bush, Congress Set for Clash," *USA Today,* May 11, 2008.

19. Interview with Mary Kay Thatcher.

20. "Committee IDs Challenges, Opportunities," *Farm Bureau News*, January 23, 2006.

21. Interview with Dick Newpher.

22. "Agriculture and Animal Rights," *Vital Speeches of the Day*, October 1, 1989.

23. "Animal Warfare: Coming to Your State Soon," *Farm Bureau News*, March 5, 2007.

24. Interview with Don Lipton.

AFBF Annual Meeting Dates and Locations: 1919 to 2009

1919	November 12–14	Chicago, Illinois
1920	March 3–4	Chicago, Illinois

(Permanent Organizational Meeting)

1920	December 6–8	Indianapolis, Indiana
1921	November 21–23	Atlanta, Georgia
1922	December 11–14	Chicago, Illinois
1923	December 10–12	Chicago, Illinois
1924	December 8–10	Chicago, Illinois
1925	December 7–9	Chicago, Illinois
1926	December 6–8	Chicago, Illinois
1927	December 5–7	Chicago, Illinois
1928	December 10–12	Chicago, Illinois
1929	December 9–11	Chicago, Illinois
1930	December 5–10	Boston, Massachusetts
1931	December 7–9	Chicago, Illinois
1932	December 5–7	Chicago, Illinois
1933	December 11–13	Chicago, Illinois
1934	December 10–12	Nashville, Tennessee
1935	December 9–11	Chicago, Illinois
1936	December 6–11	Pasadena, California
1937	December 13–15	Chicago, Illinois
1938	December 13–15	New Orleans, Louisiana
1939	December 5–7	Chicago, Illinois

1940	December 9–12	Baltimore, Maryland
1941	December 9–11	Chicago, Illinois
1942	December 7–10	Chicago, Illinois
1943	December 7–9	Chicago, Illinois
1944	December 12–14	Chicago, Illinois
1945	December 18–20	Chicago, Illinois
1946	December 10–12	San Francisco, California
1947	December 16–18	Chicago, Illinois
1948	December 14–16	Atlantic City, New Jersey
1949	December 12–15	Chicago, Illinois
1950	December 12–15	Dallas, Texas
1951	December 11–13	Chicago, Illinois
1952	December 9–11	Seattle, Washington
1953	December 15–17	Chicago, Illinois
1954	December 14–16	New York, New York
1955	December 13–15	Chicago, Illinois
1956	December 9–13	Miami Beach, Florida
1957	December 10–12	Chicago, Illinois
1958	December 9–11	Chicago, Illinois
1959	December 13–17	Chicago, Illinois
1960	December 12–15	Denver, Colorado
1961	December 12–14	Chicago, Illinois
1962	December 10–13	Atlanta, Georgia
1963	December 9–12	Chicago, Illinois
1964	December 7–10	Philadelphia, Pennsylvania
1965	December 13–16	Chicago, Illinois
1966	December 5–8	Las Vegas, Nevada
1967	December 10–14	Chicago, Illinois
1968	December 9–12	Kansas City, Missouri
1969	December 8–11	Washington, D.C.
1970	December 7–10	Houston, Texas
1971	December 6–9	Chicago, Illinois
1972	December 11–14	Los Angeles, California
1973	Changeover Year—December to January Meetings	
1974	January 14–17	Atlantic City, New Jersey
1975	January 6–9	New Orleans, Louisiana
1976	January 5–8	St. Louis, Missouri
1977	January 10–12	Honolulu, Hawaii
1978	January 9–12	Houston, Texas
1979	January 15–18	Miami Beach, Florida

1980	January 8–10	Phoenix, Arizona
1981	January 12–15	New Orleans, Louisiana
1982	January 11–14	San Diego, California
1983	January 9–13	Dallas, Texas
1984	January 8–12	Orlando, Florida
1985	January 7–10	Honolulu, Hawaii
1986	January 12–16	Atlanta, Georgia
1987	January 11–15	Anaheim, California
1988	January 10–14	New Orleans, Louisiana
1989	January 9–12	San Antonio, Texas
1990	January 8–11	Orlando, Florida
1991	January 7–10	Phoenix, Arizona
1992	January 13–16	Kansas City, Missouri
1993	January 10–14	Anaheim, California
1994	January 9–13	Ft. Lauderdale, Florida
1995	January 8–12	St. Louis, Missouri
1996	January 7–11	Reno, Nevada
1997	January 6–9	Nashville, Tennessee
1998	January 12–15	Charlotte, North Carolina
1999	January 10–14	Albuquerque, New Mexico
2000	January 9–13	Houston, Texas
2001	January 7–11	Orlando, Florida
2002	January 6–10	Reno, Nevada
2003	January 19–22	Tampa, Florida
2004	January 11–14	Honolulu, Hawaii
2005	January 9–12	Charlotte, North Carolina
2006	January 8 –11	Nashville, Tennessee
2007	January 7–10	Salt Lake City, Utah
2008	January 13–16	New Orleans, Louisiana
2009	January 11–14	San Antonio, Texas

THE AMERICAN FARM BUREAU SPIRIT

Words by
Lillian Atcherson and Florence Cheadle

Arr. by J. Oliver Riehl

Music by
Catherine Wilson and Florence Cheadle

Selected Bibliography

Alter, Jonathan. *The Defining Moment: FDR's Hundred Days and the Triumph of Hope*. New York: Simon & Schuster, 2006.

Ambrose, Stephen E. *Eisenhower: Volume Two, The President*. New York: Simon and Schuster, 1984.

Baker, Gladys. *The County Agent*. Chicago: The University of Chicago Press, 1939.

Baker, John. *Farm Broadcasting; The First Sixty Years*. Ames: The Iowa State University Press, 1981.

Beatty, Jack. *Age of Betrayal, The Triumph of Money in America, 1865–1900*. New York: Alfred A. Knopf, 2007.

Benedict, Murray R. *Farm Policies of the United States, 1790–1950*. New York: The Twentieth Century Fund, 1953.

Berger, Samuel R. *Dollar Harvest*. The Plains, VA: AAM Publications, 1978.

Bezilla, Michael. "Pennsylvania's County Agents: The Early Years of the Agricultural Extension Service," *Pennsylvania History* 53 (1986), No. 2.

Biel, Steven. *American Gothic*. New York: W. W. Norton & Company, 2005.

Block, William J. *The Separation of the Farm Bureau and the Extension Service*. Urbana: The University of Illinois Press, 1960.

Botz Dan La. *César Chávez and la Causa*. New York: Pearson Longman, 2006.

Browne, William P. *Private Interests, Public Policy, and American Agriculture*. Lawrence: University Press of Kansas, 1988.

Campbell, Christiana McFadyen. *The Farm Bureau and the New Deal*. Urbana: University of Illinois Press, 1962.

Carson, Rachel. *Silent Spring*. Boston: Houghton Mifflin Company, 1962.

Cawley, R. McGregor. *Federal Land, Western Anger.* Lawrence: University Press of Kansas, 1993.

Childs, Marquis. *The Farmer Takes a Hand, The Electrical Power Revolution in Rural America.* Garden City, NY: Doubleday & Company, 1953.

Cigler, Allan J., and Burdett A. Loomis. *Interest Group Politics.* Washington, DC: Congressional Quarterly Press, 1998.

Cochrane, Willard W., and Mary E. Ryan. *American Farm Policy, 1948–1973.* St. Paul: University of Minnesota Press, 1976.

Cochrane, Willard W. *The Development of American Agriculture.* Minneapolis: University of Minnesota Press, 1993.

CQ Press. *National Party Conventions 1831–2004.* Washington DC: Congressional Quarterly, 2005.

Culver, John C., and John Hyde. *American Dreamer, A Life of Henry A. Wallace.* New York: W. W. Norton & Company, 2000.

Davis, Kenneth S. *FDR: The New Deal Years 1933–1937.* New York: Random House, 1986.

Davis, P. O. *One Man . . . Edward Asbury O'Neal III of Alabama.* Auburn: The Alabama Polytechnic Institute, 1945.

De Toledano, Ralph. *Little Cesar.* Washington, DC: Anthem Books, 1971.

Dean, John W. *Warren G. Harding.* New York: Henry Holt and Company, 2004.

Dean, Virgil W. *An Opportunity Lost, The Truman Administration and the Farm Policy Debate.* Columbia: University of Missouri Press, 2006.

DeGroot, Gerard J. *The First World War.* New York: Palgrave, 2001.

Derks, Scott. *Working Americans 1880–1999: Volume I, The Working Class.* Lakeville, CT: Grey House Publishing, Inc., 2000.

Diggins, John Patrick. *Ronald Reagan: Fate, Freedom and the Making of History.* New York: W. W. Norton & Company, 2007.

Egan, Timothy. *The Worst Hard Time.* Boston: Houghton Mifflin Company, 2006.

Epstein, Richard A. *Supreme Neglect.* New York: Oxford University Press, 2008.

Ferrell, Robert H. *The Presidency of Calvin Coolidge.* Manhattan: University Press of Kansas, 1998.

Ferris, William G. *The Grain Traders*. East Lansing: Michigan State University Press, 1988.

Fite, Gilbert C. *George N. Peek and the Fight for Farm Parity*. Norman: University of Oklahoma Press, 1954.

Franklin, Peter D. *On Your Side: The Story of the Nationwide Insurance Enterprise*. Columbus, OH: Nationwide Mutual Insurance Company, 1994.

Friedman, Milton, and Rose D. Friedman. *Free To Choose*, San Diego: Harcourt Brace, 1980.

Frohnen, Bruce, Jeremy Beer, and Jeffrey O. Nelson. *American Conservatism*. Wilmington, DE: ISI Books, 2006.

Fursenko, Alexander, and Timothy Naftali. *Khrushchev's Cold War*. New York: W. W. Norton & Company, 2006.

Galbraith, John Kenneth. *The Affluent Society*. New York: Signet Books, 1969.

Galbraith, John Kenneth. *The Great Crash of 1929*. New York: Time, Inc., 1961.

George-Warren, Holly. *Farm Aid: A Song for America*. Emmaus, PA: Rodale, Inc., 2005.

Gerber, James. *International Economics*, third edition. Boston: Pearson Education, Inc., as Addison Wesley, 2005.

Gould, Lewis L. *Grand Old Party*. New York: Random House, 2003.

Gould, Lewis L. *The Most Exclusive Club: A History of the Modern United States Senate*. New York: Basic Books, 2005.

Groves, D. B., and Kenneth Thatcher. *Farm Bureau in Iowa: The First Fifty*. Lake Mills, IA: Graphic Publishing Company, 1968.

Groves, Ernest R. *Rural Problems of Today*. New York: Association Press, 1918.

Hage, Wayne. *Storm Over Rangelands*. Bellevue, WA: Free Enterprise Press, 1989.

Hamby, Alonzo L. *Man of the People: A Life of Harry S. Truman*. New York: Oxford Press, 1995.

Hamilton, Nigel. *Bill Clinton: Mastering the Presidency*. New York: Public Affairs, 2007.

Hannaford, Peter. *The Quotable Calvin Coolidge: Sensible Words for a New Century*. Bennington, VT: Images from the Past, Inc., 2000.

Hansen, John Mark, *Gaining Access: Congress and the Farm Lobby, 1919–1981.* Chicago: The University of Chicago Press, 1991.

Hardach, Gerd. *The First World War 1914–1918,* Berkeley: University of California Press, 1977.

Harl, Neil E. *The Farm Debt Crisis of the 1980s.* Ames: Iowa State University Press, 1990.

Harlow, Ralph V. *The Growth of the United States, Volume II: The Expansion of the Nation 1865–1943.* New York: Henry Holt and Company, 1947.

Hayek, F. A., *The Road to Serfdom.* Chicago: The University of Chicago Press, 1994.

Hayward, Steven F., *The Age of Reagan.* Roseville, CA: Prima Publishing, 2001.

Hicks, John D. *The Populist Revolt, A History of the Farmers' Alliance and People's Party,* Lincoln: University of Nebraska Press, 1961.

Hoekman, Bernard M., and Michel M. Kostecki. *The Political Economy of the World Trading System.* New York: Oxford University Press, 2001.

Hood, Ken. *Spice for Speakers, Sports, & Squares.* Danville, IL: The Interstate Printers and Publishers, Inc., 1976.

Howard, Robert P. *James R. Howard and the Farm Bureau.* Ames: Iowa State University Press, 1983.

Hubbard, Preston J. *Origins of the TVA, The Muscle Shoals Controversy 1920–1932,* New York: W. W. Norton & Company, 1961.

Hughes, Jonathan, and Louis P. Cain. *American Economic History,* sixth edition. Boston: Addison Wesley, 2003.

Irwin, Will. *Herbert Hoover: A Reminiscent Biography.* New York: The Century Company, 1928.

Jamison, Andrew. *Seeds of the Sixties.* Berkeley: University of California Press, 1994.

Kile, O. M. *The Farm Bureau Movement.* New York: The Macmillan Company, 1921.

Kile, O. M. *The Farm Bureau Through Three Decades.* Baltimore, MD: The Waverly Press, 1948.

Knutson, Ronald D., J. B. Penn, Barry L. Flinchbaugh, and Joel Outlaw, *Agricultural and Food Policy,* sixth edition. Upper Saddle River, NJ: Prentice-Hall, 2007.

Leifel, Dan, and Norma Maney. *The Diamond Harvest: A History of the Illinois Farm Bureau.* Bloomington: Illinois Agricultural Association, 1990.

Leifel, Dan, with Barbara Kay Stille and Steve Simms. *"Improving the Economic Well-being of Agriculture:" A History of the Illinois Farm Bureau.* Bloomington: Illinois Agricultural Association, 2005.

Lincoln, Murray D. *Vice President in Charge of Revolution*, New York: McGraw-Hill, 1960.

Lomborg, Bjorn. *The Skeptical Environmentalist.* Cambridge, UK: Cambridge University Press, 2001.

Manchester, William. *The Glory And the Dream: A Narrative History of America: Volumes I and II, 1932 to 1972.* Boston: Little, Brown and Company, 1974.

Mann, Charles C., and Mark L. Plummer. *Noah's Choice.* New York: Alfred Knopf, 1995.

McConnell, Grant. *The Decline of Agrarian Democracy.* Berkeley: University of California Press, 1953.

McDowell, Gary L., and Sharon L. Noble. *Reason and Republicanism.* Lanham, MD: Rowman & Littlefield Publishers, 1997.

McFall, Ken. *The Peeled Zero.* Oklahoma City: Sooner Printing, 1992.

McNamee, Thomas. *The Return of the Wolf to Yellowstone.* New York: Henry Holt and Company, 1997.

Meados, Donella H., Dennis Meadows, Jorgen Randers, and William W. Behrens III. *The Limits to Growth.* New York: Universe Books, 1974.

Nash, George H. *The Life of Herbert Hoover, Master of Emergencies 1917–1918.* New York: W. W. Norton & Company, 1996.

Nelson, Gaylord. *Beyond Earth Day: Fulfilling the Promise.* Madison: The University of Wisconsin Press, 2002.

Paarlberg, Don. *American Farm Policy: A Case Study of Centralized Decision-making.* New York: John Wiley & Sons, 1964.

Paarlberg, Don, and Philip Paarlberg. *The Agricultural Revolution of the 20th Century.* Ames: Iowa State University Press, 2000.

Pach, Chester J., Jr., and Elmo Richardson. *The Presidency of Dwight D. Eisenhower.* Lawrence: University Press of Kansas, 1991.

Paddock, William, and Paul. *Famine 1975!* Boston: Little, Brown and Company, 1967.

Parmet, Herbert S. *JFK: The Presidency of John F. Kennedy.* New York: The Dial Press, 1983.

Patterson, James T. *Restless Giant: The United States from Watergate to Bush v. Gore.* New York: Oxford University Press, 2005.

Peterson, Trudy H. *Agricultural Exports, Farm Income and the Eisenhower Administration.* Lincoln: University of Nebraska Press, 1979.

Phillips, Michael K., and Douglas W. Smith. *The Wolves of Yellowstone.* Stillwater, MN: Voyaguer Press, 1996.

Pombo, Richard, and Joseph Farah. *This Land Is Our Land: How to End the War on Private Property.* New York: St. Martin's Press, 1996.

Rasmussen, Wayne D., ed. *Agriculture in the United States, A Documentary History.* New York: Random House, 1975.

Reichley, A. James. *The Life of the Parties, A History of American Political Parties.* New York: The Free Press, a Division of Macmillan, Inc., 1992.

Renshaw, Patrick. *The Wobblies.* Chicago: Ivan R. Dee, 1999.

Reeves, Thomas C. *Twentieth Century America.* New York: Oxford University Press, 2000.

Rosenbaum, Walter A. *Environmental Politics and Policy.* Washington: CQ Press, 2004.

Sandburg, Carl. *The Complete Poems of Carl Sandburg.* New York: Harcourt, Brace, Jovanovich, 1970.

Schaller, Michael. *Right Turn: American Life in the Reagan-Bush Era 1980–1992.* New York: Oxford University Press, 2007.

Schlesinger, Arthur M., Jr. *The Coming of the New Deal.* Cambridge, MA: Riverside Press, 1958.

Schowengerdt, Margaret. *Missouri Farm Bureau . . . Yesterday . . . Today . . . Tomorrow . . .* Jefferson City: Missouri Farm Bureau, 1988.

Schriftgiesser, Karl. *The Farmer from Merna.* New York: Random House, 1955.

Simon, William E. *A Time for Truth.* New York: McGraw Hill, 1978.

Simons, L. R. *New York State's Contribution to the Organization and Development of the County Agent Farm Bureau Movement.* Cornell Extension Bulletin 993, 1957.

Smith, Jean Edward. *FDR.* New York: Random House, 2007.

Sperber, A.M. *Murrow: His Life and Times.* New York: Freundlich Books, 1986.

Steinbeck, John. *Of Mice and Men.* New York: Penguin Books, 1993.

Sterling, Bryan B., and Frances N. Sterling. *Will Rogers Speaks.* New York: M. Evans & Company, 1995.

Trani, Eugene P., and David L. Wilson. *The Presidency of Warren G. Harding.* Lawrence: University Press of Kansas, 1977

Truman, Harry S. *Memoirs by Harry S. Truman: Volume Two, Years of Trial and Hope.* Garden City, NY: Doubleday & Company, Inc., 1956.

United States Department of Agriculture. *1940 Yearbook of Agriculture: Farmers in a Changing World.* Washington DC: USDA, 1940.

Wagner, Steven. *Eisenhower Republicanism: Pursuing the Middle Way.* DeKalb: Northern Illinois University Press, 2006.

Watts, Steven. *The People's Tycoon: Henry Ford and the American Century.* New York: Alfred A. Knopf, 2005.

Whelan, Elizabeth M. *Toxic Terror.* Buffalo, NY: Prometheus Books, 1993.

White, Richard D. *Kingfish, The Reign of Huey P. Long.* New York: Random House Publishing, 2006.

Witcover, Jules. *Party of the People.* New York: Random House, 2003.

Woell, Melvin L. *Farm Bureau Architects Through Four Decades.* Dubuque, IA: Kendall/Hunt Publishing Company, 1990.

Interviews

Jack Angell
Virgil Applequist
Patrick Batts
Harry Bell
William Broderick
Dean Brown
Dave Conover
Bob Delano
Don Donnelly
Dan Durheim
Brad Eckart
Keith Eckel
Bill Eckmann
Terry Francl
Chris Garza
Terry Gilbert
Gene Hall
Rolland Hayenga
Ken Hood
John Hosemann
John Keeling
Dean Kleckner
Ross Korves
Rick Krause
Don Lipton

Carl Loop
Rankin Lusby
Woodrow Luttrell
Mark Maslyn
Dave Mayfield
Murray Miles
Cecil Miller, Jr.
Warren Newberry
Dick Newpher
Sue Palmore
Don Parrish
Jim Porterfield
Julie Anna Potts
Marsha Purcell
Don Rawlins
Linda Reinhardt
Bob Shepard
Bob Stallman
Tom Steever
Mary Kay Thatcher
Bob Vice
Ron Warfield
Bob Wilson
Betty Wolanyk
Patricia Wolff

Index